Uncle John's Bathroom Reader®

Puzzle Book #1

Edited by
Stephanie Spadaccini

The Bathroom Readers' Institute
Portable Press
San Diego, CA, and Ashland, OR

For my children,
Michael, Jim, Angela, and David

UNCLE JOHN'S
BATHROOM READER
PUZZLE BOOK #1

For information, write
The Bathroom Readers' Institute
5880 Oberlin Drive, San Diego, CA 92121

email: *unclejohn@advmkt.com*

Project Team:

Allen Orso, Publisher
JoAnn Padgett, Director, Editorial and Production
Mana Monzavi, Design and Composition
Amanda Wilson, Design and Composition
Ellen Ripstein, Project Editor

Cover design by Michael Brunsfeld *(brunsfeldo@comcast.net)*

ISBN: 1-59223-022-9

Printed in the United States of America
Second printing: February 2004
Third printing: April 2004
Fourth printing: August 2005

05 06 07 08 09 10 9 8 7 6 5 4

CONTENTS

CRISS-CROSS PUZZLES

WORD SEARCH PUZZLES

ANAGRAMS

QUIZZES & MORE WORDPLAY

BEHAVE YOURSELF!

FAMOUS PEOPLE...

Editor:

Stephanie Spadaccini is a longtime puzzle constructor, and the project editor of the *Uncle John's Bathroom Reader Plunges into...* series. Her puzzles appear regularly in *People* and *AARP* magazine. A former managing editor of *Games* magazine and writer on TV's *Jeopardy!*, Stephanie now devotes most of her spare time to learning the hula.

Contributors:

Alan Arbesfeld has been constructing crossword puzzles for over 25 years. His puzzles have appeared in *The New York Times, Los Angeles Times, Games* magazine, and *Attache Magazine,* as well as numerous crossword puzzle compilations.

Michael Ashley is a veteran contributor of 25 years to *Games* magazine. His puzzles have also appeared in *The New York Times*, *The Washington Post, The Wall Street Journal,* and other places too numerous to count. His eighth collection of quotation puzzles, *Random House Crostics*, will be published in November 2003.

Patrick Berry is a freelance puzzle constructor, whose work has appeared in *The New York Times, The Wall Street Journal, Harper's, The New Yorker, Games* magazine, and a variety of other publications. In his free time he plays the guitar, though not well.

Mark Danna is a full-time puzzle maker. He has written six word search books, cowrites a rhyming puzzle syndicated by United Media, has had crosswords published in *The New York Times,* and has created a variety of puzzles for *Games* magazine, where he was an associate editor.

Francis Heaney's puzzles have appeared in many publications, including *Games* magazine and *The New York Times.* Other works of his can be seen in *More Mirth of a Nation: The Best Contemporary Humor, 101 Damnations: The Humorist's Tour of Personal Hells,* and the websites Modern Humorist and McSweeney's.

Nancy Mandl confesses to being a lapsed librarian and dedicated web-surfer. She greatly enjoyed constructing puzzles for this edition, her very first venture into puzzleland.

FOREWORD

Stephanie Spadaccini, the editor of this book (and the author of some of its puzzles), has been creating crosswords since the 1970s, when she and I were both starting out in the puzzle business. At the crossword magazine company where I worked in Stamford, Connecticut, Stephanie's puzzles stood out above just about everyone else's. They were fresher, lighter, funnier, and more skillfully made.

At the time, Stephanie lived in Darien, next door to Stamford, so I had an idea: Let's start a club of crossword enthusiasts! I called her up, she was game, and thus was born the Fairfield County Puzzlers. The group eventually grew to more than twenty-five members in the area, and for many years we met monthly at each other's homes to talk about puzzles and play original word games.

Through the years Stephanie and I have remained friends and colleagues. Like me, she went on to edit for *Games* magazine. Unlike me, she moved to California and wrote for *Jeopardy!* And her original crosswords have continued to appear in all the top publications in the field.

In this book, Stephanie has compiled brand-new puzzles and quizzes by Patrick Berry, Michael Ashley, Francis Heaney, Mark Danna, and other leading names in the business—including her own. These all happen to be friends of mine as well. It's a small world.

The reputations of the above are your guarantee of many hours of pleasurable solving!

—Will Shortz
Editor of *The New York Times*
crossword puzzles

PREFACE

How fortunate do we feel at Portable Press? *Extremely.*

We have two great teams of talented people: the Bathroom Readers' Institute in Ashland, Oregon, and the Bathroom Readers' Hysterical Society in San Diego, California. These teams produce great books that we hope our devoted and loyal fans find both informative and entertaining, and that they have supported—to the tune of nearly four million sold.

This has allowed us to move beyond the confines of North America—we are spreading the word in Australia, and soon the United Kingdom...and then the world. We're always looking for new ways to delight, confound, and inform our readers, and we hope our latest entry will prove to be as enjoyable to read as it was to create.

During the process of developing our first two *Uncle John Bathroom Reader Plunges into...* books, it was our good fortune to develop a working relationship with the extremely talented writer and editor Stephanie Spadaccini—who by chance happened to be a former managing editor of *Games* magazine.

Hmmm... an idea began to make its way through the murky depths of our brains. Let's take the kinds of fabulous facts and information found in all of our books (over 7,000 pages at this point), and create a puzzle book—a puzzle book that will amuse and challenge. Let's utilize the formidable Ms. Spadaccini's talents to develop a book that will have something for everyone, from the novice to the aficionado.

And here you have it. With puzzles from easy to hard, from long to short, and from fun to thoughtful, we hope that this book will test your puzzle-solving mettle and provide you with hours of amusement.

Please enjoy!

And let us know what you think by writing to us at: unclejohn@advmkt.com, or Portable Press, 5880 Oberlin Dr., San Diego, California 92121.

Flushed with pride,
Uncle Al
Publisher, Portable Press

INTRODUCTION

When I first started editing the *Uncle John Bathroom Reader Plunges into...* series, I knew in a flash that I had in my hands the most perfect source for a puzzle book on earth. But I didn't do anything about it until my good friend (and unofficial literary agent) Jack Jennings suggested that I talk it up with the Uncle John's folks. Where, as it turned out, Uncle Al (of the Bathroom Readers' Hysterical Society) had long been thinking the very same thing.

The book I had in mind was one that anyone—including the severely puzzle-impaired—could pick up and play with. And because of my background in puzzles and quizzes, I also yearned to attract those diehards who disdain anything that has the nerve to appear in any newspaper west of the Hudson River.

All right, I thought, I'll get some of those East Coast puzzle people involved. So I called another friend, Susan West, of *Games* magazine. Susan was kind enough to share her "A" list, a group of puzzle constructors who actually turned out to be from all corners of the U.S., not just Brooklyn. I set my new recruits loose among the *Uncle John Bathroom Readers* that have been published in the last fifteen years, and waited for the puzzles to come in.

The results were beyond my imagining. This huge puzzle book you hold in your hands is jam-packed with all of the fascinating, and very often goofy, infotainment that Uncle John is famous for—but it's presented in brand-new ways. And all of the puzzles and quizzes were written by some of the best constructors and quiz writers in the country.

So here's the plan. We want to start you out with some easy, breezy puzzles and quizzes. Then—watch out!—because things are going to get progressively tougher. But that's just in general. In particular, you'll find all sorts of brain squeezers and teasers sprinkled throughout our brand-new baby, *The Uncle John's Bathroom Reader Puzzle Book #1.*

And don't be afraid to try a puzzle you've never tried before. You might like it!

So again, thanks to Jack, without whom it might never have happened; Susan West at *Games*; Merl Reagle, for his splendid advice; Ellen Ripstein and David Levinson Wilk, for their impeccable editing. Thanks to JoAnn, Allen, Mana, and Amanda of the Portable Press; and finally, thanks to my brilliant contributors. And oh, yes. To my old pal Willie, whose loyalty to a friend won out over the questionable use of his well-respected name between the covers of a "bathroom" book.

—Stephanie Spadaccini

THE ANAGRAMMIES

In which we present some of this year's winners of our own prestigious wordplay awards, the AnaGrammies—those neat anagrams that, when the letters are jumbled, the meaning remains close to the same. May we have the envelope, please?

ACROSS

1 *General Hospital* is one
5 Washing machine cycle
9 Incident
14 Loser to the Tortoise
15 Dorothy's dog in *The Wizard of Oz*
16 Crowbar, e.g.
17 Elevator inventor
18 Rainbow shapes
19 Farm machinery manufacturer John ___
20 Anagram of HALT WITH WONDER
23 Ancient
24 Patriotic ladies (abbr.)
25 They begin the alphabet
28 Lovers' ___
31 Hug
36 Arid
38 Be the boss or the best
40 Ill-fated luxury liner the *Andrea* ___
41 Anagram of NO UNTIDY CLOTHES
44 *Goldfinger* actress Shirley
45 Itty-bitty
46 Precipice
47 The magic word
49 Apiece
51 Musket's ending
52 What you hear with
54 *Back to the Future* actress Thompson
56 Anagram of IS LIT FOR SEAMEN
64 Buy, buy, buy
65 Kidney or lima
66 "Hey, what's the big ___"?
67 Fancy name for a pie
68 ___ *Reader*
69 Drapery hangers
70 Stayed on one's feet
71 *The* ___ *of Katie Elder*
72 Ultimatum word that follows "or"

DOWN

1 The ___ must go on
2 Vow, like the Hippocratic one
3 Song for Jessye Norman
4 Sauce for pasta
5 Norm
6 After-dinner drink
7 Hankering
8 Snooped (around)
9 Fabled city of gold
10 Take a hard right, e.g.
11 Mr. Knievel
12 Dweeb
13 "*Uno, due,* ___..."
21 Sick
22 WWII army gal (abbr.)
25 Take ___ in the right direction
26 Joy of *The View*
27 Greek island
29 Night in Paris
30 Cow from old commercials
32 Part in a play
33 Wear down
34 Burn slightly
35 *When I Need You* singer Leo
37 Baseball player Slaughter
39 Sicilian volcano
42 Not cared for
43 Tornadolike storms
48 Single cereal kernel
50 "___ So Fine" (1963 #1 hit)
53 Picture puzzle
55 Flaming
56 Dick and Jane's dog
57 Air prefix
58 Division word
59 *Panic Room* actor Jared
60 Herbie or Horace
61 Hit TV show *American* ___
62 Cincinnati team
63 Effortlessness
64 Aves

ANSWER, PAGE 187

DOG DOO! GOOD GOD!

A palindrome is a word or phrase that's spelled the same backward and forward. Word enthusiasts like to say that the first palindrome was uttered in the Garden of Eden when Adam first laid eyes on Eve: "Madam, I'm Adam." (Note that our foremother Eve had a palindromic name, as do people named Otto, Bob, and Anna. As does the sentence "Step on no pets.") Get it?

Your task is to complete the following phrases by filling in the blanks. All the letters you need are there. If the answers don't make a lot of sense to you, remember that in a palindromic world, they're sheer perfection.

1. Dennis _ _ _ _ _ _.
2. Was it a rat _   _ _ _?
3. 'Tis in a Desoto _ _ _ _ _   _   _ _ _.
4. Red rum, sir, _ _   _ _ _ _ _ _.
5. Dammit, _'_   _ _ _!
6. Do geese _ _ _   _ _ _?
7. A slut nixes _ _ _   _ _   _ _ _ _ _.
8. Lapses? Order _ _ _   _ _ _ _ _, _ _ _.
9. "Desserts," I _ _ _ _ _ _ _ _.
10. If I had a _ _-_ _…
11. Ed, I saw Harpo Marx _ _ _   _ _ _ _ _   _   _ _ _ _ _.
12. Yawn. Madonna fan? _ _   _ _ _ _   _ _ _.
13. Lisa Bonet ate _ _   _ _ _ _ _.
14. Do nine men interpret? "_ _ _ _   _ _ _,"   _   _ _ _.
15. Are we not drawn onward, we few, _ _ _ _ _   _ _ _ _ _ _   _ _   _ _ _   _ _ _?

ANSWER, PAGE 211

* * * * *

PALINDROMIC PEOPLE

Then there are the people who have palindromic names—but only when they're used in sentences like the following. Fill in the first name that begins each of these classic palindromic sentences.

1. _______, am I mayor?
2. _______ and Edna dine.
3. _______ won no wallets
4. _______, I stay away at six A.M.
5. _______, did I moan?
6. _______ is as selfless, as I am, Ron.

ANSWER, PAGE 196

THE KING'S THINGS

Back before we had Michael Jackson to kick around, Elvis Presley served most of our eccentric rock star needs. Here are some of the things Elvis demanded be kept at Graceland at all times. Can you find all 22 of the capitalized words and phrases in the grid?

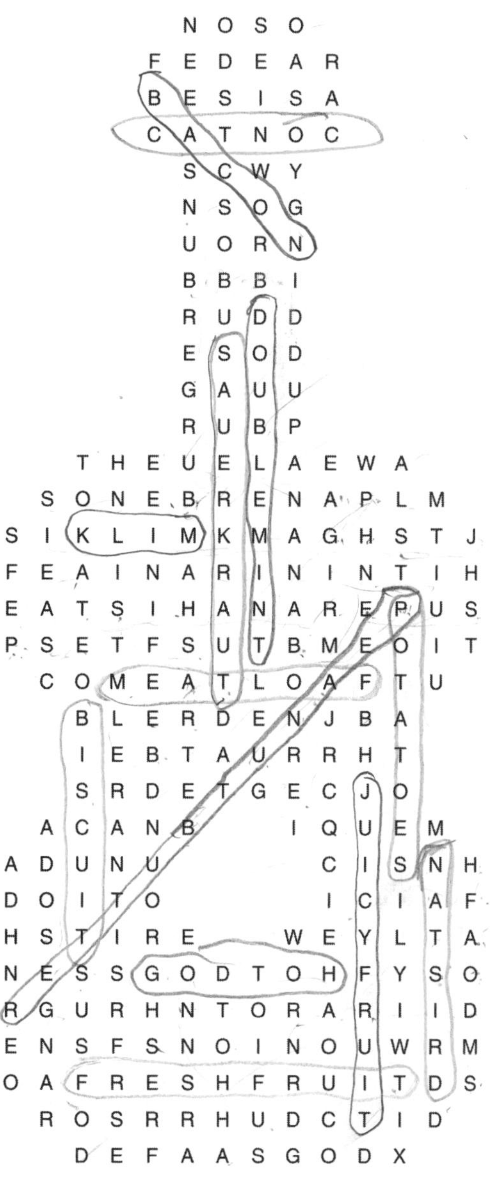

BACON
BANANA PUDDING
Six cans of BISCUITS
BROWNIES
CIGARETTES
CONTAC
DRISTAN
FRESH FRUIT

FRESH GROUND BEEF
HAMBURGER BUNS
HOT DOGS
JUICY FRUIT and
DOUBLEMINT gum
MEATLOAF
MILK
ONIONS

PEANUT BUTTER
Case of PEPSI
POTATOES
SAUERKRAUT
SUCRETS
SUPER ANAHIST

ANSWER, PAGE 187

THE CHIMP WHO SAVED EARLY MORNING TV

Here's the story of one of the most famous celebrities of TV's early years—an adorable chimpanzee with a fan base that would make Mel Gibson drool. The chimp, J. Fred Muggs, single-handedly saved the morning news/talk show when he became TV's first animal superstar in the early 1950s. But if you want to find out the real story you'll have to pick the correct answers from among the three choices in each set of parentheses.

When television was just getting started, few people thought an early morning program like ***(Good Morning America, The Early Show, The Today Show)*** could succeed…and it almost didn't; at first hardly anyone watched it. But Pat Weaver, the brains behind the show, and father of **(James Dean, Dennis Weaver, Sigourney Weaver)**, refused to give up.

In 1953, Weaver added a new cast member—J. Fred Muggs, who dressed like a human and acted like an ape, sometimes running wild on the set as host **(Dave Garroway, Ernie Kovacs, Arthur Godfrey)** watched in amusement—even though he actually hated sharing the spotlight with an ape.

Owner/trainer Buddy Mennella had raised Muggs like a son. As a result, Muggs was toilet-trained and enjoyed wearing clothes, except for **(shoes, long sleeves, hats)** which he would shed if he had to wear them for too long. Muggs's more popular routines on the show included impersonations of celebrities like Jack Benny, Popeye the Sailor, and **(Mighty Mouse, Judy Garland, General George Patton)**. The chimp was an avid finger-painter. His crowning achievement came when one of his paintings became a ***(Time, TV Guide, Mad)*** magazine cover.

J. Fred overslept and missed his first scheduled appearance in 1953. When he arrived at **(NBC, ABC, CBS)** the producers told him "Forget it." But ten minutes later, they realized they'd made a mistake—the show needed the chimp.

They ran after J. Fred and found him in a nearby drugstore eating a **(banana, cheese sandwich, donut)**, while Mennella drank a cup of coffee. Pushing aside a young man who was playing with Fred, they grabbed the chimp and trainer and brought them back to the studio. They should have grabbed the young man, too. He was **(Paul Newman, Andy Warhol, James Dean)**.

Muggs mugged so much for the TV camera while the audience listened to a radio broadcast of **(Queen Elizabeth's coronation, the London Olympics, an interview with Winston Churchill)** that the incident was brought up during a session of the House of Commons, and the London stop in Muggs's 1954 World Tour had to be canceled.

Muggs left the show in 1957 and went to work in a Florida **(amusement park, department store, wax museum)**. He retired in 1975.

UPDATE: Muggs's trainer Buddy Mennella died in 2002. He was survived by his pal J. Fred, who, as of this writing, lives with his common-law chimpette, Phoebe B. Beebe, in a lovely 2,400 square foot home in Citrus Park, Florida. We thought you'd want to know.

ANSWER, PAGE 212

HONK IF YOU LOVE PEACE AND QUIET

We've disguised three bumper sticker sayings in the puzzles below. Drop the letters from each vertical column—but not necessarily in the order in which they appear—into the empty squares below them to spell out the sayings, reading from left to right. Words may wrap around from one line to the next; black squares signify the spaces between words. Enjoy the ride—and no tailgating!

1.

P	T		M		N	T	E			E	T		W		Y
L	O	I	S	E	S	S	I	C		I	I	Y	G	A	O
N	D	N	T	I	W	O	R	K	B	A	N	N	W	O	U
N	O	■	S	E	N	S	E	■	B	E	I	N	G	■	O
P	T	I	M	I	S	T	I	C	■	I	T	■	W	O	U
L	D	N	T	■	W	O	R	K	■	A	N	Y	W	A	Y

2.

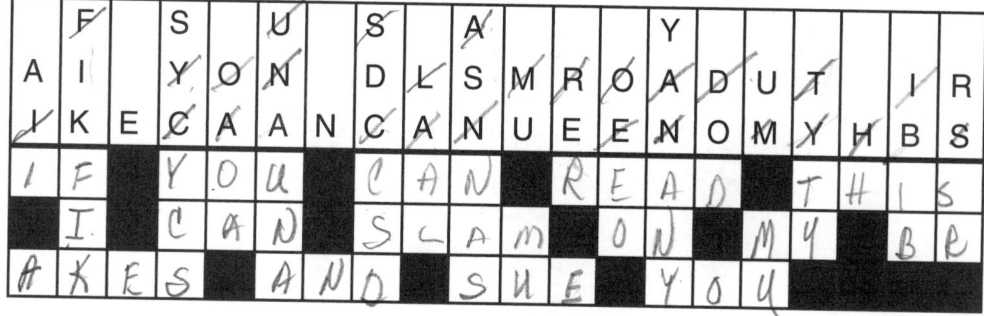

F S U S A Y
A I Y O N D L S M R O A D U T I R
I K E C A A N C A N U E E N O M Y H B S
I F ■ Y O U ■ C A N ■ R E A D ■ T H I S
■ I ■ C A N ■ S L A M ■ O N ■ M Y ■ B R
A K E S ■ A N D ■ S U E ■ Y O U

3.

U				O		S		E				R	N	L	Y				
Y	N	U	E	A	R	N	W	R	O	R	E	A	L	V	E			Y	A
R	O	L	T	N	E	V	E	T	A	R	D	U	I	T	I	L	L	E	O
Y	O	U	■	N	E	V	E	R	■	R	E	A	L	L	Y	■	L	E	A
R	N	■	T	O	■	S	W	E	A	R	■	U	N	T	I	L	■	Y	O
U	■	L	E	A	R	N	■	T	O	■	D	R	I	V	E	■	■	■	■

ANSWER, PAGE 192

SO YOU THINK YOU'VE SEEN A UFO

This is an excerpt from a checklist we published in *Uncle John's Bathroom Reader Plunges into the Universe*, in the hopes that it would save you some embarrassment before you told all your buddies at the bar that you'd seen a UFO. But this time we've taken some of the more important words, mixed up the letters, and placed them under the blanks. So before you make a darn fool of yourself, you'll have to figure out exactly what to watch out for.

1. Make sure it's not ___ ___ ___ ___ ___.
   N V U S E

2. Make sure it's not a ___ ___ ___ ___ ___ ___.
   T E M R O E

3. Make sure it's not ___ ___ ___ ___ ___ ___ ___ ___ ___ ___ ___ ___ ___ ___ ___ ___ ___.
   L G A N F I L P E C A S K J N U

4. Make sure it's not a ___ ___ ___ ___ ___.
   D O L U C

5. Make sure it's not a ___ ___ ___ ___ ___ ___ ___ ___ ___ ___ ___ ___ ___ ___.
   T R A E H W E O N L A B O L

6. Make sure it's not ___ ___ ___ ___ ___ ___ ___ ___ ___ ___ ___ ___ ___ ___ ___ ___ ___.
   T Y L I M A R I C F A R T I A R

7. Make sure it's not an ___ ___ ___ ___ ___ ___ ___ ___ ___ ___ ___ ___ ___ ___ ___ ___ ___ ___ ___.
   C R I L T C E L A E G S H A D R E I C

ANSWER, PAGE 187

A LITTLE LIST

Can you unscramble the letters below to figure out where danger lurks inside your car, be it RV, SUV, or VW? The lap you save may be your own.

The 3 Most Dangerous Foods to Eat in a Car

1. ___ ___ ___ ___ ___ ___
   E C F E O F

2. ___ ___ ___ ___ ___
   A S C O T

3. ___ ___ ___ ___ ___
   I I H L C

ANSWER, PAGE 193

SNAP, CRACKLE, FLOP

For every successful cereal like Frosted Flakes or Wheaties, there are hundreds of bombs like Banana Wackies and Ooboperoos. Here are a few of those legendary cereal flops, along with a few we made up. Can you separate the Wheaties from the chaff and find the fakes?

Mysterios (1959): Each box contained one of four different possible flavors—corn, chocolate, cinnamon, or "fruit." Not any particular fruit…just fruit. Anyway, since most kids were interested in one flavor more than the others, their parents generally just bought cereals that were the flavor their kids wanted.

Kellogg's Kream Crunch (1963): Frosted-oat loops mixed with cubes of freeze-dried vanilla-orange or strawberry ice cream. According to a Kellogg's exec: "The product kind of melted into gooey ice cream in milk. It just wasn't appetizing."

Sugar Smiles (1953): General Mills' first try at sugar cereal. A bizarre mixture of plain Wheaties and sugar-frosted Kix. Slogan: "You can't help smiling the minute you taste it."

Dinos (early 1990s): After the success of Fruity Pebbles, Post tried naming a cereal after the Flintstones' pet dinosaur. "A question that came up constantly," recalls a Post art director, "was 'We've got Cocoa Pebbles and Fruity Pebbles…so what flavor is Dino?'…It sounds like something Fred would be getting off his lawn instead of something you'd want to be eating."

Grape Ape (1976): The Saturday morning cartoon show this cereal was based on didn't last very long, but it lasted longer than the cereal. An adman for Kellogg's said, "It tasted like someone poured milk into grape juice."

Day-O (late 1960s): "The world's first calypso-inspired presweetened cereal," from General Mills.

Post Jelly Donuts (1964): The "donuts" in this cereal weren't very donut-y, but they *were* filled with jelly. Unfortunately, the donuts tended to crack in the box during shipping, and the jelly leaked out, making one big sticky mess.

Ooops (early 1970s): General Mills had so many bombs, they came up with a cereal they actually *said* was based on a mistake. The jingle went: "Ooops, it's a crazy mistake, Ooops, it's a cereal that's great!"

Kellogg's Corn Crackos (1967): The box featured the Waker Upper Bird perched on a bowl of candy-coated twists. An internal company memo said: "It looks like a bird eating worms; who wants worms for breakfast?"

Punch Crunch (1975): A spin-off of Cap'n Crunch. The screaming pink box featured Harry S., an exuberant hippo in a sailor suit, making goo-goo eyes at Cap'n Crunch. Many chain stores perceived the hippo as gay and refused to carry the cereal. Marveled one Quaker salesman: "How that one ever got through, I'll never understand."

ANSWER, PAGE 188

YOU AIN'T GOT IT, KID

On the basis of the evidence below, future superstars are constantly being overlooked by producers, publishers, and other big shots. (So that's some consolation for those of us who haven't made the big time yet.) See if you can guess who these remarkable rejections were referring to.

1. **What they said:** "With your voice, nobody is going to let you broadcast."
Who said it: CBS producer Don Hewitt, 1958
Rejected:
    a) Barbara Walters
    b) Julia Child
    c) Regis Philbin

2. **What they said:** "Stiff, unappealing. You ain't got it, kid."
Who said it: Columbia producer Jerry Tokovsky, 1965
Rejected:
    a) Sylvester Stallone
    b) Al Pacino
    c) Harrison Ford

3. **What they said:** "You have a chip on your tooth, your Adam's apple sticks out too far, and you talk too slow."
Who said it: A Universal Pictures exec, 1959
Rejected:
    a) Clint Eastwood
    b) Sean Connery
    c) Don Knotts

4. **What they said:** "That girl doesn't have a special perception or feeling which will lift that book above the curiosity level."
Who said it: An anonymous publisher, 1952
Rejected:
    a) *To Kill a Mockingbird*
    b) *The Diary of Anne Frank*
    c) *The Bell Jar*

5. **What they said:** "Go learn to cook. Your book will never sell."
Who said it: A literary agent in the early 1970s
Rejected:
    a) Toni Morrison
    b) Danielle Steel
    c) Betty Friedan

6. **What they said:** "The band's okay, but if I were you, I'd get rid of the singer with the tire-tread lips."
Who said it: A BBC radio producer at a 1963 audition
Rejected:
    a) The Kinks
    b) The Pretty Things
    c) The Rolling Stones

7. **What they said:** "His ears are too big. He looks like an ape."
Who said it: Talent scout Darryl F. Zanuck
Rejected:
    a) Peter Lorre
    b) Clark Gable
    c) Humphrey Bogart

8. **What they said:** "Can't act. Can't sing. Balding. Can dance a little."
Who said it: A studio exec in the late 1920s
Rejected:
    a) Gene Kelly
    b) James Cagney
    c) Fred Astaire

ANSWER, PAGE 188

BROADWAY BABIES

Behind the scenes of some long-long-long-running musicals, and how they made it to the bright lights and the big city.

1	2	3	4	5	■	6	7	8	9	■	10	11	12	13
14					■	15				■	16			
17					■	18				■	19			
■	■	20			21					22				
■	■	■	23			■	■	24			■	25		
26	27	28				29	30	■	31		32	■	■	■
33			■	34				35	■	36		37	38	39
40			41	■	42				43	■	44			
45				46	■	47				48	■	49		
■	■	■	50		51	■	52				53			
54	55	56	■	57		58	■	■	59			■	■	■
60			61				62	63				64	■	■
65				■	66				■	67			68	69
70				■	71				■	72				
73				■	74				■	75				

ACROSS

1 Merest remnant of a sandwich
6 Dance done by lei people?
10 Junk e-mail
14 "Is that your ___ answer?"
15 Perched on
16 Sacred
17 Bandmaster/composer John Philip ___
18 Green citrus fruit
19 There's lots of it in spinach
20 Musical based on a TV drama called *I, Don Quixote*
23 700, in old Rome
24 Catch
25 Possesses
26 Rodgers and Hammerstein's first collaboration, originally called *Away We Go!*
31 Just out
33 Corporate VIP
34 Gives off
36 Coffee-break time, maybe
40 Pitfall
42 Aunt in 26 Across
44 Foundation
45 Desi or Lucie
47 Thin strips of wood
49 Race with two winners
50 Nothing
52 Kern, Hammerstein, and Ziegfeld collaboration based on an Edna Ferber novel
54 Busy worker in Apr.
57 Dustin's *Rain Man* costar
59 *The Producers* producer Brooks
60 The Frenchman who wrote it was inspired by the hit show *Oliver!*
65 Opera solo
66 List entry
67 They need mowing
70 Disencumbers
71 Nothing
72 Heep of *David Copperfield*
73 Bass and Guinness
74 Messy stuff
75 Tiny tribesman

DOWN

1 Outfield positions (abbr.)
2 S.A. vacation spot
3 *E pluribus* ___
4 Ancient fortress in Israel
5 DuBois of *A Streetcar Named Desire*
6 50%
7 Gas or electric (abbr.)
8 *Death of a Salesman* character Willy
9 Tarzan is one
10 Leg part
11 Veranda
12 Welcome, in Waikiki
13 Mimicking birds
21 "___ all ye faithful..."
22 Assist in a crime
26 Prefix meaning "eight"
27 *The King and I* actress Deborah
28 Bank transaction
29 Paper factory
30 Bodybuilder Charles
32 One of the Ws in www
35 Adam and Eve's third son
37 Eur. alliance
38 Largest continent
39 Be introduced to
41 Give a bad review
43 Slanted square, for short
46 Pasta variety
48 Increase in size, as a bump
51 Trailing the winner
53 ___-eyed (tired)
54 Red Cross founder Barton
55 Danger
56 Parenthetical remark
58 "Heavy" kind of rock
61 Church service
62 Renovate
63 "Do I have to draw you ___?"
64 Drink greedily
68 '60s war zone, to a vet
69 Not outspoken

ANSWER, PAGE 188

IF THEY MARRIED

In *Uncle John's Ahh-Inspiring Bathroom Reader*, we finally found a use for celebrities...well, not the whole celebrity, just the name. Fill in the blanks to find out what the celebs' married names would be.

1. If Bo Derek married Don Ho, she'd be __ __   __ __.

2. If Yoko Ono had married Sonny Bono, she'd be __ __ __ __   __ __ __   __ __ __ __.

3. If Dolly Parton had married Salvador Dali, she'd be __ __ __ __ __   __ __ __ __.

4. If Oprah Winfrey married Deepak Chopra, she'd be __ __ __ __ __   __ __ __ __ __ __.

5. If Olivia Newton-John married Wayne Newton, then divorced him to marry Elton John, she'd be __ __ __ __ __ __   __ __ __ __ __ __-__ __ __ __   __ __ __ __ __ __   __ __ __ __.

6. If Sondra Locke had married Eliot Ness, then divorced him to marry Herman Munster, she'd be __ __ __ __ __ __   __ __ __ __ __   __ __ __ __   __ __ __ __ __ __ __.

7. If Bea Arthur married Sting, she'd be __ __ __   __ __ __ __ __.

8. If Liv Ullmann married Judge Lance Ito, then divorced him to marry Billy Beaver (game show host), she'd be __ __ __   __ __ __   __ __ __ __ __ __.

9. If Shirley Jones had married Tom Ewell, then Johnny Rotten, then Nathan Hale, she'd be __ __ __ __ __ __ __   __ __ __ __ __   __ __ __ __ __ __   __ __ __ __.

10. If Ivana Trump had married, in succession, actor Orson Bean, King Oscar (of Norway), Louis B. Mayer (of MGM fame), and Norbert Wiener (mathematician), she'd be __ __ __ __ __   __ __ __ __   __ __ __ __ __   __ __ __ __ __   __ __ __ __ __ __.

11. If Javier Lopez married Keiko the whale, and Edith Piaf married Rose Tu the elephant, they'd be __ __ __ __ __ __   __ __ __ __ __ and __ __ __ __ __   __ __.

12. If Tuesday Weld married Hal March III, she'd be __ __ __ __ __ __ __   __ __ __ __ __   __ __ __.

13. If Snoop Dogg married Winnie the Pooh, he'd be __ __ __ __ __   __ __ __ __   __ __ __ __.

ANSWER, PAGE 188

SNACK FOOD OF THE GODS

Directions: The grid contains a quotation that reads from left to right. The words in it wrap around to the next line; the black squares signify the spaces between the words.

Start by answering as many of the clues as you can. Write your answers on the numbered dashes, then transfer the letters to the correspondingly numbered squares in the puzzle grid. Work back and forth between the grid and the word list until the full quotation appears in the grid.

As an extra-added bonus (or a tool to use if you get stuck), if you read the first letters of the words in the word list in sequence, you'll find an acrostic—a hidden message about the subject of the quotation.

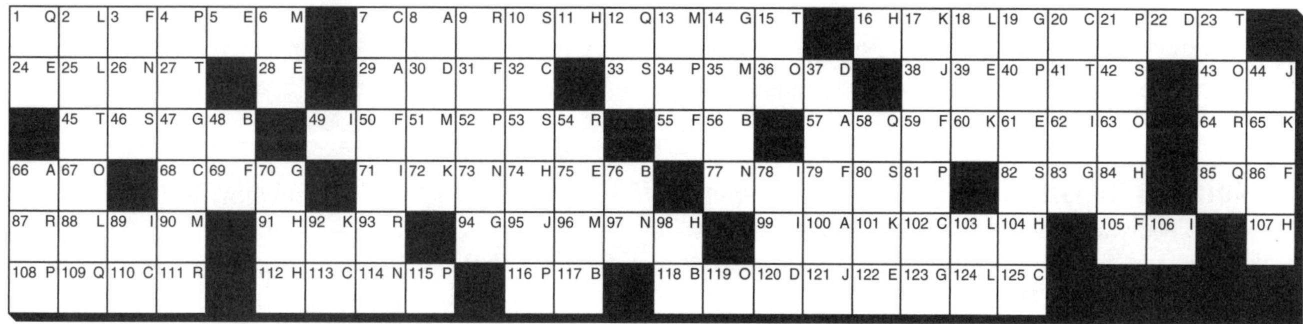

A. Home of Arizona State University

29 100 8 57 66

B. Tests by lifting

48 118 56 117 76

C. Event first observed internationally on April 22, 1970 (2 wds.)

20 102 110 68 113 125 7 32

D. Source of turpentine, tar, and pitch

120 30 37 22

E. Round of applause

122 5 28 24 39 61 75

F. Luxury hi-rise feature

59 86 31 3 69 55 79 105 50

G. Voltaire's most popular novel

47 83 14 123 19 94 70

H. Stubborn

74 16 84 112 11 98 107 91 104

I. Magazine for the young working mother

62 89 71 99 106 78 49

J. 1994 title role for Jodie Foster

44 95 38 121

K. Star of *Up in Smoke*

60 92 17 72 101 65

L. The Melancholy Dane

25 2 103 18 124 88

M. Butted up against

51 13 96 35 6 90

N. Hometown of Gerald Ford and Malcolm X

97 73 114 77 26

O. Oliver Stone's 1995 biopic

63 43 119 36 67

P. Cleverly creative

116 108 21 81 52 115 4 40 34

Q. Star of *Up in Smoke*

12 85 58 1 109

R. Room to move

54 9 93 64 87 111

S. Director of *The Pink Panther*

53 33 82 46 10 42 80

T. Mrs. Peel's partner

15 27 45 41 23

ANSWER, PAGE 188

TWISTED TITLES

California Monthly, the magazine for alumni of the University of California at Berkeley, features a game called *Twisted Titles*, in which readers are asked to send the title of a book, film, play, etc., with just one letter changed—and include a brief description of the new work they envision. Can you figure out what letter in each title was changed, based on its new description?

LITTLE RED RIDING HOOD:
Marxist midget shelters Hoffa.

DON'T SIT UNDER THE APPLE TREE:
The Andrews Sisters experience middle-age spread.

JUDE THE OBSCURE:
Wally and the Beaver's reclusive mom tells all.

THE CAT IN THE HAT:
Dr. Seuss introduces toddlers to the facts of life.

MY LIFE AS A DOG:
Pinocchio reflects on his childhood.

THE NEW TESTAMENT:
Bible of the "Me" generation.

DANCES WITH WOLVES:
Western epic starring the Three Stooges.

PATRIOT GAMES:
The DAR does the IRA.

'TIL DEATH DO US PART:
Vows exchanged in New York City gridlock.

NEVER THE TWAIN SHALL MEET:
Sam Clemens becomes a vegetarian.

CANTERBURY TALES:
Phil, Oprah, Geraldo, and now, *GEOFF!*

CLUB MED:
High jinks at Hyannisport.

MY LEFT FOOT:
Politically correct chow.

BOYZ N THE HOOD:
Jews and blacks unite to drive the KKK out of Beverly Hills.

THE WINTER OF OUR DISCONTENT:
I'm more dysfunctional than you are.

SLEEPING WITH THE ENEMY:
A tragedy in one act.

ANSWER, PAGE 188

* * * * *

WHO WANTS A GRAMMY, ANYWAY?

As strange as it sounds, four of the artists/groups below never won a single Grammy. Pick the only one that did.

a) Jimi Hendrix
b) The Who
c) Fleetwood Mac
d) The Beach Boys
e) The Doors

ANSWER, PAGE 188

PHRASEOLOGY 101

You've heard it before…but have you ever wondered where it came from?

ACROSS

1 ___ tree (in trouble)
4 Sanctify
9 Zoo barker
13 Teases
15 Go along with
16 ___ the way (get things ready)
17 Phrase from avoiding the punishment of getting hit on the knuckles
19 Swear
20 Hollywood types
21 "___" (1964 hit song about a car)
23 Conclusion
24 First prime minister of the republic of India
25 Happy ___ clam
27 Dads
29 Phrase from the days when knees were called the same as finger joints
34 The Andes, e.g.
37 Leg joint
38 Off the right path
39 Dry as a desert
41 Novelist Anne or actress Liv
43 Sammy of baseball
44 Dracula player Bela
46 Infants
48 Enclosure
49 It's from the Spanish *sombrero galon*
52 Donkey
53 Response to a ques.
54 Makes void
58 Mr. Masterson
60 Do some tailoring
62 Sesame, for one
63 Burden
65 Phrase from the days when stagecoaches raced each other on narrow roads
68 Positive-negative separator
69 Kind of engine
70 Comedian Laurel
71 Is beholden to
72 German surrealist Max
73 Cheer at a bullfight

1	2	3	■	4	5	6	7	8	■	9	10	11	12
13			14	■	15				■	16			
17				18					■	19			
20						■	■	21		22	■	23	
24					■	25	26		■	27	28	■	■
■	■	■	29		30				31			32	33
34	35	36	■	37				■	38				
39			40	■	41			42		■	43		
44				45		■	46			47	■	48	
49						50					51	■	■
■	■	52			■	53			■	54		55	56	57
58	59		■	60	61		■	■	62				
63			64	■	65		66	67					
68				■	69					■	70		
71				■	72					■	■	73	

DOWN

1 Citified
2 Slice of the pie, e.g.
3 Take ___ (lose a lot of money)
4 Exclamations of disgust
5 Shirt size (abbr.)
6 Make a boo-boo
7 Movie tough guy Steven
8 Month after Aug.
9 Health resort
10 Listen in
11 Stratford-on-___
12 Lascivious
14 Baby carrier?
18 Place for a spare
22 Major work
25 ___-deucey
26 He played Kadiddlehopper
28 Tiny crawlers
30 *Wait ___ Dark*
31 Third planet from the Sun
32 Relaxation
33 Strikeout king Nolan
34 Beer ingredient
35 Factual
36 "John Hancock"
40 *Best in Show* contestants
42 Long times
45 Window frame
47 Christmas presence
50 Hope-Crosby costar Dorothy
51 Goes off in another direction
55 Resulted in
56 On the up-and-up
57 *The Donna Reed Show* family name
58 TV clown
59 Once again
61 Ending with kitchen or luncheon
62 Vaccination
64 Brillo competitor
66 Coffee holder
67 Corp. with an eye on TV

ANSWER, PAGE 189

WHERE'S CHARLIE?

Can you guess which famous Charles or Charlie (no Chucks) we're gossiping about here?

1. From 1925 to 1949, there were 47 movies made about the fictional Chinese detective. Six actors played him—not one was Chinese.
2. As a child, he was teased so much about the size of his ears that his great-uncle told his mother to surgically fix the "problem." She declined.
3. His father was a U.S. congressman. During a visit to the Capitol as a boy, he locked the doors of the bathroom and threw lightbulbs at the street below.
4. If he were a real person, he'd be four and a half feet tall: His head would take up two of those feet, his body another two feet, and his legs six inches. Also, his head would be two feet wide.
5. After Tonya Harding called herself the "Charles ___ of figure skating," this Charles said, "My initial response was to sue her for defamation of character, but then I realized that I had no character."
6. Born on the same day as Abraham Lincoln, he originally wanted to be a doctor, but had to give it up because he "wasn't smart enough."
7. His mansion was next door to notorious Hollywood rake John Barrymore's, so he installed a telescope to spy on his neighbor's nightly exploits.
8. When he was engaged to actress Kelly Preston, he accidentally shot her in the arm. She left him and married John Travolta.

ANSWER, PAGE 190

UNHOOKED ON PHONICS

Small crostic puzzles are solved just like the big ones (directions on page 11) but the first letter of the fill-in words **do not** spell out a hidden message.

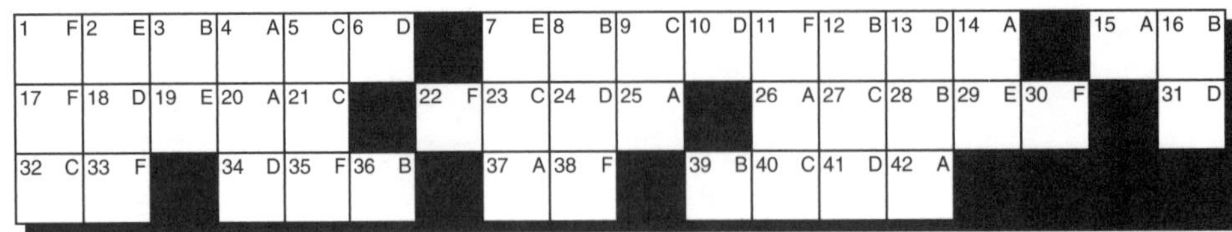

A. Censure publicly

___ ___ ___ ___ ___ ___ ___ ___
25 42 20 37 26 14 15 4

B. Hard black rubber

___ ___ ___ ___ ___ ___ ___
36 3 16 39 8 28 12

C. "Slim" Stephen King novel

___ ___ ___ ___ ___ ___ ___
21 32 40 27 9 23 5

D. Large island of myth

___ ___ ___ ___ ___ ___ ___ ___
24 6 18 34 41 31 13 10

E. Sandwich shop

___ ___ ___ ___
19 7 2 29

F. The _____ Dead (Jerry Garcia's band)

___ ___ ___ ___ ___ ___ ___ ___
35 22 1 11 33 38 17 30

ANSWER, PAGE 190

THE QUOTABLE JOHN

Our uncle is so very quotable....We took four little-known but fascinating factoids we found in Uncle John readers and translated them into cryptograms by simple letter substitution.

For instance, if we encoded UNCLE JOHN, he might end up looking like this: BRJAQ TLPR, where U = B, N = R, and so on. The letter substitutions remain constant throughout any one cryptogram, but they change from one cryptogram to the next. Here are some hints: A lot of words end in E, S, Y, R, and D; a single letter is usually an A or I; and look for words that begin with the same two-letter combination—those letters might stand for TH, as in THE, THAT, THEY, and so on. Proper nouns are preceded by an asterisk (*).

To Be Honest, Abe

OBM ROGQV: *ZWDAGZD XGOOMK KGTD OBM *CMOOVRNHQC *LKKQMRR GD LD MDPMZGEM. CGGK ROGQV, NHO XHRO L FVOB. RMPMQLZ KQLUOR GU OBM REMMAB BLPM NMMD KWRAGPMQMK.

Pick a Number, as Long as It's...

SYRWO VLZLQ. VLZLQ XV DCL VYI NB DCELL KQG BNYE, DCL DEXKQUSL KQG DCL VPYKEL, HCXRC KQRXLQD *UELLWV RNQVXGLELG DCL DHN "MLEBLRD BXUYELV."

One Guy—Four Pieces of Big Apple Pie

ETO QBIL GXWOGXII ZIXLOY OROY EQ ZIXL DQY XII DQJY *BOC *LQYA EOXKW (*KOEW, *MQMSOYW, *SFXBEW, *LXBAOOW) FW *MXYYLI *WEYXCGOYYL.

Speaking Pentagonese

TBFLXSHBGS WI TWVCKB-RFBLZ TBFLXSHBGS: SPB *V. *R. JWNBXGHBGS ALKKBT SPB QGNLRQWG WI *JXBGLTL L "FXBTLMG NBXSQALK QGRBXSQWG."

ANSWER, PAGE 189

HIM TARZAN, HER JANE

We've hidden Tarzan and Jane in the grid below—but don't go looking for them. What you'll find instead are the names of the actors and actresses who've played those roles through the years, 34 in all, reading across, down, and diagonally. We hope you won't go ape before you're done.

K	E	L	N	Y	T	F	R	R	E	L	B	A	T	Y	E	S	P	M	E	D	P
E	C	R	E	I	P	K	C	A	J	S	E	N	R	A	B	A	N	N	A	O	J
R	D	O	C	J	O	Y	C	E	M	A	C	K	E	N	Z	I	E	F	U	L	A
E	A	N	Y	W	D	L	O	G	Y	N	O	T	B	A	R	Q	E	W	I	G	N
D	T	J	O	H	N	N	Y	W	E	I	S	S	M	U	L	L	E	R	P	A	E
O	L	K	J	U	H	S	T	N	W	O	R	B	A	S	S	E	N	A	V	R	M
B	G	M	A	R	N	O	L	O	U	I	S	E	L	O	R	R	A	I	N	E	A
U	Y	M	D	A	F	A	O	N	D	O	R	F	R	N	B	E	L	T	A	I	R
S	E	A	N	L	I	M	T	O	A	W	O	T	E	O	G	L	G	A	L	N	C
T	N	R	E	L	U	C	I	A	B	K	T	E	H	T	U	L	O	N	L	E	H
E	O	H	R	O	F	E	I	N	L	E	R	E	P	S	N	I	R	T	E	D	O
R	H	C	B	P	O	R	T	E	N	I	N	A	O	U	G	M	D	R	W	E	K
C	A	S	P	E	R	V	A	N	D	I	E	N	T	H	A	Y	O	A	O	I	N
R	M	A	R	N	Z	E	E	N	D	W	E	K	S	A	I	N	N	H	D	D	O
A	K	L	U	E	R	B	K	M	K	E	Z	D	I	I	G	N	S	Y	C	Y	R
B	C	R	I	G	E	P	A	R	R	M	U	I	R	N	Y	E	C	H	A	L	M
B	O	A	C	C	H	R	Y	U	A	R	E	T	H	I	G	D	O	T	M	I	O
E	J	K	U	L	K	N	A	F	O	B	U	R	C	G	V	S	T	O	E	N	T
W	O	R	N	E	A	M	I	N	T	E	X	A	R	R	K	E	T	R	I	V	Z
S	B	R	Y	E	F	F	E	E	K	O	S	E	L	I	M	A	R	O	D	A	E
G	W	E	L	M	O	L	I	N	C	O	L	N	L	V	L	P	I	D	N	O	R
S	T	N	E	P	Y	R	G	S	I	R	R	O	M	N	E	L	G	E	A	F	R

The Tarzans:
BRUCE BENNETT
BUSTER CRABBE
CASPER VAN DIEN
CHRISTOPHER LAMBERT
DENNY MILLER
ELMO LINCOLN
FRANK MERRILL
GENE POLLAR
GLEN MORRIS
GORDON SCOTT
JACK PIERCE
JOCK MAHONEY
JOHNNY WEISSMULLER
LEX BARKER
MILES O'KEEFFE
P. DEMPSEY TABLER
RON ELY
TONY GOLDWYN

The Janes:
ANDIE MACDOWELL
BO DEREK
BRENDA JOYCE
DOROTHY HART
ENID MARKEY
JANE MARCH
JOANNA BARNES
JOYCE MACKENZIE
KARLA SCHRAMM
LOUISE LORRAINE
LYDIE DENIER
MAUREEN O'SULLIVAN
MINNIE DRIVER
NATALIE KINGSTON
VANESSA BROWN
VIRGINIA HUSTON

ANSWER, PAGE 189

BE THE BEATLES

Back in the 1960s, the Beatles were constantly proving they could do more than just write brilliant pop songs. At press conferences, for instance, they were masters of the witty, quirky retort. Here's your big chance to be your favorite Beatle. See if you can pick the actual responses from the choices given.

1. **Reporter:** Does all the adulation from teenage girls affect you?
   John:
   a) Oh, is that adulation? I thought they were frightened of us.
   b) When I feel my head start to swell, I look at Ringo and know perfectly well we're not supermen.
   c) It's certainly made me more handsome.

2. **Reporter:** What do you think of Beethoven?
   Ringo:
   a) He's great. Especially his poetry.
   b) His tunes could've been a bit shorter.
   c) Well, I don't think it's fair people get on us about our hair when Beethoven wore a wig.

3. **Reporter:** Would you like to walk down the street without being recognized?
   John:
   a) I don't mind the girls chasing me. I just wish they'd stop asking me where they can find Paul.
   b) We used to do that with no money in our pockets. There's no point in it.
   c) There's a street in Zaire we can go to when we want to do that.

4. **Reporter:** What do you think of the criticism that you are not very good?
   George:
   a) But we are very good! Except for Ringo, he's always stealing candy from babies, the cad.
   b) I think my mother should keep her opinions to herself.
   c) We're not.

5. **Reporter:** There's a "Stamp Out the Beatles" movement underway in Detroit. What are you going to do about it?
   Paul:
   a) We're going to start a campaign to stamp out Detroit.
   b) Try to stay out from underfoot, I suppose.
   c) Thank them. We'd be constantly catching on fire if it weren't for people stamping us out.

6. **Reporter:** Do you like topless bathing suits?
   Ringo:
   a) They make me too hot.
   b) We've been wearing them for years.
   c) They're better than topless drums.

7. **Reporter:** When you do a new song, how do you decide who sings the lead?
   John:
   a) We just get together and whoever knows most of the words sings the lead.
   b) If it's an easy song, then I sing the lead. Otherwise I'm busy concentrating on playing the guitar.
   c) How do you decide which reporter's going to ask the next question?

8. **Reporter:** Ringo, why do you wear two rings on each hand?
   Ringo:
   a) People keep putting them on my hands when I'm asleep and they won't come off.
   b) So they don't get lonely.
   c) Because I can't fit them through my nose.

9. **Reporter:** Why don't you smile, George?
   George:
   a) It's in my contract. I'm the moody one.
   b) I am smiling.
   c) I'll hurt my lips.

10. **Reporter:** What will you do when Beatlemania subsides?
    John:
    a) Take a nap.
    b) Count the money.
    c) Write some songs that aren't as good, I suppose.

ANSWER, PAGE 190

THE MONSTER LIVES!

A crossword about a monster so dear to our hearts that we still think fondly of him after all these years.

1	2	3	4	5	■	6	7	8	9	■	10	11	12	13
14					■	15				■	16			
17					■	18				■	19			
■	■	■	20		21					22				
23	24	25	■	■	26				■	27				
28			29	30			■	31	32		■	33		
34					■	■	35				36	■	■	■
■	■	37			38	39						40	■	■
■	■	■	41					■	■	42			43	44
45	46	47	■	48			■	49	50					
51			52		■	53	54			■	■	55		
56					57					58	59	■	■	■
60				■	61				■	62		63	64	65
66				■	67				■	68				
69				■	70				■	71				

ACROSS

1 Problems with a plan
6 Pleads
10 Bidding option
14 Misbehave
15 With, in Paris
16 Rapper-turned-actor
17 "The long green"
18 Gossip columnist Barrett
19 Beige color
20 The monster (and his creator) in question
23 Do a supermarket job
26 One's equal
27 West Point student
28 Commotions
31 Frank's wife between Nancy and Mia
33 Curve in the road
34 Post office purchase
35 Back of a boat
37 The woman who created 20 Across
41 Mailman's beat
42 Roof edges
45 Undergrad degs.
48 Arafat's org.
49 Servants for the very wealthy
51 Buddy, in Barcelona
53 Detach from the baby bottle
55 Took a load off
56 Actor who portrayed 20 Across
60 *Jacques ___ Is Alive and Well...*
61 Military no-show
62 The Scales, astrologically
66 Come down to earth
67 Zilch
68 Photographer Adams
69 Actress Lanchester who played 20 Across's bride
70 Ogled
71 Move from side to side

DOWN

1 Uncle ___ Wants You!
2 Sgt., e.g.
3 From ___ Z (everything)
4 Tonkin or Persian
5 Practice your punches
6 Noble's business partner
7 Conjure up, as a memory
8 Produce
9 Look over quickly
10 Michelangelo masterpiece
11 Give in to someone's wishes
12 The World ___
13 Attention-getting feats
21 Tax time (abbr.)
22 Shade that's really red
23 School transportation
24 Abbr. in a city address
25 Metric unit of weight
29 Poet Khayyam
30 Fitting
32 Speed (abbr.)
35 Beatles hit "___ Loves You"
36 *Hud* star Patricia
38 *The King and I* star Brynner
39 He's trying to get a free ride
40 Designer St. Laurent
43 Historical period
44 High-speed plane, for short
45 Talk nonsense
46 Unethical
47 Police car alarms
49 Sinatra specialty
50 Numero ___
52 Ms. Radner
54 Wear down
57 *Citizen* ___
58 Defect
59 Dandy's partner
63 Young knot-tying grp.
64 Gun the motor
65 Pub order

ANSWER, PAGE 190

WEIRD CELEBRATIONS

Which one of the following celebrations will Uncle John **not** be attending this year—because it doesn't exist?

THE ANNUAL FIRE ANT FESTIVAL
Location: Marshall, Texas
Background: Fire ants are red ants that swarm and bite—a real problem in South Texas. People in Marshall decided that since they couldn't get rid of the ants, they might as well have some fun with them.
Special Events: Fire Ant Call, Fire Ant Roundup, and a Fire Ant Chili Cook-Off in which entrants must certify in writing that their fixin's contain at least one fire ant. The ending to the festivities is the Fire Ant Stomp—not an attempt to squash the ants, but an old-fashioned street dance.

THE INTERNATIONAL STRANGE MUSIC FESTIVAL
Location: Olive Hill, Kentucky
Background: Founded to honor people who make music from nonmusical items.
Special Events: Every act is a special event. Performers have included a 15-piece orchestra of automobile horns, and a Japanese trio playing "My Old Kentucky Home" on a table (upside down, strung like a cello), teapot (a wind instrument), and assorted pots and pans (bongo drums).

THE ANNUAL CHICKEN SHOW
Location: Wayne, Nebraska
Background: Held on the second Saturday in July, featuring a crowing contest for roosters, a free omelet feed for humans, and a chicken-flying meet, fully sanctioned by the International Chicken Flying Association.
Special Events: A "Most Beautiful Beak" contest, chicken bingo, and an egg drop (participants risk egg-on-the-face by trying to catch a raw egg dropped from a fully extended cherry picker). The National Cluck-Off selects the person with the most lifelike cluck and most believable crow. Another contest offers prizes to the man and woman who sport the most chickenlike legs.

THE UGLY PICKUP PARADE AND CONTEST
Location: Chadron, Nebraska
Background: In 1987, newspaper columnist Les Mann wrote an homage to his junker 1974 pickup, "Black Beauty," claiming it was the ugliest truck on the planet. Irate ugly-truck owners wrote in, saying they could top him. So the first Ugly Truck Contest was born.
Special Events: Experts pick the Ugly Pickup of the Year. An Ugly Pickup Queen leads the three-block parade through town. Official rules: Trucks have to be street-legal, and over a decade old. They have to be able to move under their own power; a majority of the surface area has to be rust and dents; and, most important, they've got to have a good Ugly Truck name. Contestants get extra points for something *especially* ugly on their truck.

THE ANNUAL HELL'S ANGELS LOVE FEST
Location: Fairfax, California
Background: Commemorates the day in August 1972 when a swarm of Hell's Angels rode into town looking for trouble. Since the little burg was a haven for the hippie subculture, the citizens blithely welcomed the gang with smiles and daisies and within a few hours had all those tough guys wearing flowers in their hair.
Special Events: The town relives the days of flower power. The biggest attraction of the day is the parade: Hell's Angels from all over the western states converge on the town's main drag, stick a flower or two behind their ears and slowly ride down Main Street soaking up the adulation of the crowds.

ANSWER, PAGE 190

THE 10 MOST ADMIRED WOMEN IN AMERICA

You may not know it, but since 1948 the Gallup Poll has been asking Americans to name the people they admire the most. We were surprised by a lot of the choices for Most Admired Women—some we'd never heard of and some just aren't people we admire anymore. It goes to show how fleeting fame is. Here are 20 women who've appeared on the Gallup lists over the last 50+ years. When you've found them all, the leftover letters will reveal the names of a few more.

```
S O J M A R I A N A N D E R S O N
M Y E A S E R E T R E H T O M N O
T N A R N A G A E R Y C N A N I J
P N N G H E N O X I N T A P E U A
R E I A R S F O N E T P H E L Q C
I K T R I S T O S M E W E R E A K
N R A E E I H D N A G A R I D N I
C E B T L E A N R D O R R O N O E
E T R T E O S L E L A V E A L Z K
S S Y H T S S C L O A R M E B A E
S I A A O B M O T G H U E L U R N
G S N T U C E I H E R L E N H O N
R A T C Y E B E T T Y F O R D C E
A S K H A N D L S H U R L E E N D
C O R E T T A S C O T T K I N G Y
E W A R L H E L E N K E L L E R L
A C E Y B B O H P L U C A T E V O
```

ANITA BRYANT
BESS TRUMAN
BETTY FORD
CORAZON AQUINO
CORETTA SCOTT KING
GOLDA MEIR
HELEN KELLER
INDIRA GANDHI
JACKIE KENNEDY
JANE FONDA
KATE SMITH
MARGARET THATCHER
MARIAN ANDERSON
MOTHER TERESA
NANCY REAGAN
OVETA CULP HOBBY
PAT NIXON
PEARL S. BUCK
PRINCESS GRACE
SISTER KENNY

ANSWER, PAGE 191

SATURDAY NIGHT

Live…from New York, it's…a late-night show that's been on so long some of the original cast members are eligible for senior citizen privileges. See if you can fit them—and some of the newer cast members—into the grid crossword-style.

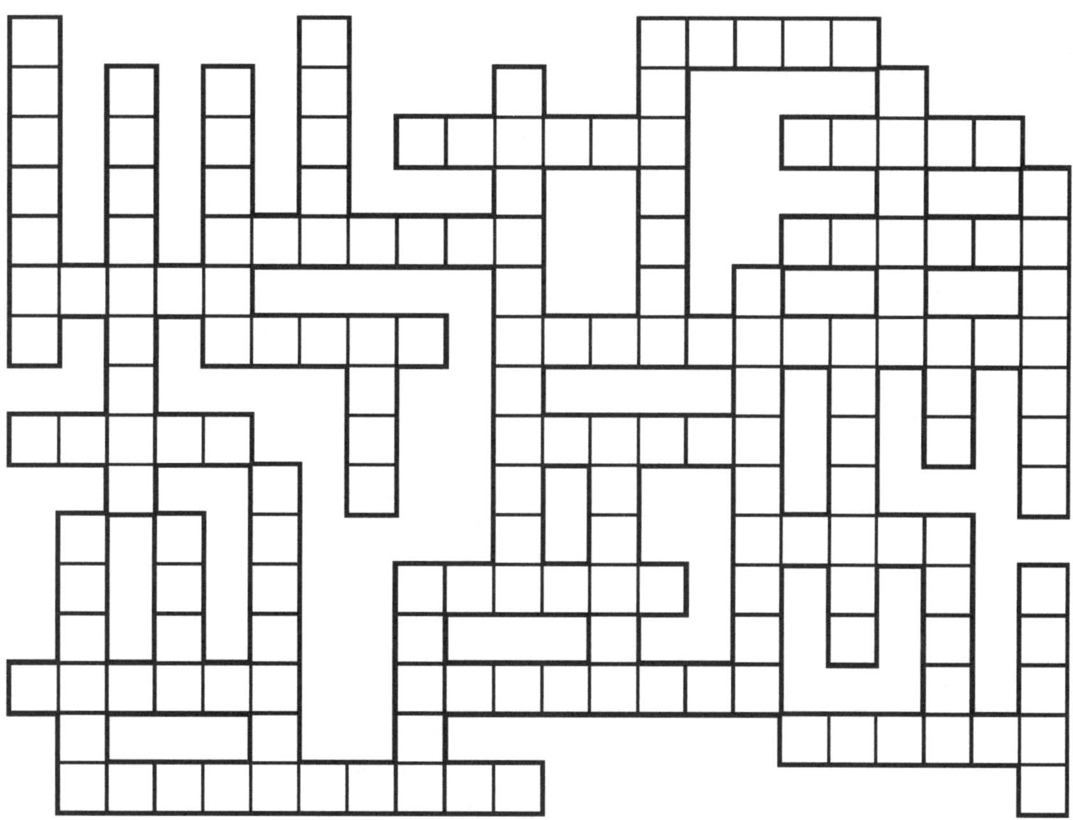

3 letter word
Tina FEY

4 letter words
Robin DUKE
Nora DUNN

5 letter words
A. Whitney BROWN
Chevy CHASE
Mary GROSS
Christopher GUEST
Mike MYERS
Cheri OTERI
Randy QUAID
Colin QUINN
Martin SHORT
David SPADE

6 letter words
Jane CURTIN
Joan CUSACK
Chris FARLEY
Dennis MILLER
Garrett MORRIS
Bill MURRAY
Laraine NEWMAN
Gilda RADNER
Robert SMIGEL
Damon WAYANS

7 letter words
John BELUSHI
Billy CRYSTAL
Chris ELLIOTT
Victoria JACKSON
Maya RUDOLPH
Harry SHEARER

8 letter word
Christine EBERSOLE

9 letter words
Michael O'DONOGHUE
Rob SCHNEIDER

10 letter word
Tim KAZURINSKY

11 letter word
Laura KIGHTLINGER

12 letter word
Julia LOUIS-DREYFUS

ANSWER, PAGE 190

YIDDISH-AMERICAN SLANG

A handful of Yiddish words have become common in the U.S. Can you match the Yiddish word (1–20) to its meaning (a–t)? What? Whaddaya mean there's too many? Quit your kvetching and do the quiz, already!

1. Bupkis
2. Chutzpa (hootz-pah)
3. Drek
4. Goniff
5. Kibitz
6. Klutz
7. Mensch
8. Meshugah (me-*shoo*-ga)
9. Noodge
10. Nosh
11. Schlemiel
12. Shiksa
13. Shlep
14. Shlock
15. Shlump
16. Shmooze
17. Shtick
18. Spritz
19. Tchotchke (chotch-key)
20. Yenta

a. A hapless individual; a person who always has bad luck; a fool
b. A non-Jewish woman
c. An act or a routine (usually associated with show business)
d. A sloppy person
e. Nothing
f. A sneaky thief; someone who takes advantage of others when able to
g. Junk; the bottom of the barrel
h. To offer unsolicited advice
i. To squirt. As a noun, a squirt of something
j. A compassionate, decent person; someone both strong and kind
k. To chat
l. A pest; as a verb, "to pester or coax"
m. A snack; as a verb, "to snack"
n. A nosy, gossipy person
o. A toy, knickknack, or worthless gizmo
p. To haul around
q. A clumsy or inept person (from the German word for "wooden block")
r. Crazy
s. Something that's poorly made, or made for low-class taste
t. Clever audacity

ANSWER, PAGE 192

* * * * *

SPEAKING OF YIDDISH...

Other than the fact that they're all Jewish, what do the following famous folks have in common? (Hint: It has to do with their careers, but not the ones they're famous for.)

Columnist Art Buchwald
Pop artist Robert Rauschenberg
Author Leon Uris
Actors Bea Arthur, Gene Hackman, and Harvey Keitel

ANSWER, PAGE 192

PHRASEOLOGY 102

More of those familiar phrases and where they came from…

ACROSS

1 Goes on the stage
5 *Trés* ___
9 Picture holder
14 The Supremes, e.g.
15 A single time
16 Foaming at the mouth
17 Phrase from the old English "bodger," a peasant chair maker whose products were of poor quality
19 Hole-___ (golfing feat)
20 Not snoozing
21 Get away from, as the police
23 Hankering
24 Perfect score in gymnastics
25 Hosp. workers
27 Actor Chaney
28 Phrase from the 18th-century soldiers who retreated because of it
34 Stationed
37 Ump's call
38 Butter substitute
39 Pipes
40 Campground behemoths (abbr.)
41 Fun-loving
42 USC rival
43 Service charge
44 Pepsi and Coke
45 Phrase from a fixed boxing match where the bettors on either side are bound to lose
48 Downed
49 Spelling contest
50 "Be Prepared" grp.
53 Understand, to a hepcat
56 Button in a bowling alley
58 Went white
60 Saying
62 It's from the shipboard practice of boiling meat and selling the slops to make money for the crew
64 Napped
65 *Born Free* lioness
66 Remainder
67 Texas battle where Davy Crockett died
68 Not shallow
69 Snack-in-a-stack cookie

DOWN

1 Up, in baseball
2 Russell of *Gladiator*
3 Atlas was one
4 Punch
5 Feather scarf
6 Kiddingly
7 Environmental studies (abbr.).
8 Unclear
9 Good buddy
10 Took off
11 *About* ___ (Hugh Grant movie)
12 Three-year-old's cry
13 Paradise
18 Pruned shrubs
22 Idiot
26 Checkers side
29 Nightclub charge
30 Nourishment
31 Jazzy Fitzgerald
32 Symbols of slipperiness
33 Plaything
34 Osso ___
35 Human rights org.
36 Take a ___ at (try)
39 Firecracker that doesn't go off
40 Took a break, courtroom-style
41 Author Wambaugh
43 Celebration
44 Direction opposite NNW
46 City on the Rio Grande
47 Kind of triangle
50 More gloomy
51 Sight or smell
52 Increase the size of
53 One of baby's first words
54 Rocker Billy
55 Strip in the Mideast
57 *Vogue* competitor
59 '60s hairstyle
61 Precious stone
63 Drain of energy

ANSWER, PAGE 192

WHICH HUNT

Life is full of choices—and some are easier to make than others. Pick the right answer to each question.

1. **Which is longer?**
   The length of the line that the average pencil can draw
   The distance that the average office chair on wheels will travel over the course of a year

2. **Which is faster?**
   The top speed of a falling raindrop
   The top speed of a honeybee in flight

3. **Which is longer?**
   The Statue of Liberty's index finger
   Big Ben's minute hand

4. **Which are there more of?**
   Dimples on a golf ball
   Sesame seeds on a Big Mac bun

5. **Which is longer?**
   The longest recorded bout of hiccups
   The longest recorded fit of sneezing

6. **Which has been adapted more times for the silver screen?**
   Hamlet
   Romeo and Juliet

7. **Which has more grooves in its edge?**
   A quarter
   A dime

8. **Which is saltier?**
   The Atlantic
   The Pacific

9. **Which group has more taste buds?**
   Children
   Adults

10. **Which TV show was more popular, overall?**
    The Addams Family
    The Munsters

11. **Which is larger?**
    England
    New England

12. **Which lasted longer?**
    The Roman Empire
    The Mayan Empire

13. **Which comprises more miles?**
    The blood vessels in the human body
    The phone lines in the Pentagon

14. **Which claimed more American lives in the 20th century?**
    Murders
    Wars

15. **Which is longer?**
    The amount of time the average MTV viewer tunes in
    The amount of time the average *Sesame Street* viewer tunes in

16. **Which will kill you first?**
    Lack of sleep
    Lack of food

17. **Which man had the larger shoe size?**
    Fred Astaire
    George Washington

18. **Which activity will use up more of your life?**
    Waiting at red lights
    Looking for misplaced objects

19. **Which is higher?**
    The point differential of the worst defeat in football history
    The highest score on a single hole of golf in tournament play

20. **Which group comprises more people worldwide?**
    Drinkers of cow's milk
    Drinkers of goat's milk

21. **Which grow faster?**
    Fingernails
    Toenails

22. **Which is more important to the average American taxpayer?**
    Taking as many deductions as possible
    Avoiding an audit

23. **Which activity burns more calories?**
    Watching TV
    Sleeping

24. **Which gives off more light?**
    A 75-watt bulb
    Three 25-watt bulbs

25. **Which contains a higher percentage of water?**
    A watermelon
    An apple

26. **Which is taller?**
    The Statue of Liberty
    The Eiffel Tower

27. **Which does the average adult male have more poundage of?**
    Muscle
    Bone

28. **Which would more Americans rather listen to, after being put on hold?**
    Music
    Silence

29. **Which product icon is older?**
    Tony the Tiger
    The Jolly Green Giant

30. **Which is more potent?**
    Rattlesnake venom
    Black widow spider venom

31. **Which would more women rather do, according to a poll?**
    Go on a shopping spree
    Have sex

32. **Which is more likely to happen to you?**
    Getting eaten by a shark
    Getting struck by lightning

33. **Which is more?**
    The average bank robbery's take
    The average American's credit card debt

34. **Which group kills more deer?**
    Hunters
    Drivers

35. **Which do Americans spend more money on?**
    Cat food
    Baby food

36. **Which do more American men prefer?**
    Boxers
    Briefs

37. **Which is louder?**
    The loudest snore on record
    The noise level of a jackhammer

38. **Which opinion is more popular among American tippers?**
    "I always leave a tip"
    "It depends on the service"

39. **Which cost more when first introduced?**
    The game of Monopoly
    The Barbie doll

40. **Which is higher?**
    The amount of money that the average American dog will cost its owner
    The cost of an average wedding

ANSWER, PAGE 193

PLAY D'OH!

Who's more quotable than Homer Simpson, America's most famous animated dad? For instructions and hints on how to solve, see page 15.

That Rain Forest Thing

EVI BVTUI WIJYTK BI VJCI IUIOEIZ THHFOFJUY FY YT BI ZTK'E VJCI ET EVFKX JUU EVI EFQI. MDYE UFXI EVJE WJFK HTWIYE YOJWI J HIB RIJWY NJOX: TDW THHFOFJUY YJB EVIWI BJY J LWTNUIQ JKZ EVIR HFAIZ FE...ZFZK'E EVIR?

What Senior Citizens Are Good For

QOY XFQXOF YQL'U LFFY GQBXVLAQLKWAX. UWFE LFFY UQ TF AKQOVUFY VLY KUJYAFY KQ AU GVL TF YFUFNBALFY CWVU LJUNAFLUK UWFE WVPF UWVU BASWU TF FHUNVGUFY RQN QJN XFNKQLVO JKF.

Women!

C YWRCM SZ KSDJ C GJJP. IUJF KWWD QWWH, IUJF ZRJKK QWWH, CMH FWV'H ZIJA WXJP FWVP WYM RWIUJP LVZI IW QJI WMJ!

Some Fatherly Advice

OIX, ZCAX UIY DMBWLSLDMWA LX ODIBWLXH ANAXWO, LW'O XIW ZCAWCAB UIY ZLX IB VIOA, LW'O CIZ GBYXR UIY HAW.

ANSWER, PAGE 192

PLAYING THE PERCENTAGES #1

Uncle John loves statistics—he's gathered a gazillion of them over the years. Now you have a chance to play with them. Place the numbers 10, 20, 30, 40, 50, 60, 70, 80, and 90 into the nine blanks below to make the statistics as accurate as possible. Some of the answers might surprise you.

_____% of witches are registered Republican

_____% of Americans are cremated when they die

_____% of extinct species are birds

_____% of a human's body weight is water

_____% of coffee drinkers drink it black

_____% of all Americans avoid public rest rooms

_____% of the Russian government's income comes from the sale of vodka

_____% of Americans will be fired from a job at least once in their lives

_____% of car-theft victims left their keys in the ignition

ANSWER, PAGE 193

PRACTICALLY NEXT DOOR

Small crostic puzzles are solved just like the big ones (directions on page 11) but the first letter of the fill-in words **do not** spell out a hidden message.

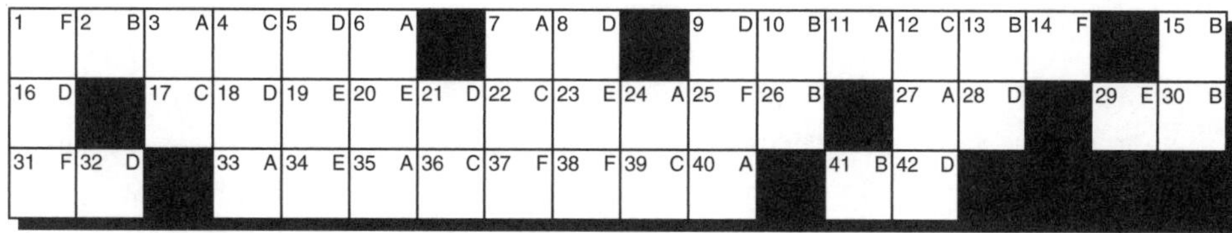

A. Mystery stories

___ 6 ___ 33 ___ 11 ___ 27 ___ 40 ___ 35 ___ 7 ___ 24 ___ 3

B. Emergency telephone connection (2 wds.)

___ 30 ___ 2 ___ 15 ___ 10 ___ 41 ___ 26 ___ 13

C. Silent (but funny) circus stars

___ 4 ___ 39 ___ 36 ___ 17 ___ 22 ___ 12

D. Special events; celebrations

___ 5 ___ 28 ___ 9 ___ 18 ___ 42 ___ 21 ___ 16 ___ 32 ___ 8

E. "You look like you've seen a _____"

___ 23 ___ 20 ___ 34 ___ 19 ___ 29

F. Hope and Crosby's costar Dorothy

___ 37 ___ 31 ___ 1 ___ 25 ___ 38 ___ 14

ANSWER, PAGE 194

ANAGRAMMIES: THE SEQUEL

Uncle John presents more winners of this year's most coveted wordplay awards.

ACROSS

1 First letter of the Greek alphabet
6 Speech you hear on a Sun.
9 Run ___ (go crazy)
13 Recovery facility
14 To be, to Henri
15 Theater seating
16 Ring-shaped coral island
17 Anagram of DIRTY ROOM
19 Chomped on
20 ___ extra cost
22 Makes up for
23 Anagram of ALAS! NO MORE Z'S
26 Part of m.p.h.
27 Alias
28 It usually tops a king
31 Maximum
34 Sen. Edwards' state
37 Luxury boat
39 City in Pennsylvania
40 Enjoy thoroughly
42 "Darn it!"
43 Smooths wood
45 "You're the ___ of my existence!"
46 Singer Horne
47 Math class
48 In favor of
50 Legendary Notre Dame coach Parseghian
52 Anagram of CASH LOST IN 'EM
58 Teheran natives
61 "Off we go ___ the wild blue yonder…"
62 Ending used with pay or Cray
63 Anagram of BAD CREDIT
65 *Hello, ___!*
67 Newspaper page, for short
68 Change for a five
69 Swallowed
70 Only
71 Closing stages
72 Office-pool worker

DOWN

1 Palestinians, e.g.
2 Allow to enter
3 Snapshot
4 Actor Holbrook
5 On fire
6 Seat at the counter
7 To ___ is human
8 Comment
9 "Hallelujah!" singers
10 A Zappa's first name
11 Shrek is one
12 Source of some pocket noise
14 Author Buchanan
18 To whom ___ concern
21 Seabirds
24 Made a choice
25 Home run king Hank
28 Farm unit
29 Asian detective who was never played by an Asian
30 Jazz singer ___ James
31 Flat-topped Southwestern hill
32 Spoken
33 Warble
35 Statesman Henry ___ Lodge
36 One of Frank's wives
38 Two-time loser to Dwight
41 Be surprised, e.g.
44 Take off
49 Gangster's gun
51 ___ Scholar
52 Nasty, as a remark
53 Bogged down
54 No ifs, ___, or buts
55 Actor Nick
56 Actress Barkin
57 Refuse
58 Wedding vows
59 Property that reverts to a previous owner, for short
60 Cain's brother
64 Former Texas governor Richards
66 Trendy kind of bran

ANSWER, PAGE 194

PERFECT FOR EACH OTHER

Want to play matchmaker? Connect each seeker (1–10) with the perfect person they're seeking (a–j) by completing the text of their ads.

WOMEN SEEKING MEN

_____ 1. **Me: Buxom blonde** with blue eyes…

_____ 2. **I like driving around with my two cats**, especially on the freeway. I make them wear little hats so that I can use the carpool lane…

_____ 3. **Cute guy with snowplow** sought by head-turnin', zany, brainy, late-30s babe to share happy time in the big driveway of love…

_____ 4. **Coldhearted, insensitive**, unconscionable, selfish, hedonistic, drunk liar…

_____ 5. **Gorgeous blonde model**, tired of being patronized…

MEN SEEKING WOMEN

_____ 6. **Mentally Ill?** Are you restrained in a straight-jacket? Do you think you're a chicken? Did you kill and eat your last boyfriend? I don't mind…

_____ 7. **I drink a lot of beer**, smoke a lot of cigars, and watch football nonstop from September to January...

_____ 8. **If it takes** a three-legged elephant with one tusk five days to cross the Sahara Desert….

_____ 9. **Award-winning poet**, 27 yrs., seeks short-term, intense, doomed relationship for inspiration…

_____ 10. **Desperate lonely loser**, SWM, 32, tired of watching TV and my roommate's hair fall out…

a. A rake for springtime a big plus!

b. How many times do I have to put an ad in to get one call?

c. I seek a woman, 18–32, to share this with.

d. Looking for sincere, understanding man. Must be willing to listen to stories of alien abduction.

e. Must be attractive, sensual, articulate, ruthless, 21–30 yrs., under 5'6". Break my heart, please.

f. Seeks depressed, unattractive SWF, 25–32, no sense of humor, for long talks about the macabre.

g. Seeks next gullible male without enough sense to stay away from me.

h. This tall, educated, professional SWM would like to meet an interesting woman!

i. Way too much time on your hands too? Call me.

j. You: elderly, marriage-minded millionaire with bad heart.

ANSWER, PAGE 194

* * * * *

SIGNALS CROSSED?

True or False: Arthur Wynne, the first crossword constructor, called his puzzle a "Word-Cross." But the typesetters inadvertently transposed the words to read "Cross-Word." And the name stuck.

ANSWER, PAGE 193

THE UNITED STATES OF APATHY

Directions for solving are on page 11.

1 E	2 J	3 C	4 G	5 P	■	6 E	7 I	8 B	9 J	10 O	11 G	■	12 K	13 N	14 H	■	15 R	16 G	17 J	18 K	19 H	20 A	21 C	■	22 E
23 I	24 H	25 P	26 R	■	27 S	28 B	29 N	30 Q	■	31 G	32 Q	33 L	34 J	35 D	36 K	37 P	38 O	39 M	■	40 M	41 C	■	42 P	43 D	44 I
■	45 I	46 H	47 J	48 P	49 A	50 D	51 C	52 S	53 B	54 M	55 R	56 G	57 E	58 O	■	59 J	60 G	61 I	62 R	63 D	64 A	65 S	66 P	67 E	68 Q
■	69 O	70 R	71 D	■	72 F	73 M	74 H	75 B	76 R	77 J	78 E	79 K	■	80 L	81 J	82 R	83 G	84 K	85 S	■	86 E	87 S	88 Q	89 F	90 O
■	91 L	92 R	93 N	94 A	95 S	96 I	97 G	■	98 S	99 L	100 P	101 F	102 G	103 Q	104 N	105 D	106 J	■	107 I	108 S	109 L	110 K	111 R	■	112 I
113 C	114 K	■	115 D	■	116 K	117 A	118 J	119 R	■	120 I	121 J	122 A	123 Q	■	124 P	125 I	126 B	127 F	128 G	129 M	130 D	■	131 K	132 D	133 C
134 S	135 G	136 H	■	137 J	138 K	139 P	■	140 H	141 K	142 N	143 S	144 R	145 J	■	146 O	147 A	■	148 P	149 N	■	■	■	■	■	■

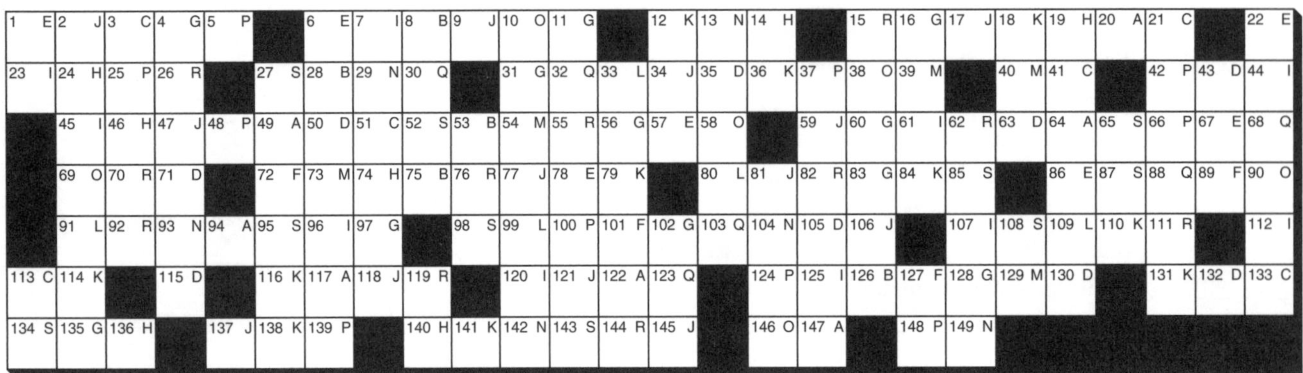

A. Custer's Last Stand state

122 147 64 49 94 20 117

B. Barbra Streisand cross-dressing role

75 28 126 53 8

C. Company that makes Tercel

51 3 133 41 21 113

D. Soar, with a little help (2 wds.)

43 115 132 130 35 105 50 71 63

E. Brent Spiner plays one in *Star Trek: TNG*

57 78 86 1 67 6 22

F. Take care of

72 101 89 127

G. Late jazz guitar great (2 wds.)

97 31 11 128 16 102 83 135 4 60 56

H. California national park named for a tree

74 136 24 140 19 46 14

I. Laughing fit to burst (2 wds.)

125 61 7 120 23 107 45 112 44 96

J. The *Beagle*'s naturalist (2 wds.)

59 2 77 118 81 34 106 145 9 17

137 121 47

K. NFL star and sportscaster born Bobby Moore (2 wds.)

12 116 18 36 79 110 141 84 138 131 114

L. Story with a moral

99 80 91 33 109

M. Those opposed

73 129 40 54 39

N. Private eye played by William Conrad on TV

93 104 29 13 149 142

O. Natural aptitude

90 69 58 38 10 146

P. Counterbalancing

139 124 100 48 5 42 37 66 25 148

Q. Verily

103 68 30 32 123 88

R. Succession

119 111 15 55 76 62 92 82 144 70 26

S. Holler one's head off (3 wds.)

27 108 98 95 65 87 85 134 52 143

ANSWER, PAGE 194

SAY CHEESE!

Mmmm. Here's a nice big slab of Swiss cheese, filled with holes...and other cheeses. See how many you can find, but be careful—words can pass through the holes, skipping over the empty spaces and coming out the other side. You'll have to be sharp as cheddar to find them all. The leftover letters will reveal something a president once had to say on the subject of cheese.

```
N H O         W C A Y B R E D E G A S N A
N O E U     L B E R I H S P O R H S Y Y T
O N G E K C G O R E     T S E C I E L L I
V E M U R O F N A         B N D A     E S
P R O V O L O N E         D Y E         L
R L Z     B N M T I     O N T G         I
H O         T A A T S D U N L O P     T T
H N         I A S L T W O O H R O U L A N
R G Z     Y N P R D L R N E D G A N I H M
E H A D Q F A A O S S I W S A O     H C O
G O R R T U J R M Y R S T I I         F N
R R E X D I     P O R T S A L         U T
U N L F R         F R A O A M N     P E E
B E L P A         E S E T U F Z E R R N R
M M A E D R     B E N E E O T O K I E I E
I M N D D C M M S O F     F R L C R A S Y
L E H E E S E E H C         M A E R C R J
E N     H M S S R N         E Y V F R U A
E         N C A S C G     O U D     A O C
H         P R     E H S J R R         B K
P T     C I         D E G E N         I T
H A V A R T         I T E R V E     H C L
C L C H E A R     R L E S S T I L T O N D
E G A R U L L N B W E N S L E Y D A L E E
```

ASIAGO
BEL PAESE
BOUGON
BOURSIN
BRIE
CAERPHILLY
CAMEMBERT
CHEDDAR
CHEVRET
COLBY
CREAM CHEESE
DUNLOP
EDAM
EMMENTAL
FARMER CHEESE
FETA
FONTINA
GJETOST
GORGONZOLA
GOUDA
GRUYERE
HAVARTI
JARLSBERG
LEICESTER
LEYDEN
LIMBURGER
LIVAROT
LONGHORN
MONTEREY JACK
MOZZARELLA
MUENSTER
NEUFCHATEL
PARMESAN
PECORINO
PORT SALUT
PROVOLONE
ROMANO
ROQUEFORT
SAGE DERBY
SHROPSHIRE BLUE
STILTON
SWISS
TILLAMOOK
TILSIT
WENSLEYDALE

ANSWER, PAGE 195

ATTACK OF THE MOVIE MONSTERS!

We warned you about them in *Uncle John's Bathroom Reader Plunges into the Universe*. Now they've been joined by some otherworldly friends—and they're all lying in wait for you in this puzzle.

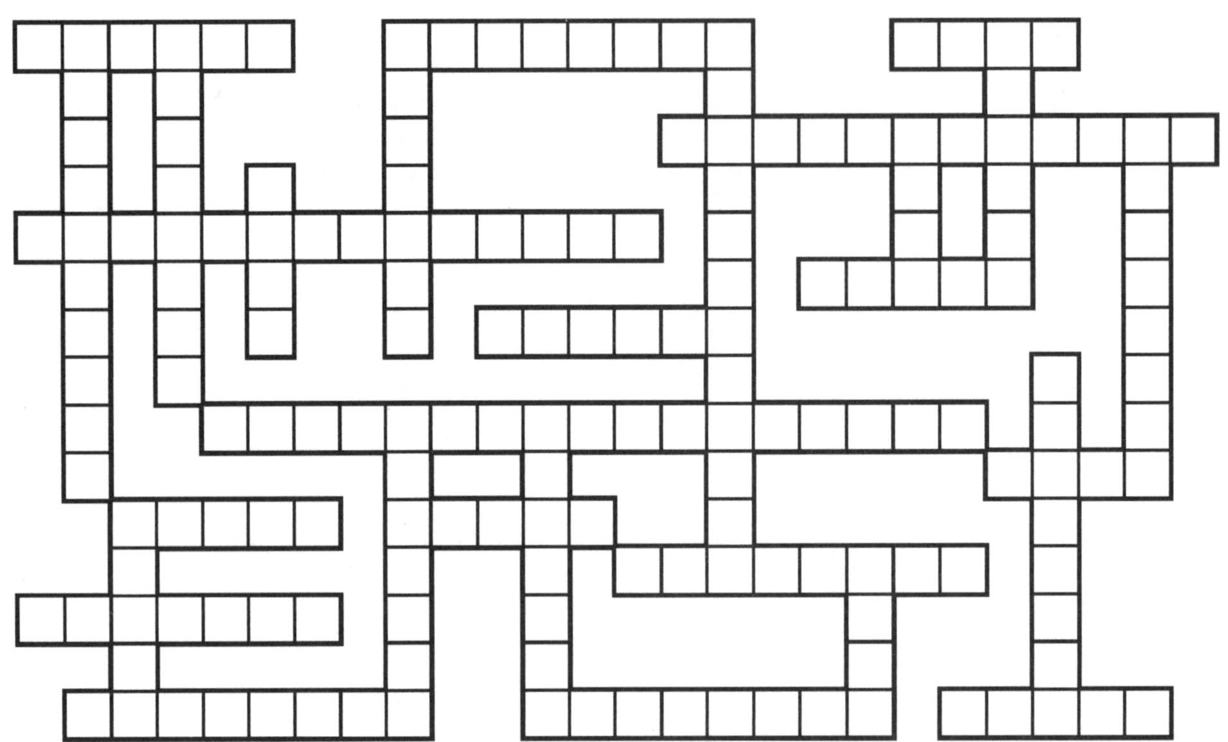

4 letter words
Jaws
Orca
Them
T-Rex
Yeti

5 letter words
Alien
Golem
Gorgo
Mummy
Rodan

6 letter words
Dragon
Gorgon
The Fly

7 letter words
Dracula
Martian
The Blob
Wolf Man

8 letter words
Arachnid
Blackula
Godzilla
Gremlins
King Kong
Triffids
Werewolf

10 letter word
Reptilicus

12 letter words
Frankenstein
Jabba the Hutt

14 letter word
Killer Tomatoes

17 letter word
Fiend Without a Face

ANSWER, PAGE 187

MR. & MS. QUIZ

For all these years, Uncle John has kept his readers up to date on the latest skirmishes in the ongoing Battle of the Sexes. Check the appropriate box to the left of each question when you've figured out which gender is more likely to…

Men	Women	
_____	_____	1. …be naturally blond?
_____	_____	2. …laugh more?
_____	_____	3. …sleep more?
_____	_____	4. …snore?
_____	_____	5. …be born at night?
_____	_____	6. …purchase men's clothing in U.S. stores?
_____	_____	7. …run stoplights?
_____	_____	8. …switch lanes without signaling?
_____	_____	9. …be left-handed?
_____	_____	10. …get migraines?
_____	_____	11. …get an ulcer?
_____	_____	12. …get hiccups?
_____	_____	13. …get struck by lightning?
_____	_____	14. …leave their hotel rooms cleaner?
_____	_____	15. …lock themselves out of their hotel rooms?
_____	_____	16. …take longer showers?
_____	_____	17. …blink more?
_____	_____	18. …stutter as a child?
_____	_____	19. …buy gifts for Mother's Day?
_____	_____	20. …fall out of bed while in the hospital?
_____	_____	21. …talk to their cars?
_____	_____	22. …hold the TV remote?
_____	_____	23. …lose the TV remote?
_____	_____	24. …have a keener sense of smell?

ANSWER, PAGE 196

I DON'T GET IT...

Of course you don't. That's because we've mixed up the answers to these perfectly awful jokes. It's your job to match each joke to its punch line. Your reward might be a laugh (or a groan) or two.

1. **Q:** What has four legs and one arm?
   A: A carrot.

2. **Q:** What is bright orange and sounds like a parrot?
   A: Ground beef.

3. **Q:** What's the most important thing to learn in chemistry?
   A: Fission chips.

4. **Q:** What do you call a midget fortune-teller who escaped from prison?
   A: A rottweiler.

5. **Q:** What do you call a cow with no legs?
   A: A buccaneer.

6. **Q:** How much do pirates pay for their earrings?
   A: The whole crew was marooned.

7. **Q:** What did the nuclear physicist have for lunch?
   A: He sold his soul to Santa.

8. **Q:** Did you hear about the dyslexic devil worshipper?
   A: He wanted to transcend dental meditation.

9. **Q:** Did you hear about the Buddhist who refused Novocain during his root canal?
   A: Never lick the spoon.

10. **Q:** Hear about the ship that ran aground carrying a cargo of red paint and black paint?
    A: A small medium at large.

ANSWER, PAGE 195

* * * * *

ODD TITLE OUT

Four of the following books are real; in fact each of them was odd enough to win *Bookseller* magazine's Odd Title of the Year award. Which is the one we had a really good time making up?

a) *Your Television's Smells, and What They Mean* (1980)
b) *Highlights in the History of Concrete* (1994)
c) *Versailles: The View from Sweden* (1988)
d) *Proceedings of the Second International Workshop on Nude Mice* (1978)
e) *How to Avoid Huge Ships* (1992)

ANSWER, PAGE 197

SON OF ANAGRAMMIES

A few more crazy, mixed-up words and phrases for you to applaud—including a guest appearance by Mr. Superstar himself.

ACROSS

1 U.S. space agency
5 "Poor me!"
9 Actress Allen or Black
14 Chooses
15 Undulating
16 Just furious
17 Anagram of HINT: HOTEL
19 Reminders sent around the office
20 *The First ___ Club*
21 Put an ___ (stop)
23 Picnic pest
24 ___ *on a Grecian Urn*
25 Word with Vegas or Cruces
27 Bleed, as colors
28 Anagram of NO MORE STARS
34 Outspoken
37 50 Across's grp.
38 Make corrections in a manuscript
39 Scandinavian inlet
40 Yes, to a sailor
41 Salty, like the sea
42 Schooling (abbr.)
43 Ted Turner has a big one
44 Relocated
45 Anagram of WOMAN HITLER
48 Small parasitic insect
49 Slithery swimmer
50 Hosp. workers
53 He used to be Clay
56 Kingdom
58 Message on your monitor
60 Damascus is its capital
62 Anagram of SO I'M CUTER
64 Between, plus
65 Member of the woodwind section
66 Happiness
67 Tubular pasta
68 Onetime attorney general Janet
69 Method (abbr.)

DOWN

1 There are ___ ways about it
2 Bug that loves roses
3 Funnyman Martin
4 Tennis great Arthur
5 Tool for punching holes
6 Last to arrive
7 "___ calling" (cosmetics company slogan)
8 *The China ___* (Jane Fonda flick)
9 Japanese robe
10 Exist
11 "___ Lama Ding Dong" (1961 oldie)
12 Noted English school
13 Cozy spot
18 Manhattan is one
22 Chicken of the Sea, really
26 One way to get information
29 Synthetic fabric
30 *Jeopardy!* creator Griffin
31 *The Sopranos* actress Falco
32 Skin of an orange
33 Sloppy spot
34 Classic name for a dog
35 Beat soundly, sports-wise
36 Part of the McDonald's logo
39 Not masc.
40 Rabble-rouser
41 Derby
43 New York canal
44 *She Done Him Wrong* star West
46 Madden
47 Matthau's "odd" partner
50 Every 24 hours
51 *The Sun Also ___*
52 Stormy precipitation
53 Pronto
54 ___ disease (illness caused by deer ticks)
55 Take out the wrinkles
57 Part of your ear
59 Coffee holders
61 Traveler's stop
63 Corp. bigwig

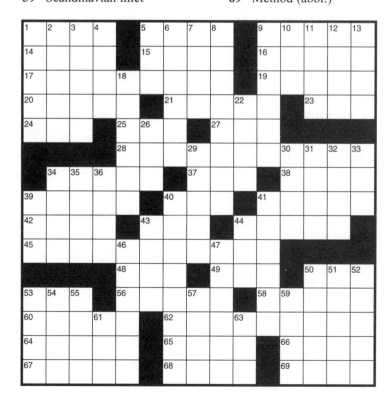

ANSWER, PAGE 196

THE SPY WHO DIDN'T CARE IF IT WAS COLD

Mata Hari went down in history as the exotic dancer who loosened many a lip during World War I. Her name is synonymous with "spy." But was she really guilty? If you want to find out the real story you'll have to pick the correct answers from among the three choices in each set of parentheses.

Mata Hari was born **(Mata Hari, Yvette Bonchance, Margaretha Geertruida Zelle)** in **(Persia, Holland, Canada)** in 1876, and it sounds like she was a wild one from the beginning. She met husband-to-be Rudolph MacLeod through a **(friend of the family, personals ad in the newspaper, chance meeting in a bar in Toronto)** and soon after joined him at his post in faraway **(Mali, Bali, Java)**. A couple of years of his company proved to be enough. She fled to **(Paris, Berlin, Madrid)** to begin her exotic dancing career.

She was an immediate success. Audiences flocked to her naughty, titillating performances to glimpse the "Oriental" dancer who shed her **(kimono, veils, sexy suit of armor)** in a naughty, titillating way. She tried to launch a serious professional dancing-acting career, and was even booked into a few **(French cabarets, English music halls, Italian opera houses)**, but people just wanted to see her take off whatever she had on. She was the "entertainment" at several notorious private parties, too.

By 1915 Hari's career was fading fast. She was doing less and less dancing on the stage and more and more of the horizontal boogie with a steady stream of men. Recently unearthed files give away the names of dozens of Mata Hari's lovers while she hovered at 40, including **(composer Giacomo Puccini, Baron Henri de Rothschild, both of the above)**.

Mata Hari was arrested by the **(French, Germans, Italians)** in 1917 and accused of spying for the **(French, Germans, Italians)**. Her accusers produced decoded messages outlining a plan to hire Mata Hari as a spy, but they were unable to produce any evidence of secrets she'd handed over. No matter. She was convicted of spying and executed by **(hanging, the guillotine, firing squad)** in 1917. Rumor has it that she **(made funny faces, pretended to faint, threw open her blouse)** to distract her executioners. In truth she went bravely, but still a slut.

Her prosecutor admitted 40 years later that **(he and his colleagues had framed her, there hadn't been enough evidence to convict her, he'd been one of her boyfriends)**. Historians pin the blame on anti-**(French, German, Italian)** hysteria, of which there was lots at the time, and also the vindictiveness of Mata Hari's prosecutors, who were probably punishing her for doing the deed with **(French, Germans, Italians)**. Those **(French, Germans, Italians)** have some funny ideas about sex—and everything else.

ANSWER, PAGE 204

PHRASEOLOGY 103

You're almost ready to graduate—to go on to bigger and better things. All you have to do is get past this one. Pick up your pencils. Begin.

ACROSS

1 Thompson and Lazarus
6 Unclothed
10 Grammar sch.
14 Show a response
15 Addict
16 Flat-bottomed boat
17 Phrase from a strong-smelling fish that was used to throw a dog off a scent in hunting
19 Computer image
20 Pittsburgh player
21 Open-faced taco
23 *The ___ King*
25 Swiss cheese has them
26 It originally was a pejorative term, meaning weather that appeared to be one season, but wasn't
32 He sang with the Belmonts
33 Hammer or saw, e.g.
34 Former dictator Amin
37 WWII battle site
41 Late, as a birthday card
43 Tennis call
44 Wyoming, from New York
46 Influence
47 Phrase from the "umbles" that commoners had to eat after the lord of the manor had his fill
51 T-bone or porterhouse
54 South Pacific island
55 Car door attachment
58 Attaches using heat
63 "Crazy" bird
64 Cowboys coined it when they noticed wild horses jerking their tails up before galloping off
66 Carry
67 "I cannot tell ___"
68 French pancake
69 Raced
70 Fix
71 Cut apart

DOWN

1 Makes a mistake
2 Track tournament
3 ___ in the shade
4 Hurt
5 Mrs. Kowalski
6 Small donkeys
7 "___ was saying..."
8 Monthly payment
9 Therefore
10 Magazine chief
11 Kind of anesthetic
12 Wear down
13 Talking birds
18 Jockey's strap
22 Outer covering
24 Crackpot
26 Worshipped one
27 Adidas rival
28 "Just ___" (27 Down's slogan)
29 Homey hotel
30 Swarm
31 Larry and Curly's partner
34 Live ___ (enjoy yourself)
35 Where you can find a hero
36 Just sitting around
38 Up and about
39 Moist
40 Fireplace residue
42 Gibbon or gorilla
45 Rubber duckie's "pond"
47 Deserved
48 One way to serve potatoes
49 Blemish
50 Purple shades
51 Adds seasoning
52 Gaggle of Girl Scouts
53 Overdo it onstage
56 Fraud
57 Scrabble piece
59 Extremely urgent
60 Abbr. on some mountaintops
61 Ready for picking
62 Ending for gang or joke
65 Martini ingredient

ANSWER, PAGE 197

DON'T!

If you were thinking of skipping this page—don't! We've disguised three important pieces of advice in the puzzles below, all of which start with the word "Don't." Just drop the letters from each vertical column—but not necessarily in the order in which they appear—into the empty squares below them to spell out the sayings, reading from left to right. Words may wrap around from one line to the next; black squares signify the spaces between words. So, what are you waiting for? Do!

1.

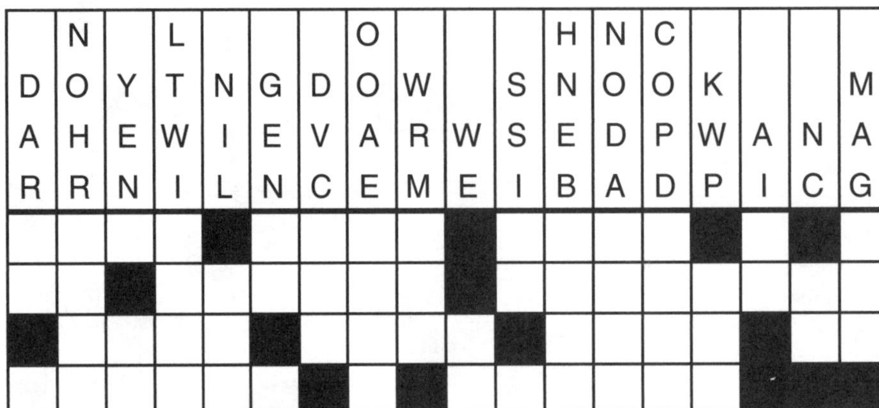

2.

3.

	L				T	O			I		G		M						
D	O			S	T	I		T	R		R	B	O	T	I			O	O
L	L	N	T	I	W	E	R	L	Y	N	A	I	N	N	L		P	E	A
P	N	F	T	H	E	S	A	O	T	H	R	A	A	U	S	I	Y	D	O
W	I	E	H	A	V	E	R	R	O	I	G	O	A	A	T	T	D	E	U

ANSWER, PAGE 197

OFF YOUR ROCKER

We'll bet you didn't know your favorite rock singers could talk, too. See if you can match the performers (a–m) to the profound (and occasionally really dumb) things they have to say (1–13).

______ 1. "I'm a mess and you're a mess, too. Everyone's a mess. Which means, actually, that no one's a mess."

______ 2. "It's really hard to maintain a one-on-one relationship if the other person is not going to allow me to be with other people."

______ 3. "I only answer to two people—myself and God."

______ 4. "I'm not a snob. Ask anybody. Well, anybody who matters."

______ 5. "There's a basic rule which runs through all kinds of music, kind of an unwritten rule. I don't know what it is."

______ 6. "Damn, I look good with guns."

______ 7. "I want to go out at the top, but the secret is knowing when you're at the top. It's so difficult in this business—your career fluctuates all the time, up and down, like a pair of trousers."

______ 8. "Just because I have my standards, they think I'm a bitch."

______ 9. "We use volume to drive evil spirits out the back of your head, and by evil spirits I mean the job, the boss, the spouse, the probation officer."

______ 10. "I should think that being my old lady would be all the satisfaction or career any woman needs."

______ 11. "God had to create disco music so that I could be born and be successful."

______ 12. "I can do anything. One of these days I'll be so complete I won't be a human. I'll be a god."

______ 13. "I can't think of a better way to spread the message of world peace than by working with the NFL and being part of Super Bowl XXVII."

a. Fiona Apple

b. Cher

c. John Denver

d. Michael Jackson

e. Mick Jagger

f. Simon LeBon

g. Ted Nugent

h. Axl Rose

i. Diana Ross

j. David Lee Roth

k. Rod Stewart

l. Donna Summer

m. Ron Wood

ANSWER, PAGE 197

PROVERBIAL WISDOM

You know that "a stitch in time saves nine," but there are countless other proverbs that you may never have heard of. We've taken some of our favorites and translated them by simple letter substitution code. In this particular puzzle, **the letter substitution stays constant throughout the whole list**. For further instructions see page 15.

GERMANY: DCZH LCZ VRY FEZJKCZA, ORRX LR SRWE NZZAZ.

INDIA: CZ LCJL KJHHRL PJHKZ KOJGTA LCZ VORRE GA WHZMZH.

ENGLAND: J NRRP JEKCZE GA XHRDH HRL QS CGA JEERDA QWL QS CGA JGT.

SPAIN: LCZ ERJP RV QS JHP QS OZJPA LR LCZ CRWAZ RV HZMZE.

CHINA: LCZ ORHNZE LCZ ZYFOJHJLGRH LCZ QGNNZE LCZ OGZ.

JAPAN: DCZH RHZ CJA HR HZZPOZ, LCEZJP GA RV OGLLOZ WAZ.

GREECE: LR ORAZ J VEGZHP, TJXZ CGT J ORJH.

IRELAND: HZMZE AZHP J KCGKXZH LR QEGHN CRTZ J VRY.

TURKEY: TZJAWEZ VRELS LGTZA, KWL RHKZ.

IRAN: LEWAL GH *NRP, QWL LGZ SRWE KJTZO.

ANSWER, PAGE 197

STATE YOUR BUSINESS!

It's not that some states are better than others, it's just that some carry particular distinctions—like the states in this puzzle. And please don't feel bad if yours isn't mentioned; we are sure it's a very nice state—after all, you live there!

1	2	3	4	■	5	6	7	■	8	9	10	11	12	13
14				■	15			■	16					
17				18				■	19					
■	■	■	20					21			■	22		
■	23	24					■	25			26			
27						■	28					■	■	■
29			■	30		31			■	32		33	34	35
36			37	■	38				39	■	40			
41				42	■	43				44	■	45		
■	■	■	46		47			■	48		49			
50	51	52					■	53						■
54			■	55			56					■	■	■
57			58			■	59					60	61	62
63						■	64			■	65			
66						■	67			■	68			

ACROSS

1 Mournful cry
5 Gov't processor of returns
8 Mailbag attachments
14 Golfer's target
15 Costa del ___
16 Busy, as a pace
17 The state with the highest population of Native Americans
19 The state with the most outhouses
20 The first state admitted to the Union
22 Always, in Byron's work
23 Cane used in furniture making
25 Apricot drinks
27 Triumphed
28 Phrase with a slash
29 Campaign
30 Coke competitor
32 The only state with a one-syllable name
36 Short news story
38 Kitchen cutting tool
40 2002 Michael Crichton book
41 The state with the most pollution
43 Painter's stand
45 First lady?
46 Blue ribbon winner
48 Hocked
50 Back rub
53 Tub occupant
54 "Honest" prez
55 The state that produces more whiskey than all the other states combined
57 The only state that was once a kingdom
59 The state with the highest divorce rate
63 Piano pieces for newbies
64 Mine yield
65 *The Grapes of Wrath* extra
66 Announcement on the news
67 Lay down the lawn?
68 "Person of the Year" mag

DOWN

1 "Guess ___!"
2 Perfect
3 Under the weather
4 Bring about
5 Like a mountain hideaway
6 Caesar was one
7 Side dish made from cabbage
8 Like network files
9 Verizon's industry
10 ___ Victor
11 Upon the ocean
12 Petty person
13 Old soldier's mementos
18 All excited
21 "___ Song" (John Denver hit)
23 Traveler's plan
24 New wing
26 "Shut your ___!"
27 Court order
28 Org. for Tin Pan Alley types
31 Kind of bakers
33 *Me, Myself &* ___ (Jim Carrey movie)
34 At no time
35 Kept a watch on
37 Apples on modern teachers' desks?
39 Placed in a new crate
42 More jittery
44 *Taxi* character ___ Gravas
47 Discriminator against the elderly
49 "I wasn't doing anything else anyway…"
50 *Politically Incorrect* host Bill
51 Subside
52 Repair, as a tear
53 Donkey used as a kitschy planter
56 New Mexico art colony
58 Hubbub
60 Slalom
61 Use a gun sight
62 Understand

ANSWER, PAGE 197

OXYMORONS

You don't need to study military intelligence to know that an oxymoron is a word or phrase that combines contradictory elements, like "military intelligence" or "plastic glasses." Your mandatory option is to find the 38 oxymorons listed below in the grid, reading across, down, and diagonally. We hope you'll find it...ahem...somewhat addictive.

```
W F O T H G I L T H G I N S I D E O U T U Q
Q O P E N S E C R E T A W E R I F R O U K D
M A R E G D O D Y T I L A E R L A U T R I V
O V W K X N G C I B L I T T L E G I A N T L
N O I T I S O P P O L A Y O L P V P H E L D
E Y R Z I N Q I L A I C E P S Y L I A D E S
Q P E I P S G I T I G H T S L A C K S U J T
Q O S O U T C V R C Q K A O I K L S D P Q S
E C I T S U J L A N I M I R C S Q G V M E D
B L D Y N D C V V C E F T W M A N I D I R D
Y A E L Y E X N O D A S E O G L J A S S E O
A N N G N N X J I C U T N C F A E I E S D N
M I T U E T Q F U D F R I E N D L Y F I R E
E G A Y Z T F V N M U M I O G E Y R X N O V
T I L T O E U I R B B R N N N K I T A G M E
I R I T R A U D R N G O I T S A B C M D O R
N O E E F C B E S D W V S O A B J F S B D A
I W N R H H Z C O T I C M H O L Y W A R N G
F C E P S E Y O H L R D N A R G Y B A B A A
E A L O E R G E T E R N A L L I F E V K R I
D O V R R Q N G A J S N O I T O M P O T S N
I S F J F Q Y M B E L M R O C K O P E R A D
```

BABY GRAND
BAKED ALASKA
CRIMINAL JUSTICE
DAILY SPECIAL
DEFINITE MAYBE
DODGE RAM
ETERNAL LIFE
EVEN ODDS
FIREWATER
FREEZER BURN
FRESH FROZEN
FRIENDLY FIRE
GOOD GRIEF
HOLY WAR
INDUSTRIAL PARK
INSIDE-OUT
JUMBO SHRIMP
LITTLE GIANT
LIVING DEAD
LOYAL OPPOSITION
NEVER AGAIN
NIGHT LIGHT
"NOW, THEN..."
OPEN SECRET
ORIGINAL COPY
PRETTY UGLY
RANDOM ORDER
RESIDENT ALIEN
ROCK OPERA
SAME DIFFERENCE
SCIENCE FICTION
SILENT SCREAM
STOP-MOTION
STUDENT TEACHER
TIGHT SLACKS
TURNED UP MISSING
VIRTUAL REALITY
WORKING VACATION

ANSWER, PAGE 198

A MOVIE STAR'S BEST FRIEND

Directions for solving are on page 11.

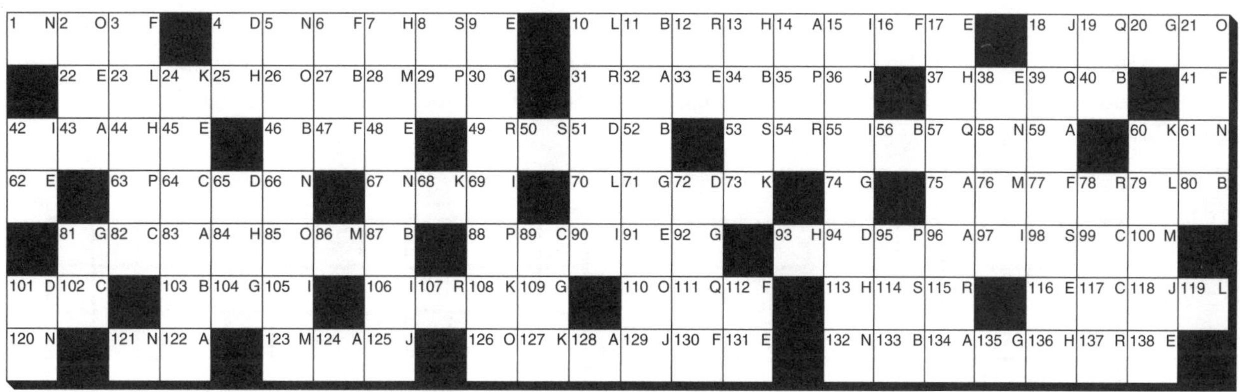

A. The first American in space (2 wds.)

134 75 83 43 122 124 14 96 32 128 59

B. The Divine Miss M (2 wds.)

27 52 103 46 40 56 133 87 34 11 80

C. Blazing (2 wds.)

102 117 89 82 64 99

D. Harlem, to Greenwich Village

65 51 101 94 4 72

E. Younger sibling of Jack and Bobby (2 wds.)

62 91 45 17 33 116 48 38 131 22 138 9

F. Oliver Stone's rock biopic (2 wds.)

112 47 16 6 41 130 77 3

G. Struggle to find the words (3 wds.)

104 109 135 20 92 81 30 74 71

H. Manage money frugally

44 93 136 113 37 84 13 25 7

I. Martha and the Vandellas #1 hit of 1963 (2 wds.)

106 69 97 90 42 55 15 105

J. Animal that sometimes dines on abalone

118 129 18 125 36

K. Take away TV privileges, e.g.

108 127 60 24 73 68

L. Jostle

79 23 10 70 119

M. Author of *The Inferno*

100 76 86 123 28

N. The world's fourth most populous country

5 120 132 61 58 66 67 1 121

O. "Who's on first?" interlocutor

26 110 126 85 21 2

P. "Live and let live," e.g.

95 88 29 63 35

Q. "Ooh, that hurt!"

57 111 39 19

R. Person who stays up till all hours (2 wds.)

137 54 78 49 31 107 115 12

S. Sorrow; grief

53 50 8 114 98

ANSWER, PAGE 198

THE ENDANGERED LIST

Humans aren't bad, really. We just occasionally rub out an entire species for no good reason at all—most of the time we don't even realize it.

We took some of the extinct animals we talked about in *Uncle John's Bathroom Reader Plunges into the Universe*, and added some that are still around but serious candidates for dead-as-a-dodo status. Can you put all 29 poor critters in their proper place in the grid? (The asterisks signify extinct species. It's the least we could do.)

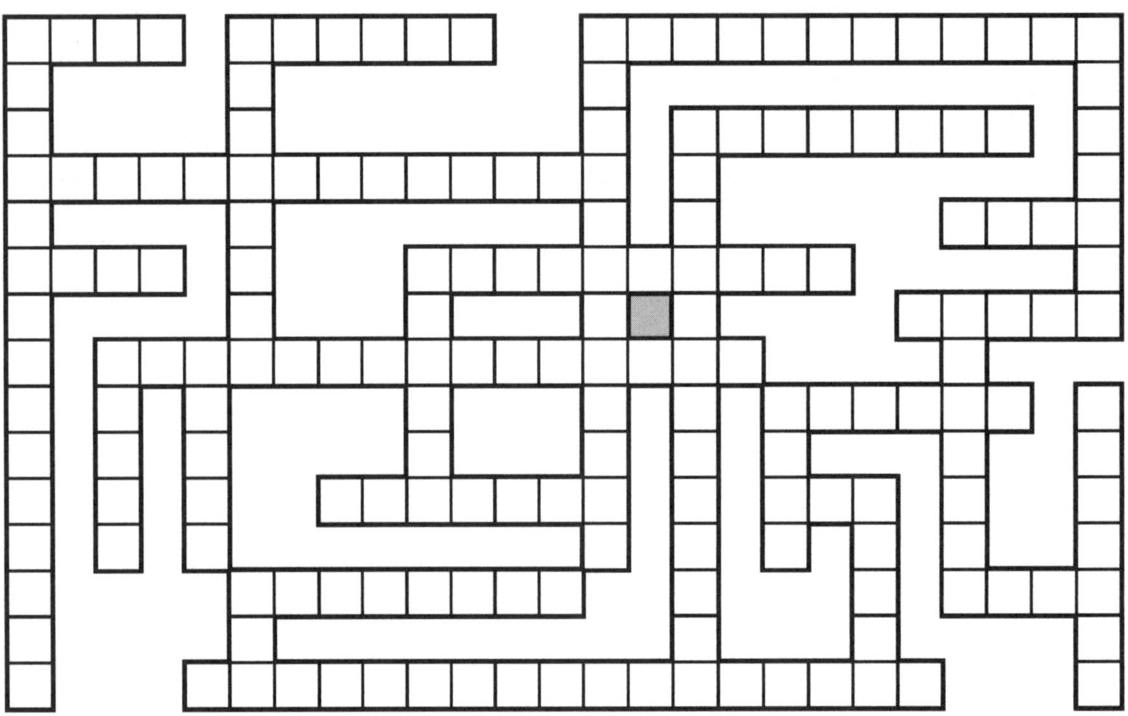

3 letter words
Moa*
Yak

4 letter words
Dodo*
Kiwi
Nene
Oryx
Puma

5 letter words
Koala
Panda
Rhino
Sloth

6 letter words
Bobcat
Condor
Ocelot

7 letter words
Gorilla
Leopard
Mammoth
Pupfish

8 letter words
Blue pike*
Cockatoo
Mastodon*

10 letter word
Chimpanzee

12 letter words
Bighorn sheep
Brown pelican

13 letter word
Chinook salmon

14 letter word
Steller's sea cow*

15 letter words
Passenger pigeon*
Peregrine falcon

17 letter word
Caribbean monk seal*

ANSWER, PAGE 199

THE SCRAWL ON THE WALL

We found this collection of graffiti written on the wall of Uncle John's john. Fill in each blank to match the beginning of a graffiti'd saying (1–13) with its logical end (a–m).

_____ 1. How do you tell the sex of a chromosome?
_____ 2. If Love is blind, and God is love and Ray Charles is blind
_____ 3. Mafia: Organized Crime
_____ 4. Flush twice
_____ 5. Death is just nature's way of telling you
_____ 6. How come nobody ever writes on
_____ 7. Did you ever feel like the whole world was a white wedding gown
_____ 8. The chicken is an egg's way of
_____ 9. If you think you have someone eating out of your hand
_____ 10. The typical Stanford undergrad is like a milk shake
_____ 11. Blessed is he who sits on a bee
_____ 12. There are those who shun elitism. Why?
_____ 13. Please do not throw cigarette butts in the toilet

a. Producing another egg.
b. It's the elitist thing to do.
c. Thick and rich.
d. It's a good idea to count your fingers.
e. Government: Disorganized Crime
f. Pull down its genes.
g. Then God plays the piano.
h. For he shall rise again.
i. It makes them hard to light.
j. It's a long way to Washington.
k. To slow down.
l. And you were a pair of muddy hiking boots?
m. Toilet seats?

ANSWER, PAGE 198

* * * * *

COUNTDOWN QUIZ

Graffiti champ: How many clues do you need to identify this guy?

1. He was the most famous graffitist in history.
2. He left his signature on the top of the torch of the Statue of Liberty, on the Marco Polo Bridge in China, and even on a Bikini atoll where an atomic bomb was to be tested.
3. He was an infantry soldier who was sick of hearing the Air Force brag about always being first on the spot.
4. His graffiti always read "(his name) was here."

ANSWER, PAGE 190

THE ANAGRAMMIES: A PREVIEW

This year's gala AnaGrammies are over—congratulations to the winners! Uncle John proudly presents a few nominees for next year's awards. Be sure to tune in…

1	2	3	■	■	4	5	6	7	■	8	9	10	11	12
13			14	■	15				■	16				
17				■	18				■	19				
20				21					22			■	■	■
23					■	■	■	24			■	25	26	27
28			■	29	30	31	32	■	33		34			
■	■	■	35					36	■	■	37			
■	38	39							40	41				■
42				■	■	43						■	■	■
44				45	46	■	47				■	48	49	50
51			■	52		53	■	■	■	54	55			
■	■	■	56				57	58	59					
60	61	62			■	63				■	64			
65					■	66				■	67			
68					■	69				■	■	70		

ACROSS

1 Recipe amt.
4 Make a trade
8 Fortune-teller's deck
13 Harvest
15 Olympic skater Lipinski
16 Isolated
17 Paquin or Pavlova
18 Greek god of war
19 Joe of frowned-upon commercials
20 Anagram of VOICES RANT ON
23 Chased up a maple?
24 You might wrestle with it
25 Use the Singer
28 Blue
29 "Shoo!"
33 Try out
35 Clears the windshield
37 Remove from office
38 Anagram of ELEVEN PLUS TWO
42 Heart
43 Strongly desires
44 Cemetery sight
47 Volcanic mountain in 53 Down
48 Gangster's gun
51 Paranormal power
52 Actor Wallach
54 Fabian's last name
56 Anagram of NO WIRE UNSENT
60 Fast
63 ___ vera
64 Waiter's first offering
65 Be crazy about
66 Bartender's twist
67 ___ *After* (Drew Barrymore movie)
68 Put a spell on
69 Number on a wine label
70 Ending with Brooklyn or Vietnam

DOWN

1 Parcels of land
2 Lady of Spain
3 Criticized
4 With 5 Down, a George Lucas epic
5 See 4 Down
6 Region
7 Everyday staple of 53 Down
8 City in Washington
9 *Harry Potter* actor Rickman
10 CD-___
11 "The loneliest number"
12 ___ Aviv
14 Work on the road
21 '50s car that went nowhere
22 Tax collecting agcy.
25 Rotated
26 Otherwise
27 Perspiring
30 104 in Roman numerals
31 ___-deucey
32 Native American shelter
34 Sounds from the pasture
35 Animal on a road sign
36 Louver
38 Piggies
39 Prepare a present
40 Vase
41 Common acronym for a mix-up
42 Revolutionary leader Guevara
45 Ranked, in a tennis tournament
46 Trains on high
48 Mourn
49 Makes amends
50 Term
53 Europe's "boot"
55 "The drinks are ___!"
56 Telegram
57 Author Wiesel
58 Capital of 53 Down, to natives
59 ___-do-well
60 "Yay, team!"
61 Summer refreshment
62 Plague or curse

ANSWER, PAGE 199

WOULD WE LIE TO YOU?

You bet we would! In this quiz, we explain the origins of some words and names that you may have wondered about. The only trouble is, we're offering too many explanations. Can you find the one true answer in each set?

1. Where did the brand name "Alpo" come from?
   a) From the name of its creator, ALfred POst.
   b) It's a simplified form of the product's original name, "All-Pro."
   c) It was the name of the product's original mascot, a St. Bernard. (The name was supposed to conjure up the Swiss Alps, where the dogs were first bred.)

2. Where did the term "rookie" come from?
   a) It's a variation on the Civil War slang "reckie," which was short for "recruit."
   b) In 17th-century England con men were known as "rooks," and their victims were called "rookees." Rookee eventually came to mean any gullible or inexperienced person.
   c) Between 1842 and 1890, Scotland Yard's new trainees were taught by Chief Inspector Rook. His students came to be known as "Rookies," and the name endured even after Rook's death.

3. Why are jackrabbits called jackrabbits?
   a) Their ears were thought to resemble donkey ears. The "jack" comes from jackass.
   b) Their fur was used to trim soldiers' leather coats, which were called jacks. (Incidentally, that's also where the term "jacket" comes from.)
   c) They were named after Jack Bonney, a famous runner of the 19th century.

4. Why is Chicago called "The Windy City"?
   a) Uh…because it's windy there? The average wind speed in Chicago is 10.3 mph.
   b) In the 1860s a powerful ward boss named Peter Charles Windy controlled most of Chicago, prompting critics to ironically dub it "Windy's City." The name endured (with a slight alteration) even after Windy's death, and probably because the city is actually windy.
   c) The 1893 Chicago World's Columbia Exposition was supposed to commemorate Columbus's discovery of America, but local politicos used it mainly as an opportunity to hype Chicago. Their claims were so boastful and overblown that a New York City newspaper editor christened Chicago "the windy city."

5. Why is "clink" a slang term for a jail?
   a) It refers to the clink of the key in a cell door's lock.
   b) There was once a famous jail on Clink Street in London.
   c) It's a mispronunciation of "clinic." Reformatories used to be known as clinics.

ANSWER, PAGE 199

HOT STUFF

In *Uncle John's Bathroom Reader Plunges into the Universe* we actually explained why there's so much sand in the Sahara. Of course, there are a lot of other things, too, including flora and fauna—and that's what inspired this puzzle. See if you can fit the 41 words in the list—all having to do with deserts—into the grid so they interlock like a crossword. All the words are used exactly once.

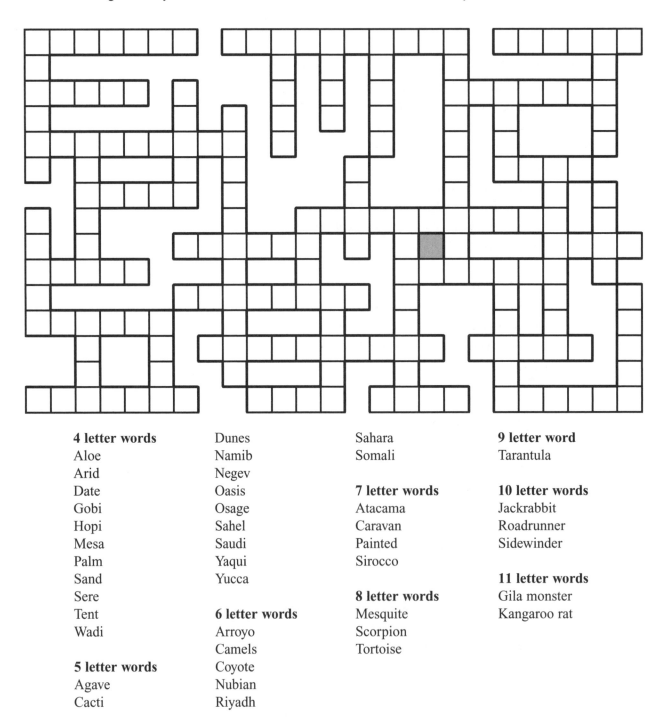

4 letter words
Aloe
Arid
Date
Gobi
Hopi
Mesa
Palm
Sand
Sere
Tent
Wadi

5 letter words
Agave
Cacti
Dunes
Namib
Negev
Oasis
Osage
Sahel
Saudi
Yaqui
Yucca

6 letter words
Arroyo
Camels
Coyote
Nubian
Riyadh
Sahara
Somali

7 letter words
Atacama
Caravan
Painted
Sirocco

8 letter words
Mesquite
Scorpion
Tortoise

9 letter word
Tarantula

10 letter words
Jackrabbit
Roadrunner
Sidewinder

11 letter words
Gila monster
Kangaroo rat

ANSWER, PAGE 199

TOP TEN HITS

Our best-of compilation album below includes 43 songs that were—in their day—one of the top ten songs of the year. Look for them in the grid, reading across, down, and diagonally. Once you've found them all, the leftover letters will reveal an interesting opinion from a very opinionated singer. Then consult your inner disc jockey and see if you can remember who recorded them all; we've provided the year (or years) the songs hit the charts to help jog your memory.

S U N E V

C E M A F R T L H

E A K D M U M I O S E T B

R L C U O Y R O F L E E F I U

T L A M W O G W H Y M E A A R L T

M B L Y U G I G L M S I Y D E E E

E T S T E S O R E H T T E Q U I L A P

E H T E R T S L A T H E V V P I C R K

G I E N I F O S S E H G O M H O U T S O P

S R S F O R G T G M O I F Y D A L E I X E

P I I S W E A R J E   L S S P B R E N E E

S S G O D D N U O H T I I H E O N W H C R

I T N E E H M H A O C I S A K Y R I E S C

B E E T P L E H A V N T R M Y M N A I

M A N I A C S L F O I R O T H T D V U

N E N T R O H P T E N N N E A Y E

R F U R A O E N A K S A R L I T N

H E Y P A U L A S N F A L N T

R R P U G N I M O C A O A

B O O U D L T R D

V O D C K

BEAT IT (1983)
CALL ME (1980)
CENTERFOLD (1982)
COMING UP (1980)
CREEP (1995)
DON'T (1958)
EL PASO (1960)
FAITH (1988)
FAME (1975)
GET BACK (1969)
GROOVIN' (1967)
HELLO (1984)
HELP! (1965)
HE'S SO FINE (1963)
HEY PAULA (1963)
HOUND DOG (1956)
HURTS SO GOOD (1982)
I FEEL FOR YOU (1985)
I GET AROUND (1964)
I SWEAR (1994)
JUMP (1984 and 1992)
KYRIE (1986)
LADY (1981)
LE FREAK (1979)
LET'S GET IT ON (1973)
LIGHT MY FIRE (1967)
MANIAC (1983)
MY GIRL (1965)
MY SHARONA (1979)
PHYSICAL (1982)
PRETTY WOMAN (1964)
REUNITED (1979)
SHE LOVES YOU (1964)
TEARS IN HEAVEN (1992)
TEQUILA (1958)
THE ROSE (1980)
THE SIGN (1994)
TSOP (1974)
VENUS (1959)
VOGUE (1990)
WHY ME (1973)
WINDY (1967)
YMCA (1979)

ANSWER, PAGE 200

INTERNATIONAL LANGUAGE LESSON

What some familiar words mean in the faraway places and times they came from.

ACROSS

1 Camel feature
5 Bootlegged stuff
10 Priority memo letters
14 Neighborhood
15 Green Mountain Boys leader ___ Allen
16 Lucy Lawless role
17 Figure skater Katarina
18 They're known as "quick little fellows" in China
20 It means "empty orchestra" in Japanese
22 Practice with a target
23 Juicy tabloid headline
24 CD-___
25 Airport abbr.
26 "…after this word from our ___"
31 It's known as "little water" in Russia
34 It means "poison" in Latin
35 Laurel & Hardy, e.g.
36 Woodwinds member
37 King of Judea known as "the Great"
38 "*Ja* ___!"
39 Come out on top
40 It means "forbidden" in Arabic
41 It means "fox" in Spanish
42 One of the Virgin Islands
44 Pricey coat
45 2001 Will Smith film
46 Hypes
50 Randy Newman's paean to a city
54 It means "jumping flea" in Hawaiian
55 It means "big soup" in Italian
57 Tiny hill builders
58 Traveling the Atlantic
59 Less fresh
60 Lawn-Boy competitor
61 Premiere attendees
62 Simpleton
63 History text topics

DOWN

1 War advocates
2 Bathsheba's husband
3 Paris's underground railway
4 Hand-clapping game
5 Ted Danson sitcom
6 "None of the above" choice
7 "So that's your game!"
8 Hits with a taser
9 Conceal
10 Self-evident truths
11 Religious splinter group
12 "Diana" singer Paul
13 It's visitable with a time machine
19 Animated characters
21 Gumbo veggie
26 Begets
27 High school dance
28 Sneaker problem
29 German industrial region
30 Unaccompanied
31 Altar readings
32 Short bio, of a sort
33 "Cut it out!"
34 "At This Moment" singer Billy ___
37 Loser to Burr in a famous duel
38 Burn the midnight oil
40 Plot problems
41 Tribesman of Natal
43 Attack
44 Flimflam man's specialty
46 Adjusted the pitch of
47 Guerrero gent
48 Extreme
49 Cuban money
50 New Apple of 1998
51 She plays Phoebe on *Friends*
52 Singles
53 "Alice's Restaurant" singer Guthrie
56 Eccentric

ANSWER, PAGE 201

TOM SWIFTIES

Tom Swift was the hero in a series of adventure books for boys. The author relied heavily on adverbs to describe how Tom was feeling at any given moment, a style that inspired "Tom Swifties," punny sentences like "'I hate pizza,' Tom said crustily."

In this quiz, we'd like you to end each sentence (1–10) with the adverb (a–j) that makes the best Tom Swifty.

_____ 1. "A thousand thanks, Monsieur," Tom said...

_____ 2. "Don't you like my new refrigerator?" Tom asked...

_____ 3. "I prefer to press my own clothes," Tom said...

_____ 4. "I'll have to send that telegram again," Tom said...

_____ 5. "I'm burning the candle at both ends," Tom said...

_____ 6. "It's the maid's night off," Tom said...

_____ 7. "The boat is leaking," Tom said...

_____ 8. "The criminals were escorted downstairs," Tom said...

_____ 9. "They pulled the wool over my eyes," Tom said...

_____ 10. "Welcome to Grant's Tomb," Tom said...

a. balefully

b. condescendingly

c. coolly

d. cryptically

e. helplessly

f. ironically

g. mercifully

h. remorsefully

i. sheepishly

j. wickedly

ANSWER, PAGE 201

* * * * *

FIT AS A FIDDLE

When someone's in perfect health, we say they're "fit as a fiddle." What's so fit about fiddles?

a) Before the days of mass production, good-sounding fiddles could only be made by master craftsmen, and the people who owned them took such good care of them that to be "fit as a fiddle" meant you were well put-together and well tended to.

b) The phrase was originally "fit as a fiddler" and referred to the stamina of fiddlers, who could play for a dance all night long without even getting tired.

c) In nautical parlance, a fiddle is a small barrier that can be raised around a table's edge to keep things from sliding off in rough weather. A "fit" fiddle is one that's in the upright position—i.e., ready to handle whatever a storm can dish out.

ANSWER, PAGE 201

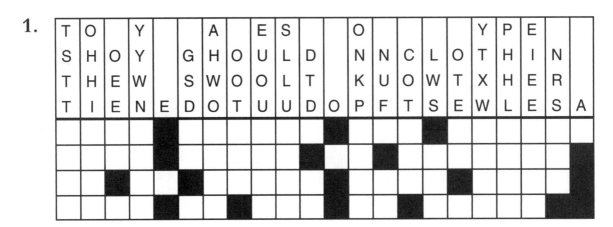

SHEER SHANDLING

A few thoughts from the man with the original "bad hair day," comedian Garry Shandling. If you need directions on how to solve this puzzle, see page 5.

1.

T	O		Y			A		E	S			O					Y	P	E		
S	H	O	Y		G	H	O	U	L	D		N	N	C	L	O	T	H	I	N	
T	H	E	W		S	W	O	O	L	T		K	U	O	W	T	X	H	E	R	
T	I	E	N	E	D	O	T	U	U	D	O	P	F	T	S	E	W	L	E	S	A
				■							■				■						
				■						■			■								■
		■			■						■					■					■
				■			■				■			■						■	■

2.

I			U	O		P			H		O	L		M	O						
O	T		L	H	R	W		T	E		E	Y		W	N		M	I	L	D	G
I	O	O	V	E	O	K	S	A	T	Y	A	N		I	H	E	N	O	M	S	O
N	M	N	S	T	I	Y	I	L	O	V	M	T	H	E	R	M	R	E	I	A	T
		■					■						■			■					
								■					■					■		■	
	■				■					■			■				■		■		
		■					■			■						■					■

3.

O		R		O		T										O		Y	A		
P		T	N	E	R	M	A	E	R	O		B	U	T		E	X	U	Y		
O	N	E	T	H	O	R	H	E	F	E	O	N	U	T	O	T	A	E	D	L	T
O	Y	S	F	T	R	S	C	N	C	Y	R	U	M	E	S	O	H	E	O	E	N
I	E	P	U	W	A	N	K	A	M	E	O	S	R	P	P	M	S	S	B	O	D
							■				■									■	
	■								■					■							■
											■				■					■	
			■					■				■			■						■
	■				■					■			■				■				

ANSWER, PAGE 201

DUBIOUS ACHIEVERS

These people actually made it into the *Guinness Book of World Records*, though whether they should be proud of it or not is another matter. But you can be proud if you correctly determine what they did to achieve their, um, honors.

1. In 1982, Randy Ober, of Bentonville, Arkansas, spat a...

    a) watermelon seed
    b) wad of tobacco
    c) silver dollar

    ...47 feet, 7 inches.

2. In 1989, Travis Johnson of Elsberry, Missouri, held nine...

    a) baseballs
    b) live guinea pigs
    c) Campbell's soup cans

    ...in one hand "without any adhesives."

3. In 1989, David Beattie and Adrian Simons of London, England, rode...

    a) skateboards
    b) escalators
    c) shopping carts

    ...for 101 hours, traveling approximately 133.19 miles.

4. In 1987, Pieter van Loggerenberg of Hoedspruit, South Africa, played...

    a) Hamlet
    b) hopscotch
    c) the accordion

    ...for 85 hours during a wildlife festival.

5. In 1981, Steve Urner of Tehachapi, California, threw a...

    a) bicycle
    b) dwarf
    c) dried cow chip

    ...more than 266 feet.

6. In 1982, N. Ravi, of Tamil Nadu, India, stood on...

    a) one foot
    b) a ball
    c) another man's shoulders

    ...for 34 hours.

7. Between 1949 and 1981, using over 50 aliases, Fred Jipp...

    a) impersonated policemen
    b) got married
    c) joined the Armed Forces and went AWOL

    ...104 times, earning 34 years in prison.

8. Since 1966, Michael Lotito of Grenoble, France, has eaten at least two pounds of...

    a) paper
    b) metal
    c) lard

    ...every day.

9. In 1986, Neil Sullivan of Cambridge, England, carried a large bag of...

    a) textbooks
    b) cats
    c) household coal

    ...34 miles, taking 12 hours and 45 minutes.

10. In 1985, two sisters, Jill Bradbury and Chris Humpish of London, England...

    a) made a bed
    b) traded clothing
    c) ate four steak-and-kidney pies

    ...in 19 seconds.

ANSWER, PAGE 201

ALMOST FAMOUS

They had successful acting careers…but might have been even more successful if it hadn't been for one single decision. Here are some stories about "the one that got away."

ACROSS

1 Drink in large gulps
5 Plaster heads
10 June honorees
14 Churchill Downs event
15 Laker who tops the seven-foot mark
16 Razor brand
17 Norway's capital
18 He swapped roles with Ray Bolger to become the Tin Man in *The Wizard of Oz* but was allergic to the facepaint
20 Magnetism
22 Golf's "Slammin' Sam"
23 Serengeti beast
24 Wrestling duos
27 His agent queered the deal to star opposite Streisand in *A Star Is Born* by demanding top billing for him
31 Luke Skywalker's guru
32 ___ Lauder
33 Exec. degree
36 Any of the Gospels
39 Sewing machine attachments
41 Susan of *L.A. Law*
42 Antitheft device
44 On the roof of
45 She was rejected for the lead in *My Fair Lady* and won an Oscar for another role the same year
48 Rave review
51 Roman triumvirate?
52 "___ we dance?"
53 Did a gofer's job
58 He would have been Indiana Jones, but was under contract to CBS
61 Ripped
62 Hydrox rival
63 Hidden hoard
64 End-of-the-week letters?
65 It lights up Broadway
66 Lavished affection (on)
67 "___ That a Shame?"

DOWN

1 Gator's cousin
2 Chopped meat dish
3 Pac-10 team
4 Ty Cobb, by birth
5 Emerges from the water
6 Latin word seen on coins
7 Puts under
8 Smidgen
9 Underhanded
10 Coleman of *WarGames*
11 Befuddled
12 Focus of Freudian analysis, often
13 The ___ (the Rat Pack's Vegas hangout)
19 High regard
21 Grp. that checks green cards
25 It can cause breathlessness
26 Joy
27 Observed closely
28 Venus's specialty
29 World War II ender
30 Arranged anew, as tiles
33 Distribute
34 Forehead
35 Egyptian snakes
37 Former French prez Charles de ___
38 First name in jazz
40 Town that a 4 Down might be from
43 Word on an incumbent's campaign poster
45 *The Jazz Singer* star
46 Made a dent in
47 Hagar creator ___ Browne
48 ___ Martin (007's car)
49 Tedious task
50 Short-but-important role
54 Reason to visit the dentist, say
55 Boo Boo's pal
56 Ireland, literarily
57 Good with one's hands
59 Digital watch technology
60 ___-tzu

ANSWER, PAGE 201

BOTTOMS UP!

They say there are more slang terms for "drunk" than any other word in the English language. Maybe that's why we had no trouble filling this beer stein to the top with 41 rich and foamy ones. When you've found them all, reading across, down, and diagonally, the leftover letters will reveal a somewhat sobering thought uttered by one of history's celebrated drinkers.

```
O N B E D E F F I P S D P
S B O X E D R R F I N C A
Q K I I T S I T O I R O R G M
U D L R O W E H T O T D A E D A
I N E Y O F D O C F R S L   W D M
F E D A F N D K A E S T Y     E H
F O U E E D E Y E E I P Z     V D
Y H S U L D S O D L A N E     A E
M A D N G G S S P I P E D     H W
U V O T N E N S N N Y D O     S E
D E K N A T O I U G Z E S     F L
M A G P T D C F J N O T P     L S
U S H I E R K I D O O S U     A I
R N L T S T E E H P W U C   U H P
D O O O L A R D Y A C B S C Z W
E O R D S E E I C I A I E O G
H T N E B H D K F N N D N
S F H B T B E S T I N K O
A U O M R D E D N D E A N
R L N O J U I C E D D D I
C L B B L O T T O E H A N
```

BENT
BLOTTO
BOILED
BOMBED
BOXED
BUSTED
CANNED
CLOBBERED
CRASHED
CROCKED
DEAD TO THE WORLD
FEELING NO PAIN
FRIED
GASSED
HALF SHAVED
HAVE A SNOOT FULL
HOOTED
IN ONE'S CUPS
JINGLED
JUICED
LUSHY
OSSIFIED
PARALYZED
PETRIFIED
PIE-EYED
PIPED
RUM-DUM
SAUCED
SCREWED
SLEWED
SLOSHED
SNOCKERED
SPIFFED
SQUIFFY
STIFF
STINKO
SWACKED
TANGLEFOOTED
TANKED
WOOZY
ZONKED

ANSWER, PAGE 202

BITE ME!

In *Uncle John's Bathroom Reader Plunges into the Universe*, readers got to ask some questions about venomous creatures—like, pound for pound, who's the most venomous? Here are 25 candidates. See if you can fit all of them into the grid so they interlock like a crossword. All the words are used exactly once. Hope you brought your bite kit.

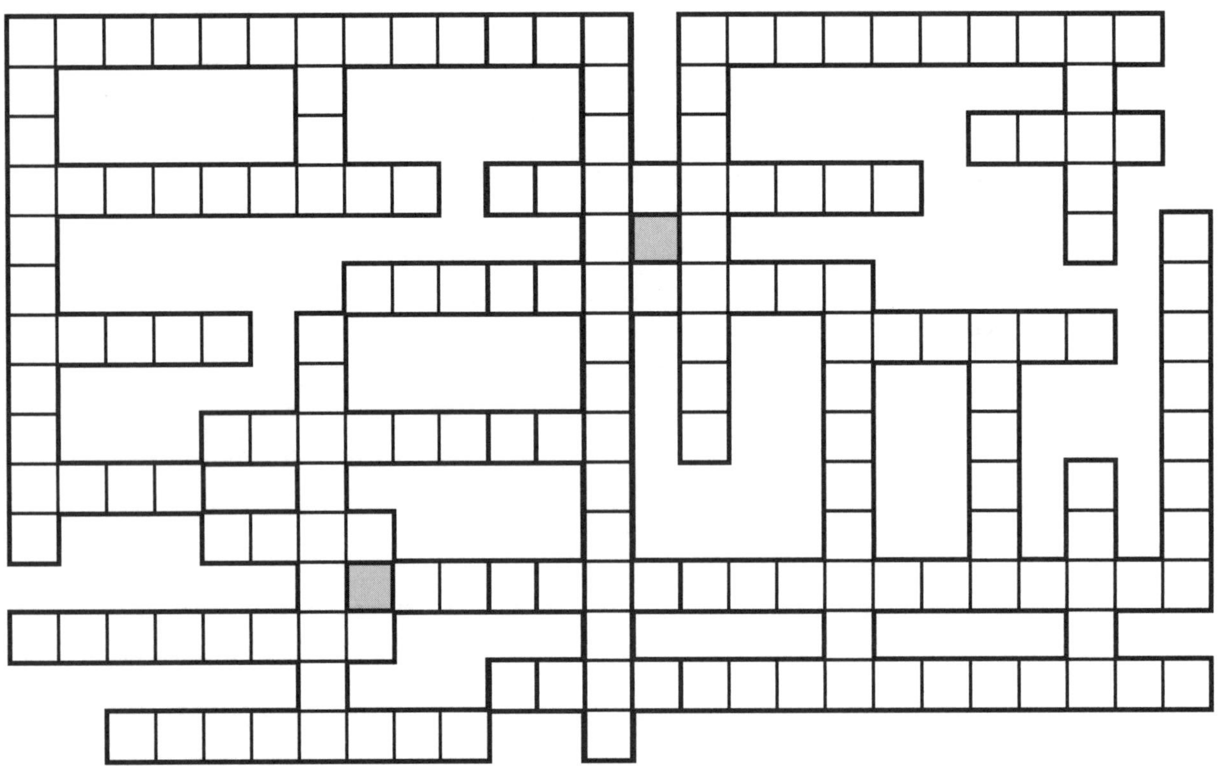

4 letter words
Fugu
Tang
Toad
Wasp

5 letter words
Krait
Mamba
Viper

6 letter words
Hornet
Urchin

8 letter words
Man of war
Platypus
Stingray

9 letter words
Boomslang
Cone snail
Funnel-web (spider)
Puff adder
Stonefish
Tarantula

10 letter word
Coral snake

11 letter words
Cottonmouth
Egyptian asp

13 letter word
Crown-of-thorns

15 letter words
Poison arrow frog
Stinging hydroid

17 letter word
Blue-ringed octopus

ANSWER, PAGE 202

PERFECT 10

The ten statements on this page are *almost* perfect, except that the ten numbers have been switched around. To help you out a little, we'll tell you that the numbers have been switched *in pairs*—i.e., if the number 1 replaced the 10, the 10 also replaced the 1. (That's just an example, of course—you can't mix a deck of cards with 1 shuffle, and Alan Shepard certainly didn't use a 10 iron on the moon!) Can you restore the perfect 10?

When Alan Shepard hit a golf ball on the moon, he used a **1** iron.

The average dairy cow produces **2** times her body weight in manure each year.

The average person looks at **3** houses before buying.

In a 1936 Ping-Pong tournament, players volleyed for over **4** hours on the opening serve.

The top speed of a chicken at full gallop is **5** mph.

In 1913, the income tax on $4,000 was **6** ¢.

Las Vegas is home to **7** of the 10 largest hotels in the U.S.

In the 1951 horror film *The Thing*, the monster was onscreen for about **8** minutes.

The average major league baseball lasts **9** pitches.

It takes **10** shuffles to thoroughly mix a 52-card deck.

ANSWER, PAGE 202

BEDTIME FOR BONZO

In the 1951 film *Bedtime for Bonzo*, Bonzo the chimp (real name: Tamba) became the only animal star ever to share top billing with a future president of the U.S. The film was one of Ronald Reagan's few box office successes. So what if you haven't seen it? Select your favorite answer from among the three given.

Ronald Reagan plays a(n) **(anthropology, psychology, zoology)** professor whose father was a **(crook, street person, politician)**. To prove that environment, not heredity, is to blame, he borrows a chimp from the zoology department and raises it like a **(puppy, son, dangerous animal)**. It backfires. When the chimp pilfers some **(campaign funds, jewelry, beer)**, Reagan is accused of **(training it to steal, stealing it himself, contributing to the delinquency of a mammal)**. Reagan winds up in jail until Bonzo's blonde nurse, as played by **(Diana Dors, Diana Lynn, Diana Rigg)** convinces the chimp to come clean. Bonzo returns the **(funds, jewelry, beer)**, Ronnie marries Diana, and they all live happily ever after.

ANSWER, PAGE 197

IT CAME FROM THE GARAGE...

It probably won't surprise you to learn that our puzzle team's favorite rock band is Phil 'n the Blanks. But if you've ever wondered how some other great bands got their names, you've come to the right place.

ACROSS

1 Esau's brother
6 On the ocean
11 Object from Saturn?
14 Despise
15 Like forks
16 KISS member Frehley
17 Band named after WWII fighter pilot slang for UFOs
19 *The ___ Squad*
20 North Sea bird
21 Author Zora ___ Hurston
22 Neighbor of Ecuador
23 Numbered rd.
24 Band named after a sociological study that the lead singer found in his mother's bookcase
27 Sail filler
28 More crafty
29 Spain, to its natives
32 Comet spotted in 1995
35 Chimney grime
36 Litter box user
37 Ewan's predecessor as Obi-Wan
38 24-karat stuff
41 Lions and Bears, e.g.
43 Big Band drummer Gene
44 ___ Marian
45 Band named by a friend concerned about the state of the band's finances
48 Crossed out
51 Like the Sahara
52 *Foundation* author Asimov
53 Inventor Whitney
54 Soak up the rays
55 Band with a Latin name that means "beyond all things" (though, in fact, it was chosen because it was the name of a friend's cat)
58 Terminus
59 At this point in time
60 Wear away
61 Lisa, to Bart
62 Makes jokes
63 Harrison and Stout

DOWN

1 *Aladdin* villain
2 ___ *a Boy* (2002 flick)
3 Strangle
4 Lifter's grunt
5 Earn, as a salary
6 Readily accessible
7 Library search criterion
8 Disrespects
9 Ending for musket
10 They're not part of the program?
11 Small part for a big name
12 Oak tree nut
13 John Updike's *Rabbit* ___
18 *The Fly* actress Davis
22 Multicolored, as a horse
25 Every one
26 Even score
27 Adulterated, with "down"
29 Medium's power
30 Former French coin
31 High-cholesterol snack from 7-11
32 Owned
33 For each
34 They do Windows?
36 Old-time trumpets used for announcements
39 Astronaut Grissom
40 Choose
41 Of birth
42 *Searching for Bobby* ___
44 Feline sounds
45 Goes out with
46 Tehran resident
47 Dressy scarf for a guy
48 Copier brand
49 Give the slip to
50 March of ___
55 Grade-schooler's sandwich, for short
56 Deli bread
57 "We ___ the World"

ANSWER, PAGE 203

THE CROSSWORD CRAZE

The first crossword puzzle appeared in the *New York World* newspaper on a Sunday, December 21, 1913. It was written by Arthur Wynne, a writer for the paper's game page. Ten years later, Richard L. Simon and M. Lincoln Schuster published the first crossword puzzle book. It sold 300,000 copies in the first year, turning college friends Simon and Schuster into major publishing house Simon & Schuster—and the crossword puzzle into a full-blown, worldwide craze.

Which of the following was not an outcome of the craze?

1. Crossword puzzles inspired a Broadway hit called *Games of 1925* and a hit song called "Crossword Mama, You Puzzle Me."

2. Clothes made of black-and-white checked fabric were the rage.

3. The B&O Railroad put dictionaries on all its mainline trains for crossword-crazy commuters.

4. In 1924, a Chicago woman sued her husband for divorce, claiming, "He was so engrossed in solving crosswords that he didn't have time to work."

5. In 1925, a New York Telephone Company employee shot his wife when she wouldn't help him with a crossword puzzle.

6. In 1926, a Budapest man committed suicide, leaving an explanation in the form of a crossword puzzle. (No one ever solved it.)

7. In 1927, a Rhode Island woman became so frustrated by a *New York Times* Sunday puzzle that she drove all the way to Manhattan and tried to assassinate the editor.

ANSWER, PAGE 203

* * * * *

JUST WING IT, KID

To "wing it" is to improvise. Why?

a) This comes from the theater. An actor who hasn't learned his part, and who only has time to study it hurriedly while waiting in the wings, is said to be "winging it."
b) It's an aviator's term that means to fly a plane while not knowing exactly where you are. In the early days of aviation, "winging it" was all too common.
c) It's a term from hunting. To wing an animal is to shoot some nonvital part of it; thus, advising someone to "wing it" is equivalent to saying, "Don't go for a direct hit—just see if you can get any kind of hit."

ANSWER, PAGE 203

A PUN? MY WORD!

If you know Uncle John, you know he loves his groaners. We've chosen a few of his favorite punny stories and converted them by simple letter substitution code, where C might equal F, or A might be Q. That sort of thing. For further instructions and hints on how to solve, see page 15.

A little girl fell into a well… RVQ RMLJBFKJ HJY XTWYQ ABT JYMS, JYT GTBLJYT HLBBQ GN RVQ QWQ VBLJWVK. AWVRMMN LJY VYDL-QBBT VYWKJGBT XRCY BPYT RVQ SFMMYQ LJY KWTM FS. "ZJN QWQV'L NBF JYMS JYT!" LJY VYWKJGBT RHEYQ LJY GBN. "JBZ," JY TYSMWYQ, "XBFMQ W GY JYT GTBLJYT RVQ RHHWHL JYT, LBB?"

A guy goes to a psychiatrist… "PMU, R EZZY ASGRWH FAZTZ SCFZBWSFRWH BZUKBBRWH PBZSXT. DRBTF, R'X S FZZYZZ; FAZW R'X S VRHVSX; FAZW R'X S FZZYZZ; FAZW R'X S VRHVSX. RF'T PBRGRWH XZ UBSQL. VASF'T VBMWH VRFA XZ?" FAZ PMUFMB BZYCRZP, "RF'T GZBL TRXYCZ. LMK'BZ FVM FZWFT."

It is well known throughout… *NSPFVGM *SWVIXS FYGF ESEOSVK IZ *TRMMRGE *FSMM'K ZGERMQ TSVS SGVMQ ASUIFSSK IZ MSGHWS OITMRPH. FYSQ YGA KXIPKIVK GPA SUSVQFYRPH. GNNIVARPH FI YRKFIVRGPK, FYIWHY, FYS VSNIVAK YGUS OSSP MIKF, KI PIOIAQ CPITK ZIV TYIE FYS *FSMMK OITMSA.

ANSWER, PAGE 203

GOOD QUESTION!

Directions for solving are on page 11.

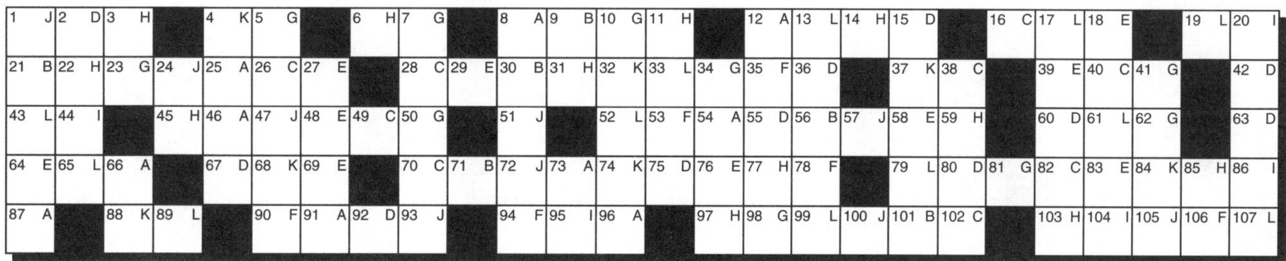

A. Most common place name in America

12 46 96 91 54 66 87 8 25 73

B. Baggy-pants rap star from Oakland

9 21 30 56 101 71

C. Most played radio song of all time

38 49 28 70 82 26 102 40 16

D. Scapegoat made to bear another's punishment (2 wds.)

63 2 92 75 55 42 15 36 60 80 67

E. Blotto and then some (3 wds.)

29 18 83 27 76 48 69 58 39 64

F. Graveyard shift periods

35 94 106 53 78 90

G. Shakespeare and Marlowe, e.g.

50 41 98 81 10 62 34 5 7 23

H. Personal quirk or tic

31 103 45 14 22 11 77 6 97 85 59 3

I. Dennis Miller's specialty

20 104 86 95 44

J. Vertical choice for an interior decorator

1 51 100 47 93 72 24 57 105

K. Middle-earth residents

84 68 88 37 4 32 74

L. Cheap, supervised lodgings (2 wds.)

89 107 61 43 33 13 17 79 19 65 99 52

ANSWER, PAGE 203

* * * * *

THAT CLEAN SLATE THING

To "start with a clean slate" is to make a fresh start. That makes sense, but what slates are we talking about?

a) Slates kept by tavern keepers to keep track of customers' debts. When a person paid off his debt, his name was erased from the board.
b) Slates used by schoolmasters to keep track of student demerits. A student who earned too many demerits in a single semester was expelled. But at the start of each new semester all demerits were removed.
c) Slates used by prison keepers to keep track of how many days each prisoner had left to serve. Prisoners who served their full sentences were cleaned from the slate.

ANSWER, PAGE 203

SAY SOMEONE'S STUPID

Unscramble the letters below each set of blanks to find out how to say someone's stupid in a whole bunch of different ways.

1. A few __ __ __ __ __ __ short of a __ __ __ __ __ __.
   W N L O S C — R U C S C I

2. A few __ __ __ __ __ short of a __ __ __ __ __ __ __ __ __.
   E F S I R — P Y A P H A E M L

3. A few __ __ __ __ __ short of a __ __ __-__ __ __ __.
   E R B E S — I S X K P C A

4. Dumber than a __ __ __ of __ __ __ __.
   O X B — R A H I

5. A few __ __ __ __ short of a __ __ __ __ __ __ __ __ __.
   S E P A — S E L R A C O S E

6. Doesn't have all his __ __ __ __ __ __ __ __ __ __ in one __ __ __.
   N C R O S E L F A K — X B O

7. __ __ __ __ __ __ __'__ clogged.
   M I C H Y S E N

8. One __ __ __ __ __ __ __ __ __ shy of a __ __ __ __ __ __ __ __.
   T O F O R P O L O — L U F L O B L W

9. One __ __ __ __ short of a __ __ __ __ __ __ __ __ __ __ __ __ __ __ __ __ __.
   C O T A — I N N A B I C O T O M T E L P A

10. A few __ __ __ __ __ __ __ __ short of a __ __ __ __ __ __ __ __ __.
    H E F A S T E R — L O W E H K U D C

11. All __ __ __ __, no __ __ __ __.
    A F O M — E R E B

12. The __ __ __ __ __ __ slid off his __ __ __ __ __ __ __.
    H S C E E E — K R C A C R E

13. Body by __ __ __ __ __ __, brains by __ __ __ __ __ __.
    S I R H F E — T E M A L T

14. Too much __ __ __ __ __ __ __ between the __ __ __ __ __ __ __ __ __ __.
    A Y G R A D E — L A G O T O S S P

15. Forgot to pay his __ __ __ __ __ __ __ __ __.
    R I N A B L I B L

16. As __ __ __ __ __ as __ __ __ __.
    M S R A T — T I B A

ANSWER, PAGE 203

TV TRIVIA

Serious couch potatoes think there's nothing trivial about the tube. Here's a few tidbits you may have missed while you were channel-surfing.

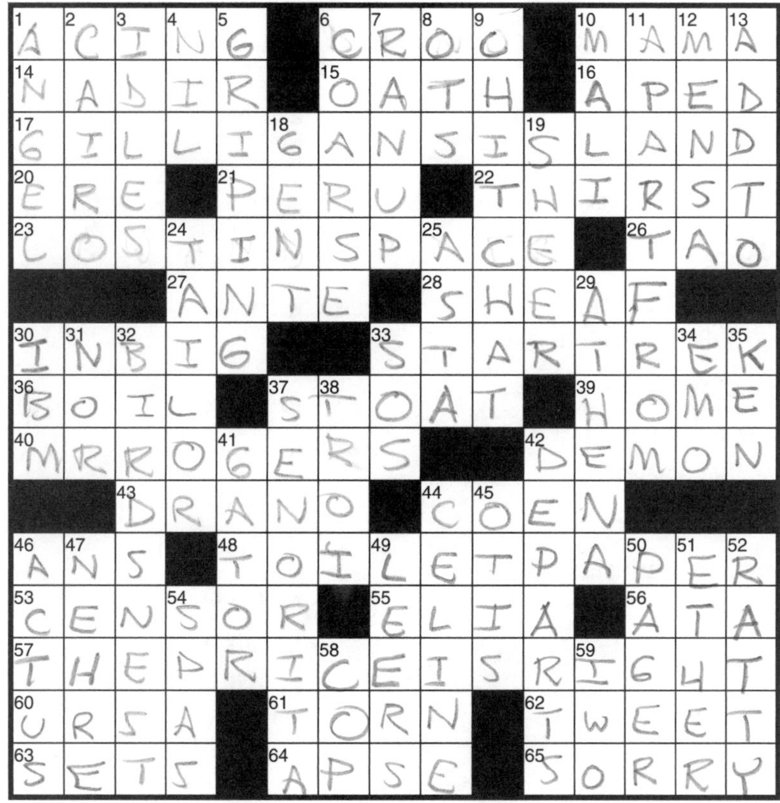

ACROSS

1 Scoring 100 on
6 Large reptile, for short
10 Baby's first word, often
14 Lowest point
15 ___ of Office
16 Mimicked
17 TV show the *San Francisco Chronicle* called "a new low in the networks' estimation of public intelligence"
20 Before, poetically
21 Nation conquered by Pizarro
22 Need for water
23 "Serious" TV adventure show that sent CBS executives into hysterics during their first screening
26 Concept originated by Lao-Tzu
27 Throw in a chip
28 Paper bundle
30 ___ trouble (up the creek)
33 Show that featured TV's first interracial kiss
36 Prepare pasta
37 Ermine, really
39 Web browser button
40 In a 1990 preschool poll, TV personality who was first choice for president
42 Speed ___ (unsafe driver)
43 Liquid-Plumr competitor
44 Last name of the brother team who made *Fargo*
46 Reply to a ques.
48 Household product that Johnny Carson created a shortage of when he joked that there was a shortage of it
53 Remover of objectionable content
55 Movie director Kazan
56 "One ___ time, please"
57 TV game show that the theme music for *Family Feud* was lifted from
60 ___ Major
61 Unable to decide
62 Songbird sound
63 Situates
64 Church area
65 "I feel terrible about this"

DOWN

1 Heavenly helper
2 Africa's most populous city
3 Runs in neutral
4 Zero
5 Complaining
6 Like sandpaper
7 Amassed, as a debt
8 Exts. to a game
9 Small talk
10 Nation south of Algeria
11 Besides
12 High-IQ club
13 Augment
18 Lady's escort
19 See-through, as fabric
24 Sew to fit
25 Nick and Nora's dog
29 Goddess of the Parthenon
30 PC Jr. manufacturer
31 Word used with "neither"
32 Bowl of eggs, sort of
33 Soap pad brand
34 Funnyman Philips
35 Starr involved in Monicagate
37 Mexican Miss
38 *Enterprise* counselor Deanna ___
41 Critter often mistaken for 6 Across
42 Takes off
44 Diva Dion
45 Singer Redding
46 Behave badly
47 Indira Gandhi's father
49 Lascivious looks
50 Cell phone predecessor
51 Old anesthetic
52 Shabby-looking
54 Health resorts
58 Whistle-blower?
59 ___ Jima

ANSWER, PAGE 204

COWBOY TALK

There's euphemisms in them thar hills! Yep, those folks in the old West sure knew how to insult somebody—in a roundabout enough way that the person might not know they were being insulted (which probably prevented a lot of unnecessary gunfights). See if you can match the phrases (1–13) to the kind of person they describe (a–m). You'll have to be "weasel smart" to get all 13.

_____ 1. "Built like a snake on stilts"
_____ 2. "Crooked enough to sleep on a corkscrew"
_____ 3. "Died of throat trouble"
_____ 4. "Fat as a well-fed needle"
_____ 5. "Fryin' size but plumb salty"
_____ 6. "Got a pill in his stomach that he can't digest"
_____ 7. "In the lead when tongues was handed out"
_____ 8. "Like a turkey gobbler in a hen pen"
_____ 9. "Like bird dung in a cuckoo clock"
_____ 10. "Like a breedin' jackass in a tin barn"
_____ 11. "Lives in a house so small he can't cuss his cat without getting fur in his mouth"
_____ 12. "Raised on prunes and proverbs"
_____ 13. "Studying to be a half-wit"

a. cheap
b. crazy
c. dishonest
d. hanged
e. noisy
f. old
g. proud
h. rare
i. religious
j. shot dead
k. poor
l. talkative
m. tall

ANSWER, PAGE 204

I LIKE GENTLE BEN IN THE 4TH

Small crostic puzzles are solved just like the big ones (directions on page 11) but the first letter of the fill-in words **do not** spell out a hidden message.

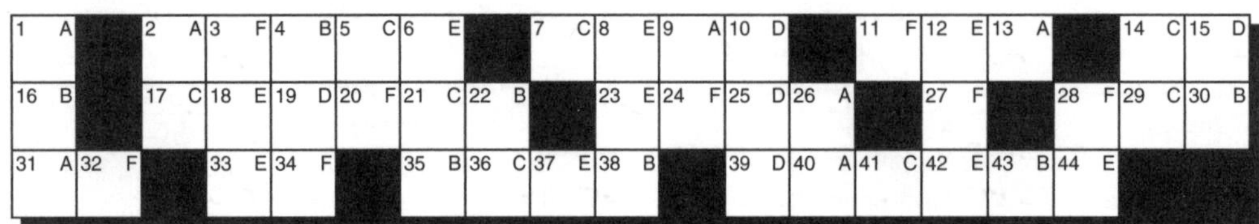

A. Early Woody Allen flick

__ __ __ __ __ __ __
2 9 26 40 13 1 31

B. Sad and lonely

__ __ __ __ __ __ __
35 43 30 38 4 22 16

C. Flounce on a woman's skirt

__ __ __ __ __ __ __ __
17 36 14 7 21 41 29 5

D. What a sweet tooth craves

__ __ __ __ __
19 15 39 25 10

E. Long slender cigar

__ __ __ __ __ __ __ __ __
44 33 6 18 23 8 37 42 12

F. England's "Iron Lady"

__ __ __ __ __ __ __ __
20 24 27 34 11 28 32 3

ANSWER, PAGE 204

THEY DIDN'T CALL HIM THE MAD MONK FOR NOTHING

At the beginning of the 20th century, Imperial Russia was like a Jenga tower with one supporting strut too few. Rasputin didn't cause the czar to fall, but he sure helped to push. Here's his story…but you'll have to work for it. Choose the correct answer from among the three in each set of parentheses.

The name "Rasputin" wasn't his given name, it was his condition: In Russian, it means **("ugly and unshaven," "debauched one," "diseased one")** and it was given to him at a young age. You'd think that being known as "Rasputin" would be a detrimental sort of thing—I mean, just imagine trying to meet people if your name was "**(Greg Pigpen, Greg Pervert, Greg What-I've-Got-Is-Catching)**."

Rasputin experienced a religious conversion at the age of 18. He joined a sect known as "Khlysty," which translates roughly as the **("Flagellants," "Flatulents," "Flat-Tops")** which means people who **(flog themselves silly, pass a lot of gas, wear funny haircuts)**. Later he chose to pursue the closeness to God that only comes through what he described as "holy passionness," which could only be reached through **(meditation, counting money, sexual exhaustion)**. This provided Rasputin the theological rationale he needed to do whatever he wanted.

Fast forward to 1903. Rasputin is the toast of the St. Petersburg movers and shakers, who regarded him the way celebrities in the 1960s regarded their swami. Sure, Rasputin was illiterate and he bathed only once a **(week, month, year)** but there sure was something about him.

Within a couple of years, Rasputin had found his way to the Czar Nikolas II and Czarina Alexandra, and he endeared himself to them by easing the pain of their **(asthmatic, hemophiliac, epileptic)** son—historians think by a form of **(faith healing, herbal medicine, hypnosis)**. He also told the royal couple that without him, they were doomed. The czar wanted to get rid of him—even managed to do it **(once, twice, six times)** but the czarina wouldn't have it.

The Russian nobles decided to get Rasputin out of the way. And thus it was in late December 1916 that the Mad Monk found himself at the home of Prince Feliks Yusupov, lured there by the promise that he'd meet **(someone's very attractive wife, Sarah Bernhardt, the richest widow in all of Russia)**. The nobles fed him poison in **(tea and cakes, champagne and caviar, beer and pretzels)**. He gobbled it all down and didn't blink. Then they **(shot, stabbed, strangled)** him and cut off his **(beard, monk's robes, you-know-what)**. He still managed to launch himself out the door. They **(shot, stabbed, strangled)** him again, wrapped him in **(his monk's robes, a carpet, a smelly old blanket)** and heaved his body into **(the trunk of a Model T, a river, the Baltic Sea)**. At which point, of course, he died. We think.

Rasputin's words came to pass, but he was true to his word; Nikolas, Alexandra, and the rest of the nobility were all dead within a couple of years, victims of **(smallpox, the Bolshevik revolution, Napoleon)**. The rest is history.

ANSWER, PAGE 204

HARSH!

Guess you can't expect famous people to be nice all the time. Here are some sharp comments from celebs who apparently woke up on the wrong side of the bed.

1.

	T			M				T	H			A	O	T	E	D			
Y	F		G	A	D		E	S	D			W	O	U	L	I		U	A
I	E	O	E	O	D	E	H	A	U	E	A	M	E	S	R	D	C	S	S
V	S	T	H	U	S	J	T	E	N	S	W	P	N	T	T	L	E	H	S
		■				■				■							■		
■			■				■				■							■	
					■						■						■		
		■				■				■									■

2.

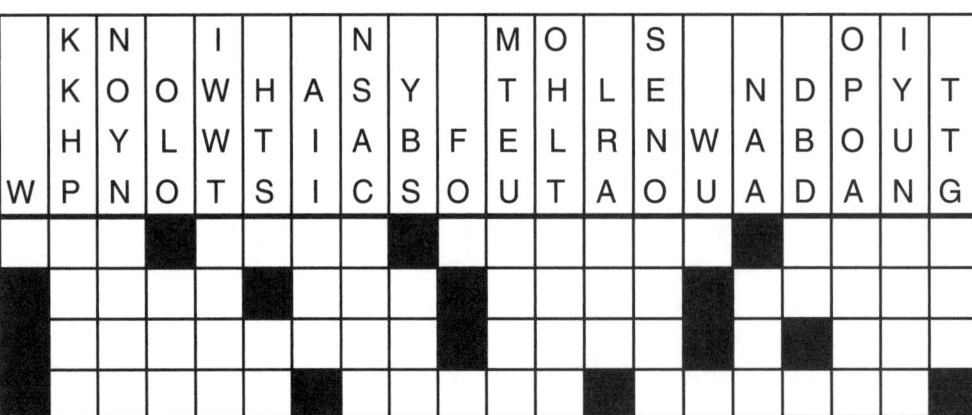

	K	N		I			N			M	O		S				O	I	
	K	O	O	W	H	A	S	Y		T	H	L	E		N	D	P	Y	T
	H	Y	L	W	T	I	A	B	F	E	L	R	N	W	A	B	O	U	T
W	P	N	O	T	S	I	C	S	O	U	T	A	O	U	A	D	A	N	G
			■					■							■				
■					■				■					■					
■									■					■		■			
■						■						■							■

3.

E	U							J		E				I	A				
M	V	E	W	F	E	T		P	R	L	H	W	A	H	S			L	E
O	A	U	S	A	S	L	O	M	L	O	E	D	T	S	N			L	N
C	M	G	H	E	O	O	C	E	A	C	N	E	T	N	C	T	S	E	B
U	I	C	H	A	R	R	H	A	A	T	K	S	O	B	E	D	A	B	E
							■									■			
		■				■							■				■		
					■						■						■		
				■					■			■				■			
			■				■									■	■	■	■

ANSWER, PAGE 204

AND IF YOU BELIEVE THAT ONE...

It's quiz time again and this time around, we're presenting you with three odd-yet-true facts and one outright lie (aren't we just terrible?). See if you can spot the lie from its three truthful companions.

1. **Patents pending**
   a) The typewriter was invented before the fountain pen
   b) The riding lawn mower was invented before the push mower
   c) The cigarette lighter was invented before the safety match
   d) The camera was invented before film

2. **Cross products**
   a) Mayonnaise makes a good skin moisturizer
   b) Cola will give your toilet a nice shine
   c) Butter is an effective burn ointment
   d) Crisco can be used to remove makeup

3. **"You wanna make something of it?"**
   a) Candy maker Milton Hershey despised the taste of chocolate
   b) Kodak founder George Eastman hated having his picture taken
   c) Beach Boys frontman Brian Wilson never surfed—in fact, he was afraid of the ocean
   d) Anna Jarvis, the creator of Mother's Day, never had children

4. **On second thought…**
   a) George Lucas originally planned to name his *Star Wars* hero Luke Starkiller
   b) "Rudolph the Red-Nosed Reindeer" was originally named Rollo
   c) Denny's restaurant used to be known as "Danny's"
   d) The first iteration of G. I. Joe was called "Fightin' George"

5. **Man of the Year?**
   a) *Time* magazine's "Man of the Year" in 1938 was Adolf Hitler
   b) *Time* magazine's "Man of the Year" in 1942 was Joseph Stalin
   c) *Time* magazine's "Man of the Year" in 1952 was Queen Elizabeth II
   d) *Time* magazine's "Man of the Year" in 1990 was Saddam Hussein

6. **Animal afflictions**
   a) Fish can get seasick
   b) Snakes can poison themselves
   c) Ducks can get the flu
   d) Fruit flies can become constipated

7. **Trans-plants**
   a) Banana trees aren't trees
   b) Banana shrubs aren't shrubs
   c) Poison oak is not an oak
   d) Poison ivy is not an ivy

8. **Gender issues**
   a) Only female mosquitoes bite
   b) Only male fireflies can fly
   c) Only female spiders spin webs
   d) Only male canaries can sing

ANSWER, PAGE 204

CURE FOR A DEPRESSION

Directions for solving are on page 11.

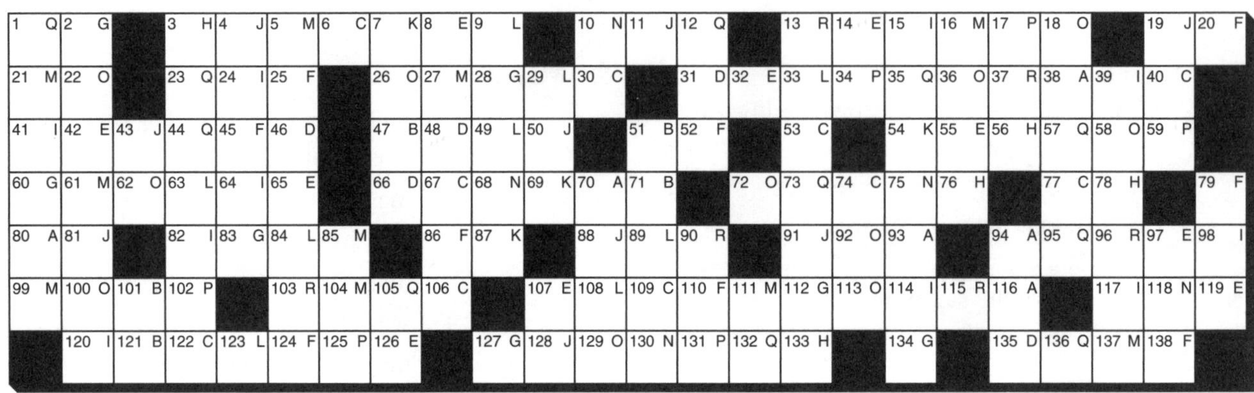

A. 1982 Best Picture biopic

116 94 70 93 80 38

B. Having debts

51 47 121 101 71

C. "The Sweater Girl" of the 1940s (2 wds.)

122 77 74 53 30 67 109 40 106 6

D. Nerd

31 135 46 48 66

E. Resumé listing

42 119 107 65 97 55 14 126 8 32

F. Best Actor nominee for *Affliction* (2 wds.)

20 124 110 138 52 86 45 79 25

G. Satisfy or relieve

112 127 60 28 134 2 83

H. Microsoft's main man

56 3 78 76 133

I. Stand-up comic who's been described as "gawky" and "bizarre" (2 wds.)

15 120 39 41 24 98 64 114 82 117

J. REM's 1991 Grammy winner (3 wds.)

43 128 88 11 91 50 19 4 81

K. Independent archipelago of some 800 islands

87 7 54 69

L. Blonde host of the TV news show *The Edge* (2 wds.)

33 9 108 123 84 63 29 89 49

M. In deep doo-doo (3 wds.)

61 16 21 111 5 99 27 104 137 85

N. Tom Wilson's comic strip creation

130 118 10 75 68

O. Budapest-born actress/celebrity christened "Sari" (3 wds.)

62 113 92 129 36 100 26 58 72 22 18

P. Drops, as a bucket in a well

131 125 59 17 34 102

Q. New York's official nickname (2 wds.)

35 95 44 73 105 132 57 12 1 23 136

R. Birthplace of Ingrid and Ingmar Bergman

37 103 90 13 96 115

ANSWER, PAGE 205

FILL IN THE LIMERICKS

You probably know a few limericks of your own (naughty, naughty) and you may recognize the following as some of Uncle John's favorites. But just how well do you remember them? See if you can fill in the blanks (one for each missing letter) to complete each little ditty.

1. A cat in despondency sighed,
And resolved to commit _ _ _ _ _ _ _;
She passed under the wheels
Of eight _ _ _ _ _ _ _ _ _ _ _ _ _
And after the ninth one she _ _ _ _.

2. There was a young fellow of Leeds,
Who swallowed six packets of _ _ _ _ _.
In a month, silly ass,
He was covered with _ _ _ _ _.
And he couldn't sit down for the _ _ _ _ _.

3. There was a young lady of Ryde,
Who ate some green apples and _ _ _ _;
The apples _ _ _ _ _ _ _ _ _ _ _
Inside the lamented,
And made cider inside her _ _ _ _ _ _.

4. There was a young athlete named Tribbling,
Whose hobby was basketball
_ _ _ _ _ _ _ _ _;
But he dribbled one day
On a busy _ _ _ _ _ _ _ _.
Now his sister is missing a _ _ _ _ _ _ _ _.

5. There was a hillbilly named Shaw
Who envied his maw and his _ _ _.
To share in their life
He adopted his _ _ _ _
And became his own
_ _ _ _ _ _ _-_ _-_ _ _.

6. A rocket explorer named Wright
Once traveled much faster than _ _ _ _ _.
He set out one day
In a relative _ _ _,
And returned on the previous _ _ _ _ _.

7. There was a young lady from Lynn
Who was sunk in original _ _ _.
When they said, "Do be good,"
She replied, "If I _ _ _ _ _....
But I'd do wrong right over _ _ _ _ _"

8. There was an old fellow named Cager
Who, as the result of a _ _ _ _ _ _,
Offered to fart
The whole oboe _ _ _ _
Of Mozart's "Quartet in F _ _ _ _ _."

9. An epicure, dining in Crewe,
Once found a large mouse in his _ _ _ _.
Said the waiter: "Don't shout,
Or wave it _ _ _ _ _,
Or the rest will be wanting one, _ _ _."

10. There was a young belle of old _ _ _ _ _ _ _ _ _
Whose garments were always in patchez.
When comment arose
On the state of her _ _ _ _ _ _ _ _,
She drawled, "When Ah itchez,
Ah _ _ _ _ _ _ _ _ _ _ _!"

ANSWER, PAGE 205

NOTABLE FIRSTS

Well, somebody's got to do it.

ACROSS

1 "Hey, there" in sailor-speak
5 Use a letter opener
9 Hungers (for)
14 Unclothed
15 Meat-filled treat
16 Winning
17 First self-made millionaire in a Communist country
19 Bizet's *Carmen*, e.g.
20 Become a duo
21 Most unseaworthy, say
23 First woman to appear in a *Playboy* centerfold
25 Site of a 1983 invasion
27 Witticism that makes people groan
28 Left in a hurry
29 He headed the USSR until 1924
32 Lukewarm
36 "___ Brute?"
38 Rented anew
40 1920s art movement
41 Paper nest builders
43 Eat soup noisily
45 Huge amount
46 Elem. school group
48 Clothing, old-style
50 First artist to refuse a Grammy
55 Hype to death
56 Parachute attachers
59 Induce thirst
60 First person to appear on the cover of *People* magazine
62 Gratuitous
63 A single time
64 Swenson of *Benson*
65 Some people have dark ones
66 Psychic
67 In a jiffy

DOWN

1 Drive the getaway car, e.g.
2 Surprise loser to the tortoise
3 They hang on trees in winter
4 Naval newbie
5 More boneheaded
6 Scientist's workroom
7 In an unfriendly way
8 Subway station purchase
9 "You're going to crash!"
10 Removed from a corkboard
11 Use the rudder
12 The *Venus de Milo*, pretty much
13 Outpouring
18 Not urban
22 Electric guitarist's need
24 Superhighways have lots of them
25 Got bigger
26 Pro ___
30 Feeling less than 100%
31 Prefix with biology or chemistry
33 Longtime *New Yorker* cartoonist
34 Clickable image
35 "___ be silly!"
37 Knockout punch
39 Move a bank balance
42 Hides away
44 One of Columbus's ships
47 Lemon or lime suffix
49 Nine Lives mascot
50 Absorb
51 One of the Mrs. Trumps
52 Dweebs
53 *Selena* star Edward James ___
54 "I Fall to Pieces" singer
57 Walt Kelly's strip
58 Tchaikovsky's ___ *Lake*
61 Expert

ANSWER, PAGE 205

WARNING LABELS

Some things in life should go without saying, but there's always the occasional nincompoop who needs to be told not to drive their car while the cardboard sun shield is still in place. See if you can match these actual warnings (1–15) to the products they originally accompanied (a–o). (Warning: This quiz should not be used as a flotation device.)

_____ 1. Avoid dropping out of windows
_____ 2. Caution: Remove infant before folding for storage
_____ 3. Caution—Risk of fire
_____ 4. Do not use as an ice-cream topping
_____ 5. Do not use to pick up anything that is currently burning
_____ 6. Do not use orally
_____ 7. Do not use for drying pets
_____ 8. Do not use as a projectile in a catapult
_____ 9. Do not use orally after using rectally
_____ 10. Never use while sleeping
_____ 11. Not intended for highway use
_____ 12. Pads cannot protect any part of the body they do not cover
_____ 13. Warning: Has been found to cause cancer in laboratory mice
_____ 14. Warning: Cape does not enable user to fly
_____ 15. Warning: This product can burn eyes

a. Air conditioner
b. Batman costume
c. Bottle of hair coloring
d. Box of rat poison
e. Compact disc player
f. Curling iron
g. Digital thermometer
h. Duraflame fireplace log
i. Microwave oven
j. Plastic, 13-inch wheelbarrow wheel
k. Portable stroller
l. Propane blowtorch
m. Shin guards
n. Toilet bowl cleaning brush
o. Vacuum cleaner

ANSWER, PAGE 205

* * * * *

STORMY WEATHER

True or false: Florida—the so-called "Sunshine State"—gets more thunderstorms and lightning than any other state in the U.S.

ANSWER, PAGE 205

PRIME-TIME PROVERBS

Real-life famous people don't have a monopoly on quotations. Lots of TV characters have said all sorts of things worth writing down. See if you can match the quotes (1–12) to the speakers (a–l).

_____ 1. "There's something neat about a sweater with a hole. It makes you look like a tough guy."

_____ 2. "Another outburst like this and I'm gonna handcuff your lips together."

_____ 3. "City women is spoiled rotten. All they think about is smearin' themselves with beauty grease. Fancy smellin' renderin's. Why, if you was to hug one of 'em, she'd squirt out of yore arms like a prune pit!"

_____ 4. "I haven't worn makeup in years. It takes away that unnatural look that we girls like."

_____ 5. "I am your father. I brought you into this world and I can take you out."

_____ 6. "I love my blubber. It keeps me warm, it keeps me company, it keeps my pants up."

_____ 7. "I'm tired of being an object of ridicule. I wanna be a figure of fear, respect, and SEX!"

_____ 8. "I'm an experienced woman; I've been around. Well...all right, I might not've been around, but I've been...nearby."

_____ 9. "If you're gonna steal, steal from kin—at least they're less likely to put the law on you."

_____ 10. "It's funny the way some people's name just suits the business they're in. Like God's name is just *perfect* for God."

_____ 11. "The roots of physical aggression found in the male species are in the DNA molecule itself. In fact, the very letters DNA are an acronym for 'Dames are Not Agressors'."

_____ 12. "The only thing I ever dream is that I just won every beauty contest in the world and all the people I don't like are forced to build me a castle in France."

a. Beaver Cleaver, *Leave It to Beaver*

b. Bret Maverick, *Maverick*

c. Cliff Claven, *Cheers*

d. Cliff Huxtable, *The Cosby Show*

e. Edith Bunker, *All in the Family*

f. Granny, *The Beverly Hillbillies*

g. Stephanie Vanderkellen, *Newhart*

h. Lily Munster, *The Munsters*

i. Mary Richards, *The Mary Tyler Moore Show*

j. Oscar Madison, *The Odd Couple*

k. Radar O'Reilly, *M*A*S*H*

l. Sgt. Wojehowicz, *Barney Miller*

ANSWER, PAGE 205

SHOOT ON A SHINGLE

American G.I.'s had to do something to make their chow palatable. So they invented slang names for pretty much everything they ate and drank.

The grid below contains 15 of those slang terms for the foods that appear in the word list. The regular names for these foods DO NOT appear in the grid—only the slang word or phrase for them does, and it's up to you to figure out what those slang words are. As hints, the spaces next to each food indicate the number of letters in each slang word; and we give you the starting letter. For example, BEANS does not appear in the grid, but AMMUNITION, its slang name, does.

As a bonus, after you've circled all the words in the grid, read the unused letters from left to right, top to bottom, to spell out a hidden message related to the puzzle theme. If you need help, turn to the answer page for the complete list of slang.

M Y S T E R Y P L A T E O
A C H A L K T T H E R N D
C W O C D E R O M R A A O
H M T E S F O M R G C L G
I O W F F E E A N A R E B
N E A M M U N I T I O N I
E B T A T E D N T E R P S
O Y E A Y D C E I D O A C
I R R E A P A S E I N R U
L T D W R E M T O W V H I
E E N S O L V E N T A S T
R U B B E R P A T C H E S
G K C I D Y E K N O D R S

BEANS: A __ __ __ __ __ __ __ __ __
BOLOGNA: D __ __ __ __ __ D __ __ __
BREAD: G __ __ W __ __ __ __ __ __
CANNED MILK: A __ __ __ __ __ __ C __ __
COFFEE: S __ __ __ __ __ __
CRACKERS: D __ __ B __ __ __ __ __ __ __
GRAPE NUTS: S __ __ __ __ __ __ __
HASH: M __ __ __ __ __ __ P __ __ __ __
KETCHUP: R __ __-E __ __
MAPLE SYRUP: M __ __ __ __ __ __ O __ __
MEATLOAF: P __ __ __ __ __ __ __ __ S __ __ __ __
PANCAKES: R __ __ __ __ __ P __ __ __ __ __ __
POWDERED MILK: C __ __ __ __
SOUP: H __ __ W __ __ __ __
SPINACH: S __ __ __ __ __ __

ANSWER, PAGE 206

TOM SWIFTIES, TOO

Can you end each sentence (1–10) with the adverb (a–j) that will make the best Tom Swifty? (If Tom Swifties are new to you, see TOM SWIFTIES on page 51.)

_____ 1. "...and you lose a few," Tom said...

_____ 2. "He only likes whole grain bread," Tom said...

_____ 3. "I forgot what to buy," Tom said...

_____ 4. "I hate seafood," Tom said...

_____ 5. "I love Chinese food," Tom said...

_____ 6. "I need a pencil sharpener," Tom said...

_____ 7. "I twisted my ankle," Tom said...

_____ 8. "I was removed from office," Tom said...

_____ 9. "I wish I were taller," Tom said...

_____ 10. "There's too much Tabasco in this chili," Tom said...

a. bluntly
b. crabbily
c. disappointedly
d. hotly
e. lamely
f. listlessly
g. longingly
h. wantonly
i. winsomely
j. wryly

ANSWER, PAGE 206

QUOTAGRAM

Here's a puzzle for experts only—or those who aspire. We've taken a quotation and anagrammed it, a little at a time. Each word should be taken in order, and its letters rearranged (if necessary) to form a quote. The blanks tell you the enumeration of each word in the quote. The first two anagrams in the puzzle have been filled in for you to show you how it's done. Happy unscrambling!

WHE/N A STU/ ___ ___ ___ ___ ___ ___ ___ ___, ___ ___ ___

4 1 6 3 2 5 9 2 2 7 2, 2 6 8

___ ___ ___ ___ ___.

4 2 2 3 4

HEW AUNTS DIP MAINS DINGO SMOTE NIGH HIES HAS FOAMED HALE SWAYED

SCARLET THAI SIT HI DUSTY

ANSWER, PAGE 206

WHAT DID YOU CALL ME?

Some very long words that describe some people with interesting quirks. Are you among them?

ACROSS

1 Chest-beating mammal
4 The ___ State (Hawaii)
9 Snake charmer's snake
14 "C'mon, be a ___!"
15 David's successor on *Late Night*
16 Leading
17 A *misodoctakleidist* is a person who hates…
20 Vocal advocate
21 Alex Haley best-seller
22 Famous fable writer
23 Murderous Genesis character
25 Howl at the moon
27 *25th Hour* director Spike
28 More than just thin
30 Walk around nervously
31 A *cardiophobe* is a person who's afraid of…
34 Money given to panhandlers
36 Small newsstands
37 An *arithmomaniac* is a person who compulsively…
39 Forearm bone
40 Piece of clothing praised in a Sisqo hit
41 Fish sans fins
44 Poker table center
45 Carrots' partner
46 Shelby ___ of country music
48 Broadcast again
50 Not out of the question
53 A *melcryptovestimentaphiliac* is a person who's compelled to steal…
55 Legal drinker
56 Capture
57 ___ Victor
58 Young girl, in British slang
59 Mitigates
60 Understand, as a joke

DOWN

1 Word after mass or sex
2 Sect member in India
3 Go by
4 Misbehave
5 *Malcolm in the Middle* mom
6 "___ upon a time…"
7 Trim, at the barbershop
8 ___ Arbor
9 Tasty rooster
10 Kent State's state
11 Repel, as an attack
12 Pillages
13 Commotion
18 Amorous murmur
19 ___ one's teeth (showing determination)
24 Darth in his pre-helmet days
26 "Absolutely!"
28 Joke writers
29 The Queen of Soul's first name
30 Avoid an F
31 *The English Patient* nurse
32 Suffix with persist
33 Dress (up)
34 River that carved the Grand Canyon
35 Found after much effort
37 Tearoom vessel
38 "___ in the highest" (church chorus)
41 Emmy Award–winning sportscaster Dick
42 Intertwine
43 Look upon lasciviously
45 Devoutness
46 Tackle box items
47 Go off course
49 Needs some TLC, say
51 Dietary standards, for short
52 *Chicago* star
53 Complete circuit of a track
54 Take advantage of

ANSWER, PAGE 206

BE KIND TO THE ANIMALS, SOMETIMES

Even if you don't believe in superstitions, they can be intriguing. Here are some very old ones relating to animals that we warned you about in *Uncle John's Great Big Bathroom Reader*. But you never listen, do you?

1.

	H	E		R			T					P				U				
T	E	A	I	F		E	P	D	L	F	C	U	R	M	C	H		M	O	
L	I	V	E	F	E	W	N	I	O	E	O	N	L	I	E	N	T	T	I	
F	H	V	L	N	G	A	I	L	G	A	P	A	S	E	A	D	I	I	N	N
						■								■				■		
■					■				■								■			■
			■					■			■		■				■			■
					■					■					■				■	■

2.

	T		Y	D	I			A				A			S		U	Y		C
I	T	E	R	O	U		F	I	N	O		E	U		A	I	R	U		K
H	O	H	L	P	W	R	I	F	R	R	Y	O	R	O	Y	H	O	U	C	D
A	F	U	R	O	E	L	L	T	O	D	V	G	O	H	D	O	L	R	L	S
		■				■					■		■						■	
										■				■						
■						■			■					■					■	
							■				■					■				

3.

R			G									B		L		A	L			
E		T	N		M	A	N	R	S		I	T	S	E		K	F	L		
A	A	N	A	E	W	W	O	Y	M	C	O	U	E	D		V	E	E	L	D
I	F	G	H	D	R	F	A	I	I	S	L	U	L	E	O	T	H	F	E	N
D	A	A	L	O	O	M	H	H	S	H	A	O	V	W	I	L	I	D	A	I
		■		■				■							■					■
	■									■			■					■		
						■				■					■					
	■				■				■						■				■	
				■			■				■								■	■

ANSWER, PAGE 206

BASKETBALL NAMES

Here's a chance for jocks to show off their knowledge of basketball lore. But even if you've never seen the game played, you can still try to figure out which of the stories about how basketball teams got their names are true, and which ones are foul lies.

Seattle SuperSonics: Named after a supersonic jet proposed by Seattle-based Boeing in the late '60s. The jet was never built, but they decided to keep the team name instead of changing it to the Seattle Scrapped Boeing Projects.

Los Angeles Lakers: Yes, you're right...there aren't any lakes in L.A. to speak of. The team was originally the Minneapolis Lakers; Minnesota is nicknamed "Land of 10,000 Lakes."

Orlando Magic: Inspired by Disney's Magic Kingdom.

New Jersey Nets: Originally the New England Nets, they got their name from the shared terminology of basketball and New England's fishing industry.

New York Knicks: Short for knickerbockers, the pants worn by Dutch settlers in New York in the 1600s.

Houston Rockets: Named for NASA. "Houston, we have a basketball team."

Indiana Pacers: Before Indiana became famous for auto racing and the Indy 500, it was famous for horse racing. The team's original owner also owned several champion harness racers, and named his team in homage to them.

Detroit Pistons: Not actually named for Detroit's auto industry. The team's founder, Fred Zollner, owned a piston factory in Fort Wayne, Indiana. In 1957, the Zollner Pistons moved to Detroit.

Los Angeles Clippers: Started out in San Diego, where great sailing boats known as clipper ships used to land 100 years ago.

Atlanta Hawks: Founded in North Carolina, the team was named after Kitty Hawk, in honor of the Wright brothers. Maybe they thought it would inspire their players to fly through the air. Instead, they flew to Atlanta.

Sacramento Kings: When the Cincinnati Royals moved to the Kansas City–Omaha area in 1972, they realized that both cities already had a team named the Royals (a baseball team in each case, but still). So they became the Kansas City Kings, and kept the name after moving to Sacramento.

ANSWER, PAGE 206

OLD WIVES' TALES

Those old wives knew what they were doing—sometimes. We've collected a few cures that—who knows?—might actually work. But if you want to try any of them, you'll first have to translate them from the simple letter substitution code we've used on them, where B might equal F, or X might be S. For further instructions and hints on how to solve, see page 15.

In this particular puzzle, **the letter substitution stays constant throughout the whole list**.

TO REDUCE FEVER:

QUTZM WSTJHQ SZTSZI SU AVUUR V MHR TZ ELH FVJY SK RSNU LVZQ.

TO TREAT GOUT:

CVJM WVUHKSSE TZ QHCR DUVII.

FOR A HEADACHE:

UNW VZ SZTSZ SOHU RSNU KSUHLHVQ. (VZSELHU INDDHIETSZ, FSFNJVU TZ ELH IHOHZEHHZEL AHZENUR, CVI ES QUTOH V ZVTJ TZES ELH IMNJJ.)

TO GET RID OF CORNS:

EVMH WUSCZ FVFHU, ISVM TE TZ OTZHDVU, VZQ FJVAH TE TZ V IVNAHU NZQHU RSNU WHQ. QVW ELH ASUZ CTEL IVJTOV HVAL QVR WHKSUH WUHVMKVIE.

FOR HEART DISEASE:

QUTZM KSGDJSOH EHV. (KSGDJSOH ASZEVTZI QTDTEVJTI, CLTAL TI NIHQ ESQVR ES ASYWVE LHVUE QTIHVIH.)

TO CURE BOILS:

AVUUR ZNEYHD TZ RSNU FSAMHE.

ANSWER, PAGE 207

WORD GEOGRAPHY

The eight words hidden in this mini-grid come from all over the planet. Figure out what the words are from the clues about their origins below and then find them in the grid. The leftover letters will reveal something you probably didn't know about the origins of another word. The eight hidden words are listed on the answer page.

T	H	E	B	W	O	R	D	S
P	W	A	I	C	I	S	N	A
M	E	O	B	H	D	J	A	F
T	E	R	L	E	E	S	Y	P
A	S	L	E	A	Z	Y	E	B
E	L	U	N	P	G	G	K	I
U	M	S	E	A	R	N	R	E
S	O	R	T	D	T	O	U	W
N	C	O	F	F	E	E	T	B

1. England's 200-year occupation of India led to many borrowed Hindi words. An Indian bangla is a one-story house, often with a roofed porch (in Hindi, a *veranda*). *Bangla*—which literally means "from Bengal"—was anglicized to _____.

2. The ancient city of Byblos was where the Phoenicians converted a plant called papyrus into a type of paper. Greeks called the paper *biblios*, after the city, and soon a *biblion* meant "a little book." In A.D. 400, the Greeks started using _____ as we know it today.

3. The Eastern European region of Silesia was known for its fine cloth. Eventually, so many low-quality imitations wound up on the market that *Silesian* turned into _____.

4. Genoa was the first city to make the denim cloth used for making _____.

5. It was in Sweden that the first leather was buffed to a fine softness. The fashionable French bought gloves of this leather and called them "*gants de* _____." The word now refers to the buffing process—not to any particular kind of leather.

6. This large European fowl is named after the country of its origin. American colonists mistakenly thought a big bird they found in the New World was the same animal…that's why we call it a _____.

7. The Old English word *ceap* (pronounced "keep") meant "to sell or barter." Because an area in London known as "_____side" was a major market where people went to barter for low prices, the word gradually took on a new pronunciation…and meaning.

8. First discovered in the town of Kaffia, these beans had traveled around the world by the 13th century, becoming *qahwah* in Arabia, and finally _____ in the New World.

ANSWER, PAGE 207

WOULD WE LIE TO YOU—TWO?

Who, us? Once again, you've got three choices—all having to do with the origins of names and phrases. Only one is correct, of course.

1. Why did the makers of Formula 409 pick the number 409?
   a) They didn't get the formula right until their 409th attempt.
   b) 409 was the number on the door of their laboratory.
   c) The number has no special significance—they just liked the way "four-oh-nine" sounded.

2. How did the rock band Blue Oyster Cult get its name?
   a) When the band landed a recording contract, they renamed themselves after the bar that had given them most of their gigs—New York's Blue Oyster Bar.
   b) The title is a sly reference to the short story "The Call of Cthulhu" by H. P. Lovecraft. In the story, the cult-god Cthulhu is described as being blue with fishlike skin. (Later descriptions of Cthulhu reveal him to be squidlike, not oysterlike, but the band liked "Oyster" better.)
   c) It's an anagram of "Cully Stout Beer." One of the band members came up with it while mindlessly doodling in a bar, and their manager liked it enough to rename the band.

3. Why are policemen referred to as "fuzz"?
   a) Policemen in London used to wear fuzzy helmets.
   b) In the 1890s, members of New York's Finest were required to cut their hair very short—a hairstyle then known as a "fuzz." (Today we'd call it a "crew cut.")
   c) It refers to the characteristic hiss of police radios.

4. How did the Three Musketeers bar get its name?
   a) The folks at the Mars candy company decided to make the bar bigger than normal candy bars, and name it after the famous trio because it was "big enough for three people to share." (Of course since the center was whipped, a lot of that extra size was air.)
   b) The bar originally came in three separate sections (one for each Musketeer), with each section featuring a different flavor of nougat: chocolate, vanilla, and strawberry. Eventually the strawberry and vanilla nougat sections were eliminated, leaving only the chocolate.
   c) The bar was originally called a Moon bar, but when *The Mickey Mouse Club* hit it big on TV in the 1950s, the Mars company paid Disney for permission to rename it "Mousketeers." Sales went up immediately—but when the show was discontinued in 1959, Mars execs feared their candy bar would be dismissed as a bygone fad. So they quietly changed the name to "Musketeers," and still later to "Three Musketeers."

5. What does chicken pox have to do with chickens?
   a) It was originally a disease of fowl, but got transmitted to humans by mosquitoes.
   b) "Chicken" is an old slang term for a young person (as in "spring chicken"). "Chicken pox" literally translates to "disease of the young."
   c) It has nothing to do with chickens—the name is a phonetic spelling of the Old English "gican pox," which simply means "itchy pox."

ANSWER, PAGE 207

RUFF TALK

A famous curmudgeon delivers an opinion that not everyone might agree with. So what else is new?

ACROSS

1 "Go to your ___!"
5 Badge of shame
11 Unit of resistance
14 1970s do
15 Deserved
16 *The Black Cat* author
17 Start of a quote by Andy Rooney
19 Earl Grey, e.g.
20 Drain declogger
21 College on the Thames
22 Long stories
24 Expose to the atmosphere
26 Zoo visitee
27 Part 2 of the quote
31 Meg of *French Kiss*
32 Sharpens
33 ___ *Misérables*
34 Blend again
35 Big game show prize
38 Bounded
39 Short haircuts
43 Part 3 of the quote
47 Outer boundaries
48 Wake up
49 Resident of Muscat
50 Crest container
52 Aykroyd of *The Blues Brothers*
53 Baseballer Swoboda
54 End of the quote
58 Business name closer
59 California's Sierra ___
60 Color
61 Storm center
62 Add spice to
63 Eon divisions

DOWN

1 Tear into, verbally
2 Time of no major elections
3 Hospital attendant
4 Comment from Bossy
5 Group twice the size of a trio
6 ___ Bell
7 Geritol supplies it
8 Wildebeest
9 Gibson of *Signs*
10 Summed numbers, in the classroom
11 Very best
12 Corn bread cooked on a farm tool
13 Disease that makes you spotty
18 Enter, as a taxi
23 Race car "stop"
25 Letters preceding an alias
26 Eddie Van Halen's brother
28 It's "wavin'" in a song from *Oklahoma!*
29 Pizzazz
30 Bring together
34 Striped jersey wearers
35 The "one" in Pepsi One
36 Money from one's ex
37 Book from Harlequin
38 Moisturizers
39 Martin Van ___
40 Lennon's love
41 Woman's private room
42 Stephen Foster's "Oh! ___"
44 Soldier material?
45 1950s *American Bandstand* idol
46 Principles
50 First word of *A Visit from St. Nicholas*
51 Menu bar option under Edit
55 Charge for services rendered
56 Eggs
57 Major telecom company

ANSWER, PAGE 207

IMAGINARY FRIENDS

Word is out—you've got some imaginary friends. You've even had them over to your house, and you never invited *us*! We'll forgive you if you can place all 29 product spokespersons in their proper spot in the grid, crossword-style. If some of them don't look familiar, you can find out who they are on the answer page.

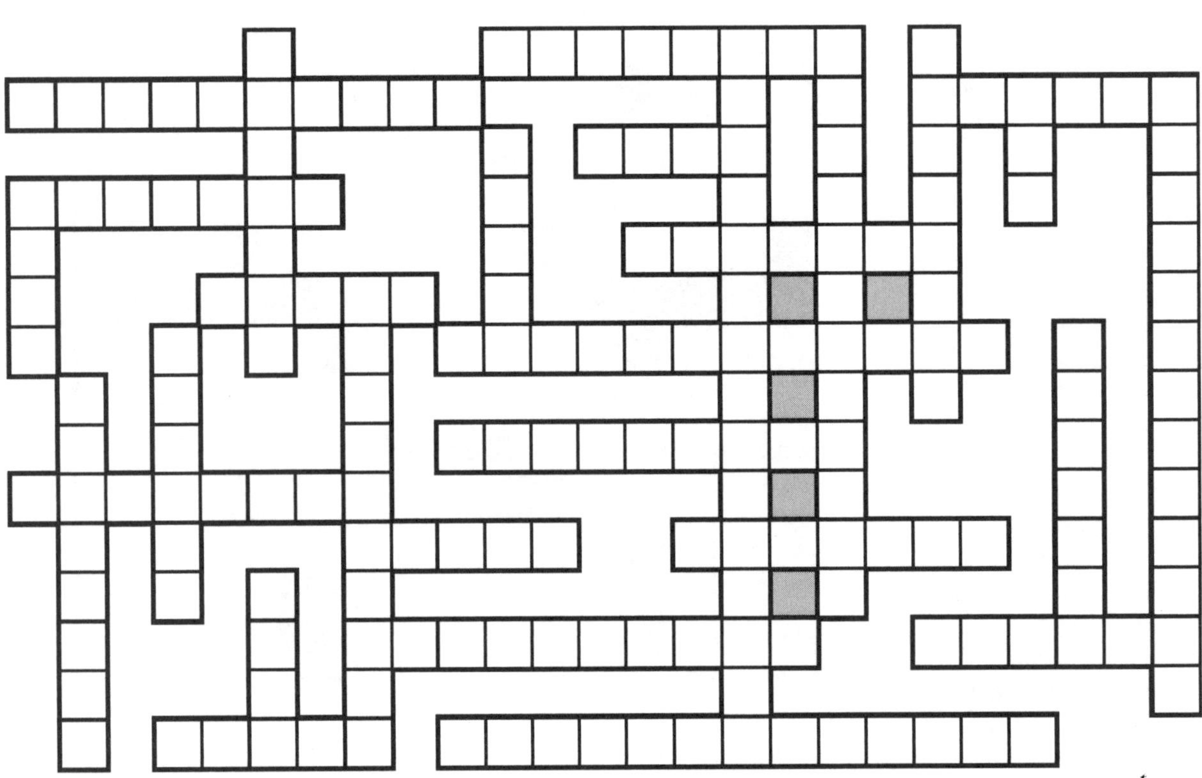

3 letter word
Pop!

4 letter words
Jack
Snap!
Tony

5 letter words
Elsie
Madge
Mikey
Rosie

6 letter words
Ernest
Nipper
Speedy

7 letter words
Charlie
Crackle!
Jifaroo
Mr. Clean
Snuggle

8 letter words
Joe Camel
Joe Isuzu
Menehune
Uncle Ben

9 letter word
Mr. Whipple

10 letter words
Aunt Jemima
Cap'n Crunch
Gerber Baby

12 letter words
Betty Crocker
Little Caesar

13 letter words
Captain Morgan
Reddy Kilowatt

15 letter word
Maytag Repairman

ANSWER, PAGE 207

AND DON'T WALK UP TO PEOPLE AND TELL THEM THEY'RE UNATTRACTIVE

Planning on traveling abroad this year? Many cultures frown on behavior we consider normal—finger pointing, yawning without covering your mouth, even eating while walking on the street. See how well you would do on a trip around the world by matching the action (1–10) to the place where you should really, really avoid doing it (a–j).

_____ 1. Stepping on doorsills. (It's believed that a domestic deity lives in them.)

_____ 2. Discussing religion or politics.

_____ 3. Giving the "O.K." sign. (It's considered obscene.)

_____ 4. Scribbling on someone's business card.

_____ 5. Sitting so that the sole of your shoe ("the lowest and dirtiest place on your body") is pointing at someone.

_____ 6. Starting a conversation with "What do you do?"

_____ 7. Taking pictures of topless or nude bathers.

_____ 8. Using your bread to soak up the juices from your meal.

_____ 9. Accepting a gift with your left hand.

_____ 10. Sucking on your chopsticks.

a. Arab countries

b. Bali

c. Brazil

d. China

e. England

f. Ireland

g. Japan

h. Kenya

i. Portugal

j. Thailand

ANSWER, PAGE 208

* * * * *

HOW DO YOU SAY...

Which language has the most words?

a) English
b) German
c) French
d) Japanese
e) Chinese
f) Esperanto

ANSWER, PAGE 208

TV HITS OF THE '70S

Where were you in the 1970s? Maybe watching the 24 TV shows hidden in the grid; all were rated in the Top Ten for at least one year in that decade. Find them all, reading across, down, forward, backward, and diagonally. The leftover letters will reveal a hidden message about those good old days of boob tubery.

```
T S L E G N A S E I L R A H C
H R T I R O N S I D E T H E M
E T H E F B I T M A U H R D E
J Y E O T Y L H K O J A K M D
E E W R D M S R O O R W M Y I
F S A S B A R E T T A A X B C
F Y L I M A F E H T N I L L A
E A T L G E S S H O N I W E L
R D O L U S P C U N N F C W C
S Y N Y N O F O A N G I E S E
O P S H S F T M H N L V R U N
N P E P M E O P T A N E H C T
S A N F O R D A N D S O N R E
E H R H K I T N S E R I N A R
E S O N E D A Y A T A T I M E
```

ALICE
ALL IN THE FAMILY
ANGIE
BARETTA
CANNON
CHARLIE'S ANGELS
GUNSMOKE
HAPPY DAYS
HAWAII FIVE-O
IRONSIDE
KOJAK
MANNIX
MARCUS WELBY, M.D.
M*A*S*H
MAUDE
MEDICAL CENTER
ONE DAY AT A TIME
PHYLLIS
RHODA
SANFORD AND SON
THE F.B.I.
THE JEFFERSONS
THE WALTONS
THREE'S COMPANY

ANSWER, PAGE 208

THE ONE & ONLY

Sometimes there's only room for one guy at the top.

ACROSS

1 Nothing more than
7 Vehicle with a meter
10 Asian cuisine
14 Earhart of aviation
15 Glovelike potholder
17 Cosmetics company
18 "New ___" (Blockbuster section)
19 The only Academy Award presenter who gave an Oscar to himself
21 A very long time
22 1958 bomb from Ford
23 Nocturnal bird
26 Marge and Homer's neighbor
27 Whale's home
29 ___ Hawkins Day
31 Ultra-good grade
33 Making a mosaic
34 The only person ever elected to a U.S. Senate seat as a write-in candidate
37 Singer Santana
38 Ness of *The Untouchables*
39 You might cry after cutting it
40 Very long time
41 Yuppie's car of choice
44 "Nice shootin', ___!"
45 Outfield encloser
49 Operatic solo
50 The only man to play in the World Series and the Super Bowl
53 Accepted, as conditions
56 Study raptly
57 Most like a ball
58 Nervous
59 Big name in techno music
60 Fish eggs
61 ___ up (full of fuel)

DOWN

1 Robin of Locksley's love
2 Come out
3 Gunned the engine
4 ___ Island (immigrant's first stop in America)
5 MGM mascot
6 Yin and ___
7 Took out the middle
8 Declares
9 Girl with a full dance card
10 Catcher of counterfeiters
11 ___ *Girl Friday*
12 Scarfed
13 "___ showtime!"
16 *Barefoot in the Park* playwright
20 Humdinger
23 Valhalla host
24 Meander
25 One of a tripod's three
27 Serve strained carrots to a baby
28 Shade trees
30 Excessively
31 Woody Guthrie's son
32 A boat, to its captain
33 Peter, Paul & Mary, for one
34 Of sound mind
35 Cereal with a rabbit mascot
36 ___ *Gold* (Peter Fonda film)
37 Folding bed
41 Guernsey and Holstein, e.g.
42 Desert hallucination
43 Ill-spent
46 Duck with a down named after it
47 "___ fast, buster!"
48 Ten times a sawbuck
49 Timber-trimming tools
50 Refuse to admit
51 Visibly shocked
52 Wendy, Michael, and John's dog
53 Activate, as an explosive
54 Viscous substance
55 "Ay, there's the ___"

ANSWER, PAGE 208

ALLENISMS

Thoughts from America's modern-day philosopher, Woody Allen. For instructions and hints on how to solve, see page 15.

1. GEXPKEWWF HF UPDZ UEX PHHELIYZ. P'N GZ EL OCHZ PQ LOZ GELO EQN XOZ'N KCHZ PQ EQN XPQR HF GCELX.

2. DTJ CAVIX UG XUNUXJX UEDA MAAX ZEX QZX KJAKIJ. DTJ MAAX AEJG GIJJK QJDDJV... CTUIJ DTJ QZX AEJG GJJR DA JEWAL DTJ CAVBUEM TAPVG RPHT RAVJ.

3. XD XG U BCIBRCOG BCSQ NCYARD LUDYW. X'Z NICOQ CJ XD. ZE BIUKQJUDWRI, CK WXG QRUDWFRQ, GCSQ ZR DWXG LUDYW.

4. AH *IUX ZUKGX UEGP IAQT LT JULT RGTFY JAIE. GACT LFCAEI F GFYIT XTMUJAO AE LP EFLT AE F *JZAJJ SFEC FRRUKEO.

5. IXH'V UWK WVVMHVNXH VX LCWV KXAO GPCXXBVMWPCMOG VMBB KXA. DAGV GMM LCWV VCMK BXXF BNFM WHI VCWV'G CXL KXA FHXL LCWV BNSM NG OMWBBK ZXNHZ VX QM BNFM.

ANSWER, PAGE 208

MISFITS QUIZ #1

Most of the answers in this quiz are so outrageous, you might have trouble believing that any of them fit their categories—but most of them do. What you're looking for is the **one answer** in each group that **doesn't** fit the category. And if you can get even half of these right, you're in a category of your own.

1. Ingredients in most toothpastes:
   a) Chalk
   b) Paraffin
   c) Cornstarch
   d) Seaweed
   e) Detergent

2. Sports featured in the 1900 Olympics:
   a) Canoeing
   b) Croquet
   c) Fishing
   d) Billiards
   e) Checkers

3. People whose creations were named after them:
   a) Jules Leotard, inventor of the leotard
   b) Dr. Charles Condom, inventor of the condom
   c) Henry Shrapnel, inventor of shrapnel
   d) Jean-Louis Caramel, inventor of caramel
   e) Adolphe Sax, inventor of the sax

4. Flavors of Jell-O manufactured (at least briefly):
   a) Cola
   b) Chocolate
   c) Celery
   d) Marshmallow
   e) Coffee

5. Names considered (but ultimately rejected) for the Seven Dwarfs:
   a) Snoopy
   b) Jumpy
   c) Dippy
   d) Woeful
   e) Flabby

6. Folk remedies for baldness, to be applied directly to the scalp:
   a) Bear grease
   b) Soup from boiled snakes
   c) Spanish fly
   d) Dog urine
   e) Beef gravy

7. Products that actually did exist (though not for long, as you might imagine):
   a) Earring Magic Ken, a Mattel doll
   b) Buffalo Chip chocolate chip cookies
   c) Mr. Crack, a snack food
   d) Ballbuster, a family-oriented game
   e) The Dictator, a make of automobile

8. Words coined by William Shakespeare:
   a) Undress
   b) Eyeball
   c) Bump
   d) Killjoy
   e) Puke

9. Actual U.S. town names:
   a) Chewgum, Montana
   b) Idiotville, Oregon
   c) Monkey's Eyebrow, Kentucky
   d) Knockemstiff, Ohio
   e) Humptulips, Washington

10. People who can claim Mary Magdalene as their patron saint:
    a) Virgins
    b) Zookeepers
    c) Meatpackers
    d) Hairdressers
    e) Pirates

ANSWER, PAGE 209

LOONEY LAWS

These are real laws from all over the U.S.A. We've mixed up some of the important words in each Looney Law so it's up to you to put the letters back in the right place in the blanks above the mixed-up letters. Otherwise, don't expect us to bail you out.

1. **Wilbur, Washington:**
   It's illegal to ride an ___ ___ ___ ___ ___ ___ ___ ___ ___ down the street.
   G L Y U S R O E H

2. **Maine:**
   It's against the law to step out of an ___ ___ ___ ___ ___ ___ ___ ___ while it's in the air.
   L E A R P A I N

3. **Star, Mississippi:**
   It's illegal to ridicule a public ___ ___ ___ ___ ___ ___.
   T E U S A T

4. **Binghamton, New York:**
   Ninth-grade boys aren't permitted to grow ___ ___ ___ ___ ___ ___ ___ ___ ___ ___.
   T C E S O H U S M A

5. **North Carolina:**
   It's against the law to ___ ___ ___ ___ ___ ___ ___ ___ ___ on a ___ ___ ___ ___ ___.
   K I N D R L K I M R A N I T

6. **Lexington, Kentucky:**
   You can't carry an ___ ___ ___ - ___ ___ ___ ___ ___ ___ ___ ___ ___ in your pocket.
   C E I M A C E R N O E C

7. **Sault Sainte Marie, Michigan:**
   You can be thrown in jail if you ___ ___ ___ ___ against the ___ ___ ___ ___.
   T I P S I N W D

8. **Massachusetts:**
   It's against the law for ___ ___ ___ ___ ___ to wear ___ ___ ___ ___ ___ ___ ___ ___.
   T O G A S S U R E R O T S

9. **Lawrence, Kansas:**
   Citizens are prohibited from carrying ___ ___ ___ ___ around in their ___ ___ ___ ___.
   E S E B A S T H

10. **Oregon:**
    You can be arrested for ___ ___ ___ ___ ___ ___ your ___ ___ ___ ___ ___ ___.
    P W G I I N H I D E S S

11. **Santa Ana, California:**
    A law makes it illegal to ___ ___ ___ ___ on ___ ___ ___ ___ ___ ___ ___.
    M S I W Y R D D A N L

12. **Hartford, Connecticut:**
    It's against the law to ___ ___ ___ ___ ___ ___ ___ your ___ ___ ___.
    C U T E A D E O D G

13. **Austin, Texas:**
    Don't even think about going ___ ___ ___ ___ ___ ___ ___ ___ without a $5 permit.
    F A R B O E T O

14. **Somerset County, Maryland:**
    There's a law that makes it illegal to ___ ___ ___ ___ ___ ___ ___ ___ ___ in the ___ ___ ___ ___.
    Y L P A R A D S C O D A R

ANSWER, PAGE 208

IT'S A LIE!

Directions for solving are on page 11.

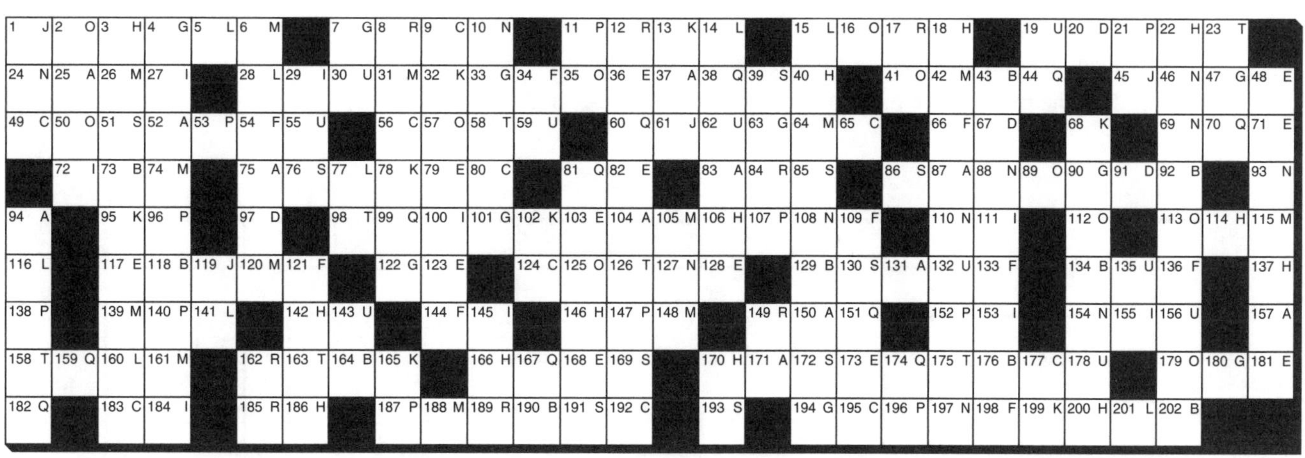

A. Dr. Evil's nemesis (2 wds.)

25 150 104 52 87 37 94 131 75 171 157 83

B. 2002 biopic role for Salma Hayek (2 wds.)

92 43 176 202 134 129 73 118 190 164

C. Differing from (3 wds.)

195 183 177 80 192 65 124 49 9 56

D. Half of this is generally deemed acceptable

91 20 97 67

E. Aerosmith's first Top 40 hit (2 wds.)

103 117 123 173 48 79 181 36 128 168 82 71

F. It's like the greatest, Daddy-O!

198 133 144 34 54 66 136 109 121

G. *Baywatch* hunk

122 180 33 47 90 63 7 4 101 194

H. Safe from a perilous situation (4 wds.)

200 22 142 106 3 166 137 186 146 18 114 170 40

I. Book subtitled *Boy Scouts and the Making of American Youth* (3 wds.)

184 111 72 27 155 145 153 100 29

J. A good thing to get out of

45 119 1 61

K. What Archie Bunker called Michael Stivic

13 32 68 78 199 102 95 165

L. Natural painkiller released through exercise

14 116 141 201 5 28 160 15 77

M. Denzel Washington's directorial debut (2 wds.)

188 74 161 115 42 26 6 31 105 148 139 64 120

N. Coin collecting

127 93 24 110 10 88 108 154 46 69 197

O. Scientist who was born the year Galileo died (2 wds.)

35 89 125 112 179 16 2 41 113 57 50

P. Oscar winner who was born a Coppola (2 wds.)

107 53 187 152 196 140 96 11 147 21 138

Q. Minnesota's moniker (2 wds.)

159 70 174 167 44 99 60 151 38 81 182

R. Soup preferred by tots

12 189 149 162 8 185 84 17

S. Sign you might see on the way to Death Valley (2 wds.)

39 193 169 85 172 86 76 130 51 191

T. U-235, e.g.

158 126 163 175 58 98 23

U. Speed-reading guru (2 wds.)

55 19 156 135 62 178 132 30 143 59

ANSWER, PAGE 209

CALLING DR. GREEN!

Herbs have been curing people for about 5,000 years—long before the days of Viagra and Claritin. We've listed 32 of them (including tobacco, which was used by Native Americans in a gazillion ways other than smoking) and lemon (which has lots of applications besides its "scurvy" reputation). Can you fit all the herbs we've listed into the grid, crossword-style?

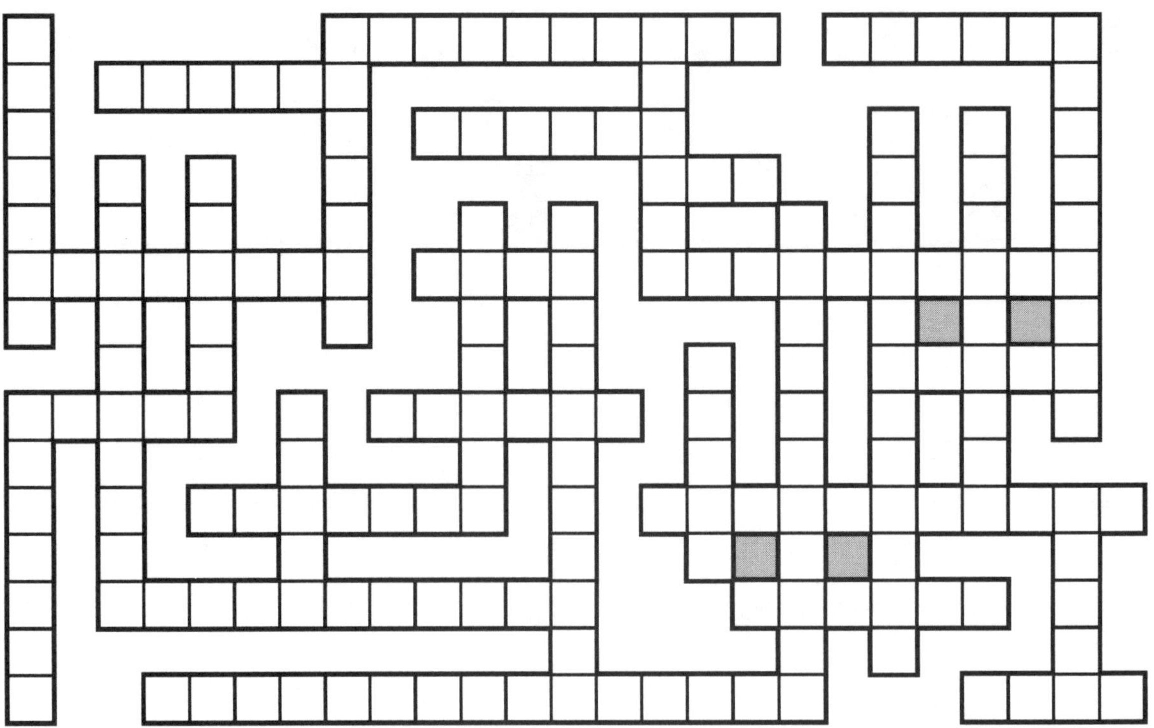

3 letter word
Rue

4 letter words
Coca
Woad

5 letter words
Clove
Lemon
Myrrh
Senna
Thyme

6 letter words
Arnica
Balsam
Fennel
Ginger
Hyssop
Myrtle
Yarrow

7 letter words
Lobelia
Parsley
Thistle
Tobacco
Verbena

8 letter word
Licorice

9 letter words
Horehound
Poppy seed

10 letter words
Eucalyptus
Pennyroyal
Watercress

11 letter words
Horseradish
Meadowsweet
Saw palmetto
St. John's wort

12 letter word
Black currant

15 letter word
Marshmallow root

ANSWER, PAGE 209

COMING UP SHORT

We feel like we're forgetting something in the lists below. It's on the tip of our tongues, darn it! There's one member of each set that we just can't remember! Can you?

The 9 Planets
Venus
Pluto
Saturn
Neptune
Mars
Mercury
Earth
Jupiter

The 8 Members of TV's Brady Family
Mike
Cindy
Jan
Bobby
Greg
Carol
Marcia

The 5 Great Lakes
Erie
Superior
Huron
Michigan

The 5 Original Members of the Rolling Stones
Bill Wyman
Mick Jagger
Brian Jones
Keith Richards

The 4 H's in the 4-H Club
Head
Hands
Health

The 13 Original U.S. Colonies
Delaware
Pennsylvania
New Jersey
Massachusetts
New York
Virginia
Connecticut
New Hampshire
Rhode Island
Maryland
North Carolina
South Carolina

The Life Savers' "5 Flavors"
Lemon
Lime
Orange
Cherry

The 4 Teletubbies
Laa-Laa
Po
Tinky Winky

ANSWER, PAGE 209

FOOD COLORING

With tongue firmly in cheek, what Tommy Smothers has to say about "natural" food coloring.

ACROSS

1 Suitcases
5 One of the "Three B's"
9 Lariat
14 Bunches and bunches
15 Souvenir from moving day
16 Olympic hurdler Moses
17 Start of a quip by Tommy Smothers
19 Nut with a "hat"
20 Junkyard transactions
21 Much-liked dessert maker
23 Got ___ (threw out)
25 Shivery sound
26 Meeting with the Dr.
29 Part 2 of the quip
34 Pigtail
36 Installed, as underground pipes
37 Suffix for hero
38 Part 3 of the quip
42 Long-running Sat. night TV show
43 "I don't ___ one way or the other"
44 Like a haunted house
45 Part 4 of the quip
48 Agatha Christie detective Parker
49 Kanga's kid
50 Oklahoma city
53 Nero or Hirohito
57 Unbridled joy
61 Local ordinance
62 End of the quip
64 Plain soup
65 "Hey, what's the big ___?"
66 1982 Jeff Bridges sci-fi flick
67 Authority
68 Nintendo competitor
69 Admission of wrongdoing, sort of

DOWN

1 Roseanne's last name
2 Not windward
3 *The ___ Must Be Crazy*
4 West Indies isl.
5 Made a "sheepish" noise
6 Uses, as information
7 "The Sweetheart of Sigma ___"
8 Former Jets owner Leon
9 Put the sofa over there instead
10 It's shown to sentries
11 Army runaway
12 It might need changing
13 Bancroft or Boleyn
18 Actor Wallach
22 Hoffman of the Chicago Seven
24 *Eye of the Needle* author
26 Immeasurable gulf
27 Flat on the ground
28 Comic Poundstone
30 Greek letter
31 Like a flame
32 ___ a million
33 Actress Zellweger
35 He traveled through time in a TARDIS
39 "Yippee!"
40 Item burned in the '70s
41 Head for, old-style
46 Good doggy's munchies
47 Unexpected
51 Morgan ___ (King Arthur's sister)
52 ___-pitch softball
53 Goes out, as the tide
54 ___ *Breckinridge*
55 Trick
56 Baseball stats
58 Lamb sandwich
59 Old-fashioned skirt stiffener
60 Wine casks
63 Hustle and bustle

ANSWER, PAGE 210

PLAYING THE PERCENTAGES #2

More statistics from Uncle John. Place the numbers 10, 20, 30, 40, 50, 60, 70, 80, and 90 into the nine blanks below to make the statistics as accurate as possible.

_____% of atheists and agnostics say they own at least one Bible

_____% of McDonald's profit comes from Happy Meals

_____% of high-school athletes say they've been hazed

_____% of Americans say they've seen a ghost

_____% of all sets of identical twins include one left-hander and one right-hander

_____% of New York cabbies are recently arrived immigrants

_____% of U.S. workers say they've had sex in the workplace

_____% of U.S. adults have dandruff

_____% of the world's oxygen supply is produced by marine plants

ANSWER, PAGE 195

MIXED MARRIAGE

Small crostic puzzles are solved just like the big ones (directions on page 11) but the first letter of the fill-in words **do not** spell out a hidden message.

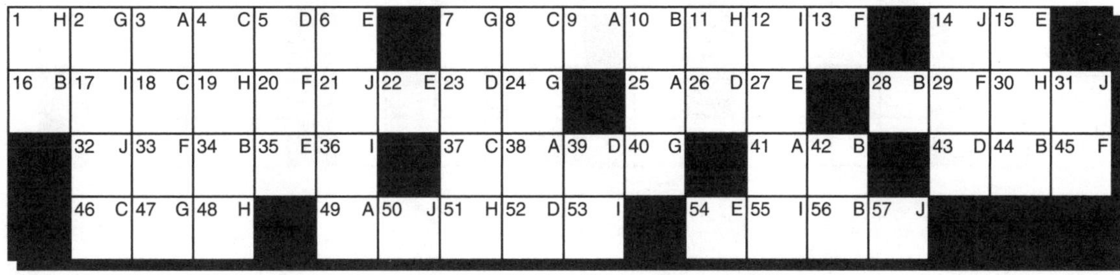

A. Oklahoman

___ ___ ___ ___ ___ ___
25 41 38 49 3 9

B. What keeps you from rushing at rush hour

___ ___ ___ ___ ___ ___ ___
28 44 16 56 42 34 10

C. Gem

___ ___ ___ ___ ___
37 18 46 8 4

D. Castro's capital

___ ___ ___ ___ ___ ___
52 26 5 39 23 43

E. Boston's old ballpark

___ ___ ___ ___ ___ ___
15 6 35 54 22 27

F. Thumb a ride

___ ___ ___ ___ ___
33 20 13 45 29

G. Least valuable chess pieces

___ ___ ___ ___ ___
7 47 2 40 24

H. Egg-coloring season

___ ___ ___ ___ ___ ___
11 51 48 1 30 19

I. Furriers' favorites

___ ___ ___ ___ ___
17 55 12 36 53

J. Wile E. _____ (Road Runner's nemesis)

___ ___ ___ ___ ___ ___
21 50 31 14 32 57

ANSWER, PAGE 210

BY GEORGE!

Carlin, that is. If you need directions on how to solve this puzzle, see page 5.

1.

I		A	N		I	R					H				T		E	N	
Y		G	E		N	N	T	S	A		I	R	M	S	L	E	O	P	
D	E	A	M	T	A	A	I	A	H	T	C	O	E	A	L	A	V	E	
V	I	E	D	I	M	O	L	T	N	E	I	A	T	P	H	E	T	E	L
	■			■				■		■									■
										■		■				■			
	■								■					■					■
				■			■						■						■

2.

R			M	O	T		H					T	U		W	I	Z	L	
Y		T	Y	L	L		W	I	M	S	I	T	E		S	E	A	L	
I		S	E	A	U		E	R	F	T	Y	O	O		R	A	N	T	E
A	F	T	E	S	L	L	A	A	N	A	H	O	H		H	E	A	E	L
		■				■					■			■					
	■					■		■						■					
	■					■				■				■					■
	■								■					■					■

3.

T					I			T		S			H	Y					
R		H	T	V	T			O	A	E	U		A	M	E		H		
I	G	T	E	A	E	R		T	H	A	L	G	G	T	P	T	D	H	G
G	O	W	H	H	E	T	O	I	H	L	D	S	H	A	Y	P	E	I	N
U	O	N	T	O	L	D	W	W	U	O	R	W	O	U	S	I	T	N	O
	■						■								■			■	
			■				■		■							■			
				■			■				■								
	■					■						■							■
		■				■						■				■	■	■	■

ANSWER, PAGE 210

UNCLE JOHN'S LISTS

You know our uncle—he loves to make lists. And the more interesting the better. Here are a few that we've anagrammed for your puzzling pleasure. Put the proper letters in the proper blanks and you'll find out what this listing business is all about.

The 5 Most Germ-Ridden Places at Work

1. __ __ __ __ __
   H O P E N

2. __ __ __ __ __ __ __
   P E S T O K D

3. __ __ __ __ __ __ __ __ __ __ __ __ __ __ __ __ __ __ __
   T R A E W I F T A O N U N L A N E D H

4. __ __ __ __ __ __ __ __ __ __ __ __ __ __ __ __ __ __ __
   V O W I R M A C E R O D O D A H L N E

5. __ __ __ __ __ __ __ __
   Y O K B A D E R

The 7 States with the Lowest Life Expectancy

1. __ __ __ __ __ __ __ __ __ __ __ __ __ __
   T U H O S N O A L A C R I

2. __ __ __ __ __ __ __ __ __ __ __
   I I I I S S S S P P M

3. __ __ __ __ __ __ __
   A R E G G I O

4. __ __ __ __ __ __ __ __ __
   S A L U I N I A O

5. __ __ __ __ __ __
   A N D A V E

6. __ __ __ __ __ __ __
   B L A M A A A

7. __ __ __ __ __ __ __ __ __ __ __ __ __
   H O T R N A R L I O C A N

ANSWER, PAGE 210

STUDYING UP ON YOUR OLOGIES

You've heard of psychology, biology, and ecology but here are some other "ologies" you may not have run across. We've listed 37 of them below followed by their subjects in parentheses. Find them all in the grid, reading across, down, and diagonally, and the leftover letters will reveal a few more you may have missed.

```
G E R O M N Y T Y O H I S T O L O G Y L
O G Y Y Y T H G E G S T A X I O L O G Y
U D Y G C G N O O D O N T O L O G Y L F
H I P P O L O G Y L A L G I T N G I M Y
E O L O L L S L G G O Y O T T H M E S T
L U Y G O L O N O R H C O R D N E D M D
M Y G Y G O L O L Y T C A D O O F Y A M
I Y O G Y M O U O S H C L L E H R G G O
N G L O E S G S M R P T O E V M L O I R
T O O L E S Y O O L O G H G E Y T L R P
H L N O H E C N T A Y S T C X U D O O H
O O I E Y O O H N F C A O V I E S T L O
L H H N I L E E A G Y L Y A L R A N O L
O C R B O R M O H T O G G L L M O O G O
G I G G O O O Y P G O T O L O G Y E Y G
Y R Y L L T H L Y L E L L L L S T D U Y
D T O O Y O F C O N C H O L O G Y W H A
T G G A S O C N I G E G T G G N T Y T H
Y Y G O L O I M E S Y R E O Y W E S O U
Y G O L O S I M T S P E C T R O L O G Y
```

ACOLOGY: (Remedies)
ANEMOLOGY: (The wind)
AXIOLOGY: (Principles, ethics, and values)
CETOLOGY: (Whales and dolphins)
CONCHOLOGY: (Shells)
DACTYLOLOGY: (Communication using finger spelling)
DENDROCHRONOLOGY: (Comparative study of the rings of trees and aged wood)
DEONTOLOGY: (Moral responsibilities)
ESCHATOLOGY: (Final events as spoken of in the Bible)
GLOTTOCHRONOLOGY: (How two languages diverge from one common source)
HELMINTHOLOGY: (Worms)
HIPPOLOGY: (Horses)
HISTOLOGY: (Tissues)
HOROLOGY: (Measuring time)
ICHTHYOLOGY: (Fish)
LIMNOLOGY: (Bodies of fresh water)
MAGIROLOGY: (Cooking)
MISOLOGY: (Hatred of reason or reasoning)
MORPHOLOGY: (The structure of organisms)
MYCOLOGY: (Fungi)
MYRMECOLOGY: (Ants)
NEOLOGY: (New words)
NOSOLOGY: (The classification of diseases)
ODONTOLOGY: (The teeth and their surrounding tissues)
OENOLOGY: (Wine)
ONEIROLOGY: (Dreams)
OOLOGY: (Eggs)
OTOLOGY: (Ears)
PHANTOMOLOGY: (Supernatural beings)
POTAMOLOGY: (Rivers)
RHINOLOGY: (Noses)
SEMIOLOGY: (Signs and signaling)
SINOLOGY: (Chinese culture)
SPECTROLOGY: (Ghosts, phantoms, or apparitions)
THEROLOGY: (Mammals)
TRICHOLOGY: (Hair)
VEXILLOLOGY: (Flags)

ANSWER, PAGE 210

THE DEVIL'S DICTIONARY

In 1911 Ambrose Bierce published *The Devil's Dictionary*, a caustic set of definitions for otherwise harmless words. The italicized clues below represent definitions from the book; can you guess the words being defined?

ACROSS

1 ___ *of Steel* (workout video)
4 Go from straight to curved
8 Bit
14 *A writer who guesses his way to the truth and dispels it with a tempest of words*
16 Prophecy provider
17 *The state or condition of a community consisting of a master, a mistress and two slaves, making in all , two*
18 Singer Bobby
19 Unmanned spacecraft
20 Least satisfactory
22 Notes held by lenders
23 Friend of Che
24 Peaches and ___
28 *Witchblade* network
29 Horatio who wrote boys' tales
30 Gasmen read it
31 Way to serve eggs
32 Rum cocktail
33 *A resumption of diplomatic relations and rectification of boundaries*
36 *To seek another's approval of a course already decided on*
37 Hooded winter jacket
38 Monster made of clay
39 Sound standard
40 Twosomes
41 Murphy's ___
44 Member of the opposition
45 He raced Cook to the Pole
46 Stare open-mouthed
47 Laundromat devices
49 Shroud of ___
50 Golfer's gofer
53 *The moral condition of a gentleman who holds the opposite opinion*
55 Most melancholy
56 *A relation into which fools are providentially drawn for their mutual destruction*
57 Novelist Sheldon
58 Priority acronym
59 First word of a Hugo title

DOWN

1 Where deodorant goes
2 Have something to do with
3 Tree-to-be
4 Party plate cheese
5 LAX board info
6 Sheer dressing gown
7 Was afraid of
8 *A short story padded*
9 Blue part of a baby blue
10 *The doctrine that everything is God, in contradistinction to the doctrine that God is everything*
11 No. in statistics
12 "Eldorado" band, briefly
13 Paneled room
15 Spheroids
21 Mal de ___
23 Movie, slangily
25 "___, Brute?"
26 Authentic
27 Native Londoner, for one
29 Collection
30 Horsehair sources
31 *Invested with a new and irresistible charm*
32 Like really old leftovers
33 1910s–1920s painting style
34 A part of
35 Word on a battery
36 Adds abrasives to
38 La ___ (NYC airport)
40 *Gidget* star Sandra
41 Not yet pupated
42 "You want ___ of me?"
43 Seller of "Biggie" fries
45 *Reverence for the Supreme Being, based on His supposed resemblance to man*
46 Island belonging to the U.S.
48 Awaken
49 Excursion
50 "Car phones" of old
51 "Prince ___" (song from *Aladdin*)
52 Firework that fizzled
54 Grp. that organizes fund-raisers

ANSWER, PAGE 211

AT HEAVEN'S DOOR

Directions for solving are on page 11.

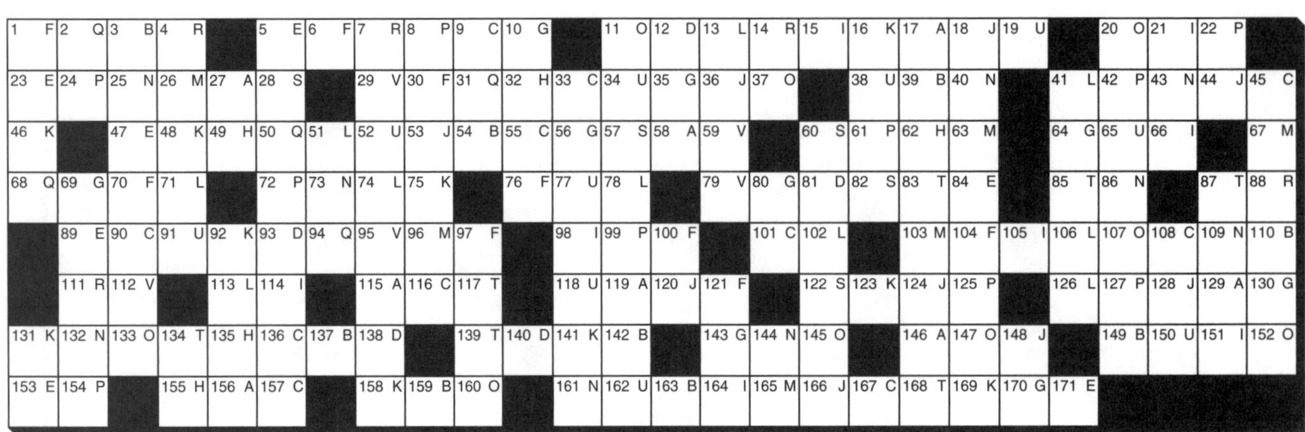

A. Rodgers and Hammerstein surprise hit musical of 1943

156 27 58 17 119 115 129 146

B. Indispensable assistant (2 wds.)

163 159 110 142 3 39 149 137 54

C. Monkees' #1 hit written by Neil Diamond (3 wds.)

108 90 116 101 55 33 136 45 9 167 157

D. Fairy-tale name

138 93 140 81 12

E. Diamond divisions

89 84 5 47 153 23 171

F. Actor who played Lex Luthor's *Superman* henchman (2 wds.)

104 70 100 1 30 6 76 97 121

G. Elizabeth Berg novel chosen for Oprah's club (2 wds.)

80 35 10 56 143 64 130 170 69

H. Destined

155 62 135 32 49

I. Enormous movie sensation of 1933 (2 wds.)

151 15 21 98 66 105 114 164

J. Nirvana's classic 1991 CD

53 36 166 120 124 128 44 18 148

K. Undecided (3 wds.)

92 131 141 158 169 46 75 48 16 123

L. The world of the Web

126 102 41 78 74 71 51 113 106 13

M. Cuddly pet

103 165 63 67 26 96

N. Buoyant Beatles #1 hit of 1964 (3 wds.)

144 86 25 40 43 161 132 109 73

O. Protagonist of Hemingway short stories (2 wds.)

147 152 133 107 11 37 20 145 160

P. He played pro hockey in four consecutive decades (2 wds.)

154 99 24 22 8 42 61 127 72 125

Q. Not concealed or secret

2 31 50 68 94

R. First word in a Hitchcock title

88 111 14 7 4

S. Units equal to one joule per second

122 82 60 57 28

T. Largest of the Ryukyu Islands

85 117 83 168 87 139 134

U. Doctors who specialize in the musculoskeletal system

162 19 38 52 34 91 65 118 77 150

V. Just swell

29 95 112 79 59

ANSWER, PAGE 211

WOULD WE LIE TO YOU—THREE?

Every chance we get. In this quiz, we explain some everyday phenomena that may have long puzzled you…the only trouble is, once again, we're offering too many explanations. Can you find the one true answer in each set?

1. In cartoons, moonshine jugs are always labeled XXX. Where does this come from?
    a) During the 1800s, breweries in Britain marked their bottles X, XX, or XXX as a sign of alcohol content. The number of X's corresponded to the potency of the drink. Naturally, hard alcohol such as corn whiskey would earn the XXX rating.
    b) Nineteenth-century reading primers contained woodcuts showing the evils of drink. To hammer the point home, bottles or kegs in the picture were marked XXX—an old symbol for poison.
    c) Small-scale whiskey brewers in rural America simply used whatever jugs were at hand when bottling their liquor for market—and if the jug in question was already labeled, say, "Molasses," the brewer simply X'ed the label out to avoid confusion.

2. Why is pink the standard color for bubble gum?
    a) Bubble gum is made from chicle, and chicle is naturally pink. Any bubble gum that isn't pink has been dyed by the manufacturer.
    b) When the first commercial batch of bubble gum was made, the manufacturer only had pink food coloring on hand. The gum was an instant hit, and other manufacturers copied it… including the color.
    c) Early bubble gum was much stickier. If a bubble popped in your face, it took a long time to remove it. So manufacturers made their gum pink.

3. Why are there buttons on coat sleeves, when there's nothing to button them to?
    a) Coat makers were tired of having customers come in and ask for replacement buttons, so they began sewing replacement buttons onto each sleeve.
    b) Those buttons were added only after the advent of dry cleaning. Dry cleaners use them to hold the sleeves away from the coat during cleaning.
    c) Believe it or not, those buttons are there to keep you from wiping your nose on your sleeve. Napoleon Bonaparte supposedly spotted a soldier using his coat sleeve as a hankie. Disgusted, he ordered new jackets for his army—this time with buttons on the sleeves, to prevent a recurrence.

4. Why is it believed that walking under a ladder brings bad luck?
    a) To early Christians, any triangle was symbolic of the Holy Trinity—including the triangle formed by leaning a ladder up against a building. Walking beneath a ladder was seen as a violation of this holy symbol.
    b) "Climbing the ladder" has been a metaphor for success since ancient Roman times. A Roman man who chose to walk past the "unclimbable" side of a ladder was indicating to the gods that he wasn't interested in being successful—a "wish" that the gods were always grimly happy to grant.
    c) In its original form, this only applied to ladders with workmen at the top of them, a safety device so that you wouldn't get hit by anything the workman happened to drop.

5. How do you dig a tunnel underwater?
    a) You dig using scuba equipment and waterproof machinery. Then, when the tunnel's finished, you pump out all the water.
    b) You dig a trench underwater, and assemble a lightweight but watertight "frame" in it. Once you've pumped all of the water out of your frame, you can begin strengthening it—from the inside, where it's dry.
    c) You dig really deep beneath the water, so you never have to deal with a flooded tunnel.

ANSWER, PAGE 211

WISE WOMEN

Some thoughtful observations from members of the stronger sex.

1.

					I	M		R		E	D			H	E			T		R	T		
G	N	O	B	O	O	Y	N	T	R	F	E		T	A	E		W	O		L	H	A	N
L	O	T	M	W	M	E	P	N	E	V	E	L	O	R	I		S	A	A	T	D	I	G
H	E	W	O	O	D	N	D	E	O	B	U	F	W	I	T	T	I	S	R	S	I	N	T
			■										■			■			■				
■							■					■					■		■				
		■							■							■							
	■			■								■				■						■	■

2.

	A	I	N	G		N		T			N				N				Y				
B	L	E	S	S		D	C	E	H		F	I	V	T	O		S	A	W	H	T		H
T	E	I	I	D	E	F	O	I	S	I	T	G	T	H	E	A	F	A	C	T	O	B	S
A	V	V	N	S	E	N	R	O	M	O	G	H	E	I	M	G	N	W	O	R	A	H	Y
							■			■				■				■				■	
					■								■			■				■			
					■					■							■						
■									■			■				■					■	■	■

3.

E			L	D					T			N				T		E					
P	O	L	Y	O		D		U	I	U		P	Y	N	T	D	U	B		G	P		
W	F	T	H	K	U	T	O	Y	C	O	A	E	O	O	L	O	M	E		T	N		A
I	Y	U	I	D	N	A	J	H	S	T	V	W	E	T	M	I	S	I	E	A	O	D	E
N	A	R	E	I	E	G	C	A	O	E	M	S	R	U	O	I	H	T	N	O	N	R	B
		■				■					■				■				■			■	
	■						■				■						■			■			
					■			■											■			■	
							■			■				■					■				■
					■								■								■	■	■

ANSWER, PAGE 211

IT'S A JUNGLE OUT THERE

Everybody knows that a black cat crossing your path means bad luck, and carrying a rabbit's foot is supposed to bring you good luck, but there are lots of more intriguing superstitions out there that have to do with animals. Here are some pretty bizarre ones that people actually once believed, and may still pay attention to, in some remote corners of the world. Check the box under "Good" or "Bad" when you think you've figured out which is which.

	Good	**Bad**
1. If a miner says the word "cat" while down in the mine	_____	_____
2. Seeing three butterflies on one leaf at the same time	_____	_____
3. Carrying a badger's tooth	_____	_____
4. Seeing a white horse	_____	_____
5. Seeing a white horse with a redheaded girl riding it	_____	_____
6. Seeing an owl during the daytime	_____	_____
7. Burning a haddock	_____	_____
8. A picture of an elephant facing a door	_____	_____
9. If a frog hops into your house	_____	_____
10. Letting a pig cross your path	_____	_____
11. Saying "white rabbit" on the first day of the month	_____	_____
12. Seeing a rabbit on your way to work	_____	_____
13. Rats leaving one house and running into another:		
a) For the new house	_____	_____
b) For the old house	_____	_____

ANSWER, PAGE 211

* * * * *

HAIL TO THE TRUE/FALSE QUIZ

True or false: George Washington was named for King George III of England.

Ronald Reagan was the only president to head a labor union.

Calvin Coolidge was the only president born on the Fourth of July.

ANSWER, PAGE 212

FALSE ADVERTISING

A cynical-but-true comment about Mom, Dad, and the kids—and what they do together—from one of our most popular comedians…

ACROSS

1 Rorschach design
5 Game show host Barker
8 Groucho's trademark hat
13 Buffet server's question
14 First lady?
15 Ancient Palestine native
16 Tag team competitor
18 Closest to retirement
19 Beginning of a quip
21 Dead heat
22 Back of the neck
23 Part 2 of the quip
28 Red pest
31 Social elitist
32 *The Sound of Music* song starter
33 Ancient kingdom in North Africa
35 Roman-born actress Sophia
37 Possess
38 Problems with the plan
39 Clean chalkboards
40 In medias ___
41 Rapper who starred in *Trespass*
42 Swine enclosure
43 End of the quip
47 Jacob's twin
48 Matterhorn or Mont Blanc
49 Author of the quip
55 Souped-up auto
56 It's between titanium and chromium on the periodic table
58 Brick red
59 Period
60 Jane Austen classic
61 *A Nightmare ___ Street*
62 Unspoken agreement
63 Gambler's problem

DOWN

1 "The Ultimate Driving Machine"
2 Bereft
3 Nabisco cookie
4 Glassware used by chemists
5 Conviction
6 Very hot room, slangily
7 Polar "mountain"
8 Relief pitchers warm up in them
9 Paul's character in *The Hustler*
10 Great Barrier ___
11 Effortlessness
12 Stump remover, maybe
15 Noted whale rider
17 Slender
20 Far from mellow
23 Parts of an archipelago
24 Derisive laugh
25 Incursion
26 Smelly
27 Pointy wheel on a cowboy boot
28 Calculators of yore
29 Dr. Watson portrayer ___ Bruce
30 Not just edible
34 Free to move
36 Reporter's workplace
44 Composer Franz Joseph ___
45 Created a breeze, handily?
46 ___ Romeo (Italian automaker)
47 Flynn of swashbuckler films
49 Folk music's Baez
50 Raison d'___
51 ___ Marriott (a.k.a. Joe Millionaire)
52 *Othello* villain
53 Juice in a gimlet
54 Unintelligent
55 Co. health plan
57 Shoe-wiping surface

ANSWER, PAGE 212

GROUNDS FOR DIVORCE

They say breaking up is hard to do, but that wasn't the case for these people. Whether they were picked on or just picky, can you figure out the real reason they all made like bananas and split?

1. In Loving, New Mexico, a woman divorced her husband because he made her...

   a) salute him and address him as "Major"
   b) feed him a Hershey's Kiss
   c) sweep the floor ahead of him

   ...whenever he walked by.

2. In Lynch Heights, Delaware, a woman filed for divorce because her husband "regularly...

   a) replaced her shampoo with Nair
   b) hid whoopee cushions in her favorite chair
   c) put itching powder in her underwear

   ...when she wasn't looking."

3. In Honolulu a man filed for divorce because his wife served...

   a) peas
   b) pineapples
   c) Spam

   ...at every meal.

4. In Hazard, Kentucky, a man divorced his wife because she "beat him whenever he...

   a) removed onions from his hamburger
   b) went to sleep
   c) left his mail on the kitchen table

   ...without first asking for permission."

5. In Frackville, Pennsylvania, a woman filed for divorce because her husband insisted on...

   a) vandalizing mailboxes
   b) shooting tin cans off her head
   c) chasing their pet cat

   ...with a slingshot.

6. One Winthrop, Maine, a man divorced his wife because she...

   a) left her underwear on the couch
   b) spit in the coffee
   c) wore earplugs

   ...whenever his mother came to visit.

7. A Smelterville, Idaho, man's wife took an even stronger approach to his elderly mother. He won a divorce after his wife

   a) bit his mother on the arm
   b) dressed up as a ghost
   c) started a small fire

   ...in an attempt to scare her out of the house.

8. In Canon City, Colorado, a woman divorced her husband because whenever...

   a) he needed to look in the passenger side mirror
   b) he saw a garage sale
   c) they drove past his girlfriend's house

   ...he made her duck under the dashboard.

9. In Bennettsville, South Carolina, a deaf man filed for divorce because his wife "was...

   a) always nagging him
   b) inarticulate
   c) flirting with other men

   ...in sign language."

10. In Hardwick, Georgia, a woman divorced her husband because he stayed home too much and...

    a) insisted on cooking dinner.
    b) was much too affectionate.
    c) wasted too much money on gifts for her.

ANSWER, PAGE 212

HANDICAP? WHAT HANDICAP?

Here are 28 people who didn't let their handicaps stand in the way of their achievements, just like you won't let a bunch of extraneous letters keep you from finding their names in this grid. Note: Only the capitalized names and parts of names are in the grid.

```
A F M Q E I N S T E I N D Q D A
P F S N T N O S I D E N O T G C
A G D V O Z Z L A B I N N A H D
S L U A P T N I A S O C T Z W W
C Z W N A E L G F S N H K I K I
A H V G C M B I L A A N L E Y P
L E B O N N X I M C S E T S N W
S L D G A I W B H N Y L J E C S
I E O H M E U R A P H S V T M Y
Y N O Y U T I J O A N O F A R C
E K W T R S D S Y M H N J R U A
N E G P T H T J C T L K I C D E
R L D I T L E V E S O O R O T S
A L E X A N D E R P O P E S J A
E E W A V N B R O W N I N G H R
K R D O R O T H E A L A N G E P
```

Ludwig von BEETHOVEN (continued to compose after going deaf)

Elizabeth Barrett BROWNING (childhood spinal injury and lung ailment)

Julius CAESAR (epilepsy)

TRUMAN CAPOTE (epilepsy)

AGATHA CHRISTIE (epilepsy)

Charles DICKENS (epilepsy)

Thomas EDISON (progressively worsening hearing difficulties)

Albert EINSTEIN (unable to speak until the age of three)

HANNIBAL (epilepsy)

JOAN OF ARC (narcolepsy)

General Philip KEARNEY (one-armed Civil War general)

HELEN KELLER (born blind, deaf, and mute)

DOROTHEA LANGE (photographer who contracted polio at age seven)

Edward LEAR (epilepsy)

JOHN MILTON (wrote *Paradise Lost* after going blind)

Lord Horatio NELSON (lost one eye and arm)

Alfred NOBEL (epilepsy)

Blaise PASCAL (epilepsy)

SAINT PAUL the Apostle (epilepsy)

ALEXANDER POPE (hunchback)

WILEY POST (made the first solo flight around the world despite having only one eye)

Franklin Delano ROOSEVELT (lost the use of his legs to polio)

SOCRATES (epilepsy)

Charles STEINMETZ (engineer, genius, and hunchback)

Harriet TUBMAN (narcolepsy)

Vincent VAN GOGH (epilepsy)

Josiah WEDGWOOD (lost his right leg to smallpox)

Woodrow WILSON (dyslexic)

ANSWER, PAGE 212

BITES OF THE ROUND TABLE

Here are some sound bites from Dorothy Parker, one of America's all-time sharpest wits. If you need directions on how to solve this puzzle, see page 5.

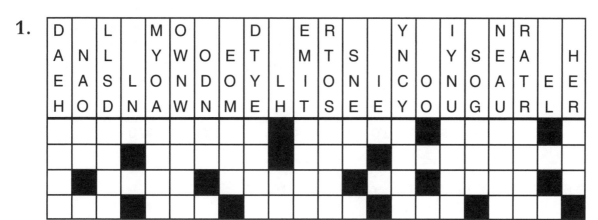

1.

D		L		M	O			D		E	R			Y		I		N	R		
A	N	L		Y	W	O	E	T		M	T	S		N		Y	S	E	A		H
E	A	S	L	O	N	D	O	Y	L	I	O	N	I	C	O	N	O	A	T	E	E
H	O	D	N	A	W	N	M	E	H	T	S	E	E	Y	O	U	G	U	R	L	R
									■						■					■	
			■						■				■								
	■					■						■			■					■	
			■				■						■					■			■

2.

R						A								D			T				
H	E	E	D	B	T	H	T		N	O	Y		T	O		I	E	I	R	H	C
E	A	K	E	R	E	N	S	T	T	A	M	A	M	A		K	S	E	T	T	H
T	H	L	I	L	E	O	U	A	H	O	H	O	N	E	T	L	O	T	P	O	S
M	I	A	P	R	E	S	E	A	W	T	F	E	T	H	E	M	E	S	P	E	E
			■					■				■			■					■	
							■			■					■			■			■
				■				■					■								
		■									■				■				■		
	■				■				■			■				■					

3.

T	A	V	E		E			G			T	O		Y	H						
E	O	C	R		I		M	E			T	E		T	A	Y		B	O		
R	E	L	U	R	T	O	S	E	O	B	U	O		S	M	V	D	S	A	O	
M	B	A	M	S	A	S	N	E	A	E	V	Y		H	B	E	E	Y	O	I	E
H	X	O	E	P	H	O	R	E	D	L	L	T	R	I	A	O	T	O	T	T	H
						■			■										■		■
				■			■			■			■				■				
				■		■							■					■			■
									■				■			■				■	
										■			■				■			■	■

ANSWER, PAGE 212

CRACKING THE CODE OF HAMMURABI

Way back in 1780 or so B.C., King Hammurabi had his favorite laws carved into an eight-foot-high stone column and displayed in Babylon, the Sin City of the ancient world. We've taken ten crimes, all punishable by death according to the code, and encrypted them using a simple letter substitution code. For instructions and hints on how to solve, see page 15. In this particular puzzle, **the letter substitution stays constant throughout the whole list**.

1. FJJAYXGE YIDRIGR IQ F JUXDR SXCTIAC WUIIQ

2. QFVYRVB FJJAYXGE YIDRIGR IQ F JUXDR

3. YCRFVXGE CTR WUIWRUCB IQ F CRDWVR IU F JIAUC

4. URJRXNXGE CTR YCIVRG WUIWRUCB IQ F CRDWVR IU F JIAUC

5. YCRFVXGE F YVFNR

6. TRVWXGE F YVFNR RYJFWR

7. TXOXGE F YVFNR

8. HURFMXGE FGO RGCRUXGE

9. JIDDXCCXGE F UIHHRUB

10. FVVISXGE JIGYWXUFCIUY CI DRRC XG BIAU CFNRUG

ANSWER, PAGE 212

SAFETY IN NUMBERS

H. L. Mencken was known for his debunking of American society, especially the people he called the "booboisie." Here's just one of his scads of satirical sayings.

ACROSS

1 Predisposed (to)
7 Flows back
11 Dream Team jersey letters
14 Build up
15 ___ Lee cheesecake
16 To the ___ degree
17 First part of a quip by H. L. Mencken
19 Egg ___ yung
20 Bleak, literarily
21 Part 2 of the quip
23 The world's largest diamond supplier
25 "___ *bien!*"
26 PowerBook, e.g.
29 The Judds's label
30 Affectionate greeting
31 Cig leavings
32 Word like "kinda"
34 "Brother, can you spare ___?"
37 Part 3 of the quip
39 Part 4 of the quip
41 *GoodFellas* protagonist ___ Hill
42 Eucharist disk
44 Talent dismissed by skeptics
45 Courteney of *Friends*
46 Creosote source
47 No way, old-style
48 First name in stunts
50 Spend a lot
54 Part 5 of the quip
56 Planetary path
60 Wisc. neighbor
61 End of the quip
63 Keanu's *The Matrix* role
64 Pay to play
65 "Religion is the ___ of the masses"
66 "This is so frustrating!"
67 Seeks the favor of
68 Liam of *Gangs of New York*

DOWN

1 *Shane* star Alan
2 Writer of sweet words?
3 Pinnacle
4 Wide-ranging
5 "Filthy" money
6 "…the veriest slave that ___ crawled…": Shelley
7 Revert to state ownership
8 Aspirin brand
9 Watchers of the "telly"
10 Miss America wears one
11 Clint Eastwood western
12 Put away for awhile
13 Ship-to-ship calls
18 Owned up to one's mistake
22 Practice piece for a musician
24 Forehead
26 SAT section
27 1975 Wimbledon winner Arthur
28 Collegiate bigwig
30 That hippie musical
32 River into which Achilles was dipped
33 To blame
35 Costa ___
36 Happen to see
38 Beastie under a bridge
40 German Mister
43 Map collections
48 *Dallas* family surname
49 More loathsome
50 Shorthand expert
51 Sauce made from basil
52 Lose it
53 Sunny *Sesame Street* regular
55 Cabbage-and-mayo dish
57 Large snakes
58 "What's gotten ___ you?"
59 High schooler
62 Spouse-to-spouse address

ANSWER, PAGE 213

PARLEZ-VOUS PENTAGONESE?

The phrases below are actual terms used by the Pentagon. Do you understand the language well enough to unscramble the plain English meaning of the military term?

1. "Disruption" ___ ___ ___ ___ ___ ___ ___
B I N M O G B

2. "Ambient noncombat personnel" ___ ___ ___ ___ ___ ___ ___ ___
S U G F R E E E

3. "Interdictional nonsuccumbers" ___ ___ ___ ___ ___ ___ ___ ___ ___ ___ ___ ___ ___ ___
M E Y E N O R V I S S U R V

4. "Force packages" ___ ___ ___ ___ ___
M O B B S

5. "Visit the site" ___ ___ ___ ___ ___ ___
O B M B T I

6. "Revisit the site" ___ ___ ___ ___ ___ ___ ___ ___ ___ ___ ___
M O B B T I N A A I G

7. "Accidental delivery of ordnance equipment" ___ ___ ___ ___ ___ ___ ___ ___ ___ ___ ___ ___ ___
S I M S H E T G A T T E R

8. "Suppression of assets" ___ ___ ___ ___ ___ ___ ___ ___ ___ ___ ___ ___
G A M I J M N A D R R A

9. "Airborne sanitation" ___ ___ ___ ___ ___ ___ ___ ___ ___ ___ ___ ___ ___
I M B O G B N K T A T A C

10. "Civilian irregular defense soldiers" ___ ___ ___ ___ ___ ___ ___ ___ ___ ___ ___
I N R E S M E E C A R

11. "Area denial weapons" ___ ___ ___ ___ ___ ___ ___ ___ ___ ___ ___ ___
S L U T R E C S B M B O

12. "Sanitizing the area" ___ ___ ___ ___ ___ ___ ___ ___ ___ ___ ___ ___ ___ ___ ___ ___
G O B B I M N G I V E R H Y E N T

13. "Servicing the target" ___ ___ ___ ___ ___ ___ ___ ___ ___ ___ ___ ___ ___ ___ ___
N I L G L I K E T H M E N Y E

ANSWER, PAGE 213

THE PRESIDENT'S PAJAMAS

…and other facts about some presidents that may not have made it into the history books.

ACROSS

1 Tasty young rooster
6 Trying experience
12 Actress Tilly
15 Topiary plants, mostly
16 Pound the pavement
17 "Strange Magic" band, for short
18 First U.S. president to throw out the first pitch of the baseball season
21 Incompetent
22 Aspirations
23 Diva's chance to shine
24 "I feel like a new ___!"
25 First U.S. president whose memoirs were a best-seller
30 Org. that aids motorists
31 1992 hit song for U2
32 U.S. president who appears on the $100,000 bill
39 Fido's foot
42 *The Return of the Native* author
43 Iwo ___
44 Kind of caviar
46 Coup d'___
47 Classic Chevy models
49 Run ___ (lose control)
50 Fame
52 "My stars!"
53 The show must go on it
54 Unit of work
55 First U.S. president born in the U.S.
58 Like Cabernets
59 Feather stole
60 U.S. president who never accepted his presidential salary
68 TV show about U.S. Navy attorneys
71 Locality
72 *Vogue* shelfmate
73 Ben Franklin's bill
75 U.S. president who owned a set of pajamas with five stars on the lapel
80 Element in pewter
81 Reach a higher state
82 Utter chaos
83 Come-___ (inducements)
84 Revolutionary leader Sun ___
85 Toothpaste brand

DOWN

1 84 Across's home nation
2 Senator Specter
3 "Lumps" in orange juice
4 Everybody's final notice
5 Ultra-secretive U.S. org.
6 "He's a man ___ word"
7 Dorm divisions
8 Use a divining rod
9 Greek H
10 Televise
11 Abbreviation akin to Inc.
12 Stiller's comic partner
13 Spritely
14 Bribed
15 Take a dip
19 Possibly will
20 Sailor's sealant
26 ___-tzu
27 Distress call
28 Haughty types
29 Actor Wilder
30 Increase
32 "This is ___ I came in"
33 Western movie, slangily
34 Sumatran ape
35 Where Lou Grant worked
36 Blade on a car window
37 Persona
38 Steven Bochco show
39 Mountain lions
40 Whiskey ___ (Hollywood club)
41 Rouse
45 Andy's *Taxi* character
47 Word before city or circle
48 Pt. of speech
51 With "house," a place of storage
53 Brutally hot day
56 Banned insecticide (abbr.)
57 Bart Simpson's granddad
60 Could do nothing but
61 Rommel of the Afrika Korps
62 Equestrian's "brakes"
63 Sack
64 Shoes to accompany a cocktail dress
65 Miss Oyl
66 Footballer Merlin
67 Singer Bobby
68 Bulldog's droopy facial features
69 Eroded
70 Microbe
74 Lymph ___
76 Indignant outburst
77 Dam-building org.
78 Morse code unit
79 Where 38 Down premiered

ANSWER, PAGE 214

UNCLE ALBERT SAYS...

Some not-very-intellectual thoughts from that cute Albert Einstein. If you need directions on how to solve this puzzle, see page 5.

1.

N	D	B		Y			A	T				M	T	
W	B	Y		I	S		I	N	D	E	H	A	E	
Y	O	O	O	D	Y		U	N	E	T	E	S	E	A
N	H	S	D	M	E	L	I	K	D	S	R	V	T	R
			■			■			■					■
						■								
			■			■				■				
					■						■			■

2.

		D					H				E	I		A
I	E	I	E	I	A		A	T	E	O	N	W		L
E	L	O	M	O	O	H	R	I	S	I	L	Y		K
I	N	V	G	E	F	T	S	E	L	P	G	S	O	N
I	S	A	M	R	W	U	D	E	N	N	I	B	E	R
	■			■		■							■	
								■						
					■					■			■	
■									■				■	
			■			■								

3.

O			M		T	O					P			A
T	R		Y	U	N	I	S	H	M	Y	E			A
R	T		P	A	C	H	N	R	E	T	S	T	F	O
U	E	M	A	R	D	T	Y	T	E	M	Y	E	F	F
T	O	H	O	U	I	E	O	M	I	M	A	N	L	F
		■							■			■		
	■			■									■	
		■										■		
		■					■			■			■	
								■						

ANSWER, PAGE 213

UNCLE JOHN'S LISTS—TWO

We keep finding more lists, but that darn Uncle John keeps scrambling the letters. Put the right letters in the right blanks.

The 7 Places You Can Legally Carry a Concealed Weapon in Utah

1. ___ ___ ___
A R C

2. ___ ___ ___ ___ ___ ___ ___
T I Y C U S B

3. ___ ___ ___ ___ ___
N A R I T

4. ___ ___ ___ ___
L A L M

5. ___ ___ ___
A B R

6. ___ ___ ___ ___ ___ ___
H R C C U H

7. ___ ___ ___ ___ ___ ___
L O C O H S

The 5 Most Interesting Things That Have Been Sold in Vending Machines

1. ___ ___ ___ ___ ___ ___ ___ ___
M U E K J Y R E

2. ___ ___ ___ ___ ___ ___ ___ ___ ___ ___ ___
A P H O D C E G S G E

3. ___ ___ ___ ___ ___ ___ ___ ___ ___
L H Y O R T W A E

4. ___ ___ ___ ___ ___ ___ ___
T E L E S E B

5. ___ ___ ___ ___ ___ ___ ___ ___ ___ ___
V E I L M I P H R S

ANSWER, PAGE 213

CLARKE'S COMMENTS

Here are a few thoughts from the eminent science fiction writer Arthur C. Clarke, author of *2001: A Space Odyssey*. Drop the letters from each vertical column—but not necessarily in the order in which they appear—into the empty squares below them to read some of Clarke's pungent comments.

1.

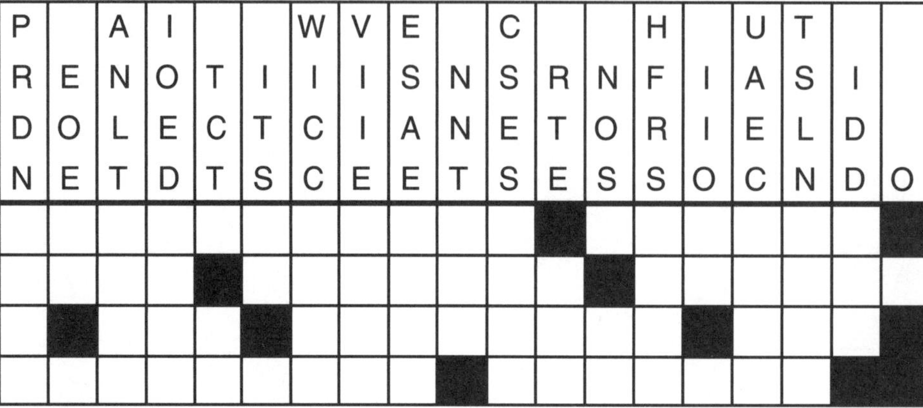

2.

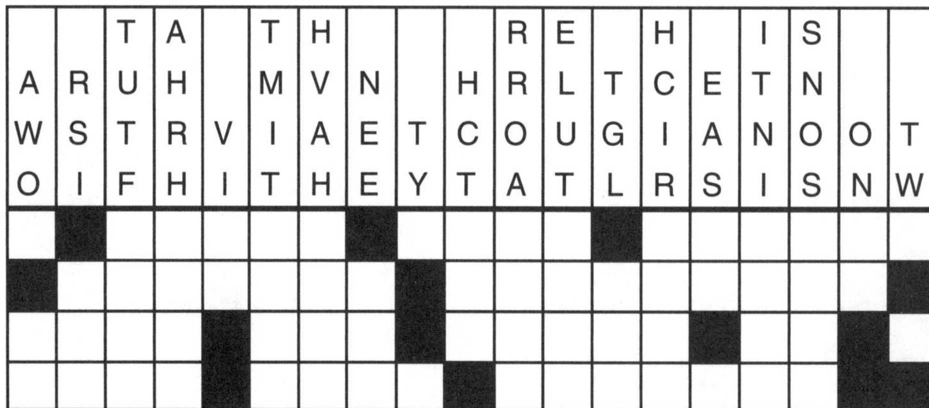

3.

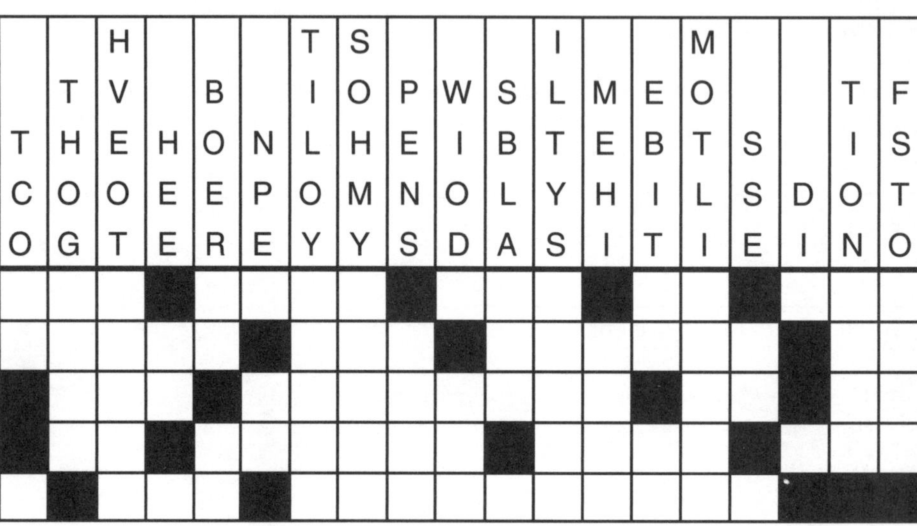

ANSWER, PAGE 213

WOULD WE LIE TO YOU—FOUR?

Yes, and we love every minute of it! More of those everyday phenomena you've been wondering about all these years. Pick the one correct answer from among the three.

1. Why are crescent moons carved into outhouse doors?
    a) These moon-shaped holes were originally bigger and designed to let moonlight in. They weren't really very useful—unless the moon was very bright, you still needed a candle—but once they became fashionable, everyone had to have one.
    b) In ancient Greece certain bodily humors were thought to cause madness, and by "evacuating" these humors regularly you stayed in favor with Selene, the moon goddess; so lavatories and chamber pots were decorated with moon symbols.
    c) Actually, the moon is the symbol for the "ladies' room"—men's outhouses originally had a sun symbol on the door. But a lot of old-time innkeepers only bothered to build a ladies' outhouse; the assumption was that men could simply nip behind a tree to do their business. The sun symbol eventually became so uncommon that it was phased out altogether.

2. Why does Santa Claus wear red?
    a) When Pope Urban II decided to canonize Nicholas of Myra, he had the poor man's remains dug up and brought to Italy. Among the remains was a fragment of red cloth. Although subsequent legends have drastically changed the type of garment Santa wears, the red color has always stayed the same.
    b) Much of the St. Nicholas legend developed in Russia, where Nick is the patron saint. The color red is a symbol of prestige in Russia—it's worn by kings, dignitaries, and members of the Church—so of course St. Nick was always shown wearing it, too.
    c) Until the 1930s, Santa Claus's clothing didn't have any fixed color. Then the Coca-Cola company ran a series of ads depicting Santa as a Coke drinker, in the hopes of boosting wintertime soda sales. The artist made Santa's suit red to match the Coke logo, and it's been red ever since.

3. The Colosseum in Rome looks like it's been hit by an earthquake. What happened to it?
    a) It was hit by an earthquake in A.D. 390. Very little of the damage was repaired before Rome itself fell to the Visigoths in A.D. 410.
    b) After the fall of Rome the Colosseum was routinely plundered for building materials. For instance, many of its stones were used to build St. Peter's Basilica across town.
    c) Nothing particularly bad happened to the Colosseum. It's just a really old building, and time takes its toll.

4. Where do the seeds for growing seedless watermelons come from?
    a) Fruit growers use a process called "grafting" to propagate seedless watermelons. They make new plants from the vines of the old ones. There are no seeds.
    b) Scientists have created an artificial seed that will grow a seedless watermelon.
    c) Grown in places with long hot growing seasons, seedless watermelons will eventually produce mature seeds.

5. What are those little squiggles you see floating on your eyes when you look at the sky?
    a) Tiny dust particles caught in the liquid that covers your eye.
    b) The remains of an artery that fed blood to your eye while you were in the womb. When your eye finished growing, the artery withered and broke apart.
    c) Very small scratches on the surface of your eyeball, caused by sharp pieces of grit. You can't avoid getting them, but don't panic—they heal over in two to three days.

ANSWER, PAGE 214

READY FOR PRIME TIME?

Just a few years ago we ran a couple of stories on weird game shows. Now you can't turn on the TV without catching a glimpse of someone being tortured or grossed out while snacking on a plate of slugs. If you've wondered where *Fear Factor* et al. came from, you can find out right here. But first, you'll have to translate the following descriptions of game shows—both foreign and domestic—from the simple letter substitution codes we've used. For further instructions and hints on how to solve, see page 15.

TV CHAMPIONS (JAPAN)

O ZXLLPGPQW YXFOGGP ECQWPNW POEK BPPU. CQP BPPU ECQWPNWOQWN EKTS "GOQEXZ, PRXH-NAPHHXQS NCJYPOQ SGTPH," OQCWKPG BPPU WKPJ "OHHCB WKPANPHRPN WC YP HCEUPZ XQ EOSPN OQZ NBCGQ OW."

THE GAME OF THE GOOSE (SPAIN)

LXCOTJODCOJ ZXUT DQXACE D WDZT HXDQE; TDLV JSDLT QTSQTJTCOJ D ENYYTQTCO LVDGGTCWT. XCT LVDGGTCWT: QTGTDJT D JTZN-CAET ZXETG YQXZ DC TRSGXENCW HTE. DCXOVTQ: OQB OX TJLDST YQXZ D HXR OVDO'J JGXFGB YNGGNCW FNOV JDCE.

FINDERS KEEPERS (U.S.)

GUOQ WUM, YQG XQFT ZX SZNPGW FI NFOUYZFI UY U WZSSGHGIY OFIYGXYUIY'X QFCXG. YQG SZNP OHGT QZWGX U JHZVG ZI YQG OFIYGXYUIY'X NZEZIR HFFP, XGYX CJ OUPGHUX, UIW YQGI NGYX EZGTGHX TUYOQ YQG OFIYGXYUIY YGUH YQG HFFP UJUHY NFFBZIR SFH ZY.

ANSWER, PAGE 214

COMMON KNOWLEDGE

More statistics from Uncle John's vast store of knowledge.

ACROSS

1 Put into port
5 University of Arizona city
11 Low-tech hair dryer
16 Toll unit for a truck
17 Available for work
18 Gulf War combatant
19 Not fatty
20 The most common school colors in the U.S.
22 The most common health complaint that Americans report to their doctors
24 Jennifer from *Dirty Dancing*
25 Time delay
26 Catch some Z's
27 A catboat has one
28 High C, e.g.
29 Nation bordering Lebanon
31 ___ Bernardino, CA
32 They're shown to newbies
33 Brownie ___ (good things to earn)
35 Theater company member
38 Sprint
39 Stylish
41 Dartmouth College town
45 Dow Jones stat, e.g.
46 The most common object involved in choking
48 Miner's find
49 Try, as a new product
51 Puncture mark
52 *Ally McBeal* actress Lucy ___
53 Chocolate/caramel/nougat treat
55 Dark furs
58 Revealed
61 Big vessel
62 Actress Witherspoon
63 Divisible by two, as a number
64 Advantage
66 Thin and flat, as rock
68 Acted as guide
69 Cut
70 The most commonly shoplifted book in the U.S.
73 The most common crime that Americans are arrested for
76 ___ *in Manhattan*
77 Computer character set
78 Speech that concludes a play
79 Singer Fitzgerald
80 Some folk dances
81 Kingdoms
82 Like Barbie's figure

DOWN

1 Painter of melting clocks
2 Yoked team
3 The most common use of gold in the U.S.
4 Star of *thirtysomething*
5 *Chinatown* screenwriter Robert ___
6 Square
7 ___ Pet (novelty item)
8 Take a load off
9 Pizza herb
10 Gets closer
11 Neat
12 Sphere
13 It's a big hit
14 See as being the same
15 Feudal lords
21 Butterfly collector's need
23 Vegans avoid it
27 Tea party attendee in *Alice in Wonderland*
28 Inadvisable act
29 Jack of nursery rhyme fame
30 "___ got mail!"
31 Dentist's direction after "Rinse"
32 General or private
34 Use steel wool
36 Hockey legend Esposito
37 Sprays a mugger
40 Red ___ (cinnamon candies)
42 The most commonly played sport in nudist parks
43 New York natives who saw a canal named after them
44 Get more out of
46 Warty creature
47 Meat served sweet-and-sour
50 Catchers of counterfeiters
54 Pibroch player's instrument
56 United ___ Emirates
57 Occasionally, old-style
58 Conehead family patriarch
59 Opposed (to)
60 Diminish
64 Go off the deep ___
65 More ominous
66 ___ Penh
67 Pantyhose brand
69 Hits the slopes
70 Cash drawer
71 *Dogfight* actress Taylor
72 Cheese coated with red wax
74 Zero
75 "Live, ___ satellite…" (newscaster's phrase)

ANSWER, PAGE 214

TOM SWIFTIES: VARIATION ON A THEME

If you've caught the other Swifties in the book, you might think they only work with words ending in "ly." Here's a variation on the original style. Finish each sentence (1–10) with the word or words (a–j) that make the most appropriate—and punniest—sentence.

_____ 1. "Get out of my hair," was Tom's…

_____ 2. "Hillbillies have a name for little valleys like this," Tom…

_____ 3. "I haven't caught a fish all day!" Tom said…

_____ 4. "I hope I can still play the guitar," Tom…

_____ 5. "I wonder what it was like being one of Zeus's daughters," Tom...

_____ 6. "I'm definitely going camping again," said Tom…

_____ 7. "It's not a candy, it's a breath mint," Tom…

_____ 8. "Oh, no! I dropped my tooth-paste," Tom said…

_____ 9. "Smoking is not permitted in here," Tom…

_____ 10. "Aha! Someone has removed the twos from this deck," Tom…

a. asserted

b. brush-off

c. crestfallen

d. deduced

e. fretted

f. fumed

g. mused

h. hollered

i. with intent

j. without debate

ANSWER, PAGE 215

* * * * *

RIGHT ON THE NOSE

The phrase "on the nose" means "exactly" or "perfectly." Why?

a) The nose is perceived as the exact center of the face, so hitting something "on the nose" is the same as hitting it dead-center, or perfectly.

b) In the early days of radio broadcasting, directors used hand signals to communicate with the crew. A finger on the nose meant that the show was exactly on schedule.

c) To a bookie, $50 "on the nose" means $50 on the favorite to win. Since favorites usually run at even odds, the bettors stand to win or lose the exact amounts of their bets.

ANSWER, PAGE 214

NUMBER TWO

Here's a crossword all about number two (which we think is pretty appropriate).

ACROSS

1 Gets quietly mad
8 Italian country house
13 Lab animal
16 Pennsylvania city
17 Bubbling away
18 Univ. URL ender
19 Most common last name in America: Smith. What's #2?
20 Most-published playwright in history: William Shakespeare. Who's #2?
22 Chimp or orang
23 Most dangerous animal in the zoo: panda. What's #2?
25 Pierced body part
26 Seaweed
28 Closes with force
29 Food that Americans hate the most: tofu. What's #2?
30 Dutch brew
33 Small inlets
34 Most-studied foreign language in the U.S.: Spanish. What's #2?
37 Go off course
40 Neon or argon, e.g.
42 Last inning
43 ___ Na Na
46 Installments
48 Richer, as milk
50 Lawyer's abbr.
51 Edmonton player
53 Unpredictable
54 Roof over one's head
56 Most popular name for U.S. high school sports teams: Eagles. What's #2?
57 Battling
59 Lousy
61 Largest internal organ in the body: liver. What's #2?
62 Arrive at
64 Arranged mtg.
68 Slips up
69 Most valuable brand name on earth: Marlboro. What's #2?
72 Fish story
73 #1 invention that Americans can't live without: car. What's #2?
75 Country that's #1 in gun ownership per capita: the U.S. What's #2?
77 Rd.
78 Permissible
79 Not observed
80 "Are we there ___?"
81 Greek island
82 Broadcasting award

DOWN

1 *Wheel* host Pat
2 Marry on the run
3 Singer Merman
4 Heavy weight
5 Hydrant hookup
6 Organic compound
7 Most rational
8 "Jump" band
9 Girder
10 Pork cuts
11 Rhythm
12 Gore and Green
13 Take away
14 Pueblo homes
15 Radio part
21 "As ___ and breathe!"
24 Begged
27 Window insets
29 Womanizer
31 Actor Patrick
32 More suspect, as dealings
33 Answer every whim of
34 At no cost
35 Sings like Eminem
36 La Salle of *ER*
38 London's Old ___
39 Concerning
41 Dump your stock
43 Location
44 ___ to the throne
45 Bow shapes
47 "Quiet on the ___!"
49 Zsa Zsa's sister
52 Like skis at a resort, e.g.
54 Taffeta sound
55 College military org.
57 Get there
58 Wal-Mart competitor
60 Make a mistake
61 Secure a climbing rope
62 Big scrape
63 Flamboyance
65 *Symposium* author
66 Yearned deeply
67 Kids' bear
69 "10-4" buddy
70 Cord
71 Actress Paquin
74 '90s R&B girl group
76 Tennis move

ANSWER, PAGE 215

PATRON SAINTS

The Roman Catholic Church has more than 5,000 saints, many of whom are "patron saints"—protectors of certain professions, sick people, and even hobbies. We've selected a few and put them in the grid, reading across, down, and diagonally. When you've found all 48 capitalized words and phrases, the leftover letters will spell a profound message from a British-born writer who was born again as a Buddhist.

```
M P S U M S A R E S I A L B U R E H S P I S
R A D R I A N I N R T O U G L Y P E O P L E
N J T E S H S A U E N T D A R E D R D A S T
E U G R N R I M E K T E S C T P R P V S S I
H L O A O T E O A O F L T C H H A E T E E B
C I S H I N N A N R D R O O I N R S K B N E
T A T T T H A M A B T T O U N Y L O Y A K K
A N E R A T A H E N M I O N I S E T A S C A
W I H A L K A R D W E N N T E S L D C T I N
D W O M E N I N L A B O R A O N I T A I S S
O D E R R M P L A P I T I N O N G X G A A U
O I S Z E Z C P L T A E H T A M I R A N E E
H L A R C S I A A N D S U S L D U G E I S N
R B L O A D D T T H I S S A R T S D T E J H
O V O A R Y S R O T C E R I D L A R E N U F
B S H D I S L I U T L N V S E T H O E G G I
H F C R A E S C L A V E R E R N I G H I G R
G V I G A N A K N A R S G W I E T O H N L E
I Q N A A T U N A S L R P A R T T S L E E O
E V E W C E A N N D O A R M S D E A L E R S
N W S O R R K A L E C O L I C D O U K R S S
H I L A R Y E H G W E H T T A M U X L S E Y
```

ADRIAN of Nicomedia, patron saint of ARMS DEALERS

ANNE, patron saint of WOMEN IN LABOR (not to be confused with John Thwing, patron saint of women in "difficult" labor—just so you know who to call out to)

Bernardino of SIENA, patron saint of HOARSENESS

BLAISE, patron saint of THROATS (he saved a child from choking)

DROGO, patron saint of UGLY PEOPLE and CATTLE

ELIGIUS, patron saint of GAS STATION workers (he miraculously cured horses, the precursors to automobiles)

ERASMUS, patron saint of SEA-SICKNESS and COLIC

FIACRE, patron saint of TAXI DRIVERS

GEORGE, patron saint of HERPES

HILARY, patron saint of SNAKEBITES

HUGH of Lincoln, patron saint of SWANS

Joseph of ARIMATHEA, patron saint of FUNERAL DIRECTORS

JULIAN the Hospitaller, patron saint of JUGGLERS

LIDWINA, patron saint of SKATERS

LOUIS IX of France, patron saint of BUTTON MAKERS

MARTHA, patron saint of DIETITIANS

MARTIN de Porres, patron saint of RACE RELATIONS

MATRONA, patron saint of DYSENTERY sufferers

MATTHEW, patron saint of ACCOUNTANTS (he was a tax collector before becoming an apostle)

NICHOLAS of Myra (also known as Santa Claus), patron saint of PAWNBROKERS

PATRICK, patron saint of ENGINEERS

Peter CLAVER, patron saint of SLAVERY

SEBASTIAN, patron saint of NEIGHBORHOOD WATCH groups

ANSWER, PAGE 215

ALPO AND GREEN SLIME

If you knew what the people who make your pizza are saying behind your back, you might decide to head for the taqueria down the street instead. Match the pizza lingo (1–19) with its meaning (a–s).

_____ 1. Alpo
_____ 2. Beef darts
_____ 3. Birthday cake
_____ 4. Blue quarters
_____ 5. Bondage pie
_____ 6. Carp
_____ 7. Cheese off!
_____ 8. Crispy critters
_____ 9. Edgar Allan pie
_____ 10. Flyers and fungus
_____ 11. Green slime
_____ 12. Hemorrhage
_____ 13. Master-baker
_____ 14. Panty liner
_____ 15. Shroomers
_____ 16. Spoodle
_____ 17. Starver
_____ 18. Vulture pie
_____ 19. Zap zits

a. Italian sausage, also known as dog food, "Puppy Chow," "Kibbles 'n' Bits," and "Snausages"
b. A saucing tool that looks like a combination spoon/ladle
c. A pizza with way too many items on it
d. A customer who orders a pizza, then tells the driver that they didn't order one but offers to buy it at a discount
e. Pizza with extra tomato sauce
f. The absorbent cardboard placed under a pizza when it's boxed
g. A friendly expletive meaning "Go away!"
h. A burnt pizza
i. A pizza with PO—pepperoni and onions
j. A pizza "with too many problems to send out to a customer," fit only as food for vultures—or employees
k. Pop the bubbles in a pizza crust as it cooks
l. An oven tender
m. A kitchen game in which coins are heated in a 550°F oven until they turn blue
n. Anchovies, also known as "guppies" and "penguin food"
o. Pepperoni (because raw slices fly like Frisbees) and mushrooms
p. A game played during slow times, in which employees hurl bits of raw beef against the walls
q. Green peppers, especially those that become slippery and slimy. Also known as "lizards" and "seaweed"
r. A pizza with S&M—sausage and mushrooms
s. Mushrooms

ANSWER, PAGE 215

HERE, DOGGIE!

There are 31 dog breeds listed below. Can you round them up and put them into the grid where they belong? Enter each word only once, crossword-style.

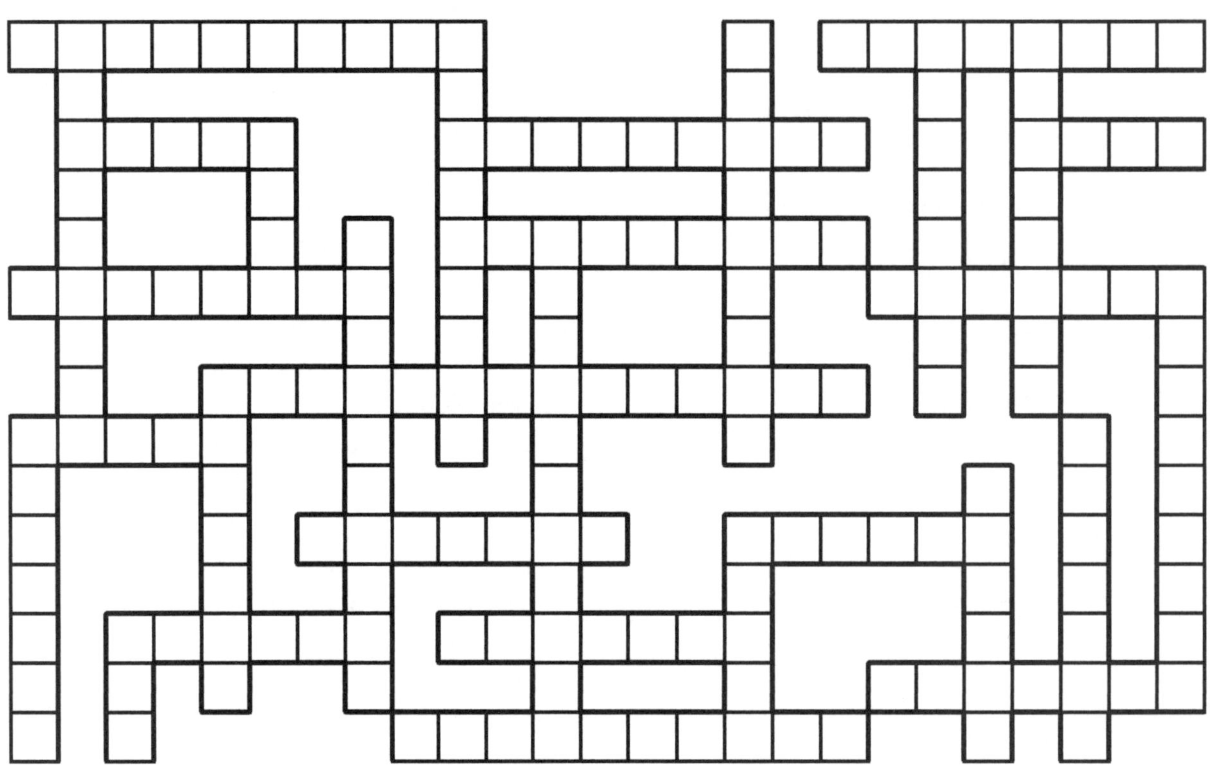

3 letter word
Pug

4 letter words
Ainu
Puli

5 letter words
Akita
Boxer
Corgi

6 letter words
Beagle
Collie
Poodle

7 letter words
Basenji
Bulldog
Griffon
Maltese
Mastiff
Pointer
Samoyed

8 letter words
Elkhound
Malamute
Papillon
Sheepdog

9 letter words
Chihuahua
Dachshund
Great Dane
Lhasa apso
Schnauzer
St. Bernard

10 letter words
Bloodhound
Pomeranian
Weimaraner

11 letter word
Bichon frise

14 letter word
German shepherd

ANSWER, PAGE 216

THERE SHE IS...

We've hidden in the grid the last names of 60 of the 74 women who've held the Miss America title. Can you find them all? Consider it your talent competition.

```
B S O W A N D Y B E O R Y A J S H O P P
E H T H Y T P E R K I N S M I T H E P R
N I T S E D H L A C A S H C N E R F A R
H N N A M R O G G L G V C H A R L E S R
A D A A A O E N I A A J A O M E S E K E
M L Y I R F I A I N K R E T T I W E R P
E E R A N M N L D P K N A C Y H L B T O
R N B W E A L E O H B C H R L E R K T O
C O U L S P R E O I E E M U T L H A E C
E S F K W B M R W E R W B R T A E I N Q
R N E E U Y A A L R G T A R R C H W R N
N H R R E E X H L L E B P M A C H A O S
I O D R E U O E A C R V A T T I X I C P
K J S E M L E P M G O N A I T B L D N R
A O E L L K L D S G N M R E F E A H C S
N E B A R A Q U I O O I S R L T F G E C
D R N U N A N I D O G T K O A B F F O K
A D B C O T C D U N O S I N N E D Y A W
E N H E R Y L L E N N O D A N Z L D R M
M E R I W E T H E R E M O B L E Y L L S
```

Susan AKIN (1986)
Donna AXUM (1964)
Angela Perez BARAQUIO (2001)
Jean BARTEL (1943)
Dorothy BENHAM (1977)
Marian BERGERON (1933)
Yolande BETBEZE (1951)
Deborah BRYANT (1966)
Marilyn BUFERD (1946)
Frances BURKE (1940)
Mary Catherine CAMPBELL (1922–23)
Gretchen CARLSON (1989)
Kellye CASH (1987)
Suzette CHARLES (1984)
Bette COOPER (1937)
Leanza CORNETT (1993)
Shirley COTHRAN (1975)
Rose COYLE (1936)
Lois DELANDER (1927)
Jo-Carroll DENNISON (1942)
Patricia DONNELLY (1939)
Nancy FLEMING (1961)
Maria FLETCHER (1962)
Judith FORD (1969)
Heather Renee FRENCH (2000)
Tawny GODIN (1976)
Margaret GORMAN (1921)
Katie HARMAN (2002)
Tara Dawn HOLLAND (1997)
Colleen HUTCHINS (1952)
Jane JAYROE (1967)
Nicole JOHNSON (1999)
Rebecca KING (1974)
Neva Jane LANGLEY (1953)
Fay LANPHIER (1925)
Rosemary LAPLANCHE (1941)
Henrietta LEAVER (1935)
Debra MAFFETT (1983)
Ruth MALCOMSON (1924)
Jacquelyn MAYER (1963)
Marian MCKNIGHT (1957)
Lynda MEAD (1960)
Terry MEEUWSEN (1973)
Jacque MERCER (1949)
Lee MERIWETHER (1955)
Marilyn MESEKE (1938)
Mary Ann MOBLEY (1959)
Bess MYERSON (1945)
Susan PERKINS (1978)
Susan POWELL (1981)
Cheryl PREWITT (1980)
Venus RAMEY (1944)
Sharon RITCHIE (1956)
Carolyn SAPP (1992)
Laurel Lea SCHAEFER (1972)
Kate SHINDLE (1998)
Bebe SHOPP (1948)
Norma SMALLWOOD (1926)
Shawntel SMITH (1996)
Marilyn VAN DERBUR (1958)

ANSWER, PAGE 216

GOODNESS!

Here we've collected some of the more unusual editions of the Bible ever created…though you probably won't be surprised at the revelation that some of the creations took place in our imagination. We have faith that you can tell the real Bibles from the ones we dreamed up.

The Geneva Bible (1560): Nicknamed the "Breeches Bible" because it was the first Bible to depict Adam and Eve wearing pants. Why? The editors thought Genesis 3:7 (the passage where Adam and Eve "sewed fig leaves together and made themselves *aprons*") was too racy…so they dumped "apron" and replaced it with "breeches."

The Wicked Bible (1631): This Bible gets its name from a typo in Exodus 20:14, which reads, "Thou shalt commit adultery." The printers were fined 300 pounds (they're just lucky they didn't also misprint "thou shalt not kill"), and the edition was immediately suppressed. Less than 10 of the original print run of 1,000 Bibles are thought to still be in existence. And they're worth a fortune.

An Aid to Memorizing the Bible (1785): Back when piety was more in fashion, there was a vogue for memorizing entire books of the Bible. The more books you could recite by heart, the more pious you were. This extra-abbreviated Bible was small enough to fit in one's pocket, and contained only the first three words of every verse in the Bible (well…except for "Jesus wept," presumably), meant to help someone jog their memory without inadvertently reading the entire verse.

The Smile Bible (1969): In the 1960s a lot of hippies found God while they were in an altered state; one of them was Ken Babbs (one of Ken Kesey's Merry Pranksters). After he got religion and read the Bible, he was appalled at the actions of the angry Old Testament God and rewrote the Bible to replace the vengefulness with nothing but peace and love. For instance, when Adam and Eve eat the forbidden fruit, they are "rewarded for their initiative" by being allowed to leave the "boring old Garden of Eden, where nothing ever happens." And in a twist worthy of *Dallas*, the entire book of Job turns out to be a dream.

The Black Bible Chronicles (1993): Subtitled *A Survival Manual for the Street*, this is a street-language version of the first five books of the Old Testament. ("Thou shalt not steal" appears as "You shouldn't be takin' from your homeboys"; "Thou shalt not kill" translates "Don't waste nobody"; and "Thou shalt not commit adultery" emerges as "Don't mess around with someone else's ol' man or ol' lady.") The book was written by a Houston, Texas, Sunday school teacher to help reach inner-city kids. "Over the years, I have found that kids just pick up on this language. For them, it's a kick. As my daughter would say, 'It's tight.'"

The Klingon Authorized Version (still in progress): The *Star Trek* fans at the Klingon Language Institute aren't satisfied with merely translating Shakespeare back into the "original Klingon." No, they've also begun the Klingon Bible Translation Project. Sample translation: John 3:16 ("For God so loved the world, that he gave his only begotten Son, that whosoever believeth in him should not perish but have everlasting life") reads: "toH qo' muSHa'pu'qu'-mo' JoH'a', wa' puqloDDaj nobpu' ghaH 'ej ghaHbaq Harchugh vay', vaj not Hegh ghaH, 'ach yln jub ghajbeh ghaH."

And now if you'll excuse us, we need to go buy more apostrophes.

ANSWER, PAGE 215

FREE ADVICE

…from some friends of Uncle John's. If you need directions on how to solve this puzzle, see page 5.

1.

	G					U	R			T		K		T
	I	N	E	Y	H	I	R		P	E	C	K	V	R
N	N	V	U	R	L	E	S	S	P	Y	C	A	E	E
A	E	O	T	N	O	T	S	U	S	O	O	U	E	M

2.

	E			H		H	C			E		I	E	
M	N		T	F	E	N	E		H	A	A	B	E	
M	B		F	A	I	E	C	H	S	I	A	T	E	
B	R	I	E	S	E	S	E	R	M	G	N	V	N	D
I	Y	E	S	P	T	B	E	E	R	E	K	T	S	G

3.

	I						T	T						
L	D	L	I		P	I	R	E		T				I
T	A	L	Y	N	E	C	O	H	N	C	O	F	B	E
U	L	E	I	S	W	A	R	U	C	T	E	C	S	F
E	H	T	S	S	G	N	S	E	T	A	O	S	H	D

ANSWER, PAGE 216

NUMEROLOGY

See if you can fill in the blanks with the correct number from the group below.

1. Researchers David Blanchflower of Dartmouth College (USA) and Andrew Oswald of the University of Warwick (Great Britain) studied 100,000 people of different ages and back grounds. They found out that happiness tends to be the lowest around age 40, and goes up after that. Furthermore, "a lasting marriage brings about the same amount of happiness as an extra $_____ in yearly income."

2. In her entire lifetime, a female hummingbird will lay at most _____ eggs.

3. The patron saint of dentists: St. Apollonia. Why? She reportedly had her teeth pulled out in A.D. _____ by an anti-Christian mob.

4. "My dog is worried about the economy because Alpo is up to 99 cents a can. That's almost $_____ in dog money."
   —Joe Weinstein

5. The most stars you can possibly see without a telescope is about _____.

6. A physician in Nairobi, after removing a bean from a young girl's ear, jammed it back in when her parents came up short on cash for the $_____ operation.

7. Thomas Jefferson wrote the Declaration of Independence in _____ days.

8. If you're an average U.S. male, you'll spend _____ hours shaving in your lifetime.

9. New Zealand sheep outnumber New Zealanders _____ to one.

10. You exhale air at an average speed of _____ miles per hour.

2 4 6 7 13 18 249

2,965 4,000 100,000

ANSWER, PAGE 216

* * * * *

ORGAN DONORS, BUT WITHOUT PERMISSION

It's kind of creepy, but a lot of the body parts of famous people are owned by museums or private collectors. Four of the following fall into that category. One is probably six feet under. Can you dig around and find it?

a) Einstein's brain
b) Napoleon's, er, "manhood"
c) Galileo's middle finger
d) Stonewall Jackson's arm
e) Lord Byron's nose

ANSWER, PAGE 216

WANNA BET?

There are a lot of poker variants in the world—way too many to fit on a single playing card (unless you write really, really small). But we managed to fit 41 of them in the ace of spades below. Care to bet how long it will take to find them all? And when you're done, the leftover letters will reveal a bit of wisdom about gambling in general.

```
S O M E E T E P N I A R B E M A L O T N E
A       L S R K E D M Z E O G N I B A W H
Y   W   E O P A S S T H E T R A S H E M E
N       V D O N E L T G E A M C B D W L E
A   S   A M A U U H E N W A Y O C R S H A
Y   G   T S M H E N A I G A B N V P N T E
L T R H O E C C A C O E M M U D O E A E N
G S O E R S N M I M S I V W D A C P C X A
U L C R Y E P R U L O Y O A D T H P I A A
E T E T W E R D O E N O T H H A V E X S E
H A R N A U J E B Y L N O N A C E R E H T
T I Y S H M U C H W   O M O S N C E M O L
D P S Y C H O Y O       N T F H A A J L T
N A T W I A S R           I O A R T A D R
A I O U T E T               L B D B C E U
D G R T A H I               L N E C K M H
A O E O N M P L     N     E Y S G U T S G
B W D V N A P A L M   A T E A A G N H S I
E P O W I E A O R       V B I N E F E A H
H O T C C F B T W O T M T Y E N L S S T D
T K S O N M Y T A O L H I N N S E T H N N
D E I N I C S T P T G E F O R U E G I A A
O R M L C B S T R I L I I N G I R B F S H
O S A U C T I O N O E N G L I S H S T U D
G A T I S L N D F I F Z E D B S T   E   N
E Y R E P A I D E H T E G N A H C   R   O
H M A S R M A R I A G E E R G L O       C
T I C T A C T O E R I A T R S T E   I   E
N T H G I R S I E C I R P E H T E       S
M F I V E C A R D S T U D W I T H A B U G
```

ABYSSINIA
ANACONDA
AUCTION
BINGO
BUDDHA'S FOLLY
CHANGE THE DIAPER
CINCINNATI
DIRTY SCHULTZ
DR. PEPPER
ELEVATOR
ENGLISH STUD
FIVE CARD STUD WITH A BUG
GROCERY STORE DOTS
GUTS
HAVE A HEART
HEINZ
HENWAY
HURRICANE
JACK THE SHIFTER
LAMEBRAIN PETE
LIMBO
LINOLEUM
MEXICAN SWEAT
MIDNIGHT BASEBALL
NAPALM
NAVY NURSE
OMAHA
PAI GOW POKER
PASS THE TRASH
PSYCHO
SECOND HAND HIGH
SPLIT POT
TEXAS HOLD 'EM
THE GOOD, THE BAD, AND THE UGLY
THE PRICE IS RIGHT
THERE CAN ONLY BE JUAN
THREE FORTY FIVE
THREE-LEGGED RACE
TIC-TAC-TOE
TRASH BIN
WOOLWORTH

ANSWER, PAGE 217

A LESSON IN PALM-READING

"Welcome to Madam Zora's. Sit down next to me and give me your hand… Oh! That's interesting…"

1	2	3	4	■	5	6	7	■	■	8	9	10	■	11	12	13
14				■	15			■	16				17			
18				19				■	20							
21			■	22				23							■	■
■	■	24	25			■	26			■	27				28	29
30	31			■	■	32				33	■	34				
35				36	■	37					38	■	■	39		
40					41		■	42				43	■	■	■	■
44						■	■	■	■	■	45		46	47	48	49
■	■	■	■	50		51	52	53	■	54						
55	56	57	■	■	58				59		■	60				
61			62	63	■	64					■	■	65			
66					67	■	68			■	69	70			■	■
■	■	71				72				73			■	74	75	76
77	78							■	79				80			
81								■	82			■	83			
84			■	85			■	■	86			■	87			

ACROSS

1 Flat-topped desert hill
5 Strike caller
8 ___ *Bilko* (Steve Martin movie)
11 Snakelike fish
14 Dumbstruck
15 Sheepish sound?
16 Burrowing crustacean
18 Wide, open palms mean you're…
20 Long, skinny hands mean you're…
21 Org. remembered in April
22 Hairy fingers mean you're…
24 "What ___ now?!"
26 Gabor of *Green Acres*
27 Begetting
30 ___ test (prototype debugging)
32 Actress Mercedes
34 Electronics brand
35 Drawbacks
37 Remove, as weeds
39 Racket string material
40 Stepping on the gas
42 Food fish with a funny name
44 Long ring fingers mean you're…
45 Narrow palms mean you're…
50 Twilled fabric
54 Boat built by Fulton
55 Quick punch
58 Mother ___ (Peace Prize winner)
60 Adoptee in *Silas Marner*
61 In any way
64 *Pride and Prejudice* hero
65 The Sex Pistols's genre
66 Impressionist Pierre Auguste ___
68 By way of
69 Iridescent gem
71 Long index fingers mean you're…
74 Tool with teeth
77 Fingers that bulge at each joint mean you're…
79 Round-shaped hands mean you're…
81 Brief breaks on long drives
82 Outback bird
83 Company that comes a-calling
84 Stomach muscles
85 "___ Drives Me Crazy" (1989 hit song)
86 Knock
87 Small salamander

DOWN

1 *The Gift of the* ___ (O. Henry tale)
2 Water pitcher
3 Lots of lines on your palm mean you're…
4 Suffix for lemon or lime
5 Sinker of ships
6 *Octopussy* actress Adams
7 Low-tech printing board
8 Bathroom bar
9 Adhesives
10 Falling-blocks video game
11 Wearing away
12 ___ de Cologne
13 Bathroom scale units (abbr.)
16 Carson's sidekick
17 Cutlass ___ (Oldsmobile model)
19 Hitter's credit
23 Civil rights leader Medgar ___
25 Ointment
28 Greenwich Village sch.
29 Acquired
30 Polar ice mass
31 Always
32 Toupee, slangily
33 Bathroom in Britain
36 Caesar and Vicious
38 Racetrack expert
41 "No" in Russia
43 Leg joint
46 Letter after iota
47 Short fingers mean you're…
48 "No" in Germany
49 Trash
51 Like fire engines
52 Aquarium floor coverings
53 Spooky
54 "I should ___ not!"
55 Cookie container
56 Had dinner
57 Highwaymen
59 Not as readily available
62 Ransacks
63 Puts restrictions on
67 Canon competitor
69 Get the better of
70 Tiger's org.
72 Back of the neck
73 ___ *la Douce*
75 Acknowledge
76 Departed
77 Person who's good with nos.
78 Bone connected to the sternum
80 Soak up the sun

ANSWER, PAGE 218

MISFITS QUIZ #2

Once again, we'd like to present you with some outrageous choices, four of which—despite their seeming outrageousness—are absolutely true and real. Your job is to find the **one answer** in each group that **doesn't** fit the category; the one we made up to fool you (heh-heh-heh).

1. Real (though exceedingly odd) plants:
   a) Starfish flower—A plant that looks and smells like a dead starfish, so that it can be pollinated by flies
   b) *Welwitschia mirabilis*—A tree with a three-foot trunk and two leaves that can grow as long as 20 feet
   c) Sugarbush—A flower with seeds that will open only if scorched by fire
   d) Strangle vine—A nocturnal plant that can encircle and trap sleeping tree mice
   e) Sandbox tree—A tree with fruit that explodes loudly when ripe, scattering the seeds up to 15 feet away

2. Actual TV show pilots:
   a) *Mickey and the Contessa*—A down-and-out European noblewoman (Eva Gabor) is hired as a housekeeper by an uncouth American basketball coach
   b) *Captain Rusty*—A 17th-century pirate (Elliott Gould) sails through the Bermuda Triangle and reemerges in present-day California, where a group of lifeguards help him adjust to modern life
   c) *The Decorator*—An interior decorator (Bette Davis) insists on moving in with her clients to get a sense of their taste, and manages to unravel their personal problems while beautifying their homes
   d) *Poochinski*—A hard-nosed cop (Peter Boyle) is murdered in the line of duty and comes back as a flatulent talking dog fighting crime alongside his former partner
   e) *Where's Everett?*—A family man (Alan Alda) adopts an invisible alien baby that has been left on his doorstep

3. Actual country music song titles:
   a) "I Wish My Beer Was As Cold As You"
   b) "I've Been Flushed from the Bathroom of Your Heart"
   c) "Mama, Get the Hammer (There's a Fly on Papa's Head)"
   d) "I've Got the Hungries for Your Love and I'm Waiting in Your Welfare Line"
   e) "You Stuck My Heart in an Old Tin Can and Shot It off a Log"

4. Things the average rat can do:
   a) Tread water for a week
   b) Fall five stories without being harmed
   c) Gnaw through lead pipes and cinder blocks
   d) Wriggle through holes the size of a quarter
   e) Scale brick walls

5. Actual (though not much sought-after) recordings:
   a) *Music to Make Automobiles By*—sound effects from an auto assembly line, backed by an orchestra
   b) "Granny's Mini-skirt"—a bluegrass "rap" song from Irene Ryan, who played Granny on *The Beverly Hillbillies*
   c) *Bobby Breaux and the Pot-Bellied Pig*—a 450-lb. boar grunts while Bobby Breaux plays slightly altered standards such as "Amazing Grease"
   d) *Where No Man Has Gone Before*—*Star Trek* alums George Takei (Sulu) and Nichelle Nichols (Uhura) sing gospel
   e) *The Sound of Combat Training*—featuring such tracks as "Inoculation" and "Mess Hall"

ANSWER, PAGE 217

WORD ROW

Remember those palindromes from the beginning of the book? Well, they're back. And forward. And up and down and diagonal. If you can find every one from this batch, feel free to shout "Yay!" in either direction. Once you've found all 46 palindromes in the grid, the leftover letters will reveal a palindrome that only a word freak could love. Proceed at your own risk.

H E N O L E M O N S N O M E L O N R R M E S

R I S E T O V O T E S I R N D I A L A I D A

E W T O O H O T T O H O O T N W O I D D T H

P O E S P I T Q T I P S W R E O S V E N A E

A N F O E A R Y O U O T L P E A O E I L I R

P T O T N X T O P N B A A A S D M N F D R D

E O P N N K A Y A K O N T S T E A O I O T E

R N A T E B I T A T I B E T A N N T E N E T

A S R S N P U T N C T L M A C N Y O D T R I

C N T N D E O T I O F A Y F K I D N I N N G

E O Y E A Y V N P L O M M A C S Y E S O A S

C T T N O O A E E U A N E T A S N V O D T O

A N R T I P M S R N P G T S T I A I N U I L

R O A E E S S I T O S I A A S N M L N M A O

D W P W F A I R D C D D L P X N O A O P S G

S T A T S E A S I I G D W S N E S I S M N I

T A S I N C R A M V D E O G S D S N I U A G

D R A W K W A R D I T I R R D L I U D D O O

R M S C T U P S E C T O M N E D I U E D R L

A B A P R O Y A M I M A Y O R V N P O U O O

T R P T E G A D N O B O N D A G E G U O S S

T O P S P O T N U R S E S R U N I N L P E T

ANNA
A TOYOTA
CIVIC
DEIFIED
DENNIS SINNED
DIAL AID
DON'T NOD
DR. AWKWARD
DUMP MUD
ED IS ON NO SIDE
EGAD! NO BONDAGE
GNU DUNG
GO, DOG
KAYAK
LIVE NOT ON EVIL
MA IS AS SELFLESS AS I AM
MR. OWL ATE MY METAL WORM
NAOMI, DID I MOAN?
NATE BIT A TIBETAN
NEVER ODD OR EVEN
NO LEMONS, NO MELON
NO, SON
NURSES RUN
PARTY TRAP
PA'S A SAP
PAST A FAT SAP
PUPILS SLIP UP
RACE CAR
RADAR
REFER
REPAPER
RISE TO VOTE, SIR
ROY, AM I MAYOR?
SEX AT NOON TAXES
SOLO GIGOLOS
SO MANY DYNAMOS
SPIT Q-TIPS
STACK CATS
STATS
SUE US
TENET
TOO HOT TO HOOT
TOP SPOT
TRACK CART
WE PANIC IN A PEW
WONTONS? NOT NOW

ANSWER, PAGE 218

LET ME WRITE SIGN—I SPEAK ENGLISH

Something to comfort you: When you're traveling in foreign countries, you may not be the only one having a hard time making yourself understood—as these examples of hotel signs from abroad show. If you need directions on how to solve this puzzle, see page 5.

1.
ON A MENU AT A POLISH HOTEL

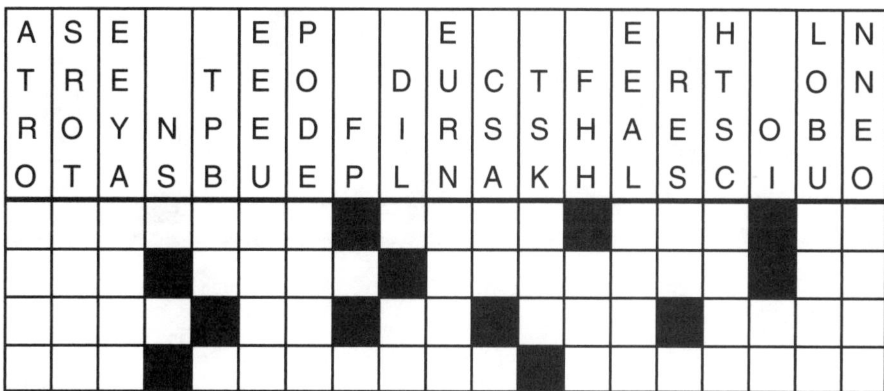

2.
AT AN ATHENS HOTEL

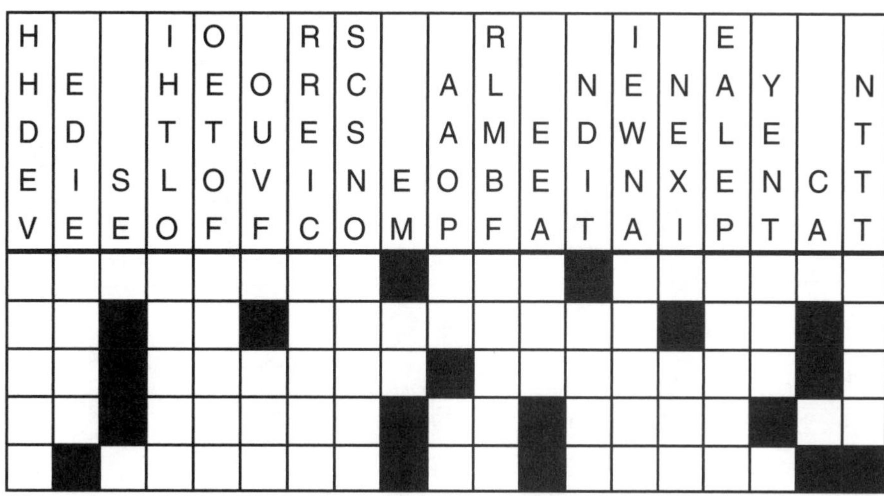

3.
IN A BUCHAREST HOTEL LOBBY

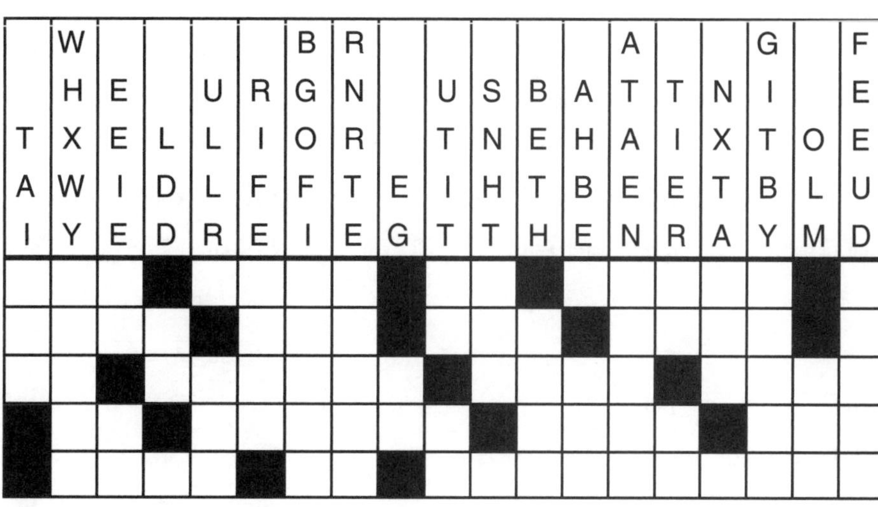

ANSWER, PAGE 217

WATCH YOUR STEP!

Directions for solving are on page 11.

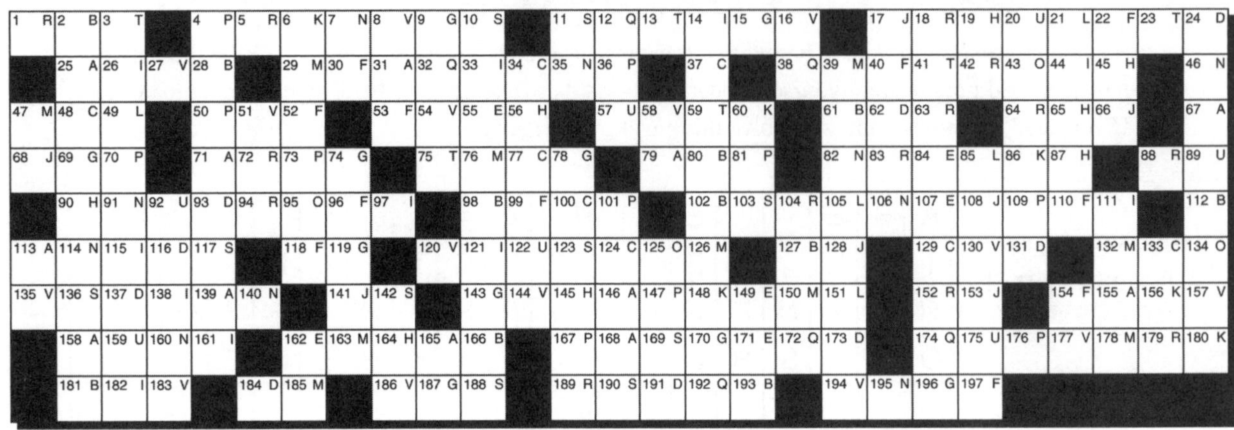

A. Small E. B. White creation (2 wds.)

158 31 113 155 165 79 67 168 25 71 146 139

B. Tony Hillerman mystery of 1984 (2 wds.)

28 80 98 112 2 181 102 193 61 127 166

C. Never (3 wds.)

37 129 133 77 48 34 124 100

D. Harris novel that introduced Hannibal Lecter (2 wds.)

173 131 116 24 93 62 191 184 137

E. Nonstick synthetic

171 162 55 84 107 149

F. Participation

40 30 99 118 53 22 96 154 52 110 197

G. Author of the novel *High Fidelity* (2 wds.)

15 170 69 78 187 196 119 9 143 74

H. Chris Elliott's 1990–1992 sitcom (3 wds.)

45 90 56 65 19 145 87 164

I. Citrus soda brand (2 wds.)

121 115 14 44 111 161 138 33 182 97 26

J. Unquestionably Gwen Stefani's band! (2 wds.)

108 141 66 153 68 17 128

K. Irate, often with "off"

60 148 6 156 86 180

L. Criminal-type caper

49 21 85 151 105

M. Leveling (2 wds.)

29 163 132 185 47 126 150 76 39 178

N. Tom Clancy novel and popular video game (2 wds.)

160 114 7 35 82 195 46 140 106 91

O. Agenda component

43 134 125 95

P. Good-natured talk or banter (hyph.)

36 109 167 81 176 101 147 50 4 70 73

Q. Homeless wanderers of the Great Depression

192 12 38 172 32 174

R. Bruce Springsteen's backup group (4 wds.)

152 72 18 83 63 88 189 179 94 1

64 104 5 42

S. Delaware's nickname and distinction (2 wds.)

142 190 11 117 103 169 10 136 123 188

T. "Western" egg dish

59 13 23 41 3 75

U. Dazed and confused (3 wds.)

89 159 175 122 57 20 92

V. Heath Ledger adventure remake of 2002 (3 wds.)

183 130 157 194 58 144 177 120 8 27

186 51 54 135 16

ANSWER, PAGE 218

WOULD WE LIE TO YOU—FIVE?

Yeah! That's the ticket! This time, the subject is phrase origins. But where the heck did they come from in the first place? Find the one true answer in each set.

1. Studying for a test is sometimes referred to as "boning up." Why?
   a) This refers to a very old analogy about knowledge: the "bones" are the underlying concepts of a subject. To "bone up" for a test therefore means to review the basics.
   b) The first and most important course taught in medical school is anatomy; every other class refers back to it in some way or another. If a med student had to refresh his old anatomy knowledge in order to pass a more advanced class, it was jokingly said that he needed to "bone up."
   c) In the early 1900s, a publishing firm named Bohn put out a guide, similar to today's Cliff's Notes, that helped students pass Greek and Latin courses. To "Bohn up" meant to study the guide, though the spelling soon changed to "bone up."

2. To "get someone's goat" is to severely aggravate them. Why?
   a) In old European farming communities, most farmers kept a goat or two to supply milk. If thieves made off with a sheep or a chicken it was a mere nuisance, but if they "got your goat" it was a severe aggravation.
   b) Nervous racehorses were often given goats as stablemates, because they had a calming effect. Once a horse became attached to its goat, it would get upset if the goat disappeared, so devious gamblers could take advantage of this fact by taking away a horse's goat the night before the race; the distraught horse always ran poorly.
   c) "Goat" was Victorian-era slang for "beard," so to "get one's goat" was to playfully pull on a man's beard. In Victorian England, touching another man's person was considered overly familiar—so tugging on a man's beard was an unpardonable offense, practiced only by the lower classes.

3. To leave someone in a desperate situation is to "leave them in the lurch." What the heck is a lurch?
   a) It's the side-to-side sway of a ship in bad weather. The lurch was twice as bad for those up on the rigging or in the crow's-nest. Any sailor caught up high when a sudden storm hit was said to have been "left in the lurch."
   b) "Lurch" is an old slang term for a debtor's prison. If you didn't have a friend or relative to come in and pay your debt, you were "left in the lurch."
   c) "Lurch" derives from *lourche*, a French game resembling backgammon. To be "in the lurch" was to be so far behind in a game that you had no chance of winning. The term was eventually applied to any situation that looked hopeless.

4. To "chew the fat" is to gab. Where did that come from?
   a) Salted pork skin was a staple food on old sailing vessels because it didn't spoil, but it was almost wholly fat. Sailors only ate it when all the other food was gone, and they generally complained while doing so—idle chatter that came to be known as "chewing the fat."
   b) Inviting a guest over to "chew the fat" was originally a jokey way of saying, "Come eat with us"—but because it was only used in dinner invitations, it encompassed the social aspects of dining. Before long, the term was used to mean "socialize," with or without food.
   c) Actually, the origin of this phrase is ridiculously simple: chewing fat involves a lot of jaw movement, and so does gabbing.

5. A smartly dressed person is said to be "dressed to the nines." Where'd we get that?
   a) For as long as our number system has been decimal, the number 10 has denoted perfection. To "dress to the nines," therefore, is to dress as closely to perfection as one can get.
   b) The "nines" are the hours between 9:00 P.M. and 10:00 P.M., when higher-born—and better-dressed—people generally arrived at country dances in old England.
   c) Actually, this phrase has nothing to do with the number nine. It's derived from the Old English expression dressed to *then eyne*, which means "dressed to the eyes."

ANSWER, PAGE 217

BOND, JAMES BOND

We've shaken and stirred some top-secret facts about 007, the world's favorite spy. For instructions and hints on how to solve, see page 15.

1. WAZ KNRFXHZNU VPMOGGT WNPHDZF *UZOM *HRMMZNT PMWR OXFPWPRMPMQ VRN *IOJZU *ERMF RM VPGJ ET WZGGPMQ APJ WAZT BZNZ ZYKZNPJZMWPMQ BPWA HOJZNO UZWXKU.

2. *JTK *WDZUJKM WQYKB ENZ KTUZ JK *AJFBG QW ENZ *VZGE *JKBJZG AL *STUZG *AQKB, TK QFKJEN-QDQMJHTD HDTGGJH. NZ VTKEZB ENZ GJUXDZGE, BYDDZGE, XDTJKZGE-GQYKBJKM KTUZ ENTE NZ HQYDB WJKB. *STUZG *AQKB GZZUZB XZFWZHE.

3. *OEQS *IQERN ZEC LRX LA NYX ATQCN MXLMUX NL CES RL NL NYX *BEHXC *DLRK QLUX. *MENQTOV *HOILLYER EUCL QXBXONXK NYX QLUX LR HLQEU IQLWRKC EC NLL FTLUXRN.

4. AHRWECR KIKG JKKHGV RWK LHBD, *TEWG *QUPPX ZEDOEJKY RWK "*TUDKJ *QEGY *RWKDK," EGK EL RWK DEJR PKZEVGHFUQBK RWKDKJ HG *WEBBXAEEY WHJREPX, UGY AUJ OUHY BKJJ RWUG LHIK WCGYPKY YEBBUPJ LEP WHJ KLLEPR.

ANSWER, PAGE 217

THE TERM-INATORS

Don't be scared. They're just some people who've coined some very familiar terms.

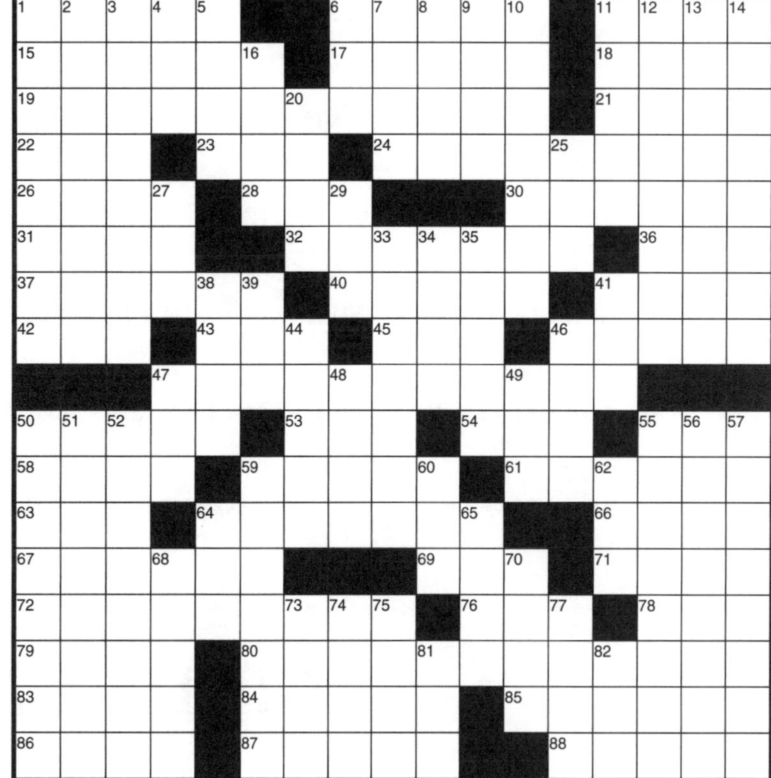

ACROSS

1 About ready to drop
6 Filmmaker Lynch
11 Head of the co.
15 Slowly, in music
17 ___ Club (beer brand)
18 Italy's San ___
19 He coined the term "G-men"
21 Muscat and ___
22 AT&T competitor
23 Zodiacal sign
24 He coined the term "gossip column"
26 Medicinal herb
28 Long sandwich
30 Without straining a muscle
31 Stylist's concern
32 Glowing
36 Penpoint
37 James of *Gunsmoke*
40 Broad smiles
41 City that makes divorce easy
42 Ahab was missing one
43 Word ignored by alphabetizers
45 Command to Fido
46 Not on the up-and-up
47 He coined the term "hike" as it's used in football
50 *Presumed Innocent* author Scott
53 Letter after sigma
54 Candied veggie
55 Glove box item
58 Fencer's blade
59 Like haughty people
61 ___ shop (second-hand store)
63 TV alien
64 Poem attributed to Homer
66 One conquered by Pizarro
67 Brandy's TV show
69 Brief snooze
71 Rams' remarks
72 He first applied the term "godfather" to mafiosos
76 Some people think it's what "pizza" means
78 Hot tub
79 Summer drinks
80 He suggested the term "hello" as a telephone greeting (to the chagrin of Alexander Graham Bell, who preferred "ahoy")
83 Golf bag pegs
84 Synagogue scroll
85 Lawn pest
86 Small whirlpool
87 Butler's love interest
88 They smell

DOWN

1 Gorgeous palace in India
2 Southern belle's exclamation
3 Sending via shortwave
4 Poached item
5 Mechanism on old telephones
6 Twosome
7 Tiny particle
8 ___ *Las Vegas* (Elvis movie)
9 Cake decorator
10 Grows dim
11 Boat fronts
12 Stayed behind
13 Corresponding the modern way
14 Blues man Williamson
16 Metal-bearing minerals
20 Time for a massage
25 Make lace
27 Before, to Wordsworth
29 Paper or plastic
33 He coined the term "nerd"
34 Four, on some clock faces
35 Keyed up
38 Put away, as carry-ons
39 Library admonition
41 *A Beautiful Mind* director Howard
44 Logbook item
46 Woman, to Sam Spade types
47 Java
48 Fedoras and derbies
49 Damage
50 Person who's on your side
51 Made available on the Net
52 Presided over a game
55 Battle of Bull Run site
56 *The Untouchables* bad guy
57 Who "them" refers to, in "Let them eat cake"
59 Get comfortable with
60 Japanese currency
62 Bro or sis
64 "Now I see!"
65 Chatters away
68 Bully's target
70 Fisherman's hangout
73 "This is not good"
74 Author ___ Neale Hurston
75 Bridge column writer Sharif
77 Garden in Genesis
81 Cry similar to 64 Down
82 Marriage ceremony words

ANSWER, PAGE 219

GOOFY HEADLINES

We've broken up some very silly—but real—headlines into consecutive three-letter strings and then rearranged the three-letter group in alphabetical order. The numbers that follow signify the number of letters in the original. For instance, if the headline was DEWEY WINS, the scrambled version would look something like this: INS EYW DEW (5 4).

1. BRI CHE ING LYT MET NIN OWA RDS RIC SGR SYS TAI TEM UDG (7 6 10 7 6 6)

2. ICE KIL LMA NER NWI POL THT VTU (6 4 3 4 2 5)

3. ACH AND BAD COC INH KRO LYH SLA URT USB (9 5, 7 5 4)

4. ABB EAT EDD HBY LCA LED MAN NAT SHO SRU TST URA USE (3 4, 7; 5 2 7 6 5)

5. AGE ARM AXE DCO ENR ERW ESF ITH JUR WIN (7 3 7 6 4 3)

ANSWER, PAGE 218

GIDDY-*UP*!

Small crostic puzzles are solved just like the big ones (directions on page 11) but the first letter of the fill-in words **do not** spell out a hidden message.

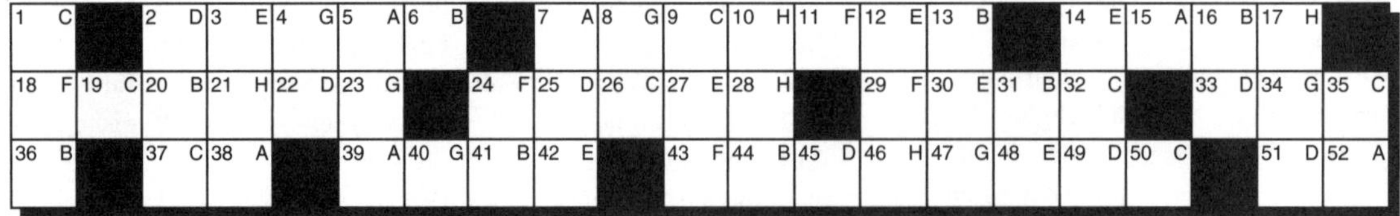

A. Railroad stations

__ __ __ __ __ __
39 7 52 15 38 5

B. Not quite "teens"

__ __ __ __ __ __ __ __
44 31 6 41 36 20 16 13

C. Classical violin great from Genoa

__ __ __ __ __ __ __ __
9 1 50 35 32 26 19 37

D. Mischievous—maybe worse

__ __ __ __ __ __ __
49 45 51 22 2 33 25

E. Big name in pizza

__ __ __ __ __ __ __
12 3 14 48 27 30 42

F. Gives, but not permanently

__ __ __ __ __
24 18 11 29 43

G. Oreo-like cookie that was introduced before Oreos

__ __ __ __ __ __
34 23 47 4 40 8

H. Environmentally friendly

__ __ __ __ __
28 21 10 17 46

ANSWER, PAGE 226

HISTORICAL HINDSIGHTS

People can be so cynical—especially about history. To see what three very smart people have said on the subject, choose a letter from each column and drop it into its correct place in the grid.

1.

M	H			E		W	R		T				O	T			
H	E	E	I	E		E	D		A	C	T	U	A	L	L	Y	
T	Y	O	N	P	A	O	T	O	Y	U	T	D	H	I	N	T	O
R	A	P	P	S	N	S	N	L	B	E	W	H	A	W	S	S	O
			■					■									■
								■				■					
		■			■					■					■		
					■						■					■	■

2.

			C			Y						O					
T	I	A	A		T	E		T	I	S	O	I	D		L	Y	
A	O	H	G	T	R	A	R	D	I	F	T	F	C	Y	O	U	
H	T	N	E	E	B	R	U	D	I	F	I	I	T	A	T	T	T
S	R	M	V	E	T	Y	N	H	H	S	F	N	R	U	N	O	T
		■					■										■
	■							■			■			■			■
					■				■					■			
■				■						■			■				
				■			■								■	■	■

3.

E			T			O		R			Y			A	A	P	
T	I		T	O	A	T		I	E	O	E			E	C	K	E
H	F	W	H	O	R	Y		A	B	B	U		P	E	E	R	L
O	N	S	L	H	E	S	E	N	S	N	A	T	T	H	V	E	N
E	S	E	D	I	T	W	L	D	E	V	T	R	P	H	O	P	P
							■			■		■					■
		■					■						■				
		■					■						■				
				■					■			■					
	■				■							■					

ANSWER, PAGE 219

WHAT'LL YA HAVE?

Today's special…a heaping serving of diner lingo.

ACROSS

1 What a cowboy calls a lady
5 Rod used to reinforce concrete
10 See 32 Down
14 Antidote
15 Guy who starred in *Memento*
16 Laundry tumbler
17 What you'll get if you order "frog sticks"
19 The *Exxon Valdez*, e.g.
20 Cry from the crow's-nest
21 ___-Roman wrestling
23 Liz Taylor said it eight times
24 Opposite of "nay"
25 Fraction of a foot
28 What you'll get if you order "Bossy in a bowl"
30 Beethoven's "Fur ___"
31 Tries a running play
32 What you'll get if you order "wax"
38 Imposes a tax
39 Features in some backyards
40 Five-digit code
43 Congregation's exclamations
44 What you'll get if you order "nervous pudding"
45 Greenie in a martini
47 ___ sequitur
48 Type of anesthetic
49 Tree-chopper
50 What you'll get if you order "hounds on an island"
53 Get less intense
56 Christmas carols
57 What you'll get if you order "an M.D."
60 The first James Bond movie
61 American sp org.
64 Bon ___ (cleanser brand)
65 Cosmetics queen Lauder
67 Des Moines residents
69 *The Simpsons* mom
71 What you'll get if you order "Noah's boy on bread"
74 Blue-pencils
75 Look up to
76 Dies ___
77 Quench one's appetite
78 Famous boy band
79 Roadhouses

DOWN

1 *Back to the Future* hero Marty
2 Halos
3 Stadium
4 Repair clothes
5 Ump
6 Where to put a Beltone
7 Nautical prison
8 Caustic
9 Go to again, as a movie
10 Mr. Onassis
11 Frasier's ex
12 "Mashed Potato Time" singer Sharp
13 Road sign symbols
15 "Hooked on ___"
16 Dunderhead
18 Hot peppers
22 First asteroid to be discovered
26 Alliance headed by Jeff Davis
27 Nag incessantly
29 Jacksonville-to-Orlando dir.
30 "___ go bragh!"
32 With 10 Across, Hawkeye Pierce's portrayer
33 Interoffice communique
34 Divisible by two
35 Pepsi and RC
36 Where Edam cheese is made
37 "Hold on Tight" band
40 Coors clear malt beverage
41 Russia's "terrible" czar
42 They're chained to bank counters
44 *Midnight Cowboy* star Voight
45 Deep red shade
46 Majors and Marvin
48 Arctic Circle residents
49 Nucleotide found in DNA
50 Greens ___ (golfer's payment)
51 Coins of India
52 "Neither rain ___ sleet…"
53 He played Mingo on *Daniel Boone*
54 Warship fleet
55 *The ___ of St. Louis*
58 Actor Hawke
59 Learns from Uncle John, say
61 Monument of heaped stones
62 From ancient Peru
63 Cremation remains
66 One of many won by *The Sopranos*
68 *Band of Brothers* conflict
70 Airfone service provider
72 Act that's confessed to
73 Semicircle

ANSWER, PAGE 219

DEAD WRONG?

Here are some stories of strange and unusual events surrounding the deaths of famous people. The only catch is that some of them are complete lies. See if you can sort out the true stories from the false.

AESCHYLUS, 456 B.C.: Died when an eagle mistook his bald head for a rock and tried to crack open a tortoise's shell on it.

ATTILA THE HUN, A.D. 453: Died of a bloody nose on the night of his wedding feast; he choked to death on the blood in his sleep.

KING JOHN, 1216: Superstitious about bathing, King John of England took only one bath per year. As luck would have it, after this year's bath he slipped on the wet floor and cracked his head on the edge of his tub, killing himself.

IVAN THE TERRIBLE, 1584: Saw a comet and believed it was a sign he would soon die. His body then became swollen for no reason his doctors could determine, and he died a short while later.

TYCHO BRAHE, 1601: After hours of heavy drinking, he needed to relieve himself, but instead sat down for dinner with guests. Unfortunately, Tycho was very polite, and etiquette of the day forbade leaving the table during dinner. His bladder burst, and he died 11 days later.

JEAN-BAPTISTE LULLY, 1687: Lully conducted his orchestra so vigorously that he stabbed himself in the toe with his baton. The injury became infected, and, because Lully refused to have his toe (or, later, his leg) amputated, the infection spread, killing him.

GEORGE WASHINGTON, 1799: It's a myth that Washington had wooden teeth. He went through many sets of dentures in his life, but never any wooden ones. But his last set of dentures was so ill-made, it actually killed him. It was held on with metal springs that constantly and excruciatingly poked his gums and lips, and eventually the irritation developed into an open sore that became fatally infected.

U.S. MAJOR GENERAL JOHN SEDGWICK, 1864: During the Civil War, General Sedgwick tried to calm his troops on the front lines by saying, "I tell you they cannot hit an elephant at this distance." Just then he was shot in the head by a sharpshooter.

CHANG AND ENG BUNKER, 1874: The famous "Siamese twins" (who were actually Chinese) adopted the name "Bunker" after joining up with P. T. Barnum and becoming American citizens. Chang eventually pushed the pair to retire, though Eng still wanted to perform. Their enmity escalated until Eng strangled Chang to death in a heated argument. Overcome with remorse, Eng killed himself.

P. T. BARNUM, 1891: Barnum wanted to read his obituary before he died. The *New York Evening Sun* was happy to oblige, and printed it under the title "Great and Only Barnum: He wanted to read his Obituary; Here it is." Barnum repaid the favor by dying two weeks later.

BABE RUTH, 1948: Babe Ruth died of cancer, which is not very interesting in itself; the interesting part is that although Ruth knew he was sick, no one ever told him what he was suffering from.

ANSWER, PAGE 219

FRUITS & VEGGIES & MORE

This puzzle was inspired by the "Fruit & Veggie Quiz" in *Uncle John's All-Purpose Bathroom Reader*. We've expanded our original list to include lots of other foods and drinks favored by those who eschew, rather than chew, meat. Can you fit all 37 of the foodstuffs listed into the grid, crossword-style?

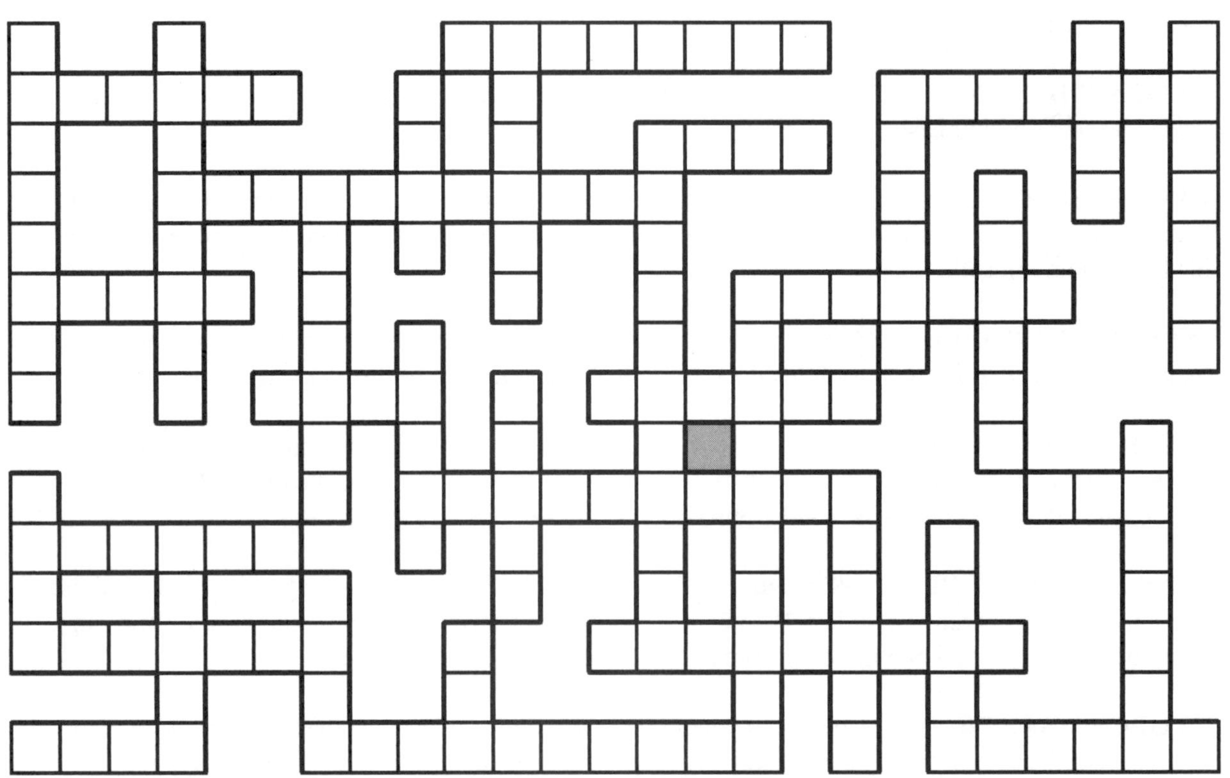

3 letter words
Poi
Tea

4 letter words
Corn
Figs
Nuts
Okra
Rice
Tofu
Yams

5 letter words
Beets
Honey
Limes
Plums
Seeds

6 letter words
Apples
Celery
Lemons
Melons
Olives
Onions
Sorrel
Squash

7 letter words
Cabbage
Granola
Lentils
Lettuce
Peaches
Soy milk

8 letter words
Avocados
Molasses
Tomatoes

9 letter word
Asparagus

10 letter words
Artichokes
Green beans
Tangerines

11 letter words
Cauliflower
Cranberries

ANSWER, PAGE 195

SPOONERISMS

Nineteenth-century Oxford academic Dr. William Spooner tripped over his tongue so many times—saying things like "you've hissed all my mystery lectures" instead of "you've missed all my history lectures"—that we now call any such switching around of sounds a Spoonerism. Dr. Spooner died in 1930 (sod rest his goal), but you can honor his memory by taking the phrases below and finding their 36 Spoonerized counterparts in the grid, reading horizontally, vertically, or diagonally. For example, if the phrase "battleships and cruisers," were on the list, you'd be looking for "cattle ships and bruisers." (If you're having trouble translating, you'll find a list of the Spoonerized phrases on the answer page.) No hidden message this time—and remember: You're looking for the Spoonerized translations in the grid!

```
T U S C D C I Z B L U S H I N G C R O W W N K
J G F Y K T H J G D G H P C F F L Q D E L A N
E K A J E L L I A R B W P X I L M U A L U K Y
G B P U F U F A P A F R I G O C R E L L K N P
W T A G H N R O P P O C H A M A W E L B N P O
A L R P V M S I S O I T S A G K P R A O E B O
V D R I S T H E B E A N D I Z Z Y O B I E I C
E B O W E R P A U L A B G W Y B I L E L O L S
T E T T D L E X I G A L T F U N E D N E F L T
H L S K I G A A J N R V I N L T H D E D A I U
E L A E A N R C N I J N N N O A B E C I N N O
S Y N W F U T E K V X Y I N G S N A S C I T R
A G D L O L R H T O P A S A T T M N E I D H T
I E K M E S Q S E H F O E U R E H M E C O E A
L N E O C E R X O S F P H C O D A E R L L F R
S E Y N A H G N Z S H L I I W T N Y H E S L B
L S S K P T E H O N A A I E N W D W T I A A Y
D J D J S F G I L S R U R U S O T F O J C N M
Y C C A G O L B A T W M S K X W A L Y T G K H
K H N I A P G N I R A O R E W O T A E K A H S
N F P L D I Z R H S I F D E M R A W F L A H U
R I N G S T A Y P U C C I H Y M T A P P O J H
Z N L Y Y U I T U O G N U L F S G A H I R G H
```

ACE OF SPADES
A SHOT IN THE DARK
BAD MANNERS
BRUSH MY HAT
CARROTS AND PEAS
CRUSHING BLOW
DEAR OLD QUEEN
DOWN TRAIN
EYE OF A NEEDLE
FILL IN THE BLANK
FLAGS HUNG OUT
FLIPPING CHANNELS

FUNNY BONE
HALF-FORMED WISH
HAZELNUT
HEALING THE SICK
IS THE DEAN BUSY
JAILBREAK
JELLY BEANS
JUNK MAIL
LIGHT A FIRE
LOVING SHEPHERD
NOBLE SONS OF TOIL
PACK OF LIES

PICK MY HAT UP
POPCORN
POURING RAIN
POWERBALL
SAVE THE WHALES
SCOUT TROOP
SLIP OF THE TONGUE
STINGRAY
TAKE A SHOWER
THREE-BEAN SALAD
WASTED TWO TERMS
WELL-OILED BICYCLE

ANSWER, PAGE 220

WHERE THE HECK DID *THAT* COME FROM?

Have you ever wondered where a certain word came from? Well, we're here to tell you. Sort of. Some of the word origins below are strictly kosher, but a few of them are from the mind of one of our near-criminal writers who's out to get you. Can you tell the real from the fake?

Debonair: From the French for "of good air." In the Middle Ages, people's health was judged partly by how they smelled. A person who gave off "good air" was presumed healthier and happier.

Jiggle: A corruption of "jigger," itself a corruption of "chigger," originally descriptive of the movements made by people suffering from itchy insect bites.

Gymnasium: Meant "to train naked" in ancient Greece, where athletes wore little or nothing.

Carnival: Literally means "Farewell, flesh." Refers to the traditional pre-Lenten feast (like Mardi Gras), after which people usually fasted.

Boor: From the same root as "boar," it seems to be the one insult related to that branch of the animal kingdom that didn't keep the same spelling (as opposed to "pig," "swine," and such).

Eleven: The Germanic ancestor of this word, *ain-lif*, translates as "one left over." That's what happens when you count to ten on your fingers and still have one left over.

Ballot: Italian term for "small ball or pebble." Italian citizens once voted by casting a small pebble or ball into one of several boxes.

Candidate: A combination of the Latin words that became "candid" and "data." Roman politicians attempted to give the impression that they were open and willing to provide any information to the public, which was certainly not always the case.

Hazard: From the Arabic words *al-zahr*, "a die," the name of a game played with dice. Then, as now, gambling was hazardous to your financial health.

Daisy: Comes from "day's eye." When the sun comes out, it opens its yellow eye.

Genuine: Originally means "placed on the knees." In ancient Rome, a father legally claimed his new-born child by sitting in front of his family and placing the child on his knee.

Gung ho: Means "very hungry" in Chinese. British colonialists in Hong Kong who loved the local cuisine heard it used to describe them, and took it as a reference to their enthusiastic eating habits.

ANSWER, PAGE 220

NOT FOR EXPORT

It's not easy selling things in the global economy—a lot of products lose something in translation. Particularly Japanese products, for some reason. Since that's where most of the unfortunately named products in the grid below came from, we've only indicated when the products originated elsewhere. Once you've found all 32 of them, the leftover letters will reveal a few more that definitely should have stayed on their own side of the globe.

```
                I P I P C
            C G R E O S O E N
        P P A E R C I U L R L E S
      H I S L M A M A P O C K E T Y
    A S J A P R P A N E N E S Y E L A
    W A T T I H C S P R P L O P P N P
  E U L G S S A F F E W L B I M B O R T
  S I S W L N I I F Z I U E R S L H R I
T N U E T O U I P S O N S O D I B I L K A
S A A S P I D C Y W P K E P O P E R S A P
U T C U E V E R Y J O Y P O P T U R B O E
F U R P O J M G P I C K L E E X H A C N A
A R A E E E D N E I R F O G N O B K N I N
  O D R F M H O M O S A U S A G E R R A
  T O P M U T A G I C W A N T T H S I E
    R I E C S P L I R T T L W E M V H
    U S M O S O B R U O Y E S A E S S
      S Y S A C W R N I T T S L I N
        G T A K R B K T L H A E T
            F Y O U Y R G D I
                R L M S Y
```

AIR SMASH (candy)
ASS GLUE (patent medicine—China)
BIMBO (donuts—Mexico)
BONGO FRIENDEE (car)
CALPIS NUDE (soft drink)
COLON PLUS (liquid detergent—Spain)
CREAP (powdered coffee creamer)
CRUNKY (chocolate)
EASE YOUR BOSOMS (coffee marketed as an antidote to stress)
EVERY JOY POP TURBO (car)
GOD-JESUS (toy robot)
HOMO SAUSAGE (beef jerky)
KOFF (beer—Finland)
KOWPIS (fermented milk drink)
LIBIDO (soda—China)
MAMA POCKETY (carrot-scented dish detergent)
MUCOS (soft drink—Philippines)
NAIVE LADY (toilet paper)
NATUROT (cookies)
PICKLE EX (candy)
PIPI (orangeade—Yugoslavia)
PLOPP (chocolate—Sweden)
POCARI SWEAT (sports drink)
POCKET WETTY (tissues)
POCKY (candy)
POLIO (laundry detergent—Czechoslovakia)
PORKY PORK (a presumably pork-flavored snack)
PSCHITT (soft drink—France)
SCRUM (car)
SLASH (gum)
SUPER PISS (solvent—Finland)
SUPER WINKY (condoms)

ANSWER, PAGE 220

AND IF YOU BELIEVE THAT ONE...TWO

Yes, we're at it again. Here are three odd-yet-true facts and one outright lie (shame on us). Can you spot the fib among the factual?

1. **Out of place**
   a) Most Panama hats are made in Ecuador
   b) The French poodle originated in Germany
   c) The English horn was invented in Austria
   d) A Dutch candy maker came up with Turkish delight

2. **Nonsensical names**
   a) Fort Worth, Texas, was never a fort
   b) Canada's Plains of Abraham are hilly
   c) Abraham Lincoln never slept in the White House's Lincoln Bedroom
   d) Russia's October Revolution is celebrated in November

3. **False advertising**
   a) There were no ponies in the Pony Express
   b) Sweet 'N' Low Soda is flavored with NutraSweet
   c) Eggo waffles don't contain any egg
   d) Kentucky Fried Chicken's Colonel Sanders was born in Indiana

4. **No, Mister President!**
   a) No man has ever been elected president twice and vice-president twice
   b) No only child has ever been elected president
   c) No bearded president has ever been a Democrat
   d) No president has been assassinated unless he was elected in a year ending with zero

5. **Spare parts**
   a) Cows have six stomachs
   b) Earthworms have five hearts
   c) Ducks have six eyelids
   d) Ants have five noses

6. **It's all relative**
   a) Alexander Graham Bell's father invented the burglar alarm
   b) Charles Darwin's cousin invented the IQ test
   c) Nelson Rockefeller's uncle bankrolled the pilot of *The Dick Van Dyke Show*
   d) Johnny Carson's brother directed *The Merv Griffin Show*

7. **Local color**
   a) The dolphins that live in the Amazon river are pink
   b) The blood of the horseshoe crab is sky-blue
   c) The sweat exuded by hot or excited hippopotami is red
   d) "Purple finches" are in fact green

8. **Late arrivals**
   a) The term "kangaroo court" was invented in the U.S., then brought to Australia
   b) Lederhosen were invented in Morocco, then brought to Bavaria
   c) Karate was invented in India, then brought to Japan
   d) Bagpipes were invented in Iran, then brought to Scotland

ANSWER, PAGE 219

THEM'S FIGHTIN' WORDS

Below are four lists of familiar words and phrases that became part of the English language during various wars or long-term occupations of foreign countries. We've put each list under a heading and used simple letter substitution to encode them, where E might equal L, D might be X, and so on. We've even solved the first word in each list to get you started. The code is exclusive to each list, but changes from one list to another.

COLONIALISM

FBCI = TREK

VKEEYLTK

VKEEYLTCCB

OCTPX

IAYIU

SYQAKPF

VKLVCLFBYFUKL VYEX

YXYBFACUT

VYWUVK

VYQAECBC

AT SEA

SABSMS = ARMADA

CSUZJ MYEJ S IZQ

PXC YD CKZ VRH

DRAGC-ASCZ

CXAJ S HFRJM ZLZ

PFZSA CKZ MZPUG

HSCCZJ MYEJ CKZ KSCPKZG

SC PFYGZ OXSACZAG

PXC SJM AXJ

HL CKZ HYSAM

WORLD WAR I

SALJAEY = FOXHOLE

GQ IJY IFYQXJYW

PGDDGQD GQ

IFYQXJ XATI

IFYQXJ UAZIJ

WJYEE WJAXV

WXFYTUGQD UYYUGYW

AMYF IJY IAB

QA-UTQ'W-ETQP

IFGB OGFY

THE KOREAN WAR

T.W.E.N. = M.A.S.H.

FWTFZZ KVHYWGQ

CZBGKD WKYGZQ

FVU ZVY

WGHEY HGRD

KNZCCDH

FVS YND PWHT

DSDFWBB-YZ-DSDFWBB

NZZKN

FHWGQJWENGQU

ANSWER, PAGE 221

SURVEY SAYS...

Remember the Fast Money round on *Family Feud*? Those answers come easy when you're sitting at home on the sofa...but imagine the pressure you'd feel on national TV. The clues in quotes and italics are actual questions asked on *Feud*, and the answers are actual answers given by flustered contestants.

ACROSS

1 On the ocean
6 Donkey's cry
10 Clothes designer Bill
15 *Something you might be allergic to*
16 Unaccompanied
17 Ward off
18 *Name a fruit that is yellow*
19 Bone alongside the radius
20 Consent (to)
21 ___ Doone
22 Diner owner on *Alice*
23 Hair-growth product
25 Newfangled crime evidence
26 Sticky substances
28 Right away
29 Noise made by a horse's hooves
30 India's first prime minister
31 Put to rest, as fear
33 Poison drinker's chaser, hopefully
36 Presider at Valhalla
37 Chew the fat
40 Boxing champ Riddick
41 Comic Sandler
43 Peaceful
45 *Something that flies that doesn't have an engine*
49 Trix, e.g.
50 Branch of phys.
51 Kevlar garment
52 Under the weather
53 Walt Kelly comic strip
55 Car door insets
58 Houston base-baller
59 Value
60 Scatters seeds
63 Attila, for one
64 Annoying one
65 *Monty Python*'s network
68 High-ranking
70 Ham radios' relatives
71 Town ___ (public announcer of old)
73 Word after curriculum or aqua
74 Model builder's need
76 *Name an item of clothing worn by the Three Musketeers*
77 Paradises
78 "Duke of ___"
79 *Name some-thing with a hole in it*
80 "Phooey!"
81 Button-eyed figure
82 Smallest amount

DOWN

1 Ohio city
2 Beauty queen's crown
3 ___ Fein
4 Halfway to married
5 Some people lie about theirs
6 *Name a song with moon in the title*
7 Subway bread
8 Advice columnist Landers
9 Celebrating anniversary #1
10 Talk big
11 Bequest
12 *Name a sign of the zodiac*
13 "___ evil, hear..."
14 *Something you do before going to bed*
15 Auctioneer's cry
22 "Mere" human being
24 Like a hooter
27 Triumphant shout
28 *Name a bird with a long neck*
30 Morticia, to Fester
32 Over again
33 Primitive calculators
34 Scientist's prize
35 Manipulate a baton
37 Parents pass them on
38 Existential depression
39 Defeats
42 Impress mightily
44 Girder securer
46 Shrill barks
47 Get (someone) dressed
48 ___ *a Crowd*
54 Reluctantly allowed
56 ___ *Doubtfire*
57 *The Candidate* director Michael
58 Obliquely
60 *A number you have to memorize*
61 Rust, for one
62 *Name something that floats in the bath*
65 Frequent flyers?
66 Infatuate, old-style
67 Off-camera workers
69 ___ *of the d'Urbervilles*
70 Ringlet
72 Author Jaffe
75 ___-Tzu (Taoism founder)
76 Hole-making tool

ANSWER, PAGE 227

PARLEZ-VOUS EUPHEMISMS?

One of Uncle John's favorite forms of speech is doublespeak. See if you can "translate" the terms used by businesses, educators, and advertisers on the left (100% guaranteed real!), and unscramble their English counterparts.

1. "Urban transportation specialist" ___ ___ ___ ___ ___ ___ ___ ___ ___
A B C V R R I D E

2. "Adverse weather visibility device"
___ ___ ___ ___ ___ ___ ___ ___ ___ ___ ___ ___ ___ ___ ___
H I D D S W E L I N W E P R I

3. "Renaturalize" ___ ___ ___ ___
N U T H

4. "Sea-air interface climatic disturbance" ___ ___ ___ ___
V A E W

5. "Judgmental lapse" ___ ___ ___ ___ ___
M E R C I

6. "Maximum incapacitation" ___ ___ ___ ___ ___ ___ ___ ___ ___ ___ ___ ___
H E D A T N Y P L E T A

7. "Physical pressure" ___ ___ ___ ___ ___ ___ ___
R O T T E R U

8. "Nutritional avoidance therapy" ___ ___ ___ ___
E D I T

9. "Induce adverse reaction" ___ ___ ___ ___
R A M H

10. "Therapeutic misadventure"
___ ___ ___ ___ ___ ___ ___ ___ ___ ___ ___ ___ ___ ___ ___ ___ ___ ___
L C A M D I E T I C C A P L A R E M

11. "Natural amenity unit" ___ ___ ___ ___ ___ ___ ___ ___
U O T O E U S H

12. "Organoleptic analysis" ___ ___ ___ ___ ___
L E M L S

13. "Intuitively counterproductive" ___ ___ ___ ___ ___ ___
D I T U S P

ANSWER, PAGE 220

APPROPRIATE AUTHORS

From the Your Name Is Your Destiny Department: See if you can match the honest-to-goodness real books (1–15) and their authors (a–o).

	Books		Authors
______	1. *The Abel Coincidence* (1969)	a.	Jane Arbor
______	2. *The Boy's Own Aquarium* (1922)	b.	William Battie, M.D.
______	3. *Causes of Crime* (1938)	c.	Walter Russell Brain
______	4. *Crocheting Novelty Potholders* (1982)	d.	Geoff Carless
______	5. *The Cypress Garden* (1969)	e.	J. N. Chance
______	6. *Diseases of the Nervous System* (1933)	f.	John Chipping
______	7. *How to Live a Hundred Years or More* (1927)	g.	Peter Elbow
		h.	George Fasting
______	8. *Illustrated History of Gymnastics* (1983)	i.	A. Fink
______	9. *Motorcycling for Beginners* (1980)	j.	Frank Finn
______	10. *Riches and Poverty* (1905)	k.	John Goodbody
______	11. *Running Duck* (1979)	l.	Paula Gosling
______	12. *The Skipper's Secret* (1898)	m.	L. G. Chiozza Money
______	13. *A Treatise on Madness* (1768)	n.	L. Macho
______	14. *Writing with Power* (1981)	o.	Robert Smellie
______	15. *Your Teeth* (1967)		

ANSWER, PAGE 221

MURPHY'S LAWS

You know about Murphy's Law—whatever can go wrong will go wrong—it's a basic learning tool of life. But it's not the only Murphy's Law. There are a few others, and the odds are you've had a run-in with them. Explain as clearly as you can what the following laws consist of. Then check the answer page where you'll not only get the answer, you'll get to see the scientific analysis of why (or whether) they hold true.

Murphy's Law of Buttered Bread

Murphy's Law of Socks

Murphy's Law of Lines

Murphy's Law of Maps

ANSWER, PAGE 222

THE COLORIZED VERSION

Directions for solving are on page 11.

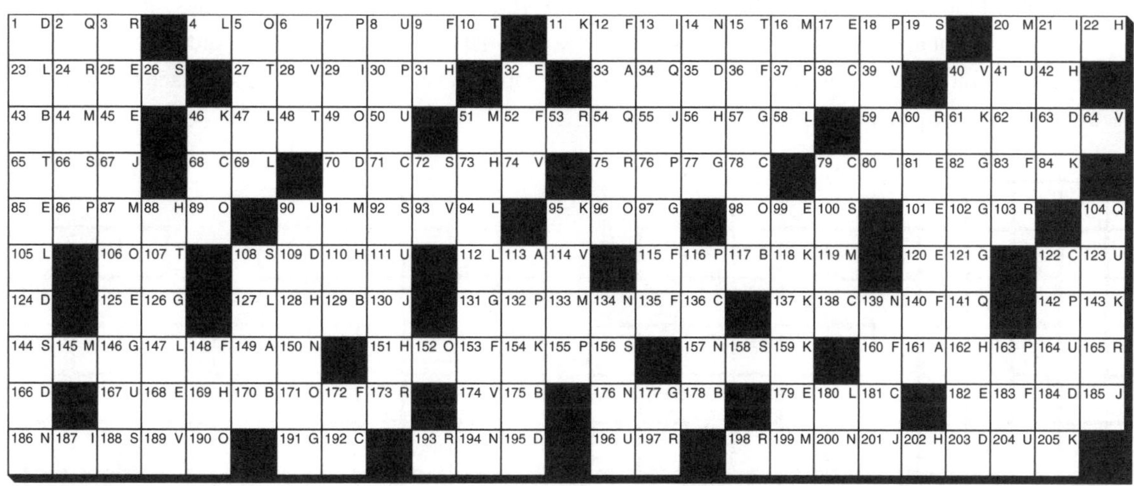

A. Longed for

113 161 33 149 59

B. Choice

117 170 175 43 178 129

C. What some toothpastes promise (2 wds.)

136 122 71 181 38 192 78 79 138 68

D. Actor who played Lurch on TV (2 wds.)

1 203 70 63 184 195 109 35 124 166

E. Founder of a large motel and restaurant chain (2 wds.)

99 17 85 32 182 168 101 125 120 25 45 81 179

F. Playwright who hung with Beckett and Genet (2 wds.)

172 52 83 183 9 12 148 135 36 140 115 160 153

G. Carly Simon's only #1 song (3 wds.)

131 177 82 97 121 57 102 77 146 191 126

H. Painter who's sometimes confused with Monet (2 wds.)

110 202 169 162 151 42 31 22 128 73 56 88

I. "Magnificent" member of the de Medicis

13 6 29 62 80 187 21

J. Dance named for a famous aviator

185 201 55 130 67

K. Arthur Ashe's autobiography (3 wds.)

143 95 46 205 84 159 118 137 154 61 11

L. *Legally Blonde* star

4 47 112 127 69 94 58 23 180 105 147

M. As dark as it gets (2 wds.)

145 87 44 20 16 51 133 91 199 119

N. World Series champions 1972–1974

194 157 139 134 14 176 186 200 150

O. Elmore Leonard spoof about Hollywood (2 wds.)

190 89 98 49 106 96 152 171 5

P. Word on a New Mexico license plate

132 18 142 86 76 163 116 7 30 155 37

Q. Egg recipe word that sounds pretty positive

104 2 54 34 141

R. George Harrison's 2002 CD

103 165 24 60 197 193 198 53 75 3 173

S. 1998 star of *Dr. Dolittle* (2 wds.)

19 156 72 188 100 144 108 66 92 158 26

T. Critter that plagued Bill Murray in *Caddyshack*

10 65 15 27 107 48

U. Spike Jonze's 2002 film starring Nicolas Cage

123 111 196 90 50 167 164 8 41 204

V. Egyptian queen often portrayed in art

189 93 40 114 39 64 174 74 28

ANSWER, PAGE 223

MOST ADMIRED MEN

We scoured the polls that the Gallup people take every year—about the men who are most admired by Americans—but couldn't find Uncle John's name in any of them. Go figure. What we did find are these 39 fellows who, in their day, made it to the top. Here's your chance to put them in their place by fitting them all into the grid crossword-style.

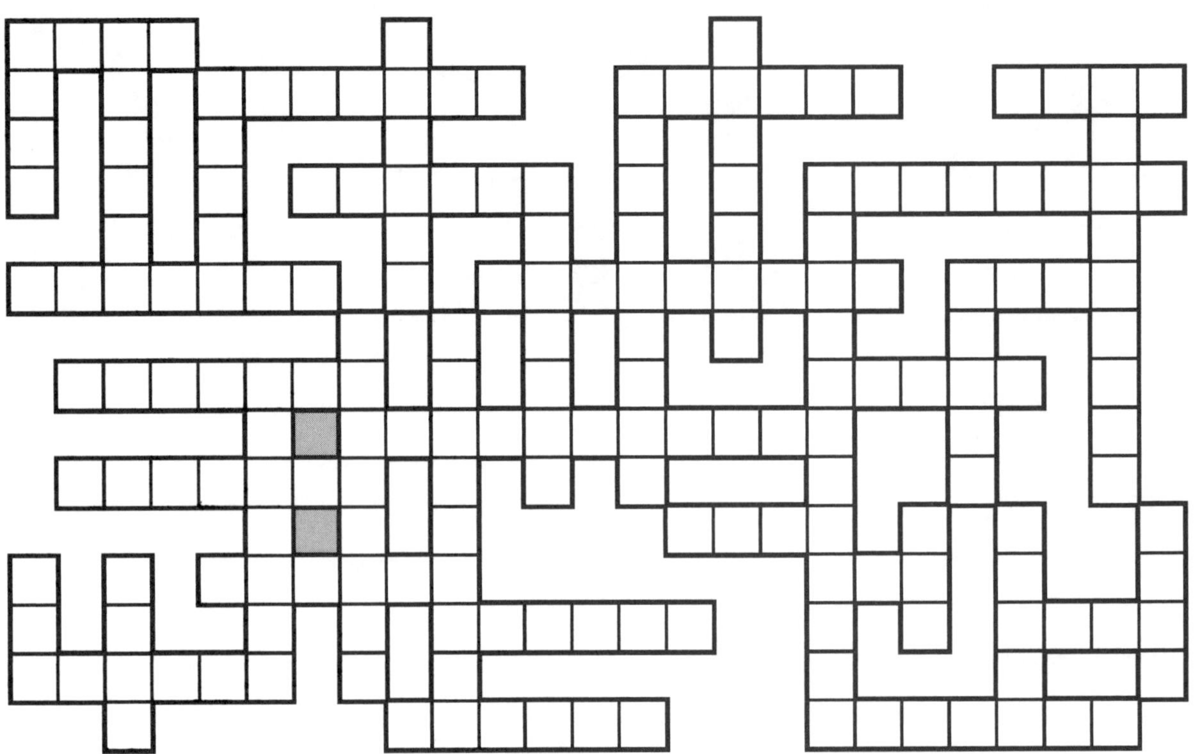

3 letter words
IKE (Dwight D. Eisenhower)
JFK (John F. Kennedy)
LBJ (Lyndon B. Johnson)

4 letter words
George BUSH (both)
Gerald FORD
Al GORE
Gary HART
Bob HOPE
Dr. Jonas SALK
Robert TAFT
Bishop Desmond TUTU

5 letter words
Spiro AGNEW
Bill GATES
John GLENN
Terry WAITE

6 letter words
Bernard BARUCH
Orval FAUBUS
Reverend Billy GRAHAM
Herbert HOOVER
Michael JORDAN
Ronald REAGAN
Harry S. TRUMAN
U THANT

7 letter words
Bill CLINTON
Everett DIRKSEN
Lee IACOCCA
Robert and Edward KENNEDY
Nelson MANDELA
Marty ROBBINS
Harold STASSEN
George WALLACE

8 letter words
Hubert HUMPHREY
George MARSHALL

9 letter words
The DALAI LAMA
Mikhail GORBACHEV
General Douglas MACARTHUR
Adlai STEVENSON

11 letter word
Nelson ROCKEFELLER

12 letter word
Dag HAMMARSKJÖLD

ANSWER, PAGE 224

PLAYING THE PERCENTAGES #3

Even more…we told you he had a gazillion. Place the numbers 10, 20, 30, 40, 50, 60, 70, 80, and 90 into the nine blanks below to make the statistics as accurate as possible.

_____% of U.S. businesses are family-owned

_____% of all forest fires are started by lightning

_____% of people say they're satisfied with their jobs

_____% of the oxygen that enters the bloodstream is used by the brain

_____% of the deaths that occur in U.S. gambling casinos are caused by "sudden heart attack"

_____% of a cat's waking hours are spent grooming itself

_____% of the potatoes grown in the U.S. are made into French fries

_____% of American homes that contain children also contain Legos

_____% of the country of Liechtenstein's GNP is generated by the sale of false teeth

ANSWER, PAGE 210

YOU'VE GOT A SLIM CHANCE

Small crostic puzzles are solved just like the big ones (directions on page 11) but the first letter of the fill-in words **do not** spell out a hidden message.

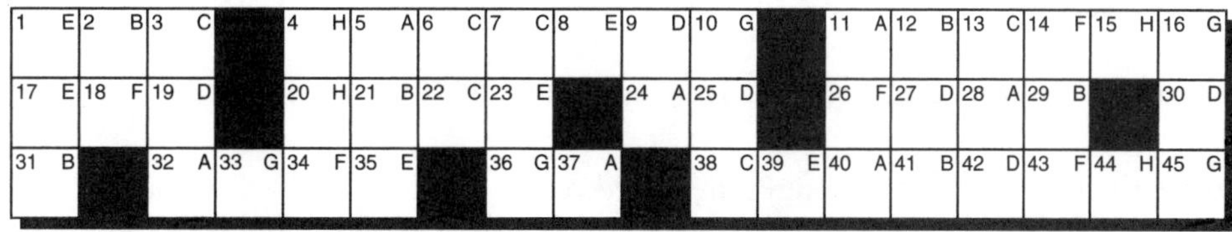

1 E	2 B	3 C		4 H	5 A	6 C	7 C	8 E	9 D	10 G		11 A	12 B	13 C	14 F	15 H	16 G
17 E	18 F	19 D		20 H	21 B	22 C	23 E		24 A	25 D		26 F	27 D	28 A	29 B		30 D
31 B		32 A	33 G	34 F	35 E		36 G	37 A		38 C	39 E	40 A	41 B	42 D	43 F	44 H	45 G

A. Movie heavy

___ ___ ___ ___ ___ ___ ___
5 32 11 28 40 24 37

B. Grits ingredient

___ ___ ___ ___ ___ ___
2 21 41 12 31 29

C. Hunky hero of *The Four Feathers*

___ ___ ___ ___ ___ ___
22 6 38 13 3 7

D. Sacred river of Asia

___ ___ ___ ___ ___ ___
9 30 27 19 42 25

E. Gauguin's second home

___ ___ ___ ___ ___ ___
1 8 35 39 23 17

F. Gunfighter's mark

___ ___ ___ ___ ___
18 26 43 34 14

G. Word with ear or peace

___ ___ ___ ___ ___
36 33 16 10 45

H. Tuckered out

___ ___ ___ ___
20 44 4 15

ANSWER, PAGE 200

MORE GOOFY HEADLINES

POLICEMAN SHOT IN BASQUE AREA. (Ow. That must have hurt.) Actually, no, it was just a real headline as silly as the ones we've disguised below by breaking up the words into consecutive three-letter groups and rearranging them in alphabetical order. The number of letters in each word of the original headline is given after the scrambled version.

1. CHI DEN EIN GAR LDS OLG REA RUS STO TFO (5'1 5 5 3 3 2 6)

2. ACE BYL GES HAR IGH MAN NGF RYC SBA STR TNI TTE UCK (3 6 2 9 5 7 7)

3. BRI DSD FIN FSI HUN ION NSH ORT PLY SUP TIS WAR (7 5 5 6 2 5 6)

4. EAT EDO EOF ERS FIC FIR IAL ILL KER NEH OSE SGR VER (4 9 7 4 8 7)

5. AIV ARW EAR ESH ING MAN MIN USE (3 5 3 6 7)

ANSWER, PAGE 219

* * * * *

WINNING HANDS-DOWN

A decisive victory is known as a "hands-down win." Where did that come from?

a) In the British Parliament, measures are voted on by asking for a show of hands "in favor," then a show of hands "opposed." If no hands are raised in opposition, either because no one's opposed or (more likely) because it's obvious from the earlier show of hands that the measure's going to pass anyway, the result is a "hands-down win."
b) It's another term for a win by knockout in boxing. The idea is that a boxer generally drops his guard during the ten-second count, and is therefore a "hands-down winner" when the fight ends. Boxers who win by technical knockout or judges' decision, on the other hand, finish the fight with their fists raised.
c) It comes from horse racing. When a jockey is so far ahead of the rest of the field that he can simply drop his reins (and, presumably, his hands) and let the horse finish the race without further spurring on, he's said to have won "hands down."

ANSWER, PAGE 200

REDUNDANT AND REPETITIOUS

Brought to you by the Department of Redundancy Department, this puzzle contains 16 two-word phrases, each of which contains a redundancy. Two such examples could be BARE NAKED or AND ETC. The word list below gives you just the first word of the phrase and the number of letters in the second word. If you can find the first word in the grid, the second word will follow. After you've circled all 16 phrases, the leftover letters in the grid will spell out a sentence that contains three additional redundancies. If you need assistance—or help—turn to the complete word list on page 225.

F O R E I G N I M P O R T S T
Y P O C E T A C I L P U D P H
G N I N R A W E C N A V D A P
A J E E C T O T N V I C D S R
C T O N E D L F C E L D O T I
I L N I W R A U S A E A U E O
L A O T N N E I S D F Q U X R
P G E S I T N V B E F E D P H
E B I B E V O O E R R I U E I
R E D A U D N G E R A D L R S
T H W L H U F E E O T L N I T
C I I A S K G I E T D B T E O
A N O T C I I R S C H U A N R
X D L O F A T E A T R E O C Y
E L A T O T M U S U N D R E K

ADDED _ _ _ _ _
ADVANCE _ _ _ _ _ _ _ _
CLOSED _ _ _ _
DUPLICATE _ _ _ _
END _ _ _ _ _ _
EXACT _ _ _ _ _ _ _
FOREIGN _ _ _ _ _ _ _
FREE _ _ _ _
JOIN _ _ _ _ _ _ _ _
LAG _ _ _ _ _ _
PAST _ _ _ _ _ _ _ _ _ _
PRIOR _ _ _ _ _ _ _
REVERT _ _ _ _
SUM _ _ _ _ _
TOTAL _ _ _ _ _ _ _ _ _ _
TRUE _ _ _ _

ANSWER, PAGE 225

ZAP!

Frank Zappa was one of the first rock musicians to admit publicly that he could think. We've taken a few of those thoughts, zapped them onto this page, and now it's up to you. Drop the letters from each vertical column—but not necessarily in the order in which they appear—into the empty squares below them to spell out the Zappaisms, reading from left to right. Words may wrap around from one line to the next; black squares signify the spaces between words.

1.

E			O	W	N				O		S			
O	M	F	O	G	H	A	T	E	E		B			C
I	V	E	R	Y	T	T	E	L	H	M	S	E		H
E	S	R	I	R	O	N	B	T	R	A	O	N	T	H
								■				■		
	■						■			■			■	
										■			■	
		■				■						■	■	■

2.

M			T			I	O			T				
M	U	U	P			N	O			I		C	O	
L	M	S	I		P	E	H	E	L	E	S	S	T	U
E	O	N	T	C	K	T	F	W	I	A	O	O	D	H
E	D	S	I	N	A	N	D	P	B	G	T	W	A	M
				■							■			
				■					■					■
					■			■			■			
	■			■				■				■		
		■			■				■				■	■

3.

	E			T	O					C				
G	L			V	V		D	O	P	C	E	P		A
T	I		T	M	E		B	E	N	E	O	U	L	C
O	B	D	I	A	O	R	B	E	N	E	Y	N	I	E
A	H	E	H	H	E	E	E	E	T	T	O	R	R	J
			■					■						
■		■					■							
			■			■			■					
		■				■							■	
		■				■					■	■	■	■

ANSWER, PAGE 216

AT SIXES AND SEVENS

When we took these lists of sevens from page 77 of *Uncle John's All-Purpose Extra Strength Bathroom Reader*, we accidentally dropped one item from each list and we were hoping you could help. Can you complete each list by adding the missing seventh item?

The 7 Wonders of the Ancient World
Great Pyramid of Giza
Hanging Gardens of Babylon
Statue of Zeus at Olympia
Temple of Artemis at Ephesus
Mausoleum at Halicarnassus
Pharos (Lighthouse) of Alexandria

The 7 Hills of Rome
Palatine
Quirinal
Viminal
Esquiline
Caelian
Aventine

The 7 Liberal Arts
Grammar
Rhetoric
Logic
Arithmetic
Geometry
Astronomy

The 7 Metals of Alchemy
Gold
Silver
Quicksilver (Mercury)
Copper
Iron
Tin

The 7 Deadly Sins
Pride
Envy
Wrath
Sloth
Avarice
Gluttony

The 7 Ancient Rivers
Nile
Oxua
Euphrates
Indus
Yaksart
Arax

The 7 Virtues
Faith
Hope
Charity
Fortitude
Prudence
Temperance

The 7 Dwarfs
Dopey
Doc
Sneezy
Grumpy
Bashful
Happy

ANSWER, PAGE 200

U.K. VS. U.S.A.

Sure, we both call it English, but sometimes it seems like our British counterparts are speaking a whole different language. We've given you a list of 41 British words; see if you can find their American equivalents in the grid, or "alphalattice," as the Brits call it. (That last comment was a complete lie; we apologize.) If you need a little help translating, you'll find the corresponding American words on the answer page.

And once you've found all the words in the grid, the leftover letters will reveal a "humourous" quote. Pip, pip, tally ho!

```
A N T O H S G N I L S E N Y A W B U S
N R N G C H E C K E R S L E I S A H M
C H E C K O U T C O U N T E R A N N E
V E M P N I T F H F L A S H L I G H T
E I T R A S A T E R I A T I L O S G D
C L R E C I F F O E C I L O P O R A N
H E A L D F D O R N H I M S A N E S O
O S P L R O R D A C C S G S E R Y O R
C E M O U L R V N H D A H A T Y W L B
O S O R G Q G E U F E A N O R U A I B
L S C T G N R E Z R V R S D U E L N A
A A E S I W E O L I F E O H Y L T E T
T L V V S R E D N E P S U S B N D T T
E O O E T E B G R S V T T O I O T E E
C M L I S L K H H U M A A S O R A I R
H I G H R I S E A P A R T M E N T R Y
I O S T T A G F E N D E R O E V O R D
P G O E M R E G G P L A N T R U C K I
S K E D S T A O C N I A R E C N U O B
```

ACCUMULATOR
AUBERGINE
BLACK TREACLE
BOBBY
BONNET
BRACES
CANDY FLOSS
CARAVAN
CASH DESK
CATAPULT
CHEMIST
CHIPS
CHUCKER OUT
CUBBYHOLE
DRAUGHTS
FAG
FASCIA PANEL
FRINGE
HOARDING
HOOTER
LAY-BY
LIFT
LORRY
MACKINTOSH
NAPPY
NOUGHT
PANTECHNICON
PATIENCE
PETROL
POLKA DOTS
PUSH CHAIR
SOLICITOR
SPANNER
SPONGE BAG
TORCH
TOWER BLOCK
TRACK
TUBE
VERGE
WAISTCOAT
WING

ANSWER, PAGE 226

CHANNEL SURFING

Rearrange the letters in each phrase to get the name of a TV show that spent at least one season as one of the top ten shows. For example, the answer to AL'S LAD (6) would be *Dallas*. Now channel your energies towards unscrambling these:

1. LET HAVE BOOT (3 4 4) ___ ___ ___ ___ ___ ___ ___ ___ ___ ___ ___
2. WE MET RUSH ORDER (6, 3 5) ___ ___ ___ ___ ___ ___, ___ ___ ___ ___ ___ ___ ___ ___
3. GRANTED (7) ___ ___ ___ ___ ___ ___ ___
4. LIFE ENDS (8) ___ ___ ___ ___ ___ ___ ___ ___
5. CANCELS FORT (6 5) ___ ___ ___ ___ ___ ___ ___ ___ ___ ___ ___
6. TALENT SHOW (3 7) ___ ___ ___ ___ ___ ___ ___ ___ ___ ___
7. KENO MUGS (8) ___ ___ ___ ___ ___ ___ ___ ___
8. NEWT WEIGHTS (3 4 4) ___ ___ ___ ___ ___ ___ ___ ___ ___ ___ ___
9. I'M A DANCE CARD (6 6) ___ ___ ___ ___ ___ ___ ___ ___ ___ ___ ___ ___
10. HENS GO ASHORE (5'1 6) ___ ___ ___ ___ ___'___ ___ ___ ___ ___ ___ ___
11. CHALLENGES AIRS (7'1 6) ___ ___ ___ ___ ___ ___ ___'___ ___ ___ ___ ___ ___ ___
12. CREATE PITCH (3 8) ___ ___ ___ ___ ___ ___ ___ ___ ___ ___ ___
13. PREY ON RAMS (5 5) ___ ___ ___ ___ ___ ___ ___ ___ ___ ___
14. I FILM YEATS (6 4) ___ ___ ___ ___ ___ ___ ___ ___ ___ ___
15. NEAR ONES (8) ___ ___ ___ ___ ___ ___ ___ ___
16. MY VERY BLOODY ENDEAVORS (9 5 7)
 ___
17. REX, OR "THE UNPERSON" (8 8)
 ___ ___ ___ ___ ___ ___ ___ ___ ___ ___ ___ ___ ___ ___ ___ ___
18. PROMOTE VIM, HE-MEN (4 11) ___ ___ ___ ___ ___ ___ ___ ___ ___ ___ ___ ___ ___ ___ ___

ANSWER, PAGE 199

SETTING THE STAGE

If you want to make it big in Hollywood, you've got to have the right kind of name. Imagine, for instance, a superstar with a moniker like, say, Arnold Schwarzenegger. Or Gwyneth Paltrow, for gosh sakes. They'd never make it to the big time.

ACROSS

1 TV show that featured Debbie Allen
5 Snake that sounds like a dance (but isn't)
10 Dreadlocks wearers
16 Half of a 2001 merger
19 Singer Brickell
20 Decorate
21 In a light, airy way
23 Roy Fitzgerald's stage name
25 Dino Crocetti's stage name
26 *Morning Edition* broadcaster
27 Ivo Levi's stage name
29 Former West German capital
30 1937 Cary Grant film
32 Proposal at the wedding
33 Baton Rouge univ.
35 Neatens up
36 Soda fountain treat
38 Scathing
42 Cosmetics company
43 Lenin's facial fuzz
44 Small hotel
45 Sense of hearing
46 Laszlo Loewenstein's stage name
49 Joseph Kubelsky's stage name
52 Davis of *Jezebel*
53 Wearisome task
55 Long in the tooth
56 Yugoslav republic
60 Lucille Le Sueur's stage name
64 Lotion ingredient
65 George Morrison's stage name
69 ___ *Thin Air* (Jon Krakauer best-seller)
70 Maurice Micklewhite's stage name
72 Gets ready to spring
74 Krazy ___
75 Square dance halls
76 Employee's request
79 Leonard Slye's stage name
82 Joseph Levitch's stage name
87 "Yes" in Ypres
88 Kauai keepsake
89 Salad leaves
91 Mug spray?
92 Part of a big delivery
94 Oddball
95 Gin-and-lime-juice drink
97 Forerunner of the CIA
98 Sufferer's sounds
99 They're used to make change
100 With 15 Down, body of water near Kazakhstan
103 Nat Birnbaum's stage name
106 30–300 gHz range
108 Bernie Schwartz's stage name
111 Taidje Khan Jr.'s stage name
113 Surgicenter visitor
114 Pal of Bert
115 ___ fixe
116 Candy that's dispensed
117 "C'mon!"
118 Passes slowly, as time
119 Running behind

DOWN

1 Plant with fronds
2 As opposed to natural, parent-wise
3 Photo reduced to pinpoint size
4 Reaction to a mouse
5 Pale purple shades
6 Certain viper
7 Model Kate
8 Ichabod's rival
9 Add explanatory passages to
10 Bureaucratic paperwork, e.g.
11 Drill sergeant's shout
12 Won't, more formally
13 Watch over
14 Movable doll part
15 See 100 Across
16 Female choir member
17 Actress Lena
18 Country singer Loretta
22 Photographer Diane
24 Overdone publicity
28 "'Fraid not"
31 Air freshener scent
33 Long and thin
34 Prismatic band seen near a waterfall
35 Barkeep's faucet
36 Siege site
37 Seldom seen
38 Enemy of Marc Antony
39 Hamstrings, e.g.
40 Bilbo portrayer Holm
41 Shriek
43 "I ___ You Babe"
47 Sports-page number

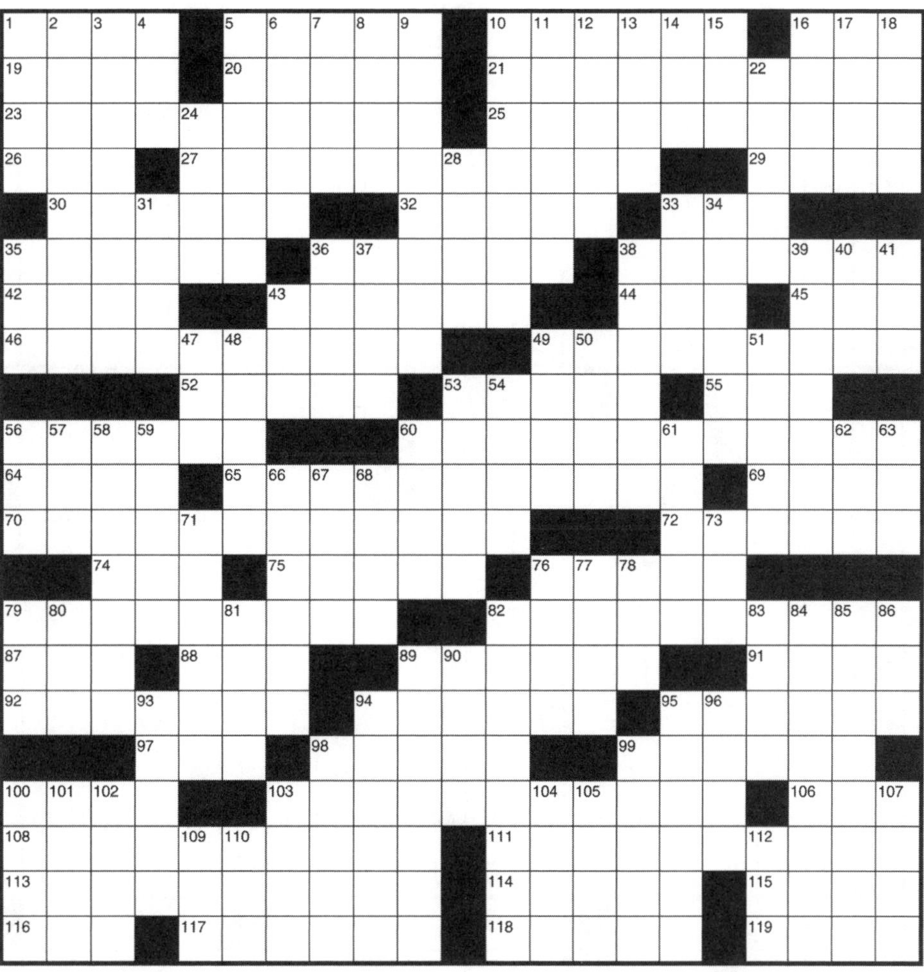

48 Amscray
49 Mitchell of folk music
50 Semicircles
51 Charmingly mischievous
53 Toe ailments
54 Loser in a fabled race
56 Ted's *Cheers* role
57 Yale alum
58 Stallone sequel of 1979
59 Joy of *The View*
60 Sign up with
61 Unable to sit still
62 Road with a no.
63 Hair arrangements
66 Even though
67 Tar Heel st.
68 Pathfinder explored it
71 Ring-shaped islands
73 Finless fish
76 Thatched roof material
77 Florentine river
78 Org. that receives returns
79 Balderdash
80 ___ *Town* (Wilder play)
81 Turns right
82 Wearing one's name and number, say
83 Jane Austen novel of 1815
84 "Flying" performer Karl
85 Sizable glacier
86 Good to go
89 Makes suitable for
90 Napkin holder
93 Tentacled animal
94 Pitching the idea of hitching
95 Comedy and drama, e.g.
96 ___-bitsy
98 Distributes
99 The boss, slangily
100 At the peak of
101 Libertine
102 Woody-Allen-as-insect film
103 Coarse particles
104 He dueled with Hamilton
105 Forearm bone
107 Thrown in
109 "Silent ___" (Coolidge's nick-name)
110 Colorado Indian
112 Zero

ANSWER, PAGE 225

MORE FREE ADVICE

…from more friends of Uncle John's. If you need directions on how to solve this puzzle, see page 5.

1.

		M	K	S					R		N			L		I			F			D
	D	O	F	N		T	S	F	O		E		F	O		T	E	A	H	E	R	D
R	F	N	E	T	N	I	E	D	A	R	F	K	O	E	F	L	F	I	W	A	E	E
A	I	I	A	S	Y	B	A	N	D	I	A	O	H	A	O	R	E	R	C	H	H	S
	■				■			■		■					■			■			■	
					■							■			■							
■						■				■		■					■			■		
■							■						■									

2.

N		B				G	F			O			W					I				
S	I	E	L	C		I	T		I	T	I		O	I		Y	W	E	L			
N	E	T	F	R	E	P	O		Y	U	T	F	E	N	C	A	E	U	S		T	U
T	U	V	E	S	T	I	N		O	N	M	N	O	O	L	M	S	E	T	S	O	I
O	T	O	R	E	T	E	L	L	S	O	U	E	T	R	E	L	O	J	U	L	T	R
					■			■				■			■					■		
					■			■				■					■					■
			■						■					■						■		
	■			■				■								■					■	
								■			■				■					■	■	■

3.

O				O									T	O		D						
T		T		U	N	U	Y	N	O	A	W		N	I		K	R	E	P	O		O
H	R	W	H	Y	O	L	T	O	T	N	Y		A	T		E	E	I	N	W	T	W
U	A	Y	H	A	T	D	O	D	W	D	S	R	T	T	K	E	R	T	N	K	Y	D
T	H	E	O	E	A	L	Y	H	U	I	T	A	L	O	H	E	A	A	N	D	H	A
			■					■				■			■					■		
		■							■			■			■				■			
	■				■					■					■						■	
			■				■					■					■				■	
	■					■					■							■				■

ANSWER, PAGE 225

LOONEY LAWS: THE QUIZ

More of those real-life, real strange laws. This time you get your choice. Select the correct answer from the three options. And be careful out there!

1. In Las Vegas, Nevada, it's against the law to pawn your...

   a) dentures
   b) hair
   c) wedding ring

2. Michigan law forbids pet owners from tying their...

   a) dogs
   b) crocodiles
   c) horses

   ...to fire hydrants.

3. In St. Louis, Missouri, it's illegal for you to drink beer...

   a) out of a bucket
   b) with no shirt on
   c) that's being poured into your mouth by someone else

   ...while sitting on the curb.

4. Cotton Valley, Louisiana, law forbids cows and horses from sleeping...

   a) in a bakery
   b) on the roof
   c) in the same building

5. It's illegal to sleep with...

   a) your boots on
   b) a teddy bear
   c) an adult of the same sex

   ...in Tulsa, Oklahoma.

6. In Natoma, Kansas, it's illegal to throw knives...

   a) between the hours of 8 A.M. and 6 P.M.
   b) at men wearing striped suits
   c) if you can't also juggle them

7. It's against the law (not to mention impossible) to...

   a) build a perpetual motion machine
   b) move objects by telekinesis
   c) whistle underwater

   ...in Vermont.

8. The law prohibits barbers in Omaha, Nebraska, from...

   a) shaving the chests of
   b) repeating the stories told by
   c) borrowing money from

   ...their customers.

9. The maximum penalty for double parking in Minneapolis, Minnesota, is...

   a) being strapped into a ducking stool and dunked into a lake
   b) working on a chain gang with nothing to eat but bread and water
   c) permanent loss of your driver's license...and your car

10. In Alabama, it's illegal to...

    a) wear lipstick
    b) paint your house
    c) play dominoes

    ... on Sunday.

ANSWER, PAGE 225

WILD KINGDOM

Hidden in these simple letter substitution messages is vital information concerning animal behavior—things you should know about before you venture into the jungle or the swamp or the deep blue sea. Come a little closer...they won't bite. For further instructions and hints on how to solve, see page 15.

1. FIJD BLN XJJ MLVYIODX DNSSVODA, BLN YKLHTHVB WIODQ WIJB'KJ JCYKJXXODA RTKJ ZLK LDJ TDLWIJK. TDM BLN'KJ KOAIW. MLVYIODX NXJ WLNRI TX T FTB WL HLDM TDM WL KJELUJ XLROTV WJDXOLDX.

2. DZDJNHYOW MDO XVTHZ VYZR CNDY ONDR'GD DFTLODA. MDYDGHZZR, OND KVGD DFTLODA ONDR HGD OND ZVYMDG HYA ZVEADG ONDR'ZZ OGEKJDO. HO UVVW, ONDR'ZZ MLXD H WNVGO, WNHGJ OVVO CNDY ONDR'GD LKJHOLDYO OV QD BDA.

3. KQTGKOC XOKL NEDAR, CE CEGWPTGWC TP'C RKNJ PE PWOO FRWPRWN PFE KQTGKOC WQAKAWJ TQ KAANWCCTMW XRLCTHKO HEQPKHP KNW KQANL EN RKMTQA K AEEJ PTGW. VDP FTPR HNEHEJTOWC, TP'C QE GLCPWNL: PRWL'NW QEP AWPPTQA KOEQA.

4. RTQF WIZANF WRCA MLWPDQIA, PTQS'DQ DQPMDFCFE PN PTQ KQDS LZIXQ RTQDQ PTQS RQDQ TIPXTQJ. IFJ PTQS ILLIDQFPZS UCFJ PTQ TNAQ WPDQIA VS PTQCD WQFWQ NU WAQZZ.

ANSWER, PAGE 226

POLI-TALKS

Some of the most memorable quotes from politicians come when they don't have a speechwriter handy.

1.

I			T			W		W				T		E			R	
I	E		O	S	N	D		O	F	A		D	H	N	O	O	E	
V	F	I	P	U	A	D		A	B	O	W	T	O	L	L	D	N	F
A	C	P	B	A	I	T	A	S	E	F	U	O	U	L	D	A	H	A

		■			■				■		■							■
	■						■			■						■		
		■					■				■				■			
				■			■						■					■

2.

U	S		T								R	R						
L	O	A	K		R	A	R	R	E	Y	I	E	G	N	T			
E	A	O	T		I	F	I	R	E	S	I	N	A	D	T			D
C	N	U	S	E	S	M	T	E	R	E	R	D	E	A	N	O	I	E
R	B	N	F	O	F	I	P	T	H	T	T	A	D	E	E	D	V	R

				■			■							■			■	
		■				■										■		■
				■				■					■				■	
					■					■						■		
				■					■						■	■	■	■

3.

L		C		F	P		I	G						M			A	
T	I	E		C	I		I	T		L	R	W	S	T	B		R	Y
Y	H	T	I	M	S	A	N	T		E	A	M	A	T	Y	A	P	N
O	T	H	A	N	I	R	S	N	N	A	E	N	A	O	F	O	N	A
L	N	E	I	M	G	G	H	E	V	R	T	H	E	A	I	E	N	O

			■						■				■			■		
						■						■				■		
						■			■		■							
	■									■					■			
			■						■									■

ANSWER, PAGE 228

YOU MUST REMEMBER THIS

Sometimes our brains need a little bit of jogging. No, not the running kind of jogging—you know what we mean. Anyway, at times like that, mnemonics come in handy. Like "Every good boy does fine," the mnemonic for remembering the notes that correspond to the lines of the treble clef: EGBDF. Can you make the connections between the mnemonics (1–14) and the lists they represent (a–n)? A little logic should do the trick, even if you can't quite recall exactly what everything stands for (goodness knows *we* can't).

_____ 1. Easter bunnies get drunk at Easter
_____ 2. God eventually let Noah drift
_____ 3. I eat green cheese
_____ 4. I'm very xenophobic; Lithuanians completely discombobulate me
_____ 5. King Hector doesn't usually drink cold milk
_____ 6. King Philip came over for good sex
_____ 7. May I have a large container of coffee?
_____ 8. My very earnest mother just served us nine pizzas
_____ 9. No plan like yours, to study history wisely
_____ 10. Old people from Texas eat spiders
_____ 11. Please excuse my dear Aunt Sally
_____ 12. Put eggs on my plate, please
_____ 13. Richard of York gave battle in vain
_____ 14. Toronto girls can flirt, and only quit to chase dwarves

a. Ascending order of Roman numerals
b. Biological groupings used in taxonomy
c. Bones of the skull
d. Colors of the rainbow
e. First books of the Bible
f. Guitar string tunings, from highest to lowest
g. Houses of the British royal family
h. Order of mathematical operations
i. Periods of the Cenozoic era
j. Planets in the solar system
k. Prefixes in the metric system, in descending order
l. Satellites of Jupiter
m. Mohs hardness scale for minerals
n. Value of pi

ANSWER, PAGE 227

* * * * *

EYE OF THE BEHOLDER

We knew she bleached her hair, but that's not all; the lovely Marilyn Monroe also enhanced her beauty in four of the following ways. What didn't she have done?

a) She heightened her hairline with electrolysis
b) She had a lump of cartilage removed from the tip of her nose
c) She had a crescent-shaped silicone implant inserted into her jaw to soften its line
d) She had her upper molars removed to emphasize her cheekbones
e) She bleached her teeth

ANSWER, PAGE 221

GOING, ABROAD

How many times have you traveled to a foreign country and accidentally brought an *Uncle John's Bathroom Reader* instead of a phrase book? Never? Well, now you can feel free to do that, because here we've provided translations of the all-important phrase "Where is the bathroom?" in 24 different languages...and then hidden them in a grid, of course (without their diacritical marks). When you've found them all, the leftover letters will tell you what you can expect in the bathrooms of a certain country.

```
L A V A C H O O K I K O W A P I T O R I E S
C D A N B E F N O U I N D I N F R A U S N C
O O E B K A M A R K E C I L D I M A N A Y A
R V I S K I N S G O E U S O N U O T D T L E
I E U O S K T A O I S A L E B T D T E E E S
E I O B U U U A T Y T O I I U M S I E L G G
H L T H T S N N O T A L E H I K O E S A D I
N B I T W O O A H E S S N Y E O M U T U E G
A A T E T N T N H E L R E S I A A E E T Z E
B G O N C V E G T E A A S B I L L L T A D I
O N S Y W A I K L L N L D E R A O U O R E F
A O N A B L E A T S E E D N O D H S A Y S O
T A A I D J V S F R C S A T N C E I L R T H
S S I W A A R I S H E T T O I L E T E U U A
E A P C T K O L U N S S T O R Y W H T K A S
E E R O E A T Y H E E M O N I E Y F A A L H
D L R L S I A A P J J A R T B L U T Y O E E
N I U C A K U S E D O K O D A W E I R O T R
O W O I S T D I E T O I L E T T E T A N T U
T E A R T H Z H V O R E R T O I L E T T E T
E V U I Z D E R B O D T S I M E R T O E I I
L E T P G D J E J E T O A L E T A P E R S M
```

AI HEA LUA? (Hawaiian)
CHOO KIKO WAPI? (Swahili)
DÓNDE ESTÁ EL BAÑO? (Spanish)
DOV'É IL BAGNO? (Italian)
EIFO HA'SHERUTIM? (Hebrew)
GDE ZDES TUALET? (Russian)
GDJE JE TOALET? (Bosnian)
GDZIE JEST TOALETA? (Polish)
HOL A MOSDÓ? (Hungarian)
HVOR ER TOILETTET? (Danish)
KAMAR KECIL DI MANA? (Indonesian)
KIE ESTAS LA NECESEJO? (Esperanto)
KUR YRA TUALETAS? (Lithuanian)
KUS ON VÄLJAKÄIK? (Estonian)
NASAAN ANG KASILYAS? (Tagalog)
ONDE ESTÁ O BANHEIRO? (Portuguese)
OU SONT LES TOILETTES? (French)
PIÄN-SÓ TĪ TÓ-UĪ? (Taiwanese)
TORIE WA DOKO DESU KA? (Japanese)
UBI ES LE LAVATORIO? (Interlingua)
UNDE ESTE TOALETA? (Romanian)
VU IZ DER BODTSIMER? (Yiddish)
WAAR IS HET TOILET? (Dutch)
WO IST DIE TOILETTE? (German)

ANSWER, PAGE 228

ANOTHER COUNTRY HEARD FROM

Who doesn't like country music? Heck, even if you don't, you gotta love some of them toe-tappin' titles. Like "She Got the Ring and I Got the Finger." Or "You're the Reason Our Kids Are So Ugly." Well, you know what? We've collected some favorites and plunked them down in this here puzzle. Can you chime in and finish the unfinished songs?

ACROSS

1 Right of entry
7 Gangsters' girls
12 Constructed
16 Apple computer
19 Badly built
20 Disney's redheaded mermaid
21 Milky gemstone
22 *Independence Day* craft
23 "Get Your Tongue Outta My Mouth, Cause I'm..."
26 ___ Lanka
27 Pal of Frodo
28 Amorous murmur
29 Compete
30 Disney movie set in ancient China
32 "If Heartaches Were Wine..."
40 Beer vendors check them
42 Like Billy Idol's hair
43 Christened again
44 Ivana's successor as Mrs. Trump
45 Pocket protector wearers
46 Choppers
47 "It Ain't Love, but..."
50 Paperless exams
51 2001 Will Smith film
54 Old-fashioned negative
55 Spread lotion
56 Jazz aficionados
59 A party to
60 Oscar winner for 1987's *Moonstruck*
62 Italian ice creams
63 Communion site
64 "How Can You Believe Me When I Say I Love You, When You Know..."
70 Accepted fact
71 Door-frame top
72 Geological time units
73 Finished
74 Sack-the-quarterback plays
76 Scuba tank contents
77 Victrola manufacturer
80 Sprinted
81 Where the Gutenberg Bible was printed
82 "You're a Cross..."
85 Creator of Holmes and Watson
86 Russian coin
89 Black material worn as a mourning band
90 Person who's on the poor side
93 They used to be fillies
94 Sex drives
96 "If You See Me Gettin' Smaller..."
99 Rap sheet entry
100 Device that connects to a TV
101 Gerund ender
102 Ungentlemanly fellow
105 Important luau attendee
106 "I Don't Know Whether to..."
114 Espionage writer Fleming
115 1960s musical
116 "Our Gang" girl
117 Germanic tribesman
118 Chicago trains
119 Ending for thermo or rheo
120 Knife blade metal
121 Place to hide an ace

DOWN

1 Makes inquiries
2 Green, furry "Pet"
3 Energy from outer space
4 Actors Asner and Harris
5 "Star Wars" inits.
6 Adjusted wristwatches to match
7 McCheese's title
8 Spanish gold
9 Lucy of *Charlie's Angels*
10 Table supporter
11 Certain East Europeans
12 Lady seen on runways
13 "Calling all cars" broadcast
14 Calendar square
15 The periodic table's 100-odd
16 Koran studier
17 Building with a steeply-sloped roof
18 Invented, as a word
24 "Ye ___!"
25 Slippery
31 Four Corners state
33 Surrealist Salvador
34 Chex variety
35 "Previously owned"
36 PBS without the video
37 Nickelodeon viewer
38 Pay for everyone's meal
39 Shoes no good for running
40 "You can count on me!"
41 Info
45 Capture
46 Hiker's path
48 Obstacle for a skier
49 Overcook

50 Based on the number 8
51 Prefix seen with climax
52 Bread purchase
53 Concerning
56 "57 Varieties" company
57 Make someone happy
58 Prepares apples for baking
59 Misfortunes
60 Chatty trucker
61 Hatchery bird
62 Overdone glamour
63 *The Fountainhead* author Rand
64 Dr. Frankenstein's assistant
65 ___ *Zapata!*
66 Smooth
67 Skirt cut
68 *Star Wars* princess
69 The break of day
74 Stagnant backwater
75 Pleasing vocal qualities
76 One or eleven at the blackjack table
77 Teach anew
78 Guitar neck attachment
79 Greek war god
81 Crown wearers
82 Ingrid's *Casablanca* role
83 Frozen yogurt chain
84 Vivacity
85 Art ___
86 Devices used with muzzle-loading firearms
87 Web addr.
88 Nectar harvester
90 Flower child
91 Like some heart muscles
92 Antiwar hand gestures
93 Great Lakes st.
94 "My Ding-a-___" (#1 Chuck Berry hit)
95 Fort Knox bars
97 Tennis champ Chris
98 Type of infection
103 Sea of ___ (Black Sea arm)
104 Unit of force
107 Feed-bag seed
108 *Crimes and Misdemeanors* star Farrow
109 Wrestling surface
110 Before, poetically
111 Hooray for Jose!
112 Warner Bros. collectible
113 Regret

ANSWER, PAGE 228

WANNA WRESTLE?

If you want to wrestle with the best of them, you'll first have to wrestle with this quiz. Match the insider words and phrases (1–19) with their meanings (a–s).

_____ 1. Face
_____ 2. Heel
_____ 3. Feud
_____ 4. Turn
_____ 5. Potato (verb)
_____ 6. Stiff
_____ 7. Run-in
_____ 8. Blade
_____ 9. Juice
_____ 10. Job
_____ 11. Post (verb)
_____ 12. Hardway juice
_____ 13. Heat
_____ 14. Pop
_____ 15. Bump
_____ 16. Jobber
_____ 17. Clean job
_____ 18. Screw-job
_____ 19. Shoot

a. Injure a wrestler in the head
b. Blood
c. One wrestler really trying to hurt another
d. Run someone into the ring post
e. A sudden rise in the enthusiasm of a crowd
f. A "good guy"
g. A wrestler who's hired to lose to the featured wrestler
h. An ending that isn't clean, where someone wins by cheating
i. Intervention by a nonparticipant
j. A staged loss
k. Level of enthusiasm of a crowd
l. When a bad guy changes his persona to a good guy or vice versa
m. A "bad guy"
n. A staged loss that doesn't involve illegal wrestling moves
o. A grudge match
p. A move the results in the wrestler falling out of the ring
q. A move intended to cause real injury
r. Blood from an unintentional injury
s. Intentionally cut yourself to produce blood

ANSWER, PAGE 189

* * * * *

THEY'RE PLOTTING AGAINST ME

The CIA is pretty sneaky. What? You didn't know? Well, back in the 1960s they were cooking up a batch of plots against Fidel Castro…Which of the following was not one that they considered?

a) Spread rumors in Cuba that the Second Coming is imminent, and that Castro is the Antichrist
b) Have 5,000 pieces of junk mail sent to him daily
c) Put itching powder in his scuba suit and LSD on his mouthpiece, to drive him crazy and make him drown
d) Surprise him at the beach with an exploding conch shell
e) Put thalium salts in his shoes and cigars to make his beard and hair fall out

ANSWER, PAGE 189

GETTING THE LAST WORD

Everyone wants their last words to be memorable, but especially the famous, because they know that their words may someday show up in a quiz like this. (At least that's what we think.) Can you use your instincts and your knowledge of history to match the parting shots (1–18) to the person who uttered them (a–r)? (No fair using a Ouija board.)

_____ 1. "All my possessions for a moment of time."
_____ 2. "Am I dying or is this my birthday?"
_____ 3. "Curtain! Fast music! Light! Ready for the last finale! Great! The show looks good!"
_____ 4. "Don't let it end like this. Tell them I said something."
_____ 5. "Drink to me!"
_____ 6. "Either that wallpaper goes, or I do."
_____ 7. "Get my swan costume ready."
_____ 8. "Go on, get out. Last words are for fools who haven't said enough."
_____ 9. "How were the receipts today at Madison Square Garden?"
_____ 10. "I owe much; I have nothing; the rest I leave to the poor."
_____ 11. "I have offended God and mankind because my work didn't reach the quality it should have."
_____ 12. "I knew it. I knew it. Born in a hotel room—and God damn it—died in a hotel room."
_____ 13. "I am about to—or I am going to—die: either expression is correct."
_____ 14. "I know you have come to kill me. Shoot, coward, you are only going to kill a man."
_____ 15. "I've had eighteen straight whiskies, I think that's the record...."
_____ 16. "Is it the Fourth?"
_____ 17. "Shoot me in the chest and don't make a mess of it!"
_____ 18. "Thomas Jefferson still survives."

a. Anna Pavlova
b. Benito Mussolini
c. Dominique Bouhours (French grammarian)
d. Dylan Thomas
e. Ernesto "Che" Guevara
f. Eugene O'Neill
g. Florenz Ziegfeld
h. François Rabelais
i. John Adams
j. Karl Marx
k. Lady Nancy Astor
l. Leonardo da Vinci
m. Oscar Wilde
n. P. T. Barnum
o. Pablo Picasso
p. Pancho Villa
q. Queen Elizabeth I
r. Thomas Jefferson

ANSWER, PAGE 227

WHAT MAKES A GOOD VILLAIN?

Directions for solving are on page 11.

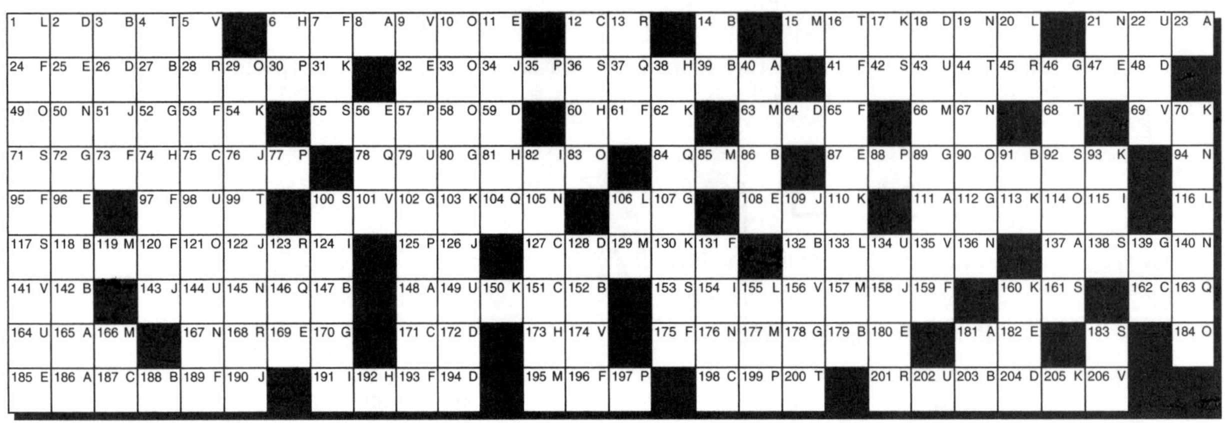

A. Giving the go-ahead

23 111 137 186 8 148 181 165 40

B. Song from *Peter Pan* (3 wds.)

179 147 3 142 91 39 27 132 118 152 188 14 203 86

C. Remarkable or strange occurrences

75 127 162 187 171 12 151 198

D. Aussie-born star of *Mulholland Dr.* (2 wds.)

48 2 172 18 64 26 128 204 194 59

E. Lesley Gore hit of 1964 (4 wds.)

25 185 56 180 87 169 108 47 32 182 96 11

F. Soviet Nobel Peace Prize winner of 1990 (2 wds.)

65 193 73 131 175 95 189 53 196 7 120 61 41 97 159 24

G. Isak Dinesen's memoirs of her time in Kenya (3 wds.)

102 178 170 139 107 112 89 52 46 72 80

H. Marked increase or improvement

192 6 60 74 38 81 173

I. Wise ones

191 124 82 154 115

J. 1973 Al Pacino-Gene Hackman movie collaboration

158 143 190 126 34 122 76 51 109

K. Earth's underdeveloped or impoverished nations (3 wds.)

130 205 54 31 160 103 17 150 62 110 113 70 93

L. Midsized Honda

133 116 155 106 20 1

M. Elope (3 wds.)

129 157 85 177 195 15 119 66 166 63

N. Rodgers and Hart query from *Babes in Arms* (3 wds.)

140 94 50 176 19 145 136 167 21 105 67

O. Collects into one sum

121 29 184 33 83 49 58 114 90 10

P. Striped bass

197 125 57 77 88 199 35 30

Q. Church get-together

146 78 104 163 84 37

R. Large shrimp or prawn

13 123 168 201 45 28

S. 2002 reality show with marriage in mind (2 wds.)

36 117 92 153 183 100 42 161 55 71 138

T. Self-evident truths

68 200 4 16 44 99

U. Grammy winners for *OK Computer*

79 149 134 98 202 144 22 43 164

V. Presented as a special event

206 101 174 9 69 156 141 135 5

ANSWER, PAGE 228

ACRONYMANIA

There seems to be some sort of SNAFU—all the 59 acronyms have fallen out of the grid below. OTOH, you might enjoy replacing them yourself, so we guess it's A-OK after all.

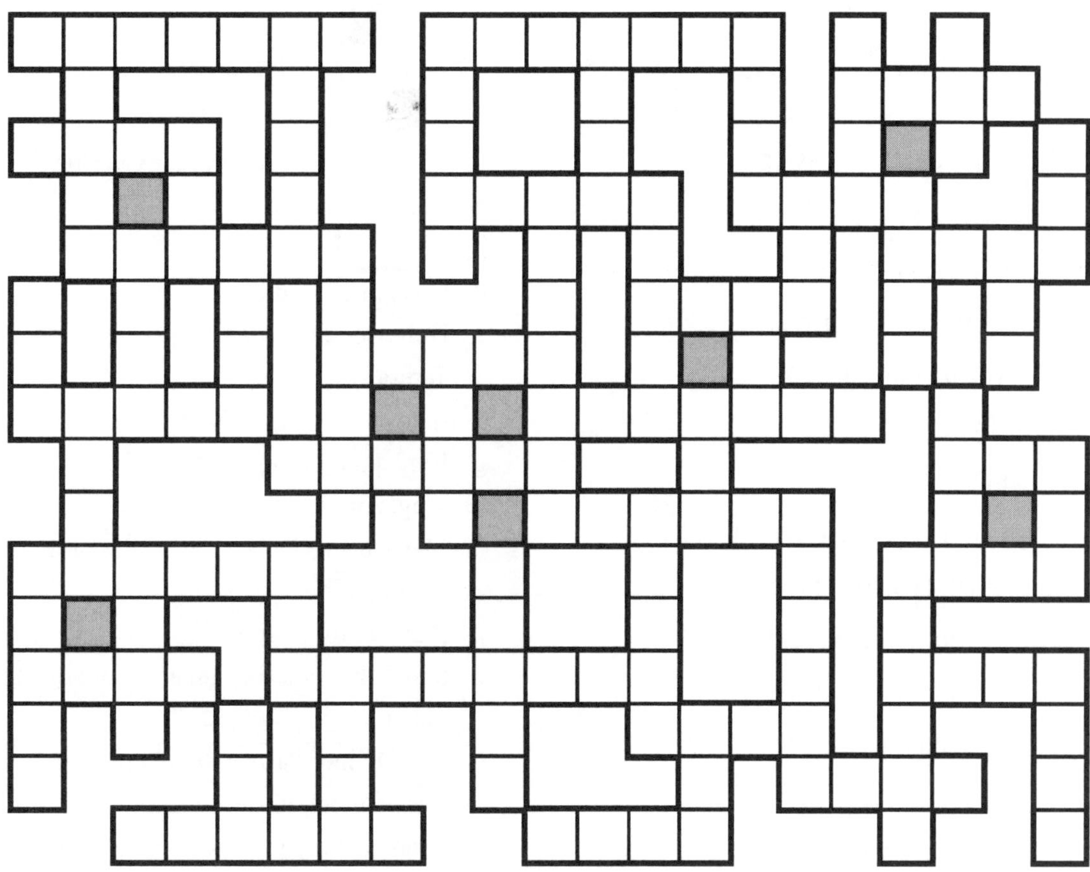

3 letter words
ADD
AKA
FAQ
FYI
LSD
PBS
PDQ
PGA
POW
QED
RBI
REM
TNT

4 letter words
AM/FM
ASAP
AWOL
FEMA
FWIW
GATT
GIGO
IMHO
NASA
NATO
OPEC
OSHA
PMRC
RCMP
SALT
SCTV
SCUD
SPCA
SWAK
SWAT
TGIF
TTFN
WASP

5 letter words
AFAIK
ASCAP
AWACS
CD-ROM
COBOL
EPCOT
NAACP
SEALS
TASER
WAVES

6 letter words
CANOLA
NASCAR
NASDAQ
POSSLQ
QANTAS
QUASAR
SOWETO
UNIVAC

7 letter words
CAT SCAN
CB RADIO
NABISCO
WYSIWYG

8 letter word
INTERPOL

ANSWER, PAGE 222

TWISTED TITLES 2

Here's a tougher version of the TWISTED TITLES you may have come across earlier in the book. The titles and names below (1–15) have been changed by one letter, and the summaries (a–o) describe those new titles. For example, if you figured out that we'd changed the movie title *Witness* to *Witless*, you could match *Witness* to a description like "A dumb cop solves a murder."

See if you can figure out what the titles were changed to and then match all the original titles with their new descriptions.

_____ 1. A BRIDGE TOO FAR
_____ 2. BORN FREE
_____ 3. CAR AND DRIVER
_____ 4. 50 WAYS TO LEAVE YOUR LOVER
_____ 5. HAIR
_____ 6. I CHING
_____ 7. I GET A KICK OUT OF YOU
_____ 8. MRS. DOUBTFIRE
_____ 9. PREPARATION "H"
_____ 10. SPORTS ILLUSTRATED
_____ 11. THE GOLD RUSH
_____ 12. TOP GUN
_____ 13. WAR AND PEACE
_____ 14. WHAT KIND OF FOOL AM I?
_____ 15. WHEN I SAY NO I FEEL GUILTY

a. AAA gets a new automotive critic
b. Chiropractic anthem
c. Connie tries a new greeting on TV
d. Couch potato dies of thirst
e. Hollywood does the biography of Mother Teresa
f. Innovative ways to beat the recession
g. Limbaugh is shipped to Alaska
h. Magazine features automotive nonsense
i. Marilyn shocks her classmates at their 25th reunion
j. *Playboy* for pygmies
k. Self-help book for Santas who laugh too much
l. The Donner Party's marching song
m. The original, unsightly Broadway cast is removed only to appear again in three to four days
n. The baby's finally asleep
o. To reduce the swelling of an inflated ego

ANSWER, PAGE 227

* * * * *

UNCLE POTATO HEAD?

What's the potato's closest edible relative?

a) Eggplant
b) Yam
c) Cauliflower

ANSWER, PAGE 225

EQUATION ANALYSIS HUNT

The original "Equation Analysis Test" was created by Will Shortz for *Games* magazine; it quickly became one of the most widely reproduced puzzles ever. You've probably seen it before—but just in case, here's how it works: Take the equation 26 = L. of the A. Think about it for a minute. Got it? It stands for 26 = LETTERS of the ALPHABET. Here's another: 6 = P. in a P. T. Which can be solved as 6 = POCKETS in a POOL TABLE. There you go.

Of course, we had to take the test one step further. We've listed some of our favorite equations below. Once you've solved each equation, find the words in the grid. For instance, after solving 6 = POCKETS in a POOL TABLE, you can look for POCKETS and the full phrase POOL TABLE.

Note: You can also use the grid for help solving the equations, since you have the first letters of each word and phrase. Once you've found them all, you shall be rewarded: The leftover letters will reveal a quote about math. (Sorry it couldn't have been something a little more expensive, but we're on a tight budget here.) Solve this one and you deserve 3 = C. (Cheers, that is.)

```
P S R E B M U N M O H S S C A L E A L B E
L R E T E I S E E R G E D N S G T H N E D
A D I V S E Y N A L I B A B A S A A A I I
Y I D N E V M S I F G N L C I R C L E S A
E V G P T I P C E O T N M H E Y M F L A M
R I T A O L H H Z O D I A C T O E D M O O
S N A E N T O T I T C I T T C H S O A N N
G E S L H C N A V B H E I T H I E L N Y D
O C S T H G I N N A I B A R A G P L E V A
L O D N H E E E R L E V N S D P I A L T S
D M R A I N S D N L E H S Y I E R R T T H
I E N I E E N O T T R D R A O B T R A D E
L D E G A E Y T O E W O N D E R S R F J C
O Y V S S P I Q R A E O L A C T S I O Q I
C V O S I L U T Y M K L R I A D R K G U M
K N H B E A R S O E E F I L R N E O E A D
S T T U R N N D Y E R T S T D R G A N R N
N D E T M E T S Y S R A L O S D N K E T I
G R E A T T O M A T O E S I E T I M R S L
Y R B S E S L F A M E R I C A N F L A G B
S A S E S U M K E E R G K N D Y M O L R E
```

1 = G. L. for M.
1 = L. to L.
2 = Q. in a H. D.
3 = B. in "G."
3 = B. M.
4 = Q. in a G.
4 = S. for a G.
4 = S. in a Y.
5 = F. on a H.
7 = W. of the A. W.
8 = G. T. in a L. B. C.
9 = C. of H. in the "D. C."
9 = G. M.
9 = P. in the S. S.
9 = S. by B.
10 = H. of a D. on the M. S.
11 = P. on a F. T.
12 = N. in an O.
12 = S. of the Z.
13 = S. on the A. F.
20 = N. on a D.
40 = D. of R. in the G. F.
40 = T. (with A. B.)
54 = C. in a D. (with the J.)
88 = P. K.
90 = D. in a R. A.
101 = D.
1001 = A. N.

ANSWER, PAGE 229

HIDDEN TALENTS

You've probably heard of all the famous names in this puzzle, but you might be surprised at some of their lesser known claims to fame.

ACROSS

1 Mulder's employer
4 Beat until fluffy
8 Stadium in Flushing, NY
12 ___ kwon do
15 Tear-stained, say
18 Hardwood tree
19 Right-hand person
20 He worked as the London correspondent of the *New York Tribune*
22 Rhoda Morgenstern's mom
23 He designed Italy's flag
26 Negligent
27 Lunch or dinner
28 "Woe is me!"
29 Cinnamon roll shapes
31 He wrote the "Stuck on Me" Band-Aid jingle
35 Natural gas compound
37 Baseball card stats
38 Baddies of Middle Earth
39 *Mad About You* infant
43 Miner's finds
44 Chicken ___ king
45 Kiddies' alphabet blocks, usually
46 He loved Lucy
47 Gangsta rap pioneer
48 Best Supporting Actor winner for *Traffic*
50 Uncontained, as a yard
52 He was Lindbergh's first passenger in the *Spirit of St. Louis*
56 Chooses
59 Spicy Louisiana cuisine
62 Opera set in ancient Egypt
63 Oblique typestyle (abbr.)
64 "I ___ you one"
65 Wide-eyed
66 He's a descendant of Pocahontas
70 Pixy ___ (candy brand)
71 "As if it wasn't obvious!"
72 Vehix.com commodity
73 Jazz singer Laine
74 Oil magnate J. Paul ___
75 New Mexico's capital
77 He drew the Chiquita Banana lady
80 Printer's characters that look like pointing fingers
83 Family storyteller, maybe
87 What a high-top covers
89 Melville's obsessed captain
90 Deck used in fortune-telling
92 Squealer
93 Affair of honor
94 Word before barrier or boom
96 Be an accessory
97 Die like a snowman
98 One of the Gallo brothers
101 He invented wax paper
104 Makes precious (to)
107 German auto
108 "Major" constellation
109 CBS's logo
110 He came up with the Maxwell House slogan, "Good to the last drop"
116 Came first
117 The statue of St. Michael atop Norway's Trondheim Cathedral is based on him
118 "Cool!"
119 Road marker abbr.
120 Cottage covering, in day-dreams
121 "Owner of a Lonely Heart" band
122 Reef lurkers
123 Therefore
124 Boston's Red ___

DOWN

1 Swampy region
2 In the wrong
3 Chrysler model
4 One of Ward's wards
5 Hasten
6 Altar answer
7 Punishment for sins, Catholic-style
8 Single-word toast
9 Cab for Sherlock
10 Tide rival
11 High mountain
12 Protective cover
13 Clarinetist Shaw
14 Apply, as influence
15 He was the first Ronald McDonald
16 He played Mary Tyler Moore's TV boss
17 Sticker price addition
21 Some college degs.
24 Boaters' blades
25 Utter happiness
30 What Richard III would have traded his kingdom for
31 Morgan's costar in *Se7en*
32 Lament
33 ___ Day (spring holiday)
34 Used seaboots
36 Laramie-to-Cheyenne dir.
40 Golfer Hogan
41 Upper-left keyboard button

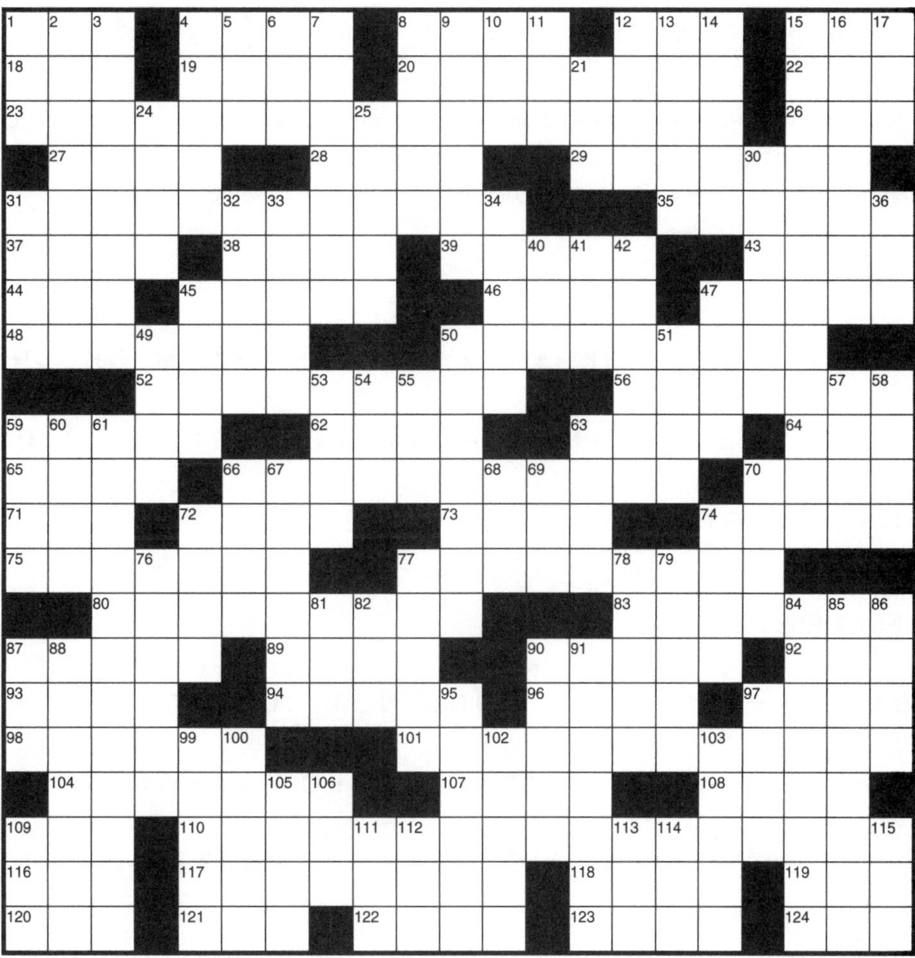

42 Isn't honest with
45 *Fargo* director Joel
47 Big PC distributor
49 Goon
50 Assisi's saint
51 Having little fat
53 Exuberant cries
54 Ornamental auto part
55 Beethoven's "___ to Joy"
57 Nincompoop
58 New and trendy
59 Rotters
60 Water, to Juan
61 He popularized James Bond in the U.S. by saying that *From Russia, With Love* was one of his favorite books
63 "Believe ___ not!"
66 Travel on a breeze
67 Bullfight rings, e.g.
68 Antlered animal
69 Orb weaver's home
70 Spotted
72 "That being the ___..."
74 Pesky little bug
76 Like a farmer's fields
77 Credit's opposite
78 Shrek and his ilk
79 Sent letters to
81 "I thought as much!"
82 Off-white shade
84 Chests of drawers
85 Residential city near Stanford
86 Business letter abbr.
87 Refreshing beverage
88 Ballet legend Rudolf
90 One who works with lions
91 Mother-of-pearl source
95 Adapted for many singers
97 Missile with multiple warheads
99 Store for future use
100 Lake ___ (Sierra Nevada resort)
102 Pro-am tournaments
103 Because of
105 Confederate soldiers
106 Turf
109 Actor Wallach
111 Colorant
112 Grand ___ Opry
113 "___ the ramparts we watched..."
114 Old sofa's problem
115 John Ritter's dad

ANSWER, PAGE 229

INDUSTRIAL ESPIONAGE

All the quotes on this page have to do with how certain companies started, or how they conduct their business. To find out their secrets, simply translate the following messages that we've converted using simple letter substitution. For further instructions and hints on how to solve, see page 15.

DING-DING-DING!

SV-SV TWVUVNHW *XVJKRX *XAJYKJ KROV MJDHJNHX NZH *HOQMUV *TMH KJX VWMPMJKNHX NZH *PVVX *ZAUVW MYH YWHKU NWAYQ.

A YEN FOR SUCCESS

V KJCQBAR-QRXXRC QJXG *HNLZNCJ *QJMJGV NQ IVT SJJG XBLH QJ LZVASR ZNT OCJGBLQ'T AVWR QJ *QJMJQV VAG JAXM BTR LVC AVWRT ERSNAANAS INQZ QZR XRQQRC "L."

WE LOVE HER, TOO!

*OGE OASEN WSU US OSLNB UAN *ENWYUN *MSBNTPW *BNHYUTSWE *OSQQTUUNN'E ANYBTWPE SW *LTNUWYQ YWZ TWEUNYZ YTBNZ BNBJWE SM *T *HSLN *HJOC YWZ *UAN *BNYH *QOOSCE.

IT'S JUST A YELLOW WEATHER INVERSION

AUOFV HQZOQF AQEIOFKQXF: FRQ *CLH *IXTQCQH *FUKQH JIOH FRQ PLOA "HKLT" DOLK UFH OQIC-QHFIFQ HQZFULX.

ANSWER, PAGE 229

HASH HOUSE

People who work in diners have a language all their own...which we've made a hash of. We've taken the examples of diner lingo and intermingled them with their real-world translations, but without scrambling them. For instance, C J O F A V F A E E can be separated into COFFEE and JAVA like this: C j O F a v F a E E. See if you can figure out what to order next.

1. A B X L U E T G R T E A E R S E
2. B H U O R T N T D H O E P G U P
3. W A I T L H L E V T E H R Y E T H W I A N Y G
4. K E N E O P L O F E F T H T E T G U R C A S E S
5. F S I P R S A R T E R L I A B D Y S
6. P H I A G B M S E T A W E N E N D T W H E S I H E C H E T S
7. H P I G L H A N A D I D R N Y
8. C U B O P I O L F H E O D T L E T A E V E S A
9. B O C W E L O R F B I E R D A S E L E D
10. T O A K N E O W U H T O E R E L D E S R
11. T A F I P I S O C H A P U E D Y D E I N S G
12. W E C S O T E W R N O M B E O L E Y T

ANSWER, PAGE 192

FOWL'S-EYE VIEW

Small crostic puzzles are solved just like the big ones (directions on page 11) but the first letter of the fill-in words **do not** spell out a hidden message.

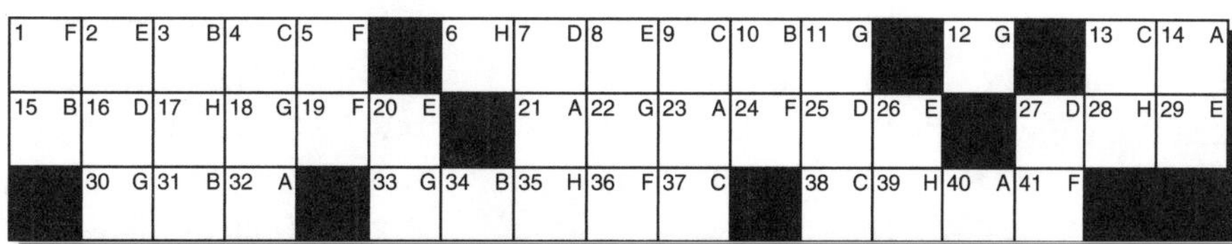

A. Your mother's brother

___ ___ ___ ___ ___
40 23 21 14 32

B. "Moolah"

___ ___ ___ ___ ___
3 34 15 10 31

C. Short, descriptive write-up

___ ___ ___ ___ ___
38 4 9 37 13

D. Dollar bills

___ ___ ___ ___
25 7 16 27

E. Lavished affection (on)

___ ___ ___ ___ ___
20 8 26 29 2

F. Andy of *60 Minutes*

___ ___ ___ ___ ___ ___
19 36 1 24 41 5

G. Cornell University locale

___ ___ ___ ___ ___ ___
18 30 11 22 33 12

H. Southern lady

___ ___ ___ ___ ___
17 6 39 35 28

ANSWER, PAGE 198

MODERN-DAY LATIN

Latin may be a dead language for most people…but not for the Vatican. In 1991 they published the *Lexicon Recentis Latinitas*, an 18,000-word dictionary updating Latin for modern usage. The italicized clues in this puzzle represent some of its entries; can you guess their English meanings?

ACROSS

1 It might hold water
5 Not suitable
10 It might hold water
15 Borrow, as a cigarette
18 "It's all the ___ to me"
19 Shock jock's venue
20 Susan Lucci's *All My Children* role
21 Actress Ward
22 *Fluxus interclusio*
24 *Infantaria*
26 Hit result, maybe (abbr.)
27 Honolulu's island
28 Watch chains
29 Low-risk investment choices
30 Nothing but
31 *Exemplar luce expressum*
34 *Autocinetorum lavatrix*
35 Real estate document
37 Permanent providers?
38 Hydrogen and others
39 Summed number
42 Without ice, to a bartender
43 Gave a broken leg, e.g.
44 Hosp. higher-ups
47 Subterranean spaces
49 Look up at the stars, say
50 With 93 Across, British playwright who wrote *Private Lives*
51 Lessen, as pain
54 *Itinerum procuratio*
58 Unruffled
59 Showed up
62 Stopped fluttering about
63 Law of motion formulator
64 Jeff Lynne's band, briefly
65 *Arbor natalicia*
68 Fruit drink
69 Toots & the Maytals's music
71 Strain or sprain symptom
72 ___ to the throne
73 Numbers on birthday cakes
74 *Coercitio mentis*
77 Maxwell House competitor
79 Hotels
80 Colleagues of Eliot Ness
81 Tough guy
84 Businesses (abbr.)
85 Boxer Julio ___ Chavez
87 Dorothy's four-legged friend
88 Resides
92 The most common first name among U.S. presidents
93 See 50 Across
95 Trouser line
96 *Memoriae amissio*
99 *Fulgor photographicus*
102 Get 100%
103 Outfought
104 Cattleman's device
105 ___ Khayyam
106 Bake sale org.
107 *Liber maxime divenditus*
109 *Aeris benzinique mixtura*
112 "Goodness me!"
113 Prefix for surgeon or toxin
114 Didn't rent
115 Sneaky stratagem
116 Moray ___
117 Watch that "takes a licking and keeps on ticking"
118 Light or dark concoctions
119 Imitated

DOWN

1 *CHiPs* actor Erik ___
2 Sang like a canary
3 Sent via AOL
4 Field arbiter
5 Dickensian villain ___ Heep
6 Tex-Mex appetizer
7 Commanding officer's assistant
8 Actress Zadora
9 Male feline
10 Dances to '40s jazz
11 James Joyce tale
12 Kids with a common parent
13 Chilled
14 '70s tennis champ Ilie ___
15 Fighting fish
16 ___ *Gold* (Peter Fonda film)
17 Cattails' habitat
21 Puts away
23 Dandyish sort
25 "The Lady ___" (Chris de Burgh hit)
28 Helvetica, e.g.
32 Bread spread
33 "The ___ is clear!"
34 Desert transport
36 Render unsticky
38 Newspaper name
40 Well-armed org.
41 Rawhide pet treat
43 Sparing no expense
44 Movie editor's creation
45 Secret ___ Ring (Ovaltine toy)
46 Cunning
48 Rend
49 Sumptuous party
50 Fresh off the lot
51 Like lemon juice

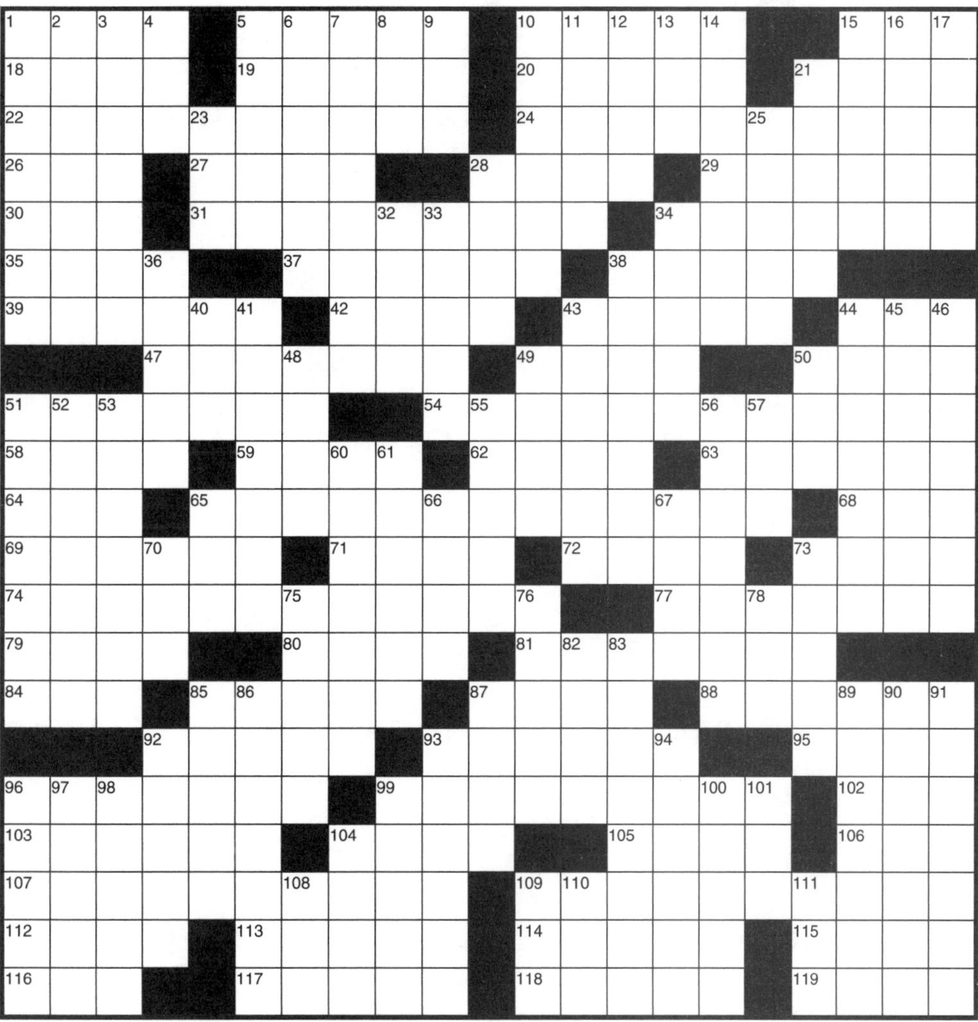

52 Italian seaport
53 "Enjoy Coca-Cola" and "Just Do It," e.g.
55 Soup-and-noodle dish
56 Type of barometer
57 "___ whiz!"
60 Noxious clouds
61 Graphic artist M. C. ___
65 Campbell's container
66 Like Twiggy
67 Lick, musically speaking
70 Enlisted men
73 ___ *of God* (1985 movie)
75 Where most of the action in *Moby Dick* takes place
76 Goes from boyhood to manhood
78 "There oughta be a ___!"
82 Four Corners state
83 Abstained from
85 They're tried
86 Renowned
87 Pond dweller
89 Rose dramatically from one's chair
90 ___ intolerant (wary of dairy)
91 Threw barbs, as during a political campaign
92 Pier made of stones
93 Bleach brand
94 Not as bright
96 Chicago Seven figure ___ Hoffman
97 Reagan Attorney General Edwin
98 Kind of spray
99 "___ Jacques"
100 Praises
101 "___, I'm freezing!"
104 Fruit with a stone
108 Hawaiian vacation keepsake
109 Corn on the ___
110 Astonishment
111 Historical period

ANSWER, PAGE 221

ROSEANNE SEZ...

A few choice thoughts from Roseanne, Uncle John puzzle-style. For instructions and hints on how to solve, see page 15.

1. DWN BPD FRCAQ DWN BPZZCSK FRS BPA WY DWNZ KZSPBL, GNF YCYFSSA DSPZL IPFSZ, DWN'ZS BPZZCSK FW P ZSJICACAX JRPCZ FRPF GNZVL.

2. VQK EJP D ZQP QX PJWTUQW. VQK EJP D ZQP QX FJDYDSFJT. U YQ AFDP UP TDVT QW PFJ DTIUBUW CQPPZJ. PDMJ PAQ DWY MJJI DADV XBQO SFUZYBJW.

3. QO XHZWNTA NTA V IKHTA YXVZ SBLNY TLP QLYXKA KI WVBYX EKTYBKD YXNY BLNDDO, BLNDDO PKBMZ. LGLBO TVSXY WLIKBL PL SK YK WLA, PL ZULTA NT XKHB PVYX KHB MVAZ.

4. U MVUJ WLSPUQT. U ZAAG DAJJAK. U WLAGG DAJJAK. RQC UJ'W WRZAK JS CKUQP SVJ SZ SGC DAAK FRQW GRNUQT RKSVQC JBA BSVWA.

5. DZK VME T SHHR MD TD, TL DZK RTQC MFK CDTSS MSTNK VZKX WE ZJCGMXQ UHWKC ZHWK LFHW VHFR, DZKX T'NK QHXK WE OHG.

ANSWER, PAGE 213

STILL CHANNEL SURFING

Haven't you gotten up off that couch yet? It must be a fascination with our top ten TV shows below, the letters to which we've, ahem, rearranged. Put them back in the right place to get the name of a TV show that spent at least one season on the list. For example, the answer to AL'S LAD (6) would be *Dallas*.

1. PRIGS IN WAGON (7 5) _______ _____
2. ESCHER (6) ______
3. HALF-MILE LITANY (3 2 3 6) ___ __ ___ ______
4. STOP ARCHENEMY (5'1 7) _____'_ _______
5. DERISION (8) ________
6. HOWDY, EASTERNER (3 6 5) ___ ______ _____
7. GOTHIC RUNT (5 5) _____ _____
8. AGONY AUNT BELCHED (7 2 2 5) _______ __ __ _____
9. LODGING SHELTER (3 6 5) ___ ______ _____
10. SCAN EVIL SCOOTER (8'1 6) ________'_ ______
11. MERCY! DUMB LAWS (6 5, 1.1.) ______ _____, _._.
12. TEACH IN DRIBLETS (4'1 10) ____'_ __________
13. THE FRETSAW'S KNOB (6 5 4) ______ _____ ____
14. YENS TEMPT (5 4) _____ ____
15. IMPUGN MA (6, 1.1.) ______, _._.
16. HOTHEADS RAKED FUZZ (3 5 2 7) ___ _____ __ _______
17. W. H. AUDEN'S EVIL SLOTH (3 2 8 4) ___ __ ________ ____
18. JAILS HAVE NO CHOICE (6 5 6) ______ _____ ______

ANSWER, PAGE 223

EVEN MORE GOOFY HEADLINES

We've ripped some headlines from the front pages of newspapers around the world, like "FEDERAL AGENTS RAID GUN SHOP, FIND WEAPONS." But if you want to read the equally silly headlines below, you'll first have to unscramble the three-letter groups we broke them up into. For instance, you'd find FED ERA LAG, etc. all mixed up, followed by numbers that signify the number of letters in the original, like the (7 6 4 3 4, 4 7) that would refer to that same silly headline.

1. AYS DCI ERS FEE MAY ORM ORS PTF SSA URD XCE (5 4 1.1. 2 4 6 3 7)

2. ANP CTP ESA FFE GBE JUM OOR PIN RIC (7 4 6 6 4)

3. ANY ASM BOY ESA GNA NCI PRE RLS SCA SGI USE (4 5 2 4 11 2 5)

4. EMI EPR ING ITU NAG NPR OBL OST SMO TEE TIO UNT (7 12 7 2 8)

5. ADW BYB EAT ELA HER RMD STO YED (5 7 2 3 7)

ANSWER, PAGE 227

...IS FOR THE MILLION THINGS...

Small crostic puzzles are solved just like the big ones (directions on page 11) but the first letter of the fill-in words **do not** spell out a hidden message.

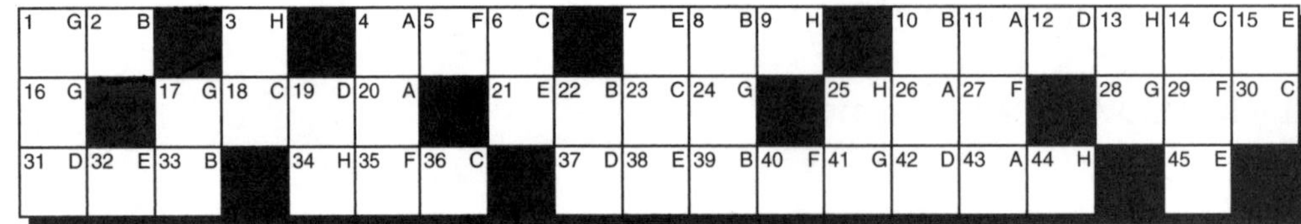

A. Close-to-the-ground dance

__ __ __ __ __
11 26 43 4 20

B. Noisy brawl

10 33 8 39 22 2

C. Mirth or merriment

18 36 23 14 30 6

D. Western classic starring Alan Ladd

19 31 42 37 12

E. The Twins of the zodiac

21 32 45 7 15 38

F. They're found at the end of fishing lines

35 5 29 40 27

G. Supervise, as an office

28 1 41 17 16 24

H. "Oh! say, can you see…," e.g.

3 9 34 25 44 13

ANSWER, PAGE 194

YOU'VE GOT THE SHAKES

You were expecting Shakespeare, maybe? Not quite. The quotes on this page were uttered by a stand-up comic named Ronnie Shakes. (We're not exactly sure who he is, but we're sure he's funny.) If you need directions on how to solve this puzzle, see page 5.

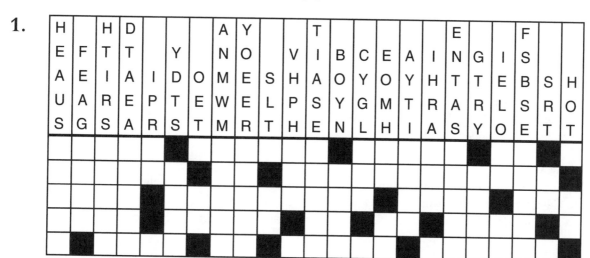

1.

H		H	D				A	Y			T						E			F		
E	F	T	T		Y		N	O		V	I	B	C	E	A	I	N	G	I	S		
A	E	I	A	I	D	O	M	E	S	H	A	O	Y	O	Y	H	T	T	E	B	S	H
U	A	R	E	P	T	E	W	E	L	P	S	Y	G	M	T	R	A	R	L	S	R	O
S	G	S	A	R	S	T	M	R	T	H	E	N	L	H	I	A	S	Y	O	E	T	T

2.

			A			G	O	I		P		T										
P		W	O	S		W	H	T		W		A	E		N	D	Y		H		S	
I	I	O	E	F		G	H	E	L	I	O	G	T	R	B	U	D		H	E	L	O
I	Y	V	H	D	T	H	O	U	K	D	N	T	O	A	T	O	F	O	P	E	C	I
T	G	T	O	O	U	T	I	N	N	G	H	W	H	A	T	H	E	T	A	O	N	L

3.

						I	R	I		G					A			W	A			
R		O	M		P	I	R	T		W	N	I			D		A	H	B	U	F	I
H	E	Y	D	E	F	O	V	E		T	I	T	M	E	I	T	M	N	E	I	L	E
S	H	T	O	E	L	E	N	E	N	E	E	E	N	H	T	V	F	C	T	Y	G	E
T	E	O	N	T	H	A	R	E	M	A	R	M	E	A	A	L	T	O	A	A	G	H

ANSWER, PAGE 194

YOU'RE MY INSPIRATION

Back in the days of the cavemen, creation myths were all about giant turtles swallowing the moon, giving birth to the earth, and generally doing lots of things turtles don't actually do. We like our creation stories better—but some of them are so mythological that they could actually be (you know us!) complete lies. Can you tell which ones were created here at Uncle John's place?

POPEYE

E. C. Segar's spinach-eating sailor was based on a beady-eyed, pipe smoking, wiry old barroom brawler named Frank "Rocky" Feigle—a legend in Segar's hometown of Chester, Illinois, around 1915. Like Popeye, Feigle was reputed never to have lost a fight. But he was no sailor; he earned his drinking money by sweeping out the local saloon.

NICOLAS CAGE

Nicolas Coppola, wanting to establish his own identity apart from the Coppola clan, changed his last name to Cage because, in his words, he has "a hard, unemotional exterior, but then you look again and there's a tiger inside. I love acting because of the effort it takes not to let the tiger loose."

PEPE LE PEW

Chuck Jones owned a cat named Twinkles, and when Twinkles went into heat for the first time, the tomcats who came to court her were joined by a skunk. In one sense, the skunk had an advantage over the cats since his presence made them all run away, but Twinkles fled as well, hiding in the house. When the skunk stayed in the front yard until Twinkles wasn't in heat anymore, Jones found such dedication inspiring—although there's no record that the skunk in his yard had a French accent.

THE SHINING

Inspired by John Lennon…or at least the term was. Stephen King came up with the idea of the "shining" as a description of psychic power after hearing Lennon's tune, "Instant Karma." King recalls: "The refrain went, 'We all shine on.' I really liked that." The book's name was originally *The Shine*, but someone pointed out to King, "You can't use that because it's a pejorative word for 'black'." So it became *The Shining.*

ROCK HUDSON

Originally named Roy Scherer, he got his stage name by combining two geographical spots: the Rock of Gibraltar and the Hudson River.

POE'S *THE RAVEN*

Prosaic as it may seem, the immortal poem was inspired by a real raven. John James Audubon owned a stuffed raven that he had attempted to paint on several occasions, but he was never perfectly happy with the results. In 1841, Audubon mounted an exhibition of his work in Philadelphia, which Poe attended. After discussing the work with the vaguely dissatisfied Audubon, he offered to attempt his own "portrait" of the bird. Audubon shipped him the bird, which now resides in the Philadelphia Library, locked in a closet, next to a sign: *The Most Famous Bird in the World.*

CHARLIE'S ANGELS

The TV series was going to be called Alley Cats until costar Kate Jackson suggested *Charlie's Angels*. Producer Aaron Spelling asked where she got the idea, and Jackson pointed to a picture of three female angels—right behind him, on the wall of his office. It wasn't even Spelling's picture; he'd inherited the office (and the picture) from Frank Sinatra.

ANSWER, PAGE 191

LEARN JAPANESE IN ONE EASY LESSON!

France has actually passed laws to keep English words from turning up as part of the French language, but Japan doesn't seem to mind at all. It's just as well, since so many of their everyday words are borrowed from English—like "baseboru" from the English "baseball."

The list below contains 35 Japanese translations—but don't look for *them* in the grid. It's their English equivalents that we've hidden in the grid reading across, down, and diagonally. When you've found them all, the leftover letters will reveal how the title of an American film was translated to "Japanese." (And if you get stuck, you can peek at a list of the English words on the answer page.)

T	P	U	C	R	H	E	H	O	X	E	S	R	S
E	A	W	B	E	H	S	I	S	C	P	G	E	R
E	G	E	U	T	T	P	O	I	N	T	O	O	R
P	E	L	T	I	A	O	V	I	T	A	M	I	N
R	E	S	T	A	U	R	A	N	T	C	S	D	Y
E	D	C	E	W	E	T	J	A	D	P	M	A	A
N	H	E	R	S	S	S	N	O	B	B	E	R	Y
L	E	C	U	A	S	T	N	A	P	E	M	T	H
L	H	O	T	E	L	A	S	E	M	A	B	T	G
A	L	E	R	R	L	R	L	U	S	A	E	U	A
B	C	A	R	D	E	S	I	G	N	S	R	A	S
S	C	H	S	W	E	L	W	D	N	O	B	D	Y
W	I	G	O	L	F	N	D	E	I	U	B	N	M
O	N	T	R	A	M	S	T	A	N	P	S	N	A

BASU
BATA
BIIRU
BITAMI
BONASU
BORU
BURAUSU
CARESU
DEZAIN
DORAMA
GASU
GORUFU
HOTERU
KADO
KAPPU
MAKUDONARUDO
MEMBA
NYUSU
PANTSU
PEJI
POINTO
RAJIO
RESUTORAN
SABISU
SEKKUSU
SOSU
SUMATO
SUMOGGU
SUNGURASU
SUNOBBARI
SUPOTSU
SUPU
SUTECCHI
TAWA
WETA

ANSWER, PAGE 223

"AND NOW, THE PUNCH LINE..."

Life is funny that way. True stories with a punch line, from various *Uncle John's Bathroom Readers*.

ACROSS

1 Move downward
8 Qualifying race
12 Length x width equals it
16 Franken and Green
19 Marc Antony's wife
20 Relaxation
21 Long-distance call?
22 Court bisector
23 What advertising slogan, used successfully in print ads for the Pfeiffer Brewing Company, didn't go over quite so well on the radio?
27 Female swine
28 Trucker who's "on the air"
29 Gather, as a crop
30 Moved upward
31 What embarrassing realization did the National Park Service come to, after paying $230,000 for a half-acre of land near D.C. in 1986?
36 Burning
39 Horse with a speckled coat
40 Film critic Shalit
41 Binary digit
42 What state motto graces the license plates made by prison inmates in Concord, New Hampshire?
46 Involuntary movement
49 Maker of Cross Your Heart bras
50 "What a ___!"
51 Adjusting, as a violin
54 Egg producers
55 Decides (to)
57 Casual Friday no-nos
59 Christopher Columbus's birthplace
60 *One Day* ___ *Time*
61 Spot for a yacht
62 Medium-sized map dot
63 Spotlessness
64 What did murderer James Rodgers ask for as his final request, while facing the firing squad?
68 Make raised designs on
71 "Holy ___!"
72 Tirade
73 Letter before sigma
76 Quagmire
77 Robin Cook's first thriller
78 Progresso product
79 Lover's ___
80 Of a single shade
82 U-shaped sink pipe
85 San Diego suburb
87 Organ supplier
88 In 1997, when the public was clamoring for campaign finance reform, most Republicans favored a proposal that eliminated all contribution limits. What was the proposal's ironic name?
90 It merged with Bell Atlantic in 1998
92 Prefix with cavity or climax
94 *The Thin Man* pooch
95 Fixed routines
96 An Australian man convicted of bank robbery was granted a retrial under an alias, to avoid prejudice on the jury's part. Why?
102 ___ *Frome*
103 Irritate
104 Fashion designer ___ Gucci
105 1989 Weird Al Yankovic film
108 A group of counterfeiters produced a near-perfect run of bogus 50,000-ruble bank-notes. But they made one mistake—what was it?
114 Afternoon meal, in Britain
115 Undersized litter member
116 Fox's *American* ___
117 Obstructed
118 Like nearly all prime numbers
119 Anxious
120 Venomous snakes
121 Tennis player Ilie

DOWN

1 Connect-the-___
2 Canyon phenomenon
3 Crock-Pot concoction
4 Metered vehicle
5 Holiday preceder
6 Sister's daughter
7 Terence Trent ___
8 Family treasures
9 Do lunch
10 Bonfire remains
11 Neon ___ (aquarium fish)
12 "Will do, captain!"
13 Comebacks
14 Inventor Whitney
15 Poe's middle name
16 What "A.D." stands for
17 Admits
18 Tampa Bay city, for short
24 "___ the World"
25 Labyrinth wall, maybe
26 "Able was I ___ I saw Elba"
31 Low cards
32 Test the weight of
33 Not easy to find
34 Extremities
35 Sobbed
36 ___ male (pack leader)
37 ___-O-Fish sandwich
38 Onetime Mrs. Trump
43 Applies more grease to
44 Boot out of school
45 "Life ___ short"
47 Month when Woodstock was held

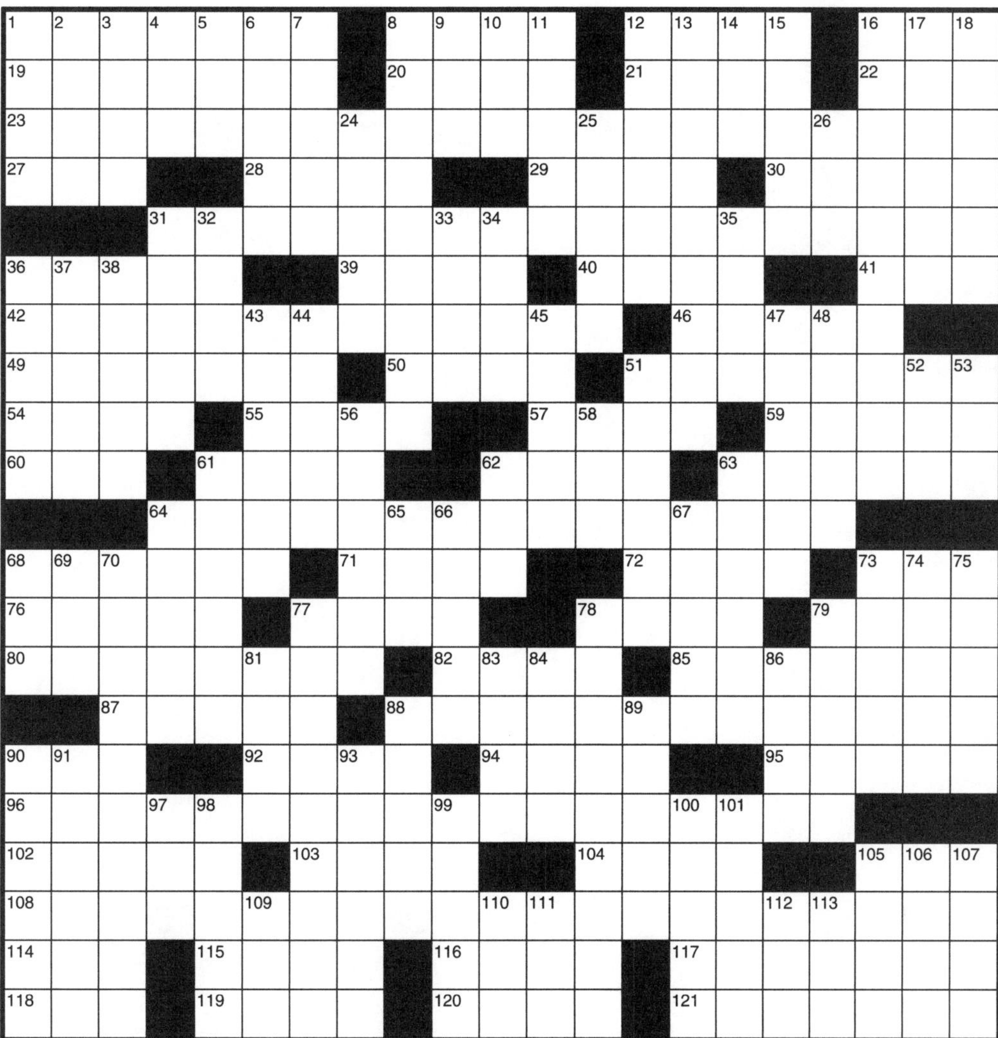

48 Hagar the Horrible's dog

51 *The Client* actor Brad ___

52 "This is ___ happening!"

53 2000 Best Supporting Actress Marcia ___ Hardin

56 Aftershock

58 ___ Jima

61 Continue

62 Take a crack at

63 Faithful correspondent

64 Chocolate syrup brand

65 Cartoon cat

66 Aristotle's tutor

67 Steel-lined bank room

68 Flightless bird

69 Aftershave user

70 Evelyn Waugh's ___ *Revisited*

73 Attended to a dead fire

74 2001 Best Actress Berry

75 Milky gemstones

77 Leaving no escape route for

78 Illegal pitches

79 Los ___ ("Don't Worry Baby" band)

81 Rich soil

83 Loud laugh

84 Furthermore

86 Violent twitch

88 Oven controls

89 Dining room centerpiece

90 Area with tenements

91 Gave to the church

93 Like scenic roads, often

97 Negative vote

98 *My Dinner with ___*

99 Old photo tint

100 Append

101 Actress Shearer

105 "___ choice" (label on packaged meat)

106 Cracks a whip at, maybe

107 Become duller

109 It's slung in dirty campaigns

110 Mag. employees

111 Cut off

112 FedEx rival

113 Fix a dislocated bone

ANSWER, PAGE 196

ANSWERS

THE ANAGRAMMIES

SO YOU THINK YOU'VE SEEN A UFO

1. Venus
2. Meteor
3. Falling space junk
4. Cloud
5. Weather balloon
6. Military aircraft
7. Electrical discharge

THE KING'S THINGS

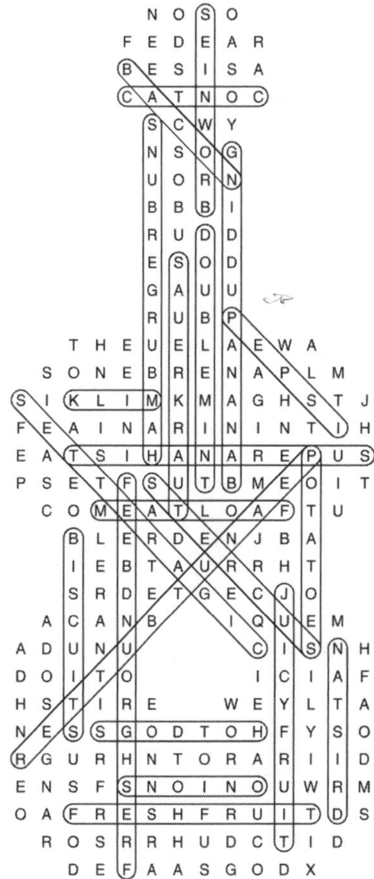

ATTACK OF THE MOVIE MONSTERS!

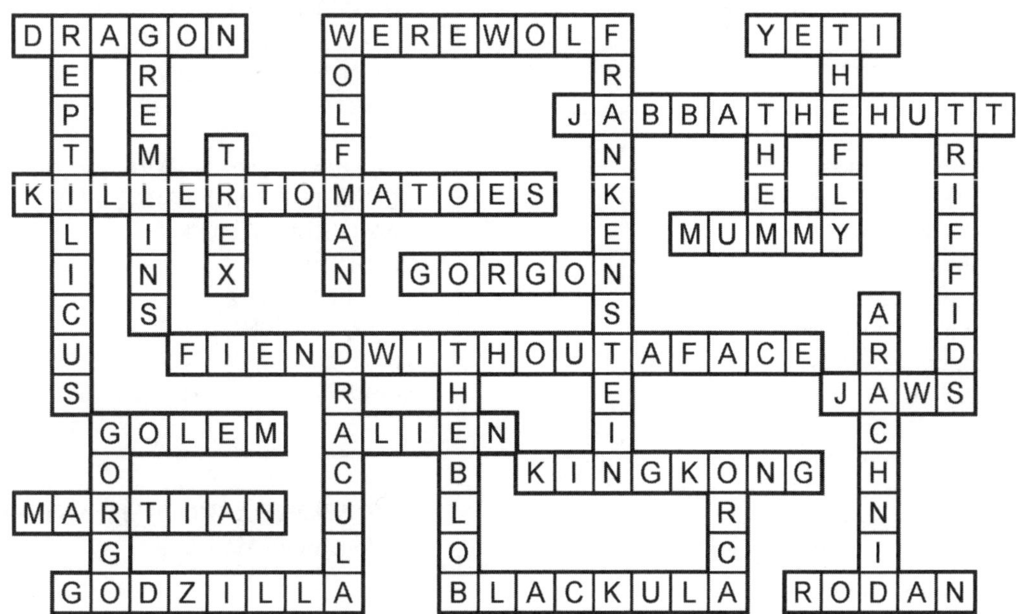

SNAP, CRACKLE, FLOP

The made-up cereals are Mysterios, Grape Ape, and Post Jelly Donuts.

YOU AIN'T GOT IT, KID

1 – a (Barbara Walters)
2 – c (Harrison Ford)
3 – a (Clint Eastwood)
4 – b (*The Diary of Anne Frank*)
5 – b (Danielle Steel)
6 – c (The Rolling Stones)
7 – b (Clark Gable)
8 – c (Fred Astaire)

BROADWAY BABIES

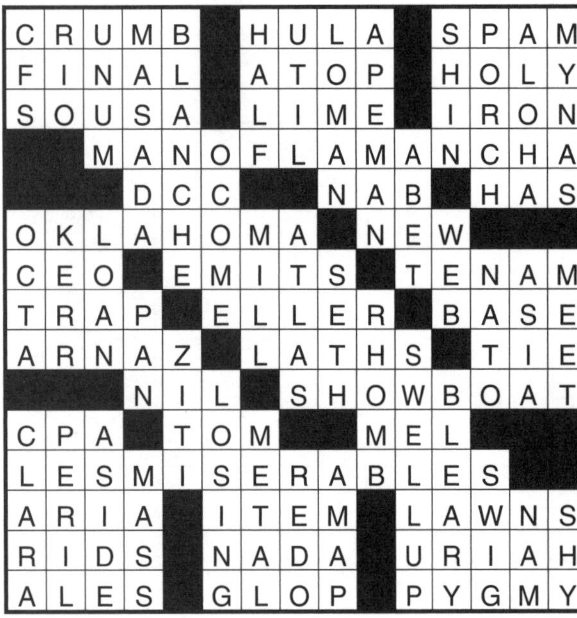

IF THEY MARRIED

1. Bo Ho
2. Yoko Ono Bono
3. Dolly Dali
4. Oprah Chopra
5. Olivia Newton-John Newton John
6. Sondra Locke Ness Munster
7. Bea Sting
8. Liv Ito Beaver
9. Shirley Ewell Rotten Hale
10. Ivana Bean Oscar Mayer Wiener
11. Javier Keiko and Edith Tu
12. Tuesday March III (3rd)
13. Snoop Dogg Pooh

SNACK FOOD OF THE GODS

The acrostic: THE POPCORN CHRONICLES

The quote: Native Americans believed that a tiny demon lived in each kernel of popcorn. When the demon's house was heated, the demon became so angry that it exploded.

The clue answers:

A. TEMPE
B. HEFTS
C. EARTH DAY
D. PINE
E. OVATION
F. PENTHOUSE
G. CANDIDE
H. OBSTINATE
I. REDBOOK
J. NELL
K. CHEECH
L. HAMLET
M. RAMMED
N. OMAHA
O. NIXON
P. INVENTIVE
Q. CHONG
R. LEEWAY
S. EDWARDS
T. STEED

TWISTED TITLES

LITTLE RED HIDING HOOD
DON'T FIT UNDER THE APPLE TREE
JUNE THE OBSCURE
THE CAT IN THE CAT
MY LIFE AS A LOG
THE NOW TESTAMENT
DUNCES WITH WOLVES
PATRIOT DAMES
'TIL DEATH DO US PARK
NEVER THE TWAIN SHALL MEAT
CANTERBURY TALKS
CLUB TED
MY LEFT FOOD
GOYZ N THE HOOD
THE WINNER OF OUR DISCONTENT
SLEEPING WITH THE ENEMA

WHO WANTS A GRAMMY, ANYWAY?

c. Fleetwood Mac

PHRASEOLOGY 101

U	P	A			B	L	E	S	S		S	E	A	L
R	I	B	S		A	G	R	E	E		P	A	V	E
B	E	A	T	T	H	E	R	A	P		A	V	O	W
A	C	T	O	R	S			G	T	O		E	N	D
N	E	H	R	U		A	S	A		P	A	S		
			K	N	U	C	K	L	E	U	N	D	E	R
M	T	S		K	N	E	E		A	S	T	R	A	Y
A	R	I	D		T	Y	L	E	R		S	O	S	A
L	U	G	O	S	I		T	O	T	S		P	E	N
T	E	N	G	A	L	L	O	N	H	A	T			
		A	S	S		A	N	S		N	U	L	L	S
B	A	T		H	E	M			S	T	R	E	E	T
O	N	U	S		T	O	U	C	H	A	N	D	G	O
Z	E	R	O		T	U	R	B	O		S	T	A	N
O	W	E	S		E	R	N	S	T			O	L	E

HIM TARZAN, HER JANE

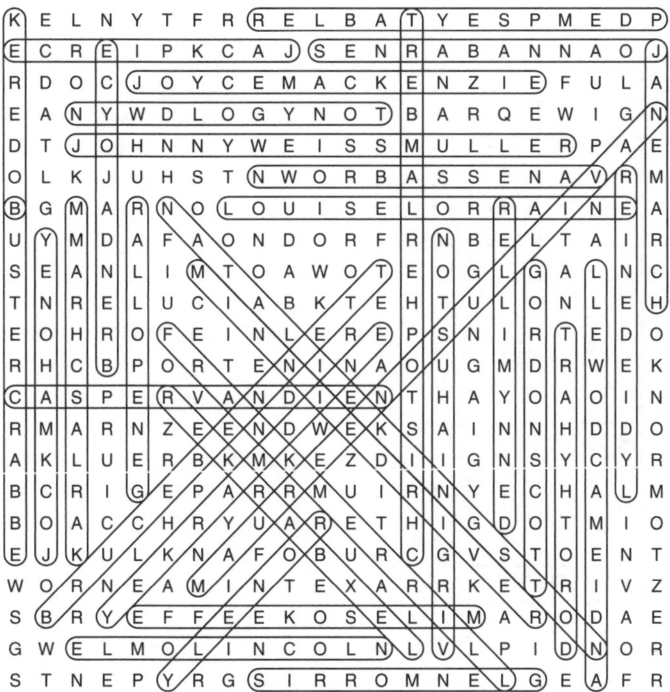

THEY'RE PLOTTING AGAINST ME

b. Have 5,000 pieces of junk mail sent to him daily

WANNA WRESTLE?

1 – f (Face: A "good guy")
2 – m (Heel: A "bad guy")
3 – o (Feud: A grudge match)
4 – l (Turn: When a bad guy changes his persona to a good guy or vice versa)
5 – a (Potato: Injure a wrestler in the head)
6 – q (Stiff: A move intended to cause real injury)
7 – i (Run-in: Intervention by a nonparticipant)
8 – s (Blade: Intentionally cut yourself to produce blood)
9 – b (Juice: Blood)
10 – j (Job: A staged loss)
11 – d (Post: Run someone into the ring post)
12 – r (Hardway juice: Blood from an unintentional injury)
13 – k (Heat: Level of enthusiasm of a crowd)
14 – e (Pop: A sudden rise in the enthusiasm of a crowd)
15 – p (Bump: A move that results in the wrestler falling out of the ring)
16 – g (Jobber: A wrestler who's hired to lose to the featured wrestler)
17 – n (Clean job: A staged loss that doesn't involve illegal wrestling moves)
18 – h (Screw-job: An ending that isn't clean, where someone wins by cheating)
19 – c (Shoot: One wrestler really trying to hurt another)

THE QUOTABLE JOHN

To Be Honest, Abe

The story: Lincoln jotted down the Gettysburg Address on an envelope. Good story, but just a myth. Several drafts of the speech have been discovered.

Pick a Number, as Long as It's...

Lucky seven. Seven is the sum of three and four, the triangle and the square, which ancient Greeks considered the two "perfect figures."

One Guy—Four Pieces of Big Apple Pie

The only baseball player ever to play for all four New York teams (Mets, Dodgers, Giants, Yankees) is Darryl Strawberry.

Speaking Pentagonese

Department of double-speak department: The U.S. government called the invasion of Grenada a "predawn vertical insertion."

THE MONSTER LIVES!

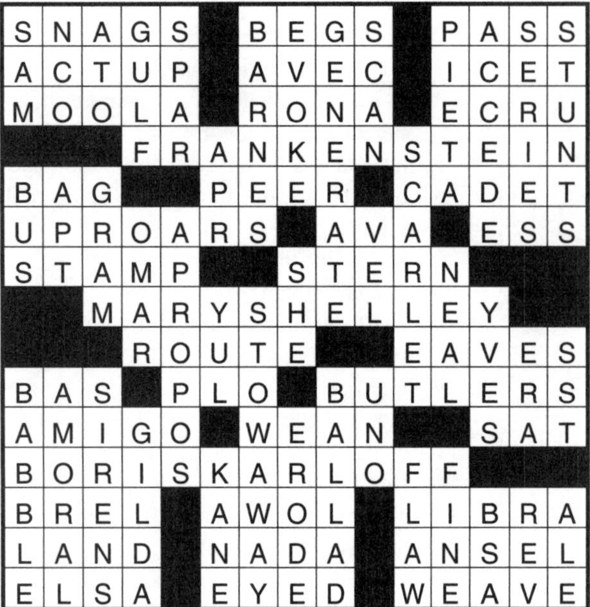

BE THE BEATLES

1 – b (When I feel my head start to swell, I look at Ringo and know perfectly well we're not supermen.)
2 – a (He's great. Especially his poetry.)
3 – b (We used to do that with no money in our pockets. There's no point in it.)
4 – c (We're not.)
5 – a (We're going to start a campaign to stamp out Detroit.)
6 – b (We've been wearing them for years.)
7 – a (We just get together and whoever knows most of the words sings the lead.)
8 – c (Because I can't fit them through my nose.)
9 – c (I'll hurt my lips.)
10 – b (Count the money.)

SATURDAY NIGHT

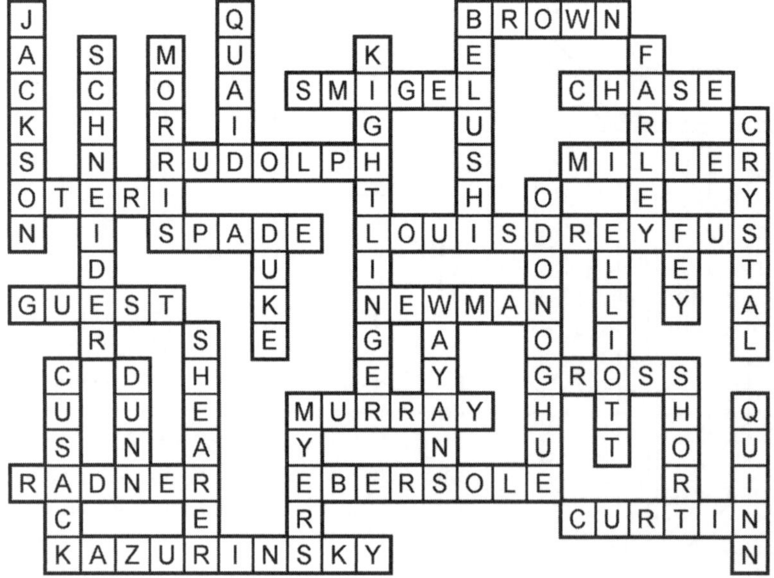

WHERE'S CHARLIE?

1. Charlie Chan
2. Prince Charles
3. Charles Lindbergh
4. Charlie Brown
5. Charles Barkley
6. Charles Darwin
7. Charlie Chaplin
8. Charlie Sheen

UNHOOKED ON PHONICS

The quote: Albert Einstein couldn't read until the age of nine.

The clue answers:

A. DENOUNCE
B. EBONITE
C. THINNER
D. ATLANTIS
E. DELI
F. GRATEFUL

WEIRD CELEBRATIONS

The Annual Hell's Angels Love Fest is the phony.

COUNTDOWN QUIZ

Kilroy

THE 10 MOST ADMIRED WOMEN IN AMERICA

The leftover letters spell: Some others on the list were Eleanor Roosevelt, Clare Boothe Luce, Helen Hayes, and Lurleen Wallace.

FYI: In case you were wondering who the heck some of these ladies are, here are thumbnail sketches of a few who might be unfamiliar.

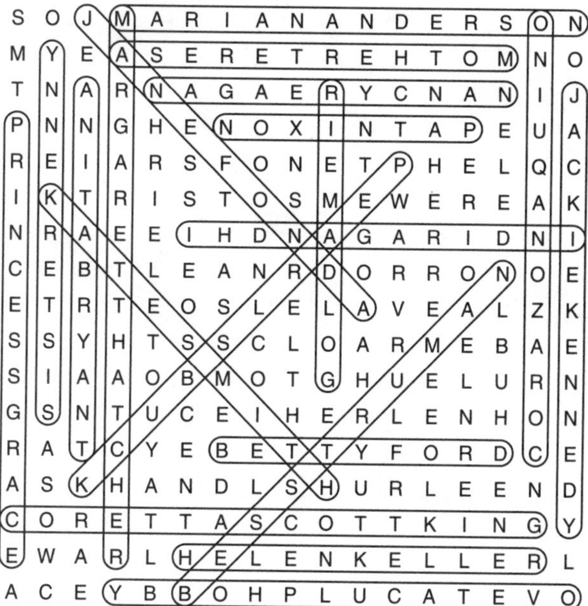

Marian Anderson (1902–1993). American singer, one of the finest contraltos of her time. First African American woman to perform in a lead role at the Metropolitan Opera, in 1955.

Corazon Aquino (1933–). Symbol of democracy. When her husband, Benino Aquino, was assassinated, she took his place in Philippine politics. Became president of the Philippines (1986–1992) restoring democratic rule after the long dictatorship of Ferdinand Marcos.

Helen Hayes (1900–1993). One of the most popular stage actresses of the 20th century. Known as "The First Lady of the American Theater."

Oveta Culp Hobby (1905–1995). Director of the U.S. Women's Army Corps (1942–1945), publisher of the *Houston Post* (1952– 1953), Secretary of Health, Education, and Welfare under President Eisenhower (1953–1955).

Sister Kenny (1880–1952). Renowned humanitarian. A nurse in the Australian medical corps during World War I, she later began a crusade to help childhood victims of polio. (Before polio could be prevented, it was among the most devastating childhood diseases.) The title of Sister was bestowed as a military rank for nurses in the Australian medical corps. Her invention of a special stretcher for moving patients in shock provided her with the funding to start her own clinic for polio victims, the Kenny Institute.

Clare Boothe Luce (1903–1987). American playwright, politician, and celebrity, often in the news and gossip columns. A congresswoman from Connecticut noted for her biting humor. Wrote the play *The Women* (rent it at your local video store). Was married to *Time/Life* magazine founder, Henry Luce.

Kate Smith (1909–1986). Another "First Lady," this time "of Radio," a widely popular singer known for her rendition of "God Bless America." (*Note:* She's the "fat lady" referred to in "It ain't over 'til the fat lady sings.")

Lurleen Wallace (1926–1968). George Wallace's wife. By law, Alabama's fiery segregationist governor George Wallace couldn't run for another term in 1966, so his wife did...and won.

YOU'RE MY INSPIRATION

Nicolas Cage's screen name is actually a tribute to both the comic book character Luke Cage (a.k.a. Power Man) and the composer John Cage.

Pepe Le Pew was inspired by smooth-talking French actor Charles Boyer, who played a character named Pepe Le Moko in the 1938 film *Algiers*.

***The Raven** was* inspired by a real raven, but the raven belonged to Charles Dickens, who received it as a gift in 1840, when he was researching ravens for *Barnaby Rudge*. The next year, Poe (at the time a literary critic in Philadelphia) savaged Dickens's use of the raven in *Rudge*, saying, "a raven could be put to far better literary use." That's when he started working on his poem. Meanwhile, Dickens's pet raven died in 1842 and was stuffed. (The bit about the Philadelphia Library is true, though.)

YIDDISH-AMERICAN SLANG

1. e; 2. t; 3. g; 4. f; 5. h; 6. q; 7. j; 8. r; 9. l; 10. m; 11. a; 12. b; 13. p; 14. s; 15. d; 16. k; 17. c; 18. i; 19. o; 20. n.

Here's the entire list, so you don't need an interpreter the next time you go to a Woody Allen movie.

Bupkis: Nothing
Chutzpa: Clever audacity
Drek: Junk; the bottom of the barrel
Goniff: A sneaky thief
Kibitz: To offer unsolicited advice
Klutz: A clumsy or inept person
Mensch: A compassionate, decent person
Meshugah: Crazy
Noodge: A pest
Nosh: A snack
Schlemiel: A hapless individual
Shiksa: A non-Jewish woman
Shlep: To haul around
Shlock: Something that's poorly made
Shlump: A sloppy person
Shmooze: To chat
Shtick: An act or a routine
Spritz: To squirt
Tchatchke: A toy, knickknack, worthless gizmo
Yenta: A nosy, gossipy person

HASH HOUSE

1. Axle grease: Butter
2. Burn the pup: Hot dog
3. All the way: With everything
4. Keep off the grass: No lettuce
5. First lady: Spare ribs
6. Pig between the sheets: Ham sandwich
7. High and dry: Plain
8. Boiled leaves: Cup of hot tea
9. Bowl of birdseed: Cereal
10. On wheels: Take-out order
11. Fish eyes: Tapioca pudding
12. Cowboy: Western omelet

PHRASEOLOGY 102

A	C	T	S	■	B	I	E	N	■	F	R	A	M	E
T	R	I	O	■	O	N	C	E	■	R	A	B	I	D
B	O	T	C	H	A	J	O	B	■	I	N	O	N	E
A	W	A	K	E	■	E	L	U	D	E	■	Y	E	N
T	E	N	■	D	R	S	■	L	O	N	■	■	■	■
■	■	■	■	G	E	T	C	O	L	D	F	E	E	T
■	B	A	S	E	D	■	O	U	T	■	O	L	E	O
D	U	C	T	S	■	R	V	S	■	J	O	L	L	Y
U	C	L	A	■	F	E	E	■	S	O	D	A	S	■
D	O	U	B	L	E	C	R	O	S	S	■	■	■	■
■	■	■	■	A	T	E	■	B	E	E	■	B	S	A
D	I	G	■	R	E	S	E	T	■	P	A	L	E	D
A	D	A	G	E	■	S	L	U	S	H	F	U	N	D
D	O	Z	E	D	■	E	L	S	A	■	R	E	S	T
A	L	A	M	O	■	D	E	E	P	■	O	R	E	O

PLAY D'OH!

That Rain Forest Thing: The whole reason we have elected officials is so we don't have to think all the time. Just like that rain forest scare a few years back: our officials saw there was a problem and they fixed it...didn't they?

What Senior Citizens Are Good For: Old people don't need companionship. They need to be isolated and studied so it can be determined what nutrients they have that might be extracted for our personal use.

Women!: A woman is like a beer. They look good, they smell good, and you'd step over your own mother just to get one!

Some Fatherly Advice: Son, when you participate in sporting events, it's not whether you win or lose, it's how drunk you get.

SPEAKING OF YIDDISH...

They all spent time as members of the U.S. Marine Corps.

HONK IF YOU LOVE PEACE AND QUIET

1. No sense being optimistic. It wouldn't work anyway.
2. If you can read this, I can slam on my brakes and sue you.
3. You never really learn to swear until you learn to drive.

WHICH HUNT

1. **The line drawn by the pencil** is 35 miles long. The average office chair on wheels will only travel 8 miles over the course of a year.
2. **A honeybee in flight** can travel up to 30 mph. The top speed of a falling raindrop is 22 mph.
3. **Big Ben's minute hand** is 11 feet long. The Statue of Liberty's index finger is 8 feet long.
4. **The dimples on a golf ball** number 350–400, depending on the make. A Big Mac bun has 178 sesame seeds on average.
5. **The longest recorded bout of hiccups** was *65 years*. The longest recorded fit of sneezing was only 978 days.
6. ***Hamlet*** has been adapted 49 times; *Romeo and Juliet*, only 27.
7. **A quarter** has 119 grooves, to a dime's 118.
8. **The Atlantic** is saltier than the Pacific.
9. **Children** have more taste buds than adults do.
10. ***The Munsters*** was more popular than *The Addams Family*.
11. **New England** is half as large as England.
12. **The Mayan Empire** lasted *six* times longer than the Roman Empire.
13. **The phone lines in the Pentagon** comprise more miles, but not by much: 68,000 miles of phone lines, compared to the human body's 60,000 miles of blood vessels.
14. **Murders** have claimed more American lives than wars in the 20th century.
15. **The average MTV viewer** tunes in for 16 minutes at a time; the average *Sesame Street* viewer, only 8 minutes.
16. **Lack of sleep** will kill you in about 10 days. Starvation takes a few weeks.
17. **George Washington**'s feet were size 13. Fred Astaire's dancing shoes were 8 ½.
18. **Looking for misplaced objects** consumes about a year of the average person's life; waiting at red lights, only six months.
19. **The point differential of the worst defeat in football history** was 222 (the score was, in fact 222–0). The highest score on a single hole of golf in tournament play is 161.
20. **Drinkers of goat's milk** are more common than drinkers of cow's milk.
21. **Fingernails** grow faster than toenails.
22. **Taking as many deductions as possible** is more important than avoiding an audit, to most American taxpayers.
23. **Sleeping**, believe it or not, burns more calories than watching TV.
24. **A 75-watt bulb** gives off more light than three 25-watt bulbs.
25. **A watermelon** is 92% water, compared to an apple's 84%. (Hey, it's right there in the name: *water*melon.)
26. **The Eiffel Tower** is more than three times taller than the Statue of Liberty.
27. **Muscle** comprises 65 pounds of the average adult male's body; bone comprises only 40 pounds.
28. **Music** is preferred to silence by most Americans on hold.
29. **The Jolly Green Giant** is much older; he was introduced in 1928. Tony the Tiger debuted in 1955.
30. **Black widow spider venom** is more potent than rattlesnake venom.
31. **Going on a shopping spree** is more appealing to women than having sex.
32. **Getting struck by lightning** is more likely to happen to you than getting eaten by a shark.
33. **The average American's credit card debt** is $3900; the average bank robbery take, only $3000.
34. **Drivers** kill more deer than hunters do.
35. **Cat food** is a bigger seller than baby food.
36. **Boxers** are preferred to briefs roughly 2 to 1.
37. **The noise level of a jackhammer**, at 95 decibels, just barely edges out the loudest recorded human snore, at 93 decibels.
38. **"It depends on the service"** is the credo of 70% of American tippers. Only 2% say they "always" leave a tip.
39. **The game of Monopoly** (introduced after the Stock Market crash of 1929) cost $4; the first Barbie doll made her debut in 1959 and cost $3.
40. **The average wedding** costs $19,000. The average American dog will cost its owner $14,600.

PLAYING THE PERCENTAGES #1

The numbers in order are: 70, 20, 90, 60, 50, 30, 10, 80, 40

SIGNALS CROSSED?

True

A LITTLE LIST

The 3 Most Dangerous Foods to Eat in a Car

1. Coffee
2. Tacos
3. Chili

PERFECT FOR EACH OTHER

1 – j (You: elderly, marriage-minded millionaire with bad heart.)
2 – i (Way too much time on your hands too? Call me.)
3 – a (A rake for springtime a big plus!)
4 – g (Seeks next gullible male without enough sense to stay away from me.)
5 – d (Looking for sincere, understanding man. Must be willing to listen to stories of alien abduction.)
6 – h (This tall, educated, professional SWM would like to meet an interesting woman!)
7 – c (I seek a woman, 18–32, to share this with.)
8 – b (How many times do I have to put an ad in to get one call?)
9 – e (Must be attractive, sensual, articulate, ruthless, 21–30 yrs, under 5'6". Break my heart, please.)
10 – f (Seeks depressed, unattractive SWF, 25–32, no sense of humor, for long talks about the macabre.)

ANAGRAMMIES: THE SEQUEL

A	L	P	H	A			S	E	R		A	M	O	K
R	E	H	A	B		E	T	R	E		L	O	G	E
A	T	O	L	L		D	O	R	M	I	T	O	R	Y
B	I	T		A	T	N	O		A	T	O	N	E	S
S	N	O	O	Z	E	A	L	A	R	M	S			
			P	E	R			A	K	A		A	C	E
M	O	S	T		N	C	A	R		Y	A	C	H	T
E	R	I	E		S	A	V	O	R		D	R	A	T
S	A	N	D	S		B	A	N	E		L	E	N	A
A	L	G		P	R	O			A	R	A			
			S	L	O	T	M	A	C	H	I	N	E	S
I	R	A	N	I	S		I	N	T	O		O	L	A
D	E	B	I	T	C	A	R	D		D	O	L	L	Y
O	P	E	D		O	N	E	S		E	A	T	E	N
S	O	L	E		E	N	D			S	T	E	N	O

YOU'VE GOT THE SHAKES

1. After twelve years of therapy my psychiatrist said something that brought tears to my eyes. He said, "No hablo ingles."
2. I was going to buy a copy of *The Power of Positive Thinking*, and then I thought: What the hell good would that do?
3. Hey, there are advantages to living in a mobile home. One time it caught on fire. We met the fire department halfway.

PRACTICALLY NEXT DOOR

The quote: Moscow is closer to Washington, D.C., than Honolulu is.

The clue answers:

A. WHODUNITS
B. HOT LINE
C. CLOWNS
D. OCCASIONS
E. GHOST
F. LAMOUR

THE UNITED STATES OF APATHY

The acrostic: MYTH AMERICA FACTOIDS

The quote: Rhode Island and Vermont didn't send delegates to the Constitutional Convention, and Maryland almost didn't, because officials there had a hard time finding anyone who wanted to go.

The clue answers:

A. MONTANA
B. YENTL
C. TOYOTA
D. HANG GLIDE
E. ANDROID
F. MIND
G. EDDIE CONDON
H. REDWOOD
I. IN STITCHES
J. CHARLES DARWIN
K. AHMAD RASHAD
L. FABLE
M. ANTIS
N. CANNON
O. TALENT
P. OFFSETTING
Q. INDEED
R. DEVOLVEMENT
S. SHOUT IT OUT

…IS FOR THE MILLION THINGS…

The quote: As a boy, Ian Fleming also gave his mother the nickname "M."

The clue answers:

A. LIMBO
B. FRACAS
C. LEVITY
D. SHANE
E. GEMINI
F. HOOKS
G. MANAGE
H. ANTHEM

SAY CHEESE!

The leftover letters spell: "How can anyone govern a nation that has two hundred and forty six different kinds of cheese?" —French president Charles de Gaulle

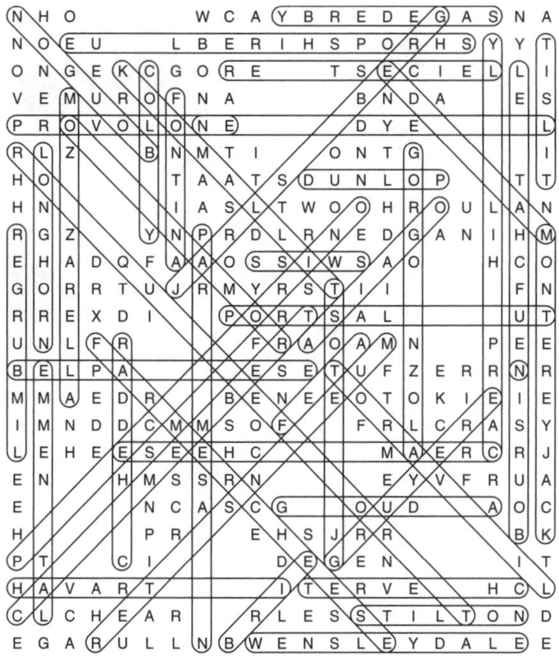

PLAYING THE PERCENTAGES #2

The numbers in order are: 60, 40, 80, 10, 20, 90, 50, 30, 70

I DON'T GET IT…

1. **Q:** What has four legs and one arm?
   A: A rottweiler.
2. **Q:** What is bright orange and sounds like a parrot?
   A: A carrot.
3. **Q:** What's the most important thing to learn in chemistry?
   A: Never lick the spoon.
4. **Q:** What do you call a midget fortune-teller who escaped from prison?
   A: A small medium at large.
5. **Q:** What do you call a cow with no legs?
   A: Ground beef.
6. **Q:** How much do pirates pay for their earrings?
   A: A buccaneer.
7. **Q:** What did the nuclear physicist have for lunch?
   A: Fission chips.
8. **Q:** Did you hear about the dyslexic devil worshipper?
   A: He sold his soul to Santa.
9. **Q:** Did you hear about the Buddhist who refused Novocain during his root canal?
   A: He wanted to transcend dental meditation.
10. **Q:** Hear about the ship that ran aground carrying a cargo of red paint and black paint?
    A: The whole crew was marooned.

FRUITS & VEGGIES & MORE

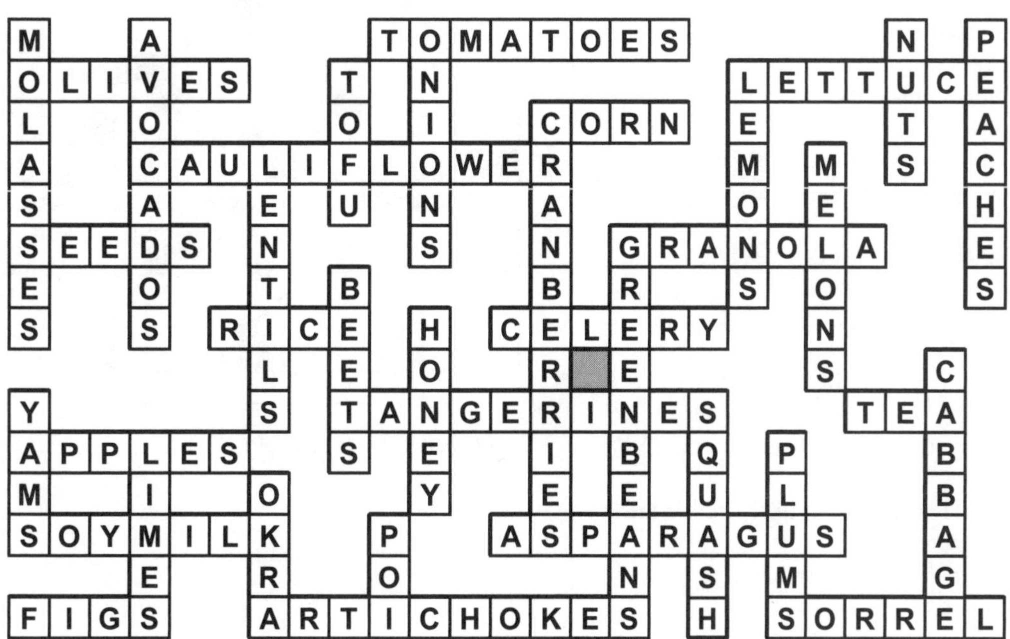

MR. & MS. QUIZ

1. **Women** are more likely to be naturally blond. One of every 14 women in America is a natural blonde; only one out of every 16 men is.
2. **Men** are more likely to laugh more. The average American male laughs 69 times a day; the average woman, 55.
3. **Women** are more likely to sleep more.
4. **Men** are more likely to snore (big surprise there).
5. **Women** are more likely to be born at night.
6. **Women** are more likely to purchase men's clothing in U.S. stores—about two-thirds of all men's clothing is bought by women.
7. **Men** are more likely to run stoplights.
8. **Women** are more likely to switch lanes without signaling.
9. **Men** are more likely to be left-handed. There are roughly 50% more left-handed males than females.
10. **Women** are more likely to get migraines.
11. **Men** are more likely to get an ulcer.
12. **Men** are more likely to get hiccups.
13. **Men** are *six times* more likely to get struck by lightning.
14. **Men** are more likely to leave their hotel rooms cleaner.
15. **Women** are more likely to lock themselves out of their hotel rooms.
16. **Women** are more likely to take longer showers—13 minutes on average, compared with the average man's 11.4 minutes.
17. **Women** blink nearly twice as much as men.
18. **Men**—we should say, boys—are four times more likely to stutter than girls are.
19. **Women** are almost twice as likely to buy gifts for Mother's Day.
20. **Men** are twice as likely to fall out of bed while in the hospital.
21. **Women** are more likely to talk to their cars.
22. **Men** are twice as likely to hold the TV remote.
23. **Men** are also twice as likely to lose the TV remote.
24. **Women** generally have a keener sense of smell.

SON OF ANAGRAMMIES

N	A	S	A		A	L	A	S		K	A	R	E	N
O	P	T	S		W	A	V	Y		I	R	A	T	E
T	H	E	H	I	L	T	O	N		M	E	M	O	S
W	I	V	E	S		E	N	D	T	O		A	N	T
O	D	E		L	A	S		R	U	N				
				A	S	T	R	O	N	O	M	E	R	S
	F	R	A	N	K		A	M	A		E	D	I	T
F	I	O	R	D		A	Y	E		B	R	I	N	Y
E	D	U	C		E	G	O		M	O	V	E	D	
M	O	T	H	E	R	I	N	L	A	W				
				N	I	T		E	E	L		D	R	S
A	L	I		R	E	A	L	M		E	M	A	I	L
S	Y	R	I	A		T	O	M	C	R	U	I	S	E
A	M	O	N	G		O	B	O	E		G	L	E	E
P	E	N	N	E		R	E	N	O		S	Y	S	T

"AND NOW, THE PUNCH LINE..."

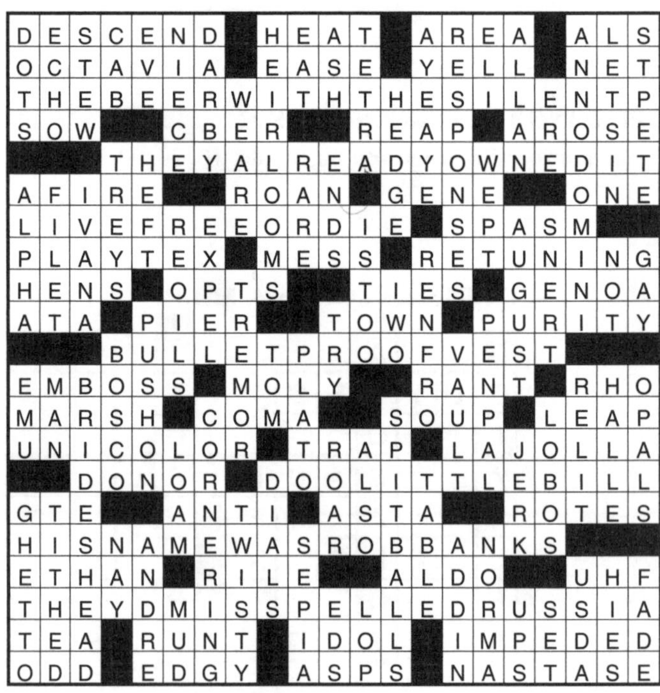

D	E	S	C	E	N	D		H	E	A	T		A	R	E	A		A	L	S
O	C	T	A	V	I	A		E	A	S	E		Y	E	L	L		N	E	T
T	H	E	B	E	E	R	W	I	T	H	T	H	E	S	I	L	E	N	T	P
S	O	W			C	B	E	R			R	E	A	P		A	R	O	S	E
			T	H	E	Y	A	L	R	E	A	D	Y	O	W	N	E	D	I	T
A	F	I	R	E			R	O	A	N		G	E	N	E			O	N	E
L	I	V	E	F	R	E	E	O	R	D	I	E		S	P	A	S	M		
P	L	A	Y	T	E	X		M	E	S	S		R	E	T	U	N	I	N	G
H	E	N	S		O	P	T	S			T	I	E	S		G	E	N	O	A
A	T	A		P	I	E	R			T	O	W	N		P	U	R	I	T	Y
			B	U	L	L	E	T	P	R	O	O	F	V	E	S	T			
E	M	B	O	S	S		M	O	L	Y			R	A	N	T		R	H	O
M	A	R	S	H		C	O	M	A			S	O	U	P		L	E	A	P
U	N	I	C	O	L	O	R		T	R	A	P		L	A	J	O	L	L	A
		D	O	N	O	R		D	O	O	L	I	T	T	L	E	B	I	L	L
G	T	E			A	N	T	I		A	S	T	A			R	O	T	E	S
H	I	S	N	A	M	E	W	A	S	R	O	B	B	A	N	K	S			
E	T	H	A	N		R	I	L	E			A	L	D	O			U	H	F
T	H	E	Y	D	M	I	S	S	P	E	L	L	E	D	R	U	S	S	I	A
T	E	A		R	U	N	T		I	D	O	L		I	M	P	E	D	E	D
O	D	D		E	D	G	Y		A	S	P	S		N	A	S	T	A	S	E

PALINDROMIC PEOPLE

1. Roy
2. Enid
3. Stella
4. Max
5. Naomi
6. Norma

PHRASEOLOGY 103

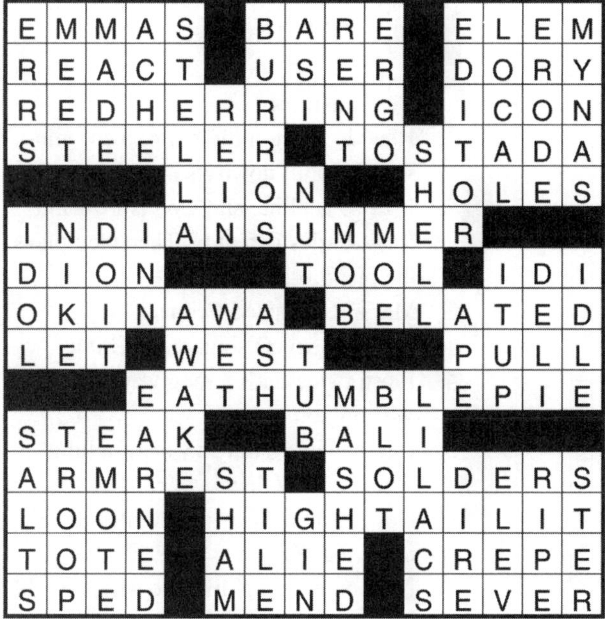

STATE YOUR BUSINESS!

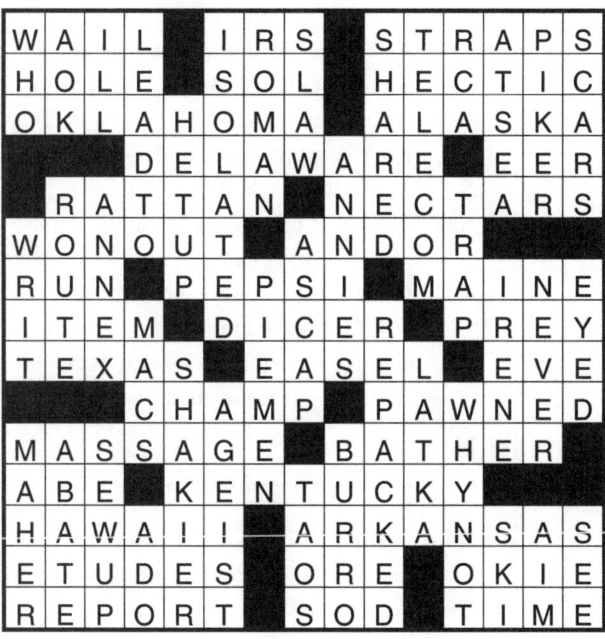

ODD TITLE OUT

a. *Your Television's Smells, and What They Mean* (the actual winner in 1980 was *The Joy of Chickens*)

BEDTIME FOR BONZO

Psychology, crook, son, jewelry, training it to steal, Diana Lynn, jewelry

PROVERBIAL WISDOM

GERMANY: When the fox preaches, look to your geese.

INDIA: He that cannot dance claims the floor is uneven.

ENGLAND: A good archer is known not by his arrows but by his aim.

SPAIN: The road of by and by leads to the house of never.

CHINA: The longer the explanation the bigger the lie.

JAPAN: When one has no needle, thread is of little use.

GREECE: To lose a friend, make him a loan.

IRELAND: Never send a chicken to bring home a fox.

TURKEY: Measure forty times, cut once.

IRAN: Trust in God, but tie your camel.

OFF YOUR ROCKER

1 – a (Fiona Apple)
2 – h (Axl Rose)
3 – b (Cher)
4 – f (Simon LeBon)
5 – m (Ron Wood)
6 – g (Ted Nugent)
7 – k (Rod Stewart)
8 – i (Diana Ross)
9 – j (David Lee Roth)
10 – e (Mick Jagger)
11 – l (Donna Summer)
12 – c (John Denver)
13 – d (Michael Jackson)

DON'T!

1. Don't ever send a man window-shopping. He'll come back carrying a window. (*A Wife's Little Instruction Book*)
2. Don't carry a grudge. While you're carrying the grudge, the other guy's out dancing. (Buddy Hackett)
3. Don't worry about people stealing an idea. If it's original, you'll have to ram it down their throats. (Howard Aiken)

OXYMORONS

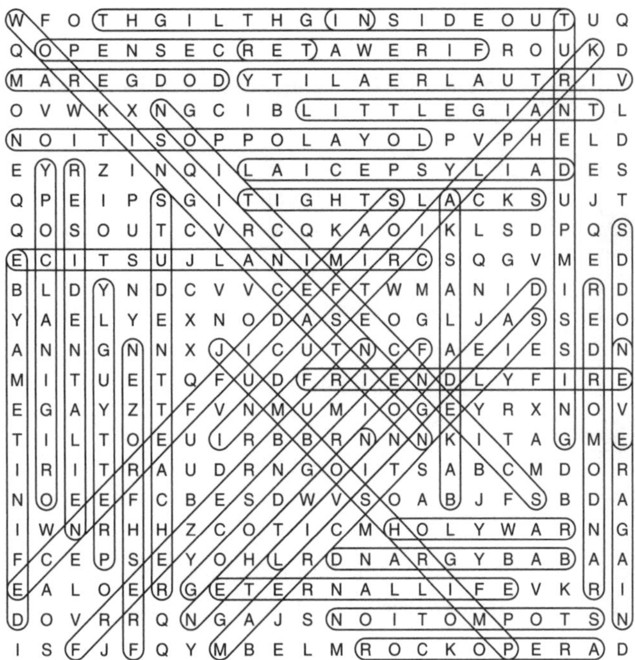

A MOVIE STAR'S BEST FRIEND

The acrostic: ABOUT THE HOPE DIAMOND

The quote: It's widely believed that Elizabeth Taylor once owned the Hope (Diamond). Not true. She owns a larger diamond, often compared to the Hope, but now known as the Burton Diamond.

The clue answers:

A. ALAN SHEPARD
B. BETTE MIDLER
C. ON FIRE
D. UPTOWN
E. TEDDY KENNEDY
F. THE DOORS
G. HEM AND HAW
H. ECONOMIZE
I. HEAT WAVE
J. OTTER
K. PUNISH
L. ELBOW
M. DANTE
N. INDONESIA
O. ABBOTT
P. MOTTO
Q. OUCH
R. NIGHT OWL
S. DOLOR

THE SCRAWL ON THE WALL

1. f; 2. g; 3. e; 4. j; 5. k; 6. m; 7. l; 8. a; 9. d; 10. c; 11. h; 12. b; 13. i.

Complete answers:

1. How do you tell the sex of a chromosome?...Pull down its genes.
2. If Love is blind, and God is love and Ray Charles is blind...Then God plays the piano.
3. Mafia: Organized Crime... Government: Disorganized Crime
4. Flush twice...it's a long way to Washington.
5. Death is just nature's way of telling you...to slow down.
6. How come nobody ever writes on... toilet seats?
7. Did you ever feel like the whole world was a white wedding gown...and you were a pair of muddy hiking boots?
8. The chicken is an egg's way of... producing another egg.
9. If you think you have someone eating out of your hand...it's a good idea to count your fingers.
10. The typical Stanford undergrad is like a milkshake...thick and rich.
11. Blessed is he who sits on a bee...for he shall rise again.
12. There are those who shun elitism. Why?...It's the elitist thing to do.
13. Please do not throw cigarette butts in the toilet...it makes them hard to light.

FOWL'S-EYE VIEW

The quote: Oddly enough, a bluebird cannot see the color blue.

The clue words:

A. UNCLE
B. DOUGH
C. BLURB
D. ONES
E. DOTED
F. ROONEY
G. ITHACA
H. BELLE

THE ENDANGERED LIST

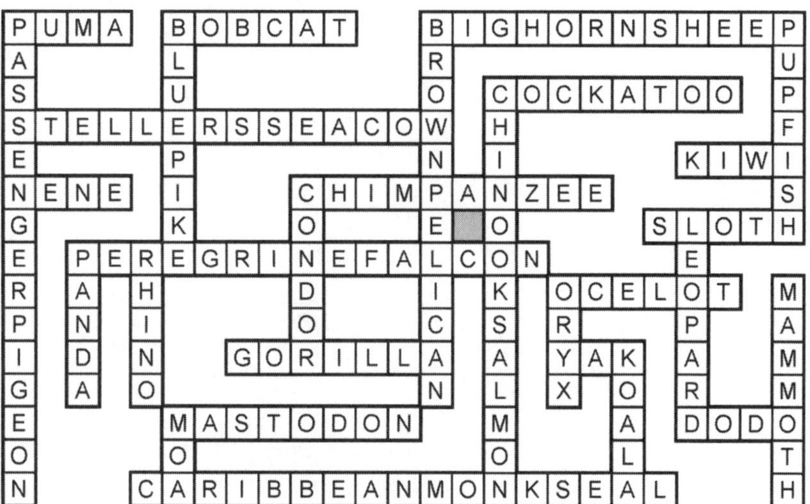

WOULD WE LIE TO YOU?

1 – b (It's a simplified form of "All-Pro.")

2 – a (It comes from the slang for "recruit.")

3 – a (Their ears resemble donkey ears.)

4 – c (Local politicians were excessively "windy" about 1893's Exposition.)

5 – b (There was a famous jail on Clink Street.)

THE ANAGRAMMIES: A PREVIEW

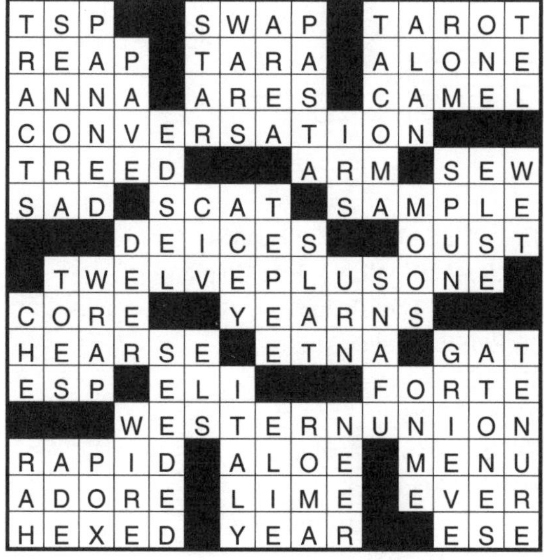

CHANNEL SURFING

1. *The Love Boat*
2. *Murder, She Wrote*
3. *Dragnet*
4. *Seinfeld*
5. *Falcon Crest*
6. *The Waltons*
7. *Gunsmoke*
8. *The West Wing*
9. *Candid Camera*
10. *Hogan's Heroes*
11. *Charlie's Angels*
12. *The Practice*
13. *Perry Mason*
14. *Family Ties*
15. *Roseanne*
16. *Everybody Loves Raymond*
17. *Northern Exposure*
18. *Home Improvement*

HOT STUFF

The Namib desert is in (where else?) Namibia, and the Sahel runs across Africa along the southern border of the Sahara. The Atacama, in South America, is the driest place on earth. Riyadh is the capital of Saudi Arabia.

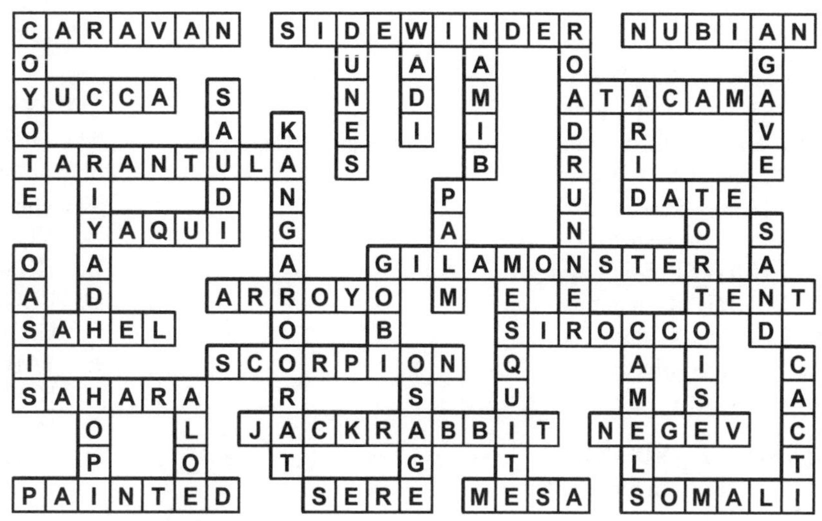

TOP TEN HITS

The leftover letters spell: "The most brutal, ugly, desperate form of expression it has been my misfortune to hear." —Frank Sinatra, about rock.

The songs and artists:

BEAT IT – Michael Jackson
CALL ME – Blondie
CENTERFOLD – J. Geils Band
COMING UP – Paul McCartney
CREEP – TLC
DON'T – Elvis Presley
EL PASO – Marty Robbins
FAITH – George Michael
FAME – David Bowie
GET BACK – The Beatles
GROOVIN' – The Rascals
HELLO – Lionel Richie
HELP! – The Beatles
HE'S SO FINE – The Chiffons
HEY PAULA – Paul and Paula
HOUND DOG – Elvis Presley
HURTS SO GOOD – John Cougar
I FEEL FOR YOU – Chaka Khan
I GET AROUND – The Beach Boys
I SWEAR – All-4-One
JUMP – Van Halen (1984), Kriss Kross (1992)
KYRIE – Mr. Mister
LADY – Kenny Rogers
LE FREAK – Chic
LET'S GET IT ON – Marvin Gaye
LIGHT MY FIRE – The Doors
MANIAC – Michael Sembello
MY GIRL – The Temptations
MY SHARONA – The Knack
PHYSICAL – Olivia Newton-John
PRETTY WOMAN – Roy Orbison
REUNITED – Peaches and Herb

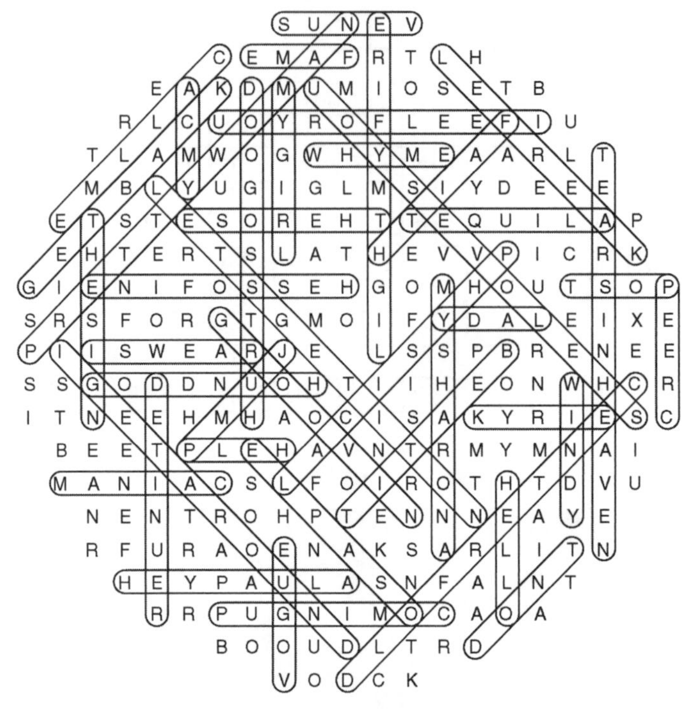

SHE LOVES YOU – The Beatles
TEARS IN HEAVEN – Eric Clapton
TEQUILA – The Champs
THE ROSE – Better Midler
THE SIGN – Ace of Base
TSOP – MFSB
VENUS – Frankie Avalon
VOGUE – Madonna
WHY ME – Kris Kristofferson
WINDY – The Association
YMCA – The Village People

AT SIXES AND SEVENS

The 7 Wonders of the Ancient World: Colossus of Rhodes
The 7 Liberal Arts: Music
The 7 Deadly Sins: Lust
The 7 Virtues: Justice
The 7 Hills of Rome: Capitoline
The 7 Metals of Alchemy: Lead
The 7 Ancient Rivers: Tigris
The 7 Dwarfs: Sleepy

WINNING HANDS-DOWN

c. It comes from horse racing.

YOU'VE GOT A SLIM CHANCE

The quote: The average lightning bolt is only an inch in diameter.

The clue answers:

A. VILLAIN
B. HOMINY
C. LEDGER
D. GANGES
E. TAHITI
F. NOTCH
G. INNER
H. BEAT

INTERNATIONAL LANGUAGE LESSON

H	U	M	P	■	B	O	O	Z	E	■	A	S	A	P
A	R	E	A	■	E	T	H	A	N	■	X	E	N	A
W	I	T	T	■	C	H	O	P	S	T	I	C	K	S
K	A	R	A	O	K	E	■	S	H	O	O	T	A	T
S	H	O	C	K	E	R	■	■	R	O	M	■	■	■
■	■	■	A	R	R	■	S	P	O	N	S	O	R	S
V	O	D	K	A	■	V	I	R	U	S	■	D	U	O
O	B	O	E	■	H	E	R	O	D	■	W	O	H	L
W	I	N	■	H	A	R	E	M	■	Z	O	R	R	O
S	T	T	H	O	M	A	S	■	F	U	R	■	■	■
■	■	■	A	L	I	■	■	T	A	L	K	S	U	P
I	L	O	V	E	L	A	■	U	K	U	L	E	L	E
M	I	N	E	S	T	R	O	N	E	■	A	N	T	S
A	S	E	A	■	O	L	D	E	R	■	T	O	R	O
C	A	S	T	■	N	O	D	D	Y	■	E	R	A	S

ALMOST FAMOUS

C	H	U	G	■	B	U	S	T	S	■	D	A	D	S
R	A	C	E	■	O	N	E	A	L	■	A	T	R	A
O	S	L	O	■	B	U	D	D	Y	E	B	S	E	N
C	H	A	R	I	S	M	A	■	■	S	N	E	A	D
■	■	■	G	N	U	■	T	A	G	T	E	A	M	S
E	L	V	I	S	P	R	E	S	L	E	Y	■	■	■
Y	O	D	A	■	■	E	S	T	E	E	■	M	B	A
E	V	A	N	G	E	L	■	H	E	M	M	E	R	S
D	E	Y	■	A	L	A	R	M	■	■	A	T	O	P
■	■	■	J	U	L	I	E	A	N	D	R	E	W	S
A	C	C	O	L	A	D	E	■	I	I	I	■	■	■
S	H	A	L	L	■	■	L	A	C	K	E	Y	E	D
T	O	M	S	E	L	L	E	C	K	■	T	O	R	E
O	R	E	O	■	C	A	C	H	E	■	T	G	I	F
N	E	O	N	■	D	O	T	E	D	■	A	I	N	T

FIT AS A FIDDLE

b. The phrase was originally "fit as a fiddler."

SHEER SHANDLING

1. They should put expiration dates on clothes so we would know when they go out of style.
2. I'm very loyal in relationships. Even when I go out with my mom I don't look at other moms.
3. Oysters are supposed to enhance your sexual performance, but they don't work for me. Maybe I put them on too soon.

DUBIOUS ACHIEVERS

1 – b (wad of tobacco)
2 – a (baseballs)
3 – b (escalators)
4 – c (the accordian)
5 – c (dried cow chip)
6 – a (one foot)
7 – b (got married)
8 – b (metal; since 1966 he has eaten 10 bicycles, a supermarket food cart, seven televisions, six chandeliers, a coffin, and a Cessna airplane)
9 – c (coal; no word on whether his eventual destination was Newcastle)
10 – a (made a bed)

TOM SWIFTIES

1 – g ("A thousand thanks, Monsieur," Tom said mercifully.)
2 – c ("Don't you like my new refrigerator?" Tom asked coolly.)
3 – f ("I prefer to press my own clothes," Tom said ironically.)
4 – h ("I'll have to send that telegram again," Tom said remorsefully.)
5 – j ("I'm burning the candle at both ends," Tom said wickedly.)
6 – e ("It's the maid's night off," Tom said helplessly.)
7 – a ("The boat is leaking," Tom said balefully.)
8 – b ("The criminals were escorted downstairs," Tom said condescendingly.)
9 – i ("They pulled the wool over my eyes," Tom said sheepishly.)
10 – d ("Welcome to Grant's Tomb," Tom said cryptically.)

BOTTOMS UP!

The leftover letters spell: "One drink is too many for me and a thousand not enough." —Irish playwright Brendan Behan

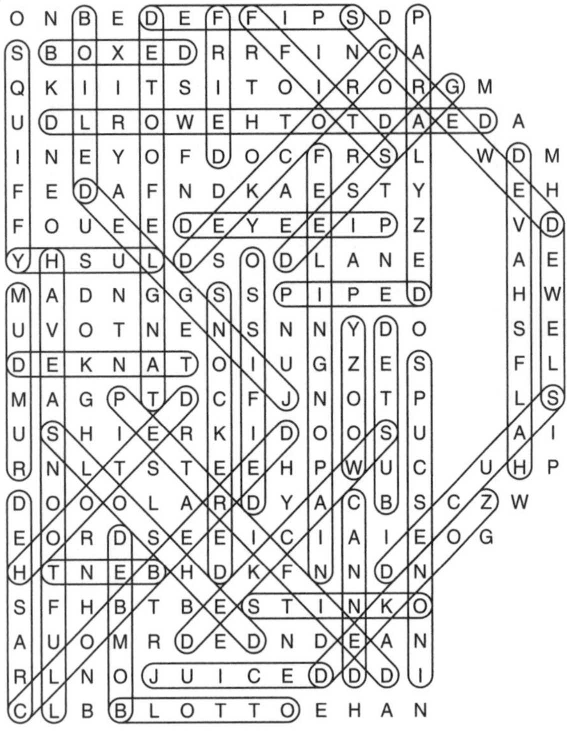

PERFECT 10

Alan Shepard used a **6** iron.

The average dairy cow produces **4** times her body weight in manure each year.

The average person looks at **8** houses before buying.

In a 1936 Ping-Pong tournament, players volleyed for over **2** hours on the opening serve.

The top speed of a chicken at full gallop is **9** mph.

In 1913, the income tax on $4,000 was **1** ¢.

Las Vegas is home to **10** of the 10 largest hotels in the U.S.

The monster in *The Thing* was onscreen **3** minutes.

The average major league baseball lasts **5** pitches.

It takes **7** shuffles to thoroughly mix a 52-card deck.

BITE ME!

The most venomous insect is the harvester ant; the most toxic fish is the reed stonefish. The winner among arachnids is the Sydney funnel-web spider. But the hands-down winner of them all is a snake called the inland taipan of Australia. Oh, hey, look. I think there's one right there by your foot.

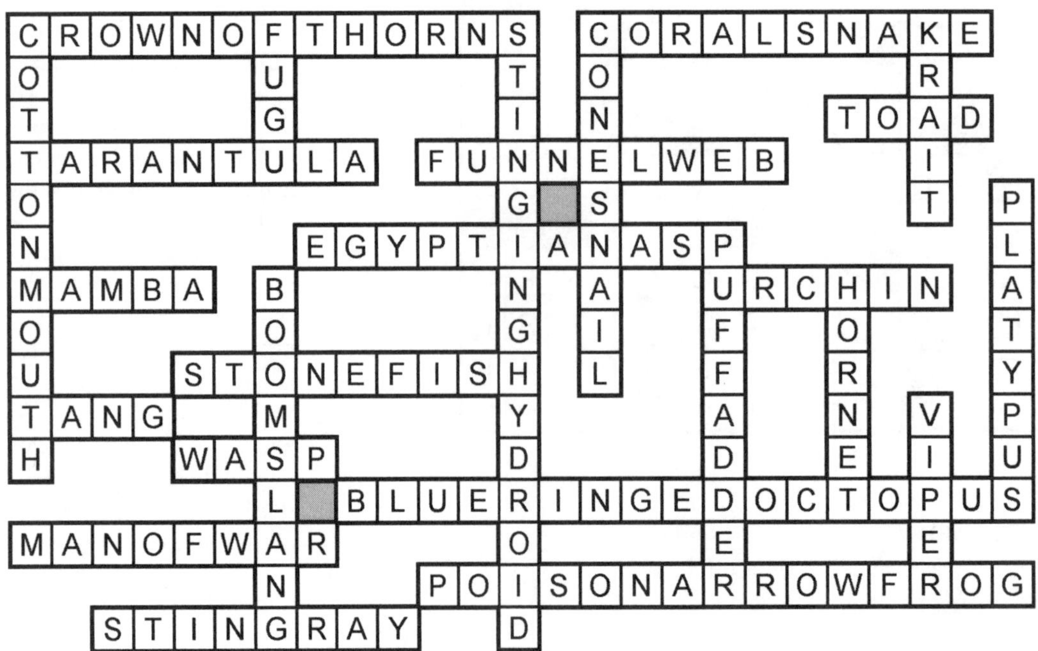

IT CAME FROM THE GARAGE…

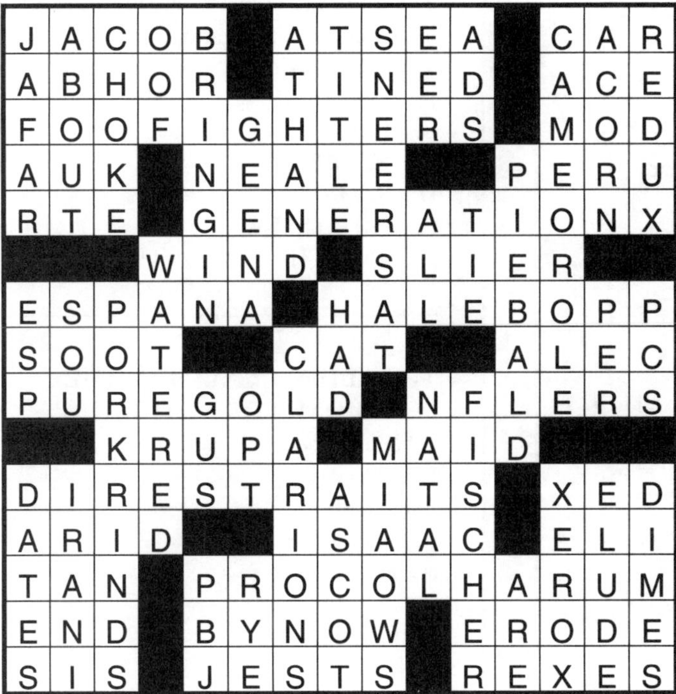

THE CROSSWORD CRAZE

Number 7 is the fake. *The New York Times* didn't start publishing crosswords until right after Pearl Harbor in 1941. Up until then, even the *Times*'s publisher, Arthur Hays Sulzberger, had to buy the rival *New York Herald Tribune* every day to get his crossword fix.

JUST WING IT, KID

a. It's an old theater expression.

A PUN? MY WORD!

A little girl fell into a well…and although she cried for help, her brother stood by and did nothing. Finally the next-door neighbor came over and pulled the girl up. "Why didn't you help her!" the neighbor asked the boy. "How," he replied, "could I be her brother and assist her, too?"

A guy goes to a psychiatrist…"Doc, I keep having these alternating recurring dreams. First, I'm a teepee; then I'm a wigwam; then I'm a teepee; then I'm a wigwam. It's driving me crazy. What's wrong with me?" The doctor replied, "It's very simple. You're two tents."

It is well known throughout…Central Europe that members of William Tell's family were early devotees of league bowling. They had sponsors and everything. According to historians, though, the records have been lost, so nobody knows for whom the Tells bowled.

GOOD QUESTION!

The acrostic: WHY WONDER WHY?

The quote: Why is it that when you transport something by car, it's called a shipment, but when you transport something by ship, it's called cargo?

The clue answers:

A. WASHINGTON
B. HAMMER
C. YESTERDAY
D. WHIPPING BOY
E. OUT TO LUNCH
F. NIGHTS
G. DRAMATISTS
H. ECCENTRICITY
I. RANTS
J. WALLPAPER
K. HOBBITS
L. YOUTH HOSTELS

THAT CLEAN SLATE THING

a. It refers to slates kept by tavern keepers.

SAY SOMEONE'S STUPID

1. A few clowns short of a circus.
2. A few fries short of a Happy Meal.
3. A few beers short of a six-pack.
4. Dumber than a box of hair.
5. A few peas short of a casserole.
6. Doesn't have all his corn flakes in one box.
7. Chimney's clogged.
8. One Froot Loop shy of a full bowl.
9. One taco short of a combination plate.
10. A few feathers short of a whole duck.
11. All foam, no beer.
12. The cheese slid off his cracker.
13. Body by Fisher, brains by Mattel.
14. Too much yardage between the goalposts.
15. Forgot to pay his brain bill.
16. As smart as bait.

TV TRIVIA

A	C	I	N	G		C	R	O	C		M	A	M	A
N	A	D	I	R		O	A	T	H		A	P	E	D
G	I	L	L	I	G	A	N	S	I	S	L	A	N	D
E	R	E		P	E	R	U		T	H	I	R	S	T
L	O	S	T	I	N	S	P	A	C	E		T	A	O
			A	N	T	E		S	H	E	A	F		
I	N	B	I	G			S	T	A	R	T	R	E	K
B	O	I	L		S	T	O	A	T		H	O	M	E
M	R	R	O	G	E	R	S			D	E	M	O	N
		D	R	A	N	O		C	O	E	N			
A	N	S		T	O	I	L	E	T	P	A	P	E	R
C	E	N	S	O	R		E	L	I	A		A	T	A
T	H	E	P	R	I	C	E	I	S	R	I	G	H	T
U	R	S	A		T	O	R	N		T	W	E	E	T
P	U	T	S		A	P	S	E		S	O	R	R	Y

COWBOY TALK

1 – m (tall)
2 – c (dishonest)
3 – d (hanged)
4 – k (poor)
5 – f (old)
6 – j (shot dead)
7 – l (talkative)
8 – g (proud)
9 – h (rare)
10 – e (noisy)
11 – a (cheap)
12 – i (religious)
13 – b (crazy)

HARSH!

1. If God had wanted us to use the metric system, Jesus would have had ten apostles. (Jesse Helms)
2. Why, this fellow don't know any more about politics than a pig knows about Sunday. (Harry S. Truman about Dwight Eisenhower)
3. Michael Jackson's album was called *Bad* because there wasn't enough room on the sleeve for *Pathetic*. (Prince)

AND IF YOU BELIEVE THAT ONE…

1 – b (The push mower predates the riding mower.)
2 – c (In spite of old wives' tales to the contrary, butter is *not* an effective burn ointment.)
3 – a (Candy maker Milton Hershey didn't despise chocolate.)
4 – d (G. I. Joe was always called G. I. Joe.)
5 – d (*Time* magazine's "Men of the Year" in 1990 were the two George Bushes.)
6 – b (Snakes can't poison themselves.)
7 – b (Banana shrubs really *are* shrubs.)
8 – c (Both male and female spiders spin webs. However, female spiders spin *better* webs.)

I LIKE GENTLE BEN IN THE 4TH

The quote: A brown bear can run faster than a horse at full gallop.

The clue answers:

A. BANANAS
B. FORLORN
C. FURBELOW
D. SUGAR
E. PANATELLA
F. THATCHER

THEY DIDN'T CALL HIM THE MAD MONK FOR NOTHING

debauched one
Greg Pervert
Flagellants
flog themselves silly
sexual exhaustion
month
hemophiliac
hypnosis
once
someone's very attractive wife
tea and cakes
shot
you-know-what
shot
a carpet
a river
the Bolshevik Revolution

THE SPY WHO DIDN'T CARE IF IT WAS COLD

Margaretha Geertruida Zelle
Holland
personals ad in the newspaper
Java
Paris
veils
Italian opera houses
both of the above
French
Germans
firing squad
threw open her blouse
there hadn't been enough evidence to convict her
German
Germans
Germans

CURE FOR A DEPRESSION

The acrostic: GOLDEN AGE OF PUZZLES

The quote: As America got deeper into the Great Depression...people went on a jigsaw puzzle buying binge. At the peak of the fad, Americans were purchasing six million puzzles a *week*.

The clue answers:

A. GANDHI
B. OWING
C. LANA TURNER
D. DWEEB
E. EXPERIENCE
F. NICK NOLTE
G. APPEASE
H. GATES
I. EMO PHILIPS
J. OUT OF TIME
K. FIJI
L. PAULA ZAHN
M. UP THE CREEK
N. ZIGGY
O. ZSA ZSA GABOR
P. LOWERS
Q. EMPIRE STATE
R. SWEDEN

NOTABLE FIRSTS

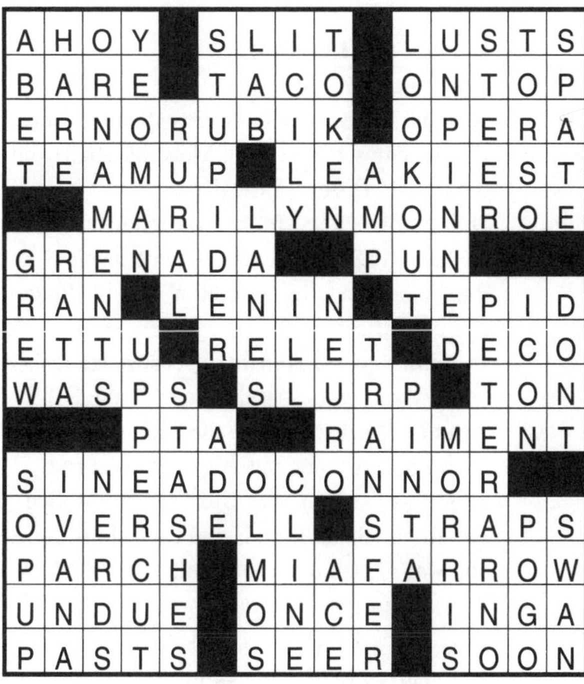

FILL IN THE LIMERICKS

1. suicide, automobiles, died
2. seeds, grass, weeds
3. died, fermented, inside
4. dribbling, highway (or freeway or roadway), sibling
5. paw, wife, father-in-law
6. light, way, night
7. sin, could, again
8. wager, part, Major
9. stew, about, too
10. Natchez, clothes, scratchez(s)

WARNING LABELS

1 – a (air conditioner)
2 – k (portable stroller—but also good advice for a Batman costume, don't you think?)
3 – h (Duraflame fireplace log)
4 – c (bottle of hair coloring)
5 – o (vacuum cleaner)
6 – n (toilet bowl cleaning brush—eeeeeyew!)
7 – i (microwave oven)
8 – e (compact disc player)
9 – g (digital thermometer—double eeeeeyew!)
10 – l (propane blowtorch)
11 – j (wheelbarrow wheel)
12 – m (shin guards)
13 – d (rat poison—is that before or after they die?)
14 – b (Batman costume)
15 – f (curling iron)

PRIME-TIME PROVERBS

1 – a (Beaver Cleaver)
2 – l (Sgt. Wojehowicz)
3 – f (Granny)
4 – h (Lily Munster)
5 – d (Cliff Huxtable)
6 – j (Oscar Madison)
7 – k (Radar O'Reilly)
8 – i (Mary Richards)
9 – b (Bret Maverick)
10 – e (Edith Bunker)
11 – c (Cliff Claven)
12 – g (Stephanie Vanderkellen)

STORMY WEATHER

True

SHOOT ON A SHINGLE

The leftover letters spell:

Other names for coffee are "battery acid" or "paint remover."

The word list:

BEANS: Ammunition
BOLOGNA: Donkey dick
BREAD: Gun wadding
CANNED MILK: Armored cow
COFFEE: Solvent
CRACKERS: Dog biscuits
GRAPE NUTS: Shrapnel
HASH: Mystery plate
KETCHUP: Red-eye
MAPLE SYRUP: Machine oil
MEATLOAF: Ptomaine steak
PANCAKES: Rubber patches
POWDERED MILK: Chalk
SOUP: Hot water
SPINACH: Seaweed

QUOTAGRAM

"When a stupid man is doing something he is ashamed of, he always declares that it is his duty." —George Bernard Shaw

***WHAT* DID YOU CALL ME?**

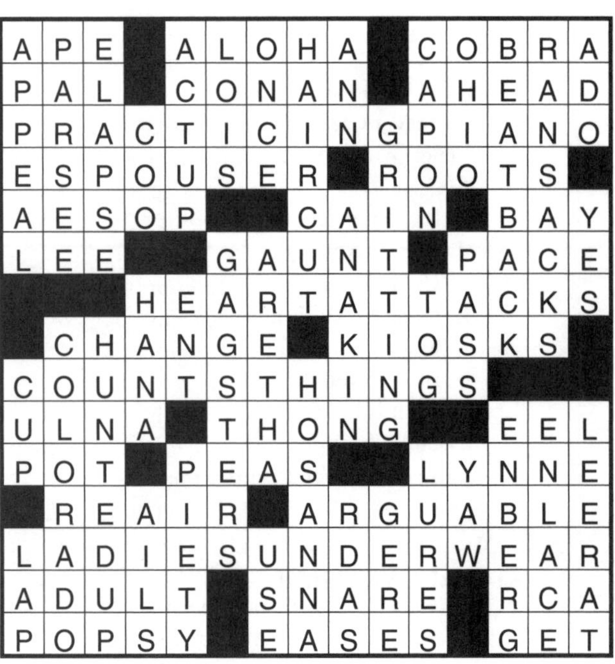

TOM SWIFTIES, TOO

1 – i ("…and you lose a few," Tom said winsomely.)
2 – j ("He only likes whole grain bread," Tom said wryly.)
3 – f ("I forgot what to buy," Tom said listlessly.)
4 – b ("I hate seafood," Tom said crabbily.)
5 – h ("I love Chinese food," Tom said wantonly.)
6 – a ("I need a pencil sharpener," Tom said bluntly.)
7 – e ("I twisted my ankle," Tom said lamely.)
8 – c ("I was removed from office," Tom said disappointedly.)
9 – g ("I wish I were taller," Tom said longingly.)
10 – d ("There's too much Tabasco in this chili," Tom said hotly.)

BE KIND TO THE ANIMALS, SOMETIMES

1. Living pigeons cut in half and applied to the feet of a man in fever will cure him.
2. If you find a hairy caterpillar, you should throw it over your shoulder for good luck.
3. If a man should kill a glowworm, it will endanger his love affair, and may cause the death of his beloved.

BASKETBALL NAMES

The fakes are:

New Jersey Nets: They were called the Nets to rhyme with the New York Mets (baseball) and the New York Jets (football).

Houston Rockets: In fact, the team started out as the San Diego Rockets, a name inspired by the theme of a "city in motion" and its "space age industries."

Indiana Pacers: So named because the team's owners wanted to "set the pace" in the NBA.

Atlanta Hawks: It's true the team wasn't founded in Atlanta, but it actually was first known as the Tri-Cities Blackhawks (Moline and Rock Island, Illinois and Davenport, Iowa), and was named after Sauk Indian chief Black Hawk, who fought settlers of the area in the 1831 Black Hawk Wars. In 1951, when the team moved to Milwaukee for a while, the name was shortened to the Hawks.

OLD WIVES' TALES

To reduce fever: Drink boiled onions or carry a key in the palm of your hand.
To treat gout: Walk barefoot in dewy grass.
For a headache: Rub an onion over your forehead. (Another suggestion, popular in the 17th century, was to drive a nail into the skull.)
To get rid of corns: Take brown paper, soak it in vinegar, and place it in a saucer under your bed. Dab the corn with saliva each day before breakfast.
For heart disease: Drink foxglove tea. (Foxglove contains digitalis, which is used today to combat heart disease.)
To cure boils: Carry nutmeg in your pocket.

WORD GEOGRAPHY

The word list:

1. Bungalow
2. Bible
3. Sleazy
4. Jeans
5. Suede
6. Turkey
7. Cheap
8. Coffee

```
T H E B W O R D S
P W A I C I S N A
M E O B H D J A F
T E R L E E S Y P
A S L E A Z Y E B
E L U N P G G K I
U M S E A R N R E
S O R T D T O U W
N C O F F E E T B
```

The leftover letters spell: The word "spa" is named after Spa, Belgium, a resort town.

RUFF TALK

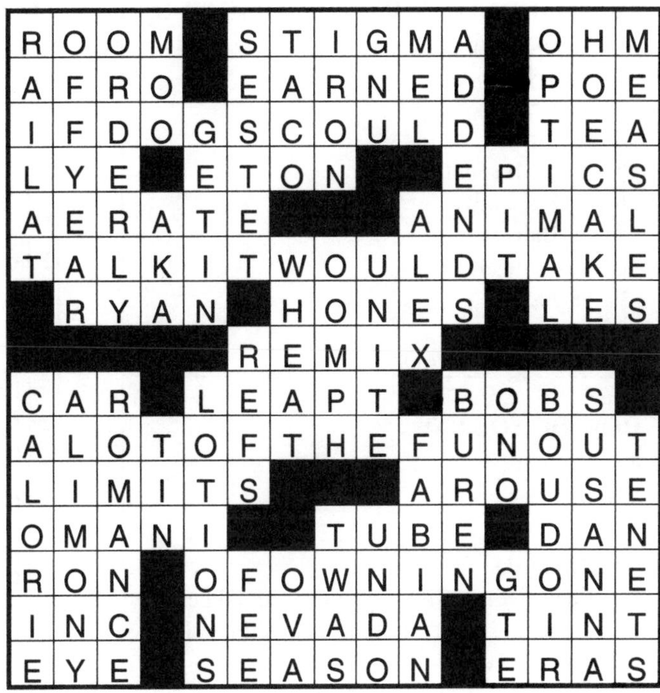

WOULD WE LIE TO YOU—TWO?

1 – a (It took 409 attempts to perfect the formula.)
2 – c (It's an anagram of "Cully Stout Beer.")
3 – a (Policemen in London used to wear fuzzy helmets.)
4 – b (The bar originally came in three sections.)
5 – c (It comes from the Old English for "itchy pox.")

IMAGINARY FRIENDS

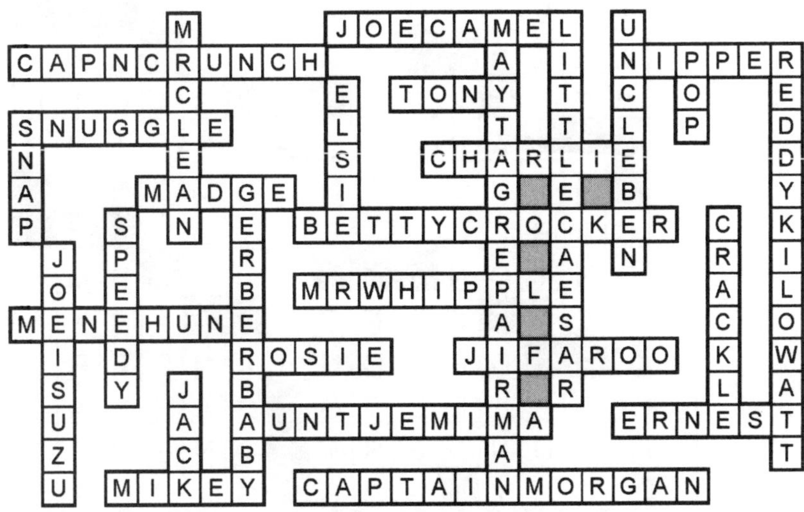

Snap!, Crackle!, and Pop! were used in commercials for Rice Krispies cereal; Jack, of course, is Jack in the Box. Then there's Tony the Tiger; Elsie the Cow; Madge the Manicurist; Mikey of Life cereal commercials; Rosie, the waitress-spokesperson for Bounty Paper Towels; Ernest, the nosy neighbor ("Hey, Vern!") of numerous commercials; Nipper, the RCA Victor dog; Speedy Alka-Seltzer; Charlie the Tuna; Jifaroo, the Jif peanut butter kangaroo; Menehune was the Hawaiian imp used in United Airlines commercials; Captain Morgan of rum fame; and Reddy Kilowatt, who's been around since 1926 and now is the spokestoon for the Northern States Power Company.

AND DON'T WALK UP TO PEOPLE AND TELL THEM THEY'RE UNATTRACTIVE

1 – j (Thailand)
2 – f (Ireland)
3 – c (Brazil)
4 – g (Japan)
5 – a (Arab countries)
6 – e (England)
7 – b (Bali)
8 – i (Portugal)
9 – h (Kenya)
10 – d (China)

HOW DO YOU SAY...

a. English

ALLENISMS

1. Basically my wife was immature. I'd be at home in the bath and she'd come in and sink my boats.
2. The world is divided into good and bad people. The good ones sleep better... while the bad ones seem to enjoy the working hours much more.
3. It is a gorgeous gold pocket watch. I'm proud of it. My grandfather, on his deathbed, sold me this watch.
4. If God would only give me some clear sign. Like making a large deposit in my name in a Swiss bank account.
5. Don't pay attention to what your school teachers tell you. Just see what they look like and that's how you know what life is really going to be like.

LOONEY LAWS

1. Ugly horse
2. Airplane
3. Statue
4. Moustaches
5. Drink milk, train
6. Ice-cream cone
7. Spit, wind
8. Goats, trousers
9. Bees, hats
10. Wiping, dishes (Oregonians are supposed to let them drip-dry)
11. Swim, dry land
12. Educate, dog
13. Barefoot
14. Play cards, road

TV HITS OF THE '70S

The leftover letters spell: *The Mary Tyler Moore Show* spun off three other hit series. (They were *Rhoda*, *Phyllis*, and *Lou Grant*. A fourth spin-off—*The Ted Knight Show*—barely lasted a month.)

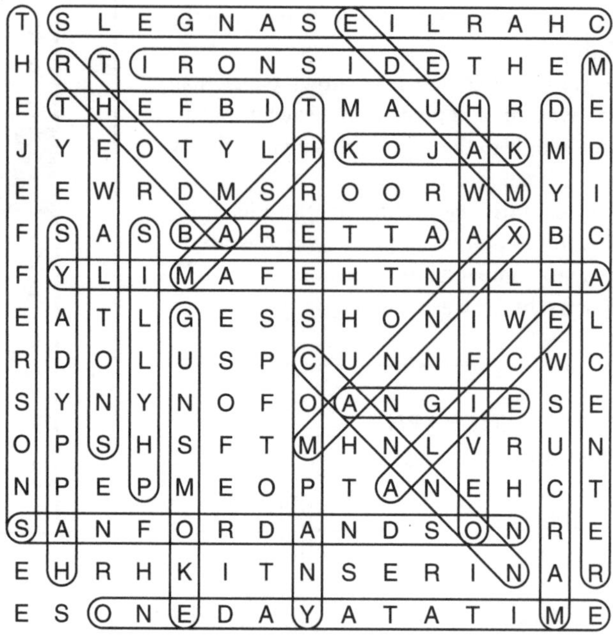

THE ONE & ONLY

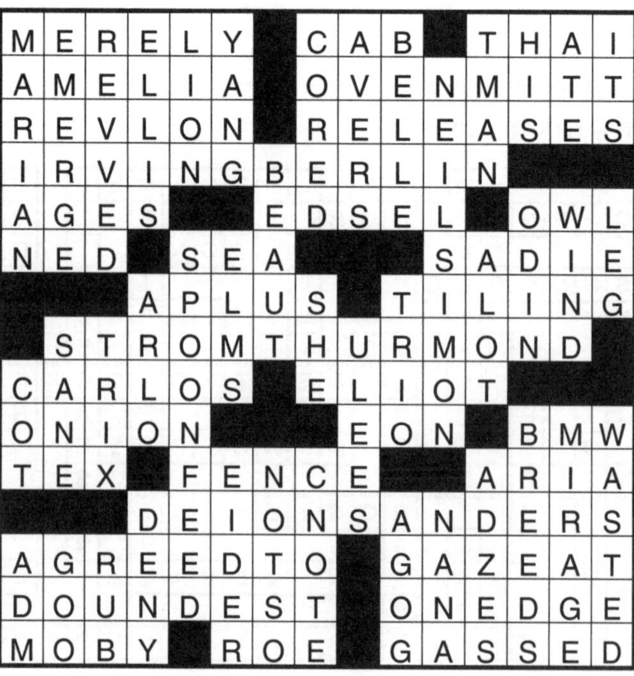

MISFITS QUIZ #1

1 – c (Cornstarch)
2 – a (Canoeing)
3 – d (Caramel)
4 – d (Marshmallow)
5 – b (Jumpy)
6 – e (Beef gravy)
7 – c (Mr. Crack. Mattel pulled Earring Magic Ken off the shelves when it realized that a lavender-mesh-shirted doll with an earring was suddenly a must-have for collectors in the gay community. Studebaker introduced the Dictator in 1934 and continued to manufacture it for three years, until the rise of Hitler and Mussolini when the name started to sound downright un-American.)
8 – d (Killjoy)
9 – a (Chewgum, Montana)
10 – b (Zookeepers)

COMING UP SHORT

The 9 Planets: Uranus
The 8 Members of TV's Brady Family: Peter
The 5 Great Lakes: Ontario
The 5 Original Members of the Rolling Stones: Charlie Watts
The 4 H's in the 4-H Club: Heart
The 13 Original U.S. Colonies: Georgia
The Life Savers' "5 Flavors": Pineapple
The 4 Teletubbies: Dipsy

IT'S A LIE!

The acrostic: A FALSEHOOD, MEANING A LIE

The quote: Before hats came into vogue...many professionals...wore distinctive hood styles. If a con man wanted to set himself up as a professional in a town where he wasn't known, all he had to do was put on the right hood. This deception came to be called a falsehood.

The clue answers:

A. AUSTIN POWERS
B. FRIDA KAHLO
C. AT ODDS WITH
D. LOAF
E. SWEET EMOTION
F. ENDSVILLE
G. HASSELHOFF
H. OUT OF THE WOODS
I. ON MY HONOR
J. DEBT
K. MEATHEAD
L. ENDORPHIN
M. ANTWONE FISHER
N. NUMISMATICS
O. ISAAC NEWTON
P. NICOLAS CAGE
Q. GOPHER STATE
R. ALPHABET
S. LAST CHANCE
T. ISOTOPE
U. EVELYN WOOD

CALLING DR. GREEN!

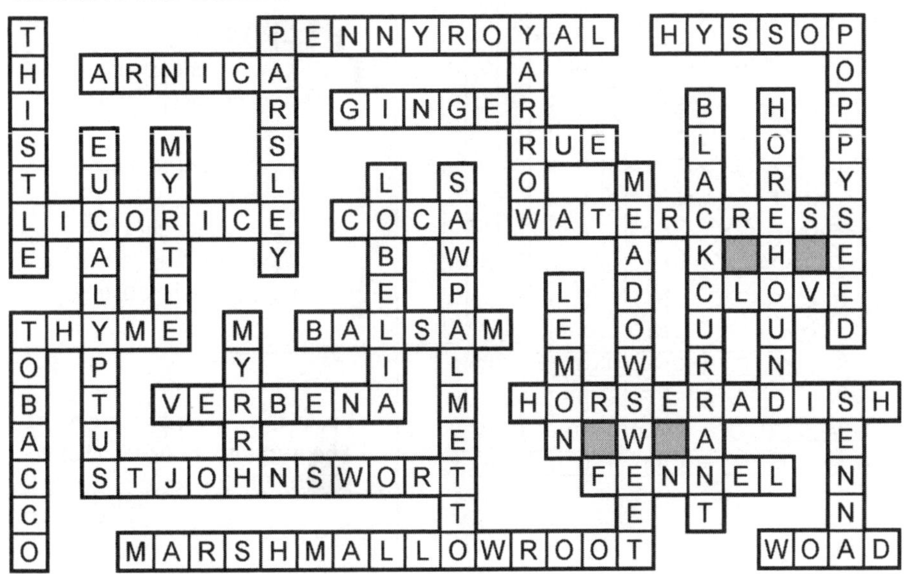

FOOD COLORING

B	A	G	S	■	B	A	C	H	■	R	I	A	T	A
A	L	O	T	■	A	C	H	E	■	E	D	W	I	N
R	E	D	M	E	A	T	I	S	■	A	C	O	R	N
R	E	S	A	L	E	S	■	S	A	R	A	L	E	E
■	■	■	R	I	D	O	F	■	B	R	R	■	■	■
A	P	P	T	■	■	N	O	T	B	A	D	F	O	R
B	R	A	I	D	■	■	L	A	I	N	■	I	N	E
Y	O	U	N	O	W	B	L	U	E	G	R	E	E	N
S	N	L	■	C	A	R	E	■	■	E	E	R	I	E
M	E	A	T	T	H	A	T	S	■	■	P	Y	N	E
■	■	■	R	O	O	■	T	U	L	S	A	■	■	■
E	M	P	E	R	O	R	■	D	E	L	I	G	H	T
B	Y	L	A	W	■	B	A	D	F	O	R	Y	O	U
B	R	O	T	H	■	I	D	E	A	■	T	R	O	N
S	A	Y	S	O	■	S	O	N	Y	■	O	O	P	S

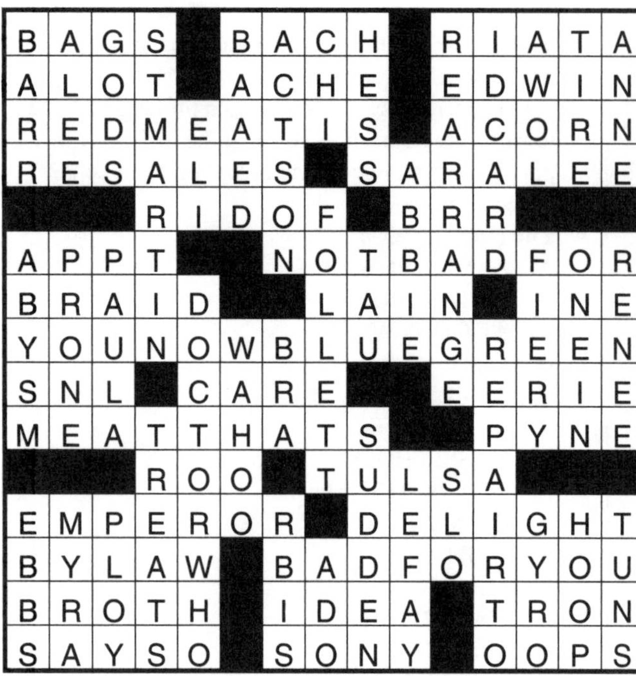

STUDYING UP ON YOUR OLOGIES

The leftover letters spell: Gerontology—the study of aging; myology—the study of muscles; speleology—the study of caves; garbology—the study of what a society throws out.

G	E	R	O	M	N	Y	T	Y	O	H	I	S	T	O	L	O	G	Y	L
O	G	Y	Y	Y	T	H	G	E	G	S	T	A	X	I	O	L	O	G	Y
U	D	Y	G	C	G	N	O	O	D	O	N	T	O	L	O	G	Y	L	F
H	I	P	P	O	L	O	G	Y	L	A	L	G	I	T	N	G	I	M	Y
E	O	L	O	L	L	S	L	G	G	O	Y	O	T	T	H	M	E	S	T
L	U	Y	G	O	L	O	N	O	R	H	C	O	R	D	N	E	D	M	D
M	Y	G	Y	G	O	L	O	L	Y	T	C	A	D	O	O	F	Y	A	M
I	Y	O	G	Y	M	O	U	O	S	H	C	L	L	E	H	R	G	G	O
N	G	L	O	E	S	G	S	M	R	P	T	O	E	V	M	L	O	I	R
T	O	O	L	E	S	Y	O	O	L	O	G	H	G	E	Y	T	L	R	P
H	L	N	O	H	E	C	N	T	A	Y	S	T	C	X	U	D	O	O	H
O	O	I	E	Y	O	O	H	N	F	C	A	O	V	I	E	S	T	L	O
L	H	H	N	I	L	E	E	A	G	Y	L	Y	A	L	R	A	N	O	L
O	C	R	B	O	R	M	O	H	T	O	G	G	L	L	M	O	O	G	O
G	I	G	G	O	O	O	Y	P	G	O	T	O	L	O	G	Y	E	Y	G
Y	R	Y	L	L	T	H	L	Y	L	E	L	L	L	L	S	T	D	U	Y
D	T	O	O	Y	O	F	C	O	N	C	H	O	L	O	G	Y	W	H	A
T	G	G	A	S	O	C	N	I	G	E	G	T	G	G	N	T	Y	T	H
Y	Y	G	O	L	O	I	M	E	S	Y	R	E	O	Y	W	E	S	O	U
Y	G	O	L	O	S	I	M	T	S	P	E	C	T	R	O	L	O	G	Y

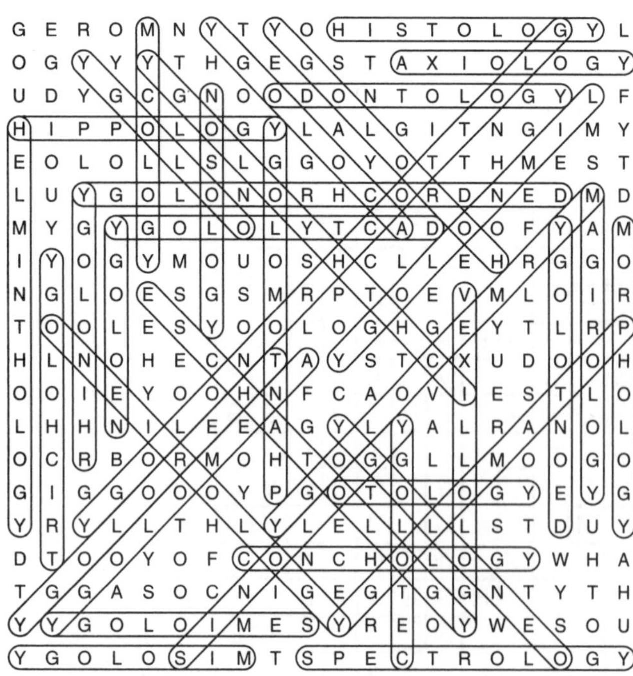

MIXED MARRIAGE

The quote: Twelve percent of Americans say they think Joan of Arc was Noah's wife.

The clue answers:

A. SOONER
B. TRAFFIC
C. JEWEL
D. HAVANA
E. FENWAY
F. HITCH
G. PAWNS
H. EASTER
I. MINKS
J. COYOTE

UNCLE JOHN'S LISTS

The 5 Most Germ-Ridden Places at Work

1. Phone
2. Desktop
3. Water fountain handle
4. Microwave door handle
5. Keyboard

The 7 States with the Lowest Life Expectancy

1. South Carolina
2. Mississippi
3. Georgia
4. Louisiana
5. Nevada
6. Alabama
7. North Carolina

BY GEORGE!

1. I am not a complete vegetarian. I eat only animals that have died in their sleep.
2. If you want to really test a faith healer, tell him you want a smaller shoe size.
3. I never thought I'd grow old. I always thought it was something that would happen to the other guy.

PLAYING THE PERCENTAGES #3

The numbers in order are: 90, 50, 10, 40, 80, 30, 20, 70, 60

THE DEVIL'S DICTIONARY

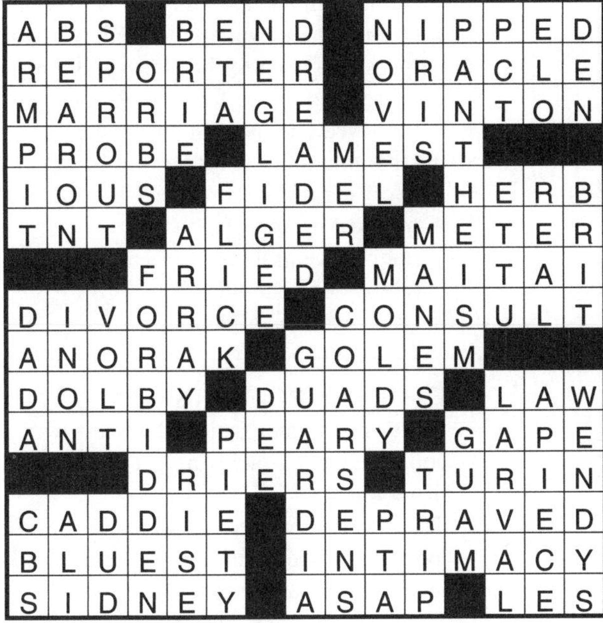

A	B	S		B	E	N	D		N	I	P	P	E	D
R	E	P	O	R	T	E	R		O	R	A	C	L	E
M	A	R	R	I	A	G	E		V	I	N	T	O	N
P	R	O	B	E		L	A	M	E	S	T			
I	O	U	S		F	I	D	E	L		H	E	R	B
T	N	T		A	L	G	E	R		M	E	T	E	R
			F	R	I	E	D		M	A	I	T	A	I
D	I	V	O	R	C	E		C	O	N	S	U	L	T
A	N	O	R	A	K		G	O	L	E	M			
D	O	L	B	Y		D	U	A	D	S		L	A	W
A	N	T	I		P	E	A	R	Y		G	A	P	E
			D	R	I	E	R	S		T	U	R	I	N
C	A	D	D	I	E		D	E	P	R	A	V	E	D
B	L	U	E	S	T		I	N	T	I	M	A	C	Y
S	I	D	N	E	Y		A	S	A	P		L	E	S

AT HEAVEN'S DOOR

The acrostic: ORIGIN OF KNOCKING ON WOOD

The quote: Both Native Americans and Greeks developed the belief (independently) that oak trees were the domain of an important god. By knocking on an oak, they were communicating with him and asking for his forgiveness.

The clue answers:

A. OKLAHOMA
B. RIGHT-HAND
C. I'M A BELIEVER
D. GRIMM
E. INNINGS
F. NED BEATTY
G. OPEN HOUSE
H. FATED
I. KING KONG
J. NEVER MIND
K. ON THE FENCE
L. CYBERSPACE
M. KITTEN
N. I FEEL FINE
O. NICK ADAMS
P. GORDIE HOWE
Q. OVERT
R. NORTH
S. WATTS
T. OKINAWA
U. OSTEOPATHS
V. DANDY

WOULD WE LIE TO YOU—THREE?

1 – a (It's an indication of high alcohol content.)
2 – b (The manufacturer only had pink food coloring on hand.)
3 – c (The buttons keep you from wiping your nose on your sleeve.)
4 – a (Walking beneath a ladder violates the "Holy Trinity" symbol.)
5 – c (You dig really deep beneath the water.)

WISE WOMEN

1. How wonderful it is that nobody need wait a single moment before starting to improve the world. (Anne Frank)
2. Blessed is the man who, having nothing to say, abstains from giving worthy evidence of the fact. (George Eliot)
3. If you just set out to be liked, you would be prepared to compromise on anything at any time, and would achieve nothing. (Margaret Thatcher)

IT'S A JUNGLE OUT THERE

1. Bad
2. Bad
3. Good
4. Bad
5. Bad
6. Bad
7. Bad
8. Good
9. Good
10. Bad
11. Good
12. Bad

13a. Good
13b. Bad

DOG DOO! GOOD GOD!

1. Dennis **sinned.**
2. Was it a rat **I saw?**
3. 'Tis in a Desoto **sedan I sit.**
4. Red rum, sir, **is murder.**
5. Damnit, **I'm mad!**
6. Do geese **see God?**
7. A slut nixes **sex in Tulsa.**
8. Lapses? Order **red roses, pal.**
9. "Desserts," I **stressed.**
10. If I had a **hi-fi…**
11. Ed, I saw Harpo Marx **ram Oprah W aside.**
12. Yawn. Madonna fan? **No damn way.**
13. Lisa Bonet ate **no basil.**
14. Do nine men interpret? **"Nine men," I nod.**
15. Are we not drawn onward, we few, **drawn onward to new era?**

FALSE ADVERTISING

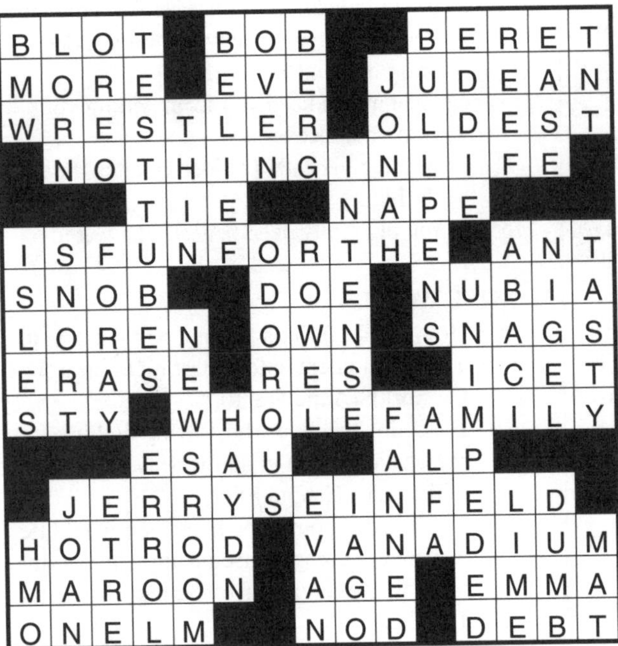

HANDICAP? WHAT HANDICAP?

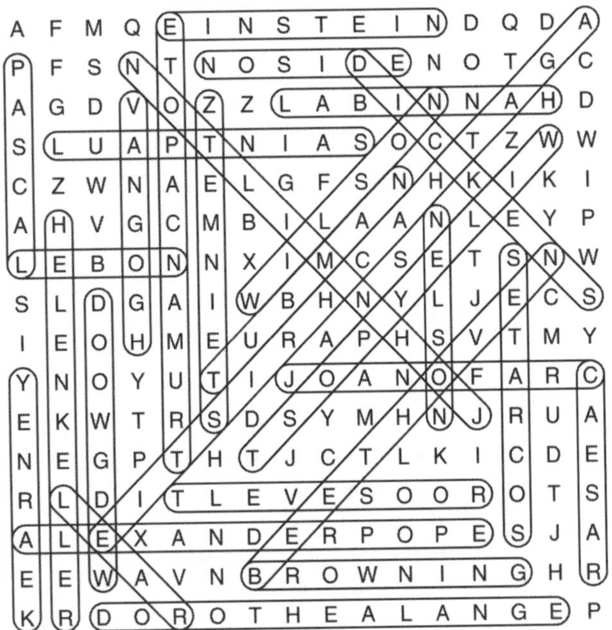

HAIL TO THE TRUE/FALSE QUIZ

George Washington was most likely named for George Eskridge, who became his mother's guardian when she was orphaned.

The other two are true. (Reagan headed the Screen Actors Guild in the '40s and '50s.)

GROUNDS FOR DIVORCE

1 – a (salute him and address him as "Major")
2 – c (put itching powder in her underwear)
3 – a (peas: pea soup for breakfast and dinner, and pea sandwiches for lunch)
4 – a (removed onions from his hamburger)
5 – b (shooting tin cans off her head)
6 – c (wore earplugs)
7 – b (dressed up as a ghost)
8 – c (they drove past his girlfriend's house)
9 – a (always nagging him)
10 – b (was much too affectionate)

BITES OF THE ROUND TABLE

1. Hollywood money isn't real money. It's congealed snow, melts in your hand, and there you are.
2. The best way to keep children at home is to make the home atmosphere pleasant and let the air out of the tires.
3. Excuse me, everybody, I have to go to the bathroom. I really have to telephone, but I'm too embarrassed to say so.

CRACKING THE CODE OF HAMMURABI

1. Accusing someone of a crime without proof
2. Falsely accusing someone of a crime
3. Stealing the property of a temple or a court
4. Receiving the stolen property of a temple or a court
5. Stealing a slave
6. Helping a slave escape
7. Hiding a slave
8. Breaking and entering
9. Committing a robbery
10. Allowing conspirators to meet in your tavern

THE CHIMP WHO SAVED EARLY MORNING TV

The Today Show
Sigourney Weaver
Dave Garroway
long sleeves
General George Patton
Mad
NBC
donut
James Dean
Queen Elizabeth's coronation
amusement park

SAFETY IN NUMBERS

PARLEZ-VOUS PENTAGONESE?

1. bombing
2. refugees
3. enemy survivors (enemy troops who survive bombing attacks)
4. bombs
5. bomb it
6. bomb it again
7. miss the target (refers to bombs that hit hospitals, schools, and so on)
8. jamming radar (also jamming radio, blowing up antiaircraft weapons, and shooting down enemy planes)
9. bombing attack
10. mercenaries
11. cluster bombs
12. bombing everything (…from enemy soldiers to sewage plants)
13. killing the enemy

ROSEANNE SEZ…

1. You may think you married the man of your dreams, but fifteen years later, you're married to a reclining chair that burps.
2. You get a lot of tension. You get a lot of headaches. I do what it says on the aspirin bottle. Take two and keep away from children.
3. My husband and I found this great new method of birth control that really, really works. Every night before we go to bed, we spend an hour with our kids.
4. I quit smoking. I feel better. I smell better. And it's safer to drink out of old beer cans laying around the house.
5. The way I look at it, if the kids are still alive when my husband comes home from work, then I've done my job.

UNCLE ALBERT SAYS…

1. Why is it that nobody understands me, and everybody likes me?
2. I am a deeply religious nonbeliever…This is a somewhat new kind of religion.
3. To punish me for my contempt for authority, Fate made me an authority myself.

UNCLE JOHN'S LISTS—TWO

The 7 Places You Can Legally Carry a Concealed Weapon in Utah

1. Car
2. City bus
3. Train
4. Mall
5. Bar (but give yourself an extra point if you guessed "bra")
6. Church
7. School

The 5 Most Interesting Things That Have Been Sold in Vending Machines

1. Emu jerky
2. Poached eggs
3. Holy water
4. Beetles
5. Live shrimp

CLARKE'S COMMENTS

1. Politicians should read science fiction, not westerns and detective stories.
2. A faith that cannot survive collision with the truth is worth many regrets.
3. The only way to discover the limits of the possible is to go beyond them into the impossible.

THE PRESIDENT'S PAJAMAS

	C	A	P	O	N		O	R	D	E	A	L		M	E	G
S	H	R	U	B	S		F	O	O	T	I	T		E	L	O
W	I	L	L	I	A	M	H	O	W	A	R	D	T	A	F	T
I	N	E	P	T		A	I	M	S				A	R	I	A
M	A	N		U	L	Y	S	S	E	S	S	G	R	A	N	T
			A	A	A					O	N	E				
W	O	O	D	R	O	W	W	I	L	S	O	N		P	A	W
H	A	R	D	Y		J	I	M	A		B	E	L	U	G	A
E	T	A	T		I	M	P	A	L	A	S		A	M	O	K
R	E	N	O	W	N		E	G	A	D		S	T	A	G	E
E	R	G		A	N	D	R	E	W	J	A	C	K	S	O	N
				R	E	D					B	O	A			
H	E	R	B	E	R	T	H	O	O	V	E	R		J	A	G
A	R	E	A				E	L	L	E		C	N	O	T	E
D	W	I	G	H	T	D	E	I	S	E	N	H	O	W	E	R
T	I	N		E	V	O	L	V	E		B	E	D	L	A	M
O	N	S		Y	A	T	S	E	N		C	R	E	S	T	

COMMON KNOWLEDGE

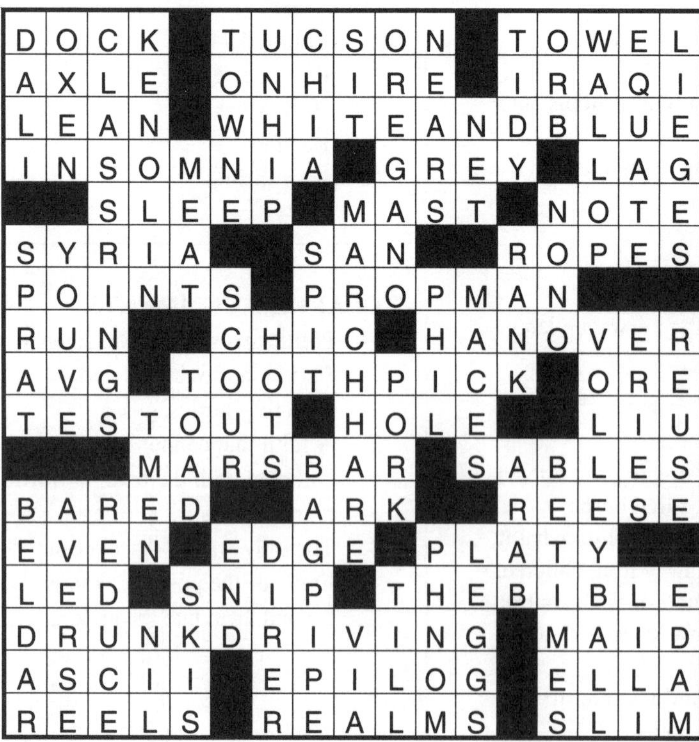

D	O	C	K		T	U	C	S	O	N		T	O	W	E	L
A	X	L	E		O	N	H	I	R	E		I	R	A	Q	I
L	E	A	N		W	H	I	T	E	A	N	D	B	L	U	E
I	N	S	O	M	N	I	A		G	R	E	Y		L	A	G
		S	L	E	E	P		M	A	S	T		N	O	T	E
S	Y	R	I	A			S	A	N			R	O	P	E	S
P	O	I	N	T	S		P	R	O	P	M	A	N			
R	U	N			C	H	I	C		H	A	N	O	V	E	R
A	V	G		T	O	O	T	H	P	I	C	K		O	R	E
T	E	S	T	O	U	T		H	O	L	E			L	I	U
			M	A	R	S	B	A	R		S	A	B	L	E	S
B	A	R	E	D			A	R	K			R	E	E	S	E
E	V	E	N		E	D	G	E		P	L	A	T	Y		
L	E	D		S	N	I	P		T	H	E	B	I	B	L	E
D	R	U	N	K	D	R	I	V	I	N	G		M	A	I	D
A	S	C	I	I		E	P	I	L	O	G		E	L	L	A
R	E	E	L	S		R	E	A	L	M	S		S	L	I	M

READY FOR PRIME TIME?

TV Champions (Japan)
A different bizarre contest each week. One week contestants chug "rancid, evil-smelling soybean gruel," another week they "allow themselves to be locked in cages and sworn at."

The Game of the Goose (Spain)
Contestants move around a game board; each space represents a different challenge. One challenge: release a semi-nude model from an exploding bed. Another: try to escape from a box that's slowly filling with sand.

Finders Keepers (U.S.)
Each day, the show is filmed on location at a different contestant's house. The film crew hides a prize in the contestant's living room, sets up cameras, and then lets viewers watch the contestant tear the room apart looking for it.

WOULD WE LIE TO YOU—FOUR?

1 – c (The moon is the symbol for the "ladies' room.")
2 – c (Santa's suit is red to match the Coca-Cola logo.)
3 – b (The Colosseum was plundered for building materials.)
4 – c (Seedless watermelons will eventually produce mature seeds.)
5 – b (The squiggles are the remains of what's called the "hyaloid artery.")

RIGHT ON THE NOSE

b. It's an old radio broadcasting expression.

TOM SWIFTIES: VARIATION ON A THEME

1 – b ("Get out of my hair," was Tom's brush-off.)
2 – h ("Hillbillies have a name for little valleys like this," Tom hollered.)
3 – j ("I haven't caught a fish all day!" Tom said, without debate.)
4 – e ("I hope I can still play the guitar," Tom fretted.)
5 – g ("I wonder what it was like being one of Zeus's daughters," Tom mused.)
6 – i ("I'm definitely going camping again," said Tom with intent.)
7 – a ("It's not a candy, it's a breath mint," Tom asserted.)
8 – c ("Oh, no! I dropped my toothpaste," Tom said, crestfallen.)
9 – f ("Smoking is not permitted in here," Tom fumed.)
10 – d ("Aha! Someone has removed the twos from this deck," Tom deduced.)

ALPO AND GREEN SLIME

1 – a (Italian sausage)
2 – p (game hurling beef)
3 – c (too many items)
4 – m (game heating coins)
5 – r (S&M—sausage and mushrooms)
6 – n (anchovies)
7 – g ("go away")
8 – h (burnt)
9 – i (PO—pepperoni and onions)
10 – o (pepperoni)
11 – q (green peppers)
12 – e (extra tomato sauce)
13 – l (oven tender)
14 – f (absorbent cardboard)
15 – s (mushrooms)
16 – b (saucing tool)
17 – d (cheapskate customer)
18 – j (problem pizza fit for vultures)
19 – k (pop the crust bubbles)

GOODNESS!

The fakes are "An Aid to Memorizing the Bible" and "The Smile Bible."

NUMBER TWO

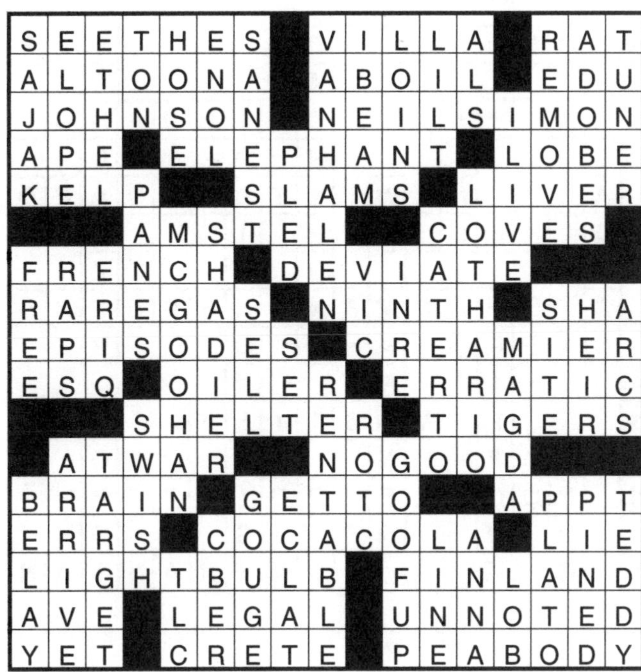

PATRON SAINTS

The leftover letters spell: "Pure Spirit, one hundred degrees proof—that's a drink that only the most hardened contemplation-guzzlers indulge in. Bodhisattvas dilute their Nirvana with equal parts [of] love and work." —Aldous Huxley

(Huxley wrote *Brave New World* in 1932. After a life crisis in the 1940s, he moved to California and threw in his lot with the Ramakrishna Mission in Hollywood, where—so the story goes—he "found himself.")

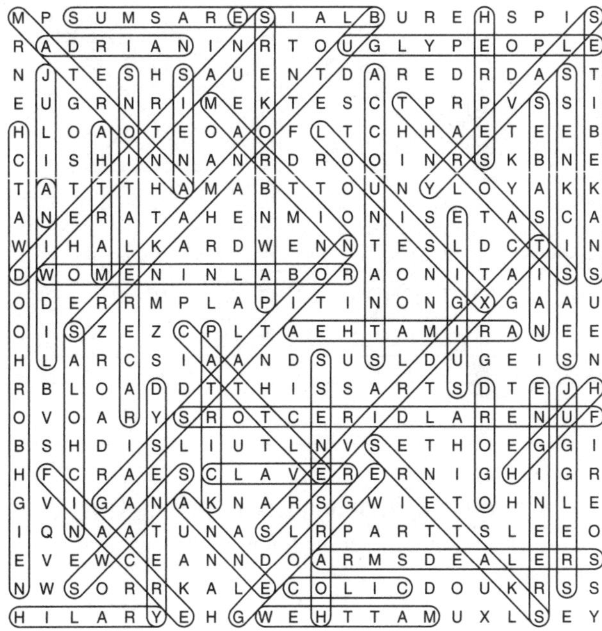

HERE, DOGGIE!

```
BLOODHOUND     S SHEEPDOG
 H       A     C   L A
 AKITA   CHIHUAHUA K PULI
 S   I   H     N   H I
 A   N W STBERNARD O L
MALAMUTE H I   U  BULLDOG
 P     I U C   Z   N O  R
 S  GERMANSHEPHERD D N  E
BOXER  A D O   R       SA
A   I  R   N        B  AT
S   F MASTIFF  COLLIE  MD
E   F  N   R   O    A  OA
N POODLE POINTER    G  YN
J U N  R   S   G  MALTESE
I G     POMERANIAN  E  D
```

NUMEROLOGY

1. 100,000
2. 2
3. 249
4. 7
5. 4,000
6. 6
7. 18
8. 2,965
9. 13
10. 4

THERE SHE IS...

```
B S O W A N D Y B E O R Y A J S H O P P
E H T H Y T P E R K I N S M I T H E P R
N I T S E D H L A C A S H C N E R F A R
H N N A M R O G G L G V C H A R L E S R
A D A A A O E N I A A J A O M E S E K E
M L Y I R F I A I N K R E T T I W E R P
E E R A N M N L D P K N A C Y H L B T O
R N B W E A L E O H B C H R L E R K T O
C O U L S P R E O I E E M U T L H A E C
E S F K W B M R W E R W B R T A E I N Q
R N E E U Y A A L R G T A R R C H W R N
N H R R E E X H L L E B P M A C H A O S
I O D R E U O E A C R V A T T I X I C P
K J S E M L E P M G O N A I T B L D N R
A O E L L K L D S G N M R E F E A H C S
N E B A R A Q U I O O I S R L T F G E C
D R N U N A N I D O G T K O A B F F O K
A D B C O T C D U N O S I N N E D Y A W
E N H E R Y L L E N N O D A N Z L D R M
M E R I W E T H E R E M O B L E Y L L S
```

FREE ADVICE

1. Never trust a man unless you've got his pecker in your pocket. (Lyndon Baines Johnson)
2. My father gave me these hints in speechmaking: Be sincere...be brief...be seated. (James Roosevelt, FDR's son)
3. The secret of dealing successfully with a child is not to be its parent. (Mell Lazarus, cartoonist: *Miss Peach, Momma*)

ZAP!

1. Everyone has the right to be comfortable on his own terms.
2. Most people wouldn't know good music if it came up and bit them in the ass.
3. The more people I have encouraged to be cynical, the better job I've done.

ORGAN DONORS, BUT WITHOUT PERMISSION

e. Lord Byron's nose (But his lungs are kept in a jar somewhere in Greece.)

WANNA BET?

The leftover letters spell: "Someone...asked me why women don't gamble as much as men...I gave the commonsensical reply that we don't have as much money. That was a true but incomplete answer. In fact, women's total instinct for gambling is satisfied by marriage."
—Gloria Steinem

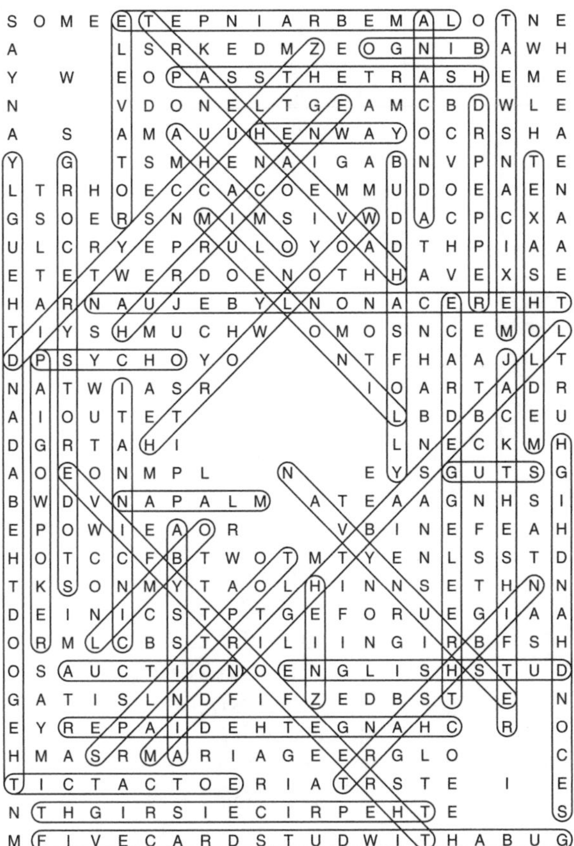

MISFITS QUIZ #2

1 – d (Strangle vine)
2 – b (*Captain Rusty*)
3 – a ("I Wish My Beer Was As Cold As You")
4 – a (Tread water for a week; but it can tread water for three days)
5 – d (*Where No Man Has Gone Before*; actually Nichelle Nichols *has* made a few albums, but no gospel albums. George Takei hasn't done any recording that we know of.)

LET ME WRITE SIGN—I SPEAK ENGLISH

1. Roasted duck let loose, beef rashers beaten up in the country people's fashion.
2. Visitors are expected to complain at the office between the hours of nine and eleven A.M. daily.
3. The lift is being fixed for the next day. During that time we regret that you will be unbearable.

WOULD WE LIE TO YOU—FIVE?

1 – c (It refers to Bohn's student guide.)
2 – b (Hyperactive racehorses didn't like losing their goats.)
3 – c ("Lurch" is derived from the French game *lourche*.)
4 – a (Sailors chattered complainingly while chewing actual fat.)
5 – c (It comes from an expression meaning "dressed to the eyes.")

BOND, JAMES BOND

1. The producers finally tricked Sean Connery into auditioning for James Bond on film by telling him they were experimenting with camera setups.

2. Ian Fleming found the name in *Birds of the West Indies* by James Bond, an ornithological classic. He wanted the simplest, dullest, plainest-sounding name that he could find. James Bond seemed perfect.

3. Cary Grant was one of the first people to say no to the James Bond role. Patrick McGoohan also rejected the role on moral grounds as too violent.

4. Without even seeing the film, John Barry composed the "James Bond Theme," one of the most recognizable themes in Hollywood history, and was paid less than five hundred dollars for his effort.

A LESSON IN PALM-READING

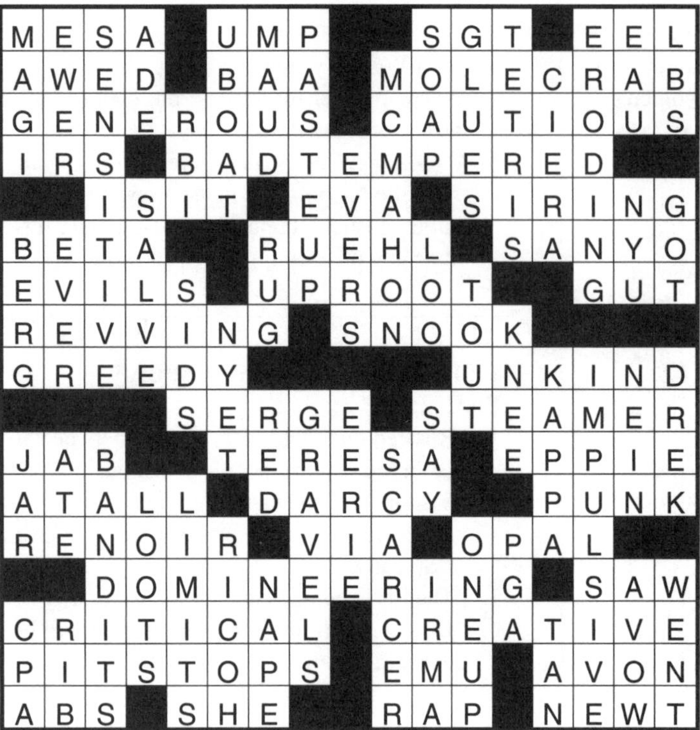

WORD ROW

The leftover letters spell: Here's another one for you: "T. Eliot, top bard, notes putrid tang emanating, is sad. I'd assign it a name: Gnat dirt upset on drab pot toilet.")

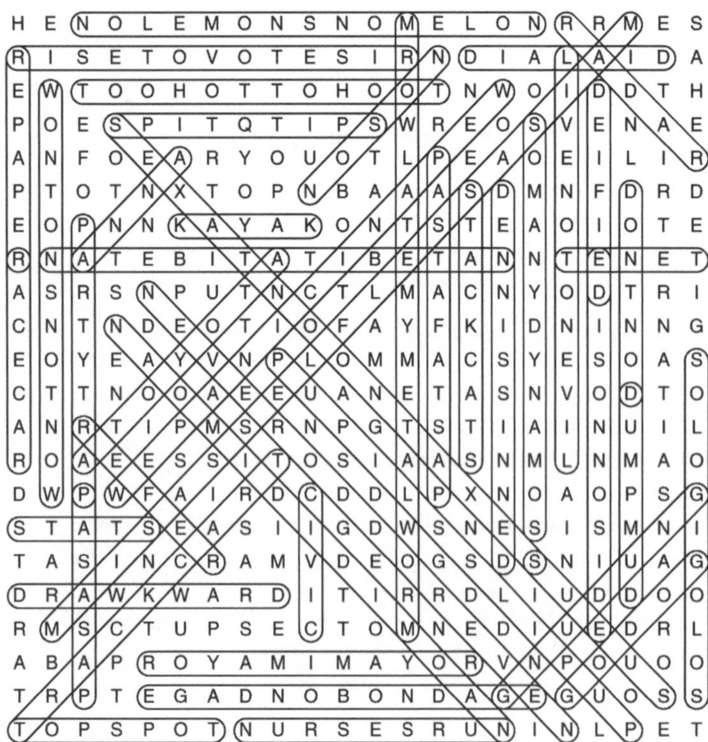

WATCH YOUR STEP!

The acrostic: STARTING ON THE RIGHT FOOT

The quote: The ancient Romans...believed that entering a building with the left foot was bad luck. They took the belief to extremes, even stationing guards or "footmen" at the entrances of buildings to make sure every visitor "started out on the right foot."

The clue answers:

A. STUART LITTLE
B. THE GHOSTWAY
C. AT NO TIME
D. RED DRAGON
E. TEFLON
F. INVOLVEMENT
G. NICK HORNBY
H. GET A LIFE
I. ORANGE CRUSH
J. NO DOUBT
K. TICKED
L. HEIST
M. EVENING OUT
N. RAINBOW SIX
O. ITEM
P. GIVE-AND-TAKE
Q. HOBOES
R. THE E STREET BAND
S. FIRST STATE
T. OMELET
U. OUT OF IT
V. THE FOUR FEATHERS

GOOFY HEADLINES

1. BRITAIN INCHES GRUDGINGLY TOWARDS METRIC SYSTEM
2. POLICE KILL MAN WITH TV TUNER
3. COCKROACH SLAIN, HUSBAND BADLY HURT
4. MAN SHOT, STABBED; DEATH BY NATURAL CAUSES RULED
5. ENRAGED COW INJURES FARMER WITH AXE

THE TERM-INATORS

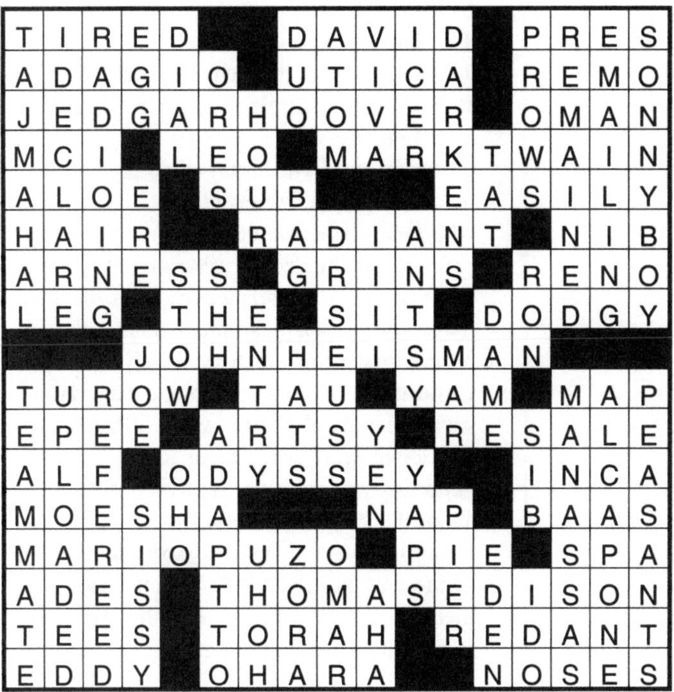

WHAT'LL YA HAVE?

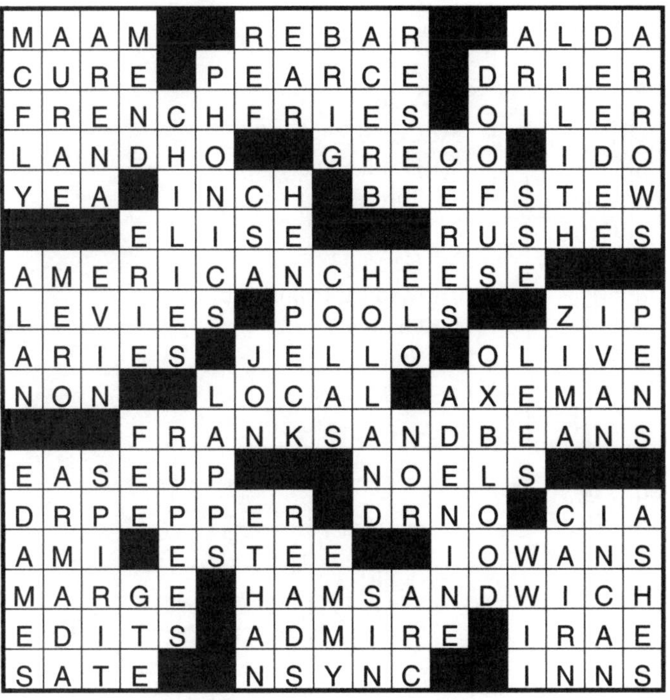

MORE GOOFY HEADLINES

1. CHILD'S STOOL GREAT FOR USE IN GARDEN
2. MAN STRUCK BY LIGHTNING FACES BATTERY CHARGES
3. BRITISH UNION FINDS DWARFS IN SHORT SUPPLY
4. FIRE OFFICIALS GRILLED OVER KEROSENE HEATERS
5. MAN MINUS EAR WAIVES HEARING

HISTORICAL HINDSIGHTS

1. The past actually happened but history is only what someone wrote down. (A. Whitney Brown)
2. So very difficult a matter is it to trace and find out the truth of anything by history. (Plutarch)
3. History is a pack of lies about events that never happened told by people who weren't there. (George Santayana)

DEAD WRONG?

The fakes are **King John**, **George Washington**, and **Chang and Eng**. King John, a glutton, died of dysentery caused by too much fruit and cider. While Washington did have a set of dentures with springs that caused him pain, he was actually bled to death by doctors who were treating him for a cold. Chang and Eng had no such disagreement; Chang died of bronchial trouble and Eng died of fright, thinking he would die, too.

AND IF YOU BELIEVE THAT ONE…TWO

1 – d (Turkish delight really did originate in Turkey.)

2 – b (The Plains of Abraham are actual plains.)

3 – c (Eggs are fourth on the list of ingredients for Eggo waffles—after enriched wheat flour, whey, and partially hydrogenated soybean oil.)

4 – a (Richard Nixon was elected president twice and vice-president twice.)

5 – a (Cows don't have six stomachs. They only have four.)

6 – c (*The Dick Van Dyke Show*'s pilot was actually bankrolled by Joseph Kennedy, JFK's father.)

7 – d (Okay, purple finches aren't really green. But they aren't purple either; they're crimson.)

8 – b (Lederhosen weren't invented in Morocco.)

SPOONERISMS

The phrases you're looking for in the grid:

A DOT IN THE SHARK
BELLY GENES
BILL IN THE FLANK
BLUSHING CROW
BOWERPAUL
BRAILLE JAKE
BUNNY PHONE
CHIPPING FLANNELS
COP PORN
FIGHT A LIAR
HAGS FLUNG OUT
HALF-WARMED FISH
HUSH MY BRAT
IS THE BEAN DIZZY
KNEE OF AN IDOL
LACK OF PIES
MAD BANNERS
MONK JAIL
NASAL HUT
NOBLE TONS OF SOIL
PARROTS AND KEYS
PAT MY HICCUP
QUEER OLD DEAN
RING STAY
ROARING PAIN
SEALING THE HICK
SHAKE A TOWER
SHOVING LEOPARD
SPACE OF AIDES
TASTED TWO WORMS
THREE-SCENE BALLAD
TIP OF THE SLUNG
TOWN DRAIN
TROUT SCOOP
WAVE THE SAILS
WELL-BOILED ICICLE

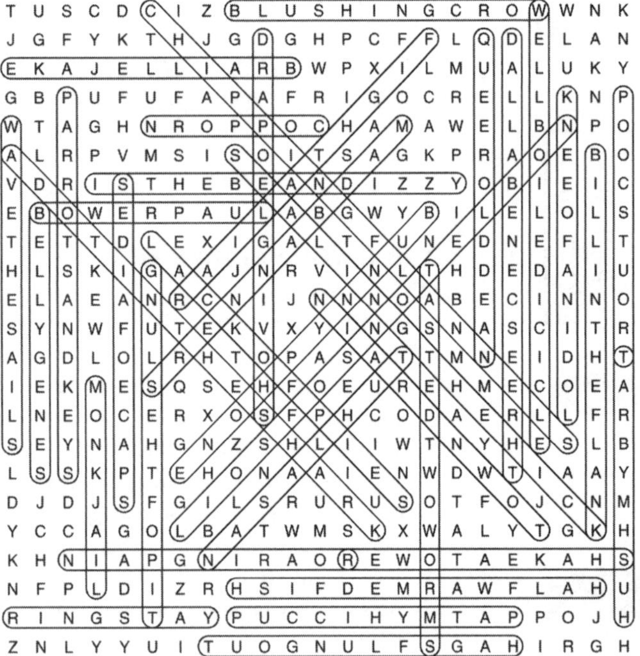

NOT FOR EXPORT

The leftover letters spell: "Green Piles" is a Japanese lawn fertilizer; "Shitto" is a spicy pepper sauce from Ghana; and from Taiwan, there's "Little Hussy," a writing tablet for girls.

WHERE THE HECK DID *THAT* COME FROM?

The fakes are:

Jiggle: Refers to the jig (the dance, that is).

Boor: Actually originally meant "farmer," and is unrelated to "boar." (A "neighbor" was a near-farmer.) The term had no pejorative meaning at first, but eventually, city-dwellers, who fancied themselves as being more refined than their country cousins, interpreted the word as "an unrefined, rude, or ill-mannered person"—so much so that the original meaning was lost entirely.

Candidate: In ancient Rome, a candidatus was "a person clothed in white." Roman politicians wore white togas to symbolize "humility and purity of motive." Still all about the PR, though.

Gung ho: Actually means "work together" in Chinese. A group of U.S. Marines used it as their motto in World War II, and it became a term to describe an enthusiastic soldier.

PARLEZ-VOUS EUPHEMISMS?

1. Cabdriver
2. Windshield wiper
3. Hunt
4. Wave
5. Crime
6. Death penalty
7. Torture
8. Diet
9. Harm
10. Medical malpractice
11. Outhouse
12. Smell
13. Stupid

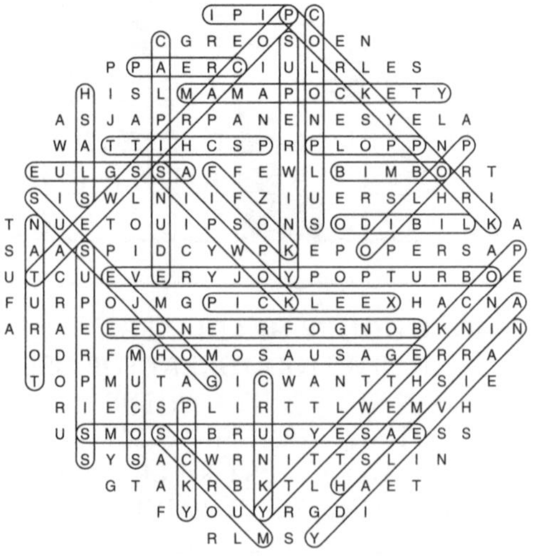

THEM'S FIGHTIN' WORDS

COLONIALISM
TREK
COMMANDO
COMMANDEER
FED UP
KHAKI
WASHOUT
CONCENTRATION CAMP
APARTHEID
CALICO
CASHMERE

WORLD WAR I
FOXHOLE
IN THE TRENCHES
DIGGING IN
TRENCH COAT
TRENCH MOUTH
SHELL SHOCK
SCREAMING MEEMIES
OVER THE TOP
NO-MAN'S-LAND
TRIP WIRE

AT SEA
ARMADA
TAKEN DOWN A PEG
CUT OF THE JIB
FIRST-RATE
TURN A BLIND EYE
CLEAR THE DECKS
BATTEN DOWN THE HATCHES
AT CLOSE QUARTERS
CUT AND RUN
BY THE BOARD

THE KOREAN WAR
M.A.S.H.
BAMBOO CURTAIN
POLICE ACTION
BUG OUT
AIR STRIKE
CHOPPER
BUY THE FARM
EYEBALL-TO-EYEBALL
HOOCH
BRAINWASHING

MODERN-DAY LATIN

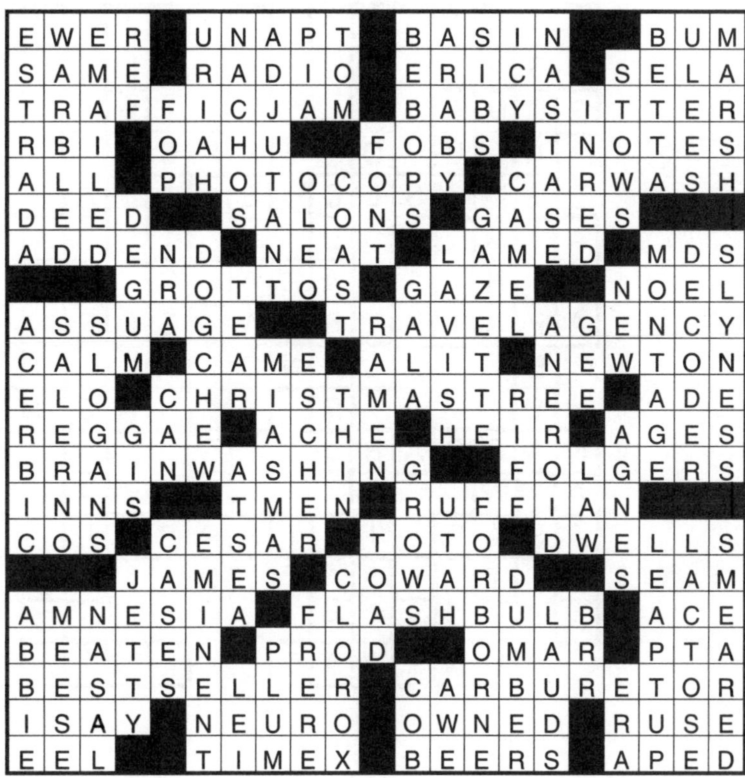

APPROPRIATE AUTHORS

1 – e (*The Abel Coincidence*, by J. N. Chance)
2 – j (*The Boy's Own Aquarium*, by Frank Finn)
3 – i (*Causes of Crime*, by A. Fink)
4 – n (*Crocheting Novelty Potholders*, by L. Macho)
5 – a (*The Cypress Garden*, by Jane Arbor)
6 – c (*Diseases of the Nervous System*, by Walter Russell Brain)
7 – h (*How to Live a Hundred Years or More*, by George Fasting)
8 – k (*Illustrated History of Gymnastics*, by John Goodbody)
9 – d (*Motorcycling for Beginners*, by Geoff Carless)
10 – m (*Riches and Poverty*, by L. G. Chiozza Money)
11 – l (*Running Duck*, by Paula Gosling)
12 – o (*The Skipper's Secret*, by Robert Smellie)
13 – b (*A Treatise on Madness*, by William Battie, M.D.)
14 – g (*Writing with Power*, by Peter Elbow)
15 – f (*Your Teeth*, by John Chipping)

EYE OF THE BEHOLDER

d. Marilyn didn't remove her upper molars to emphasize her cheekbones—that was Marlene Dietrich's beauty secret.

ACRONYMANIA

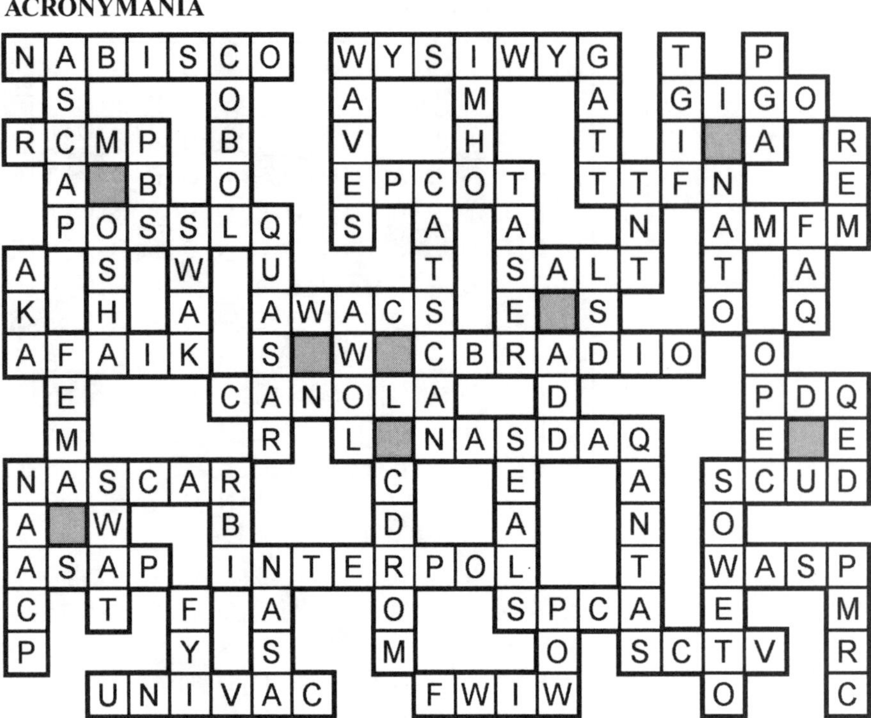

MURPHY'S LAWS

Murphy's Law of Buttered Bread: "A dropped piece of bread will always land butter side down."
Scientific analysis: The behavior of a piece of bread dropped from table height is fairly predictable: As it falls to the ground it is more likely than not to rotate on its axis; and the distance to the ground is not sufficient for the bread to rotate the full 360 degrees needed for it to land face up. So more often than not, it will land face down.

Murphy's Law of Lines: "The line next to you will move more quickly than the one you're in." (Also works with a line of traffic.)
Scientific analysis: On average, all the lanes of traffic, or lines at a K-Mart, move at roughly the same rate. That means that if there's a checkout line on either side of you, there's a two in three chance that one of them will move faster than the one you're in.

Murphy's Law of Socks: "If you lose a sock, it's always from a complete pair."
Scientific analysis: Start with a drawer containing 10 complete pairs of socks, for a total of 20 socks. Now lose one sock, creating one incomplete pair. The drawer now contains 19 socks, 18 of which belong to a complete pair. Now lose a second sock. If all of the remaining socks have the same odds of being lost, there's only 1 chance out of 18 that this lost sock is the mate of the first one that was lost. That means there's a 94.4% chance that it's from one of the complete pairs.

Murphy's Law of Maps: "The place you're looking for on the map will be located at the most inconvenient place on the map, such as an edge, a corner, or near a fold."
Scientific analysis: If you measure out an inch or so from each edge of the map and from each fold, and then calculate the total area of these portions of the map, they'll account for more than half the total area of the map. So if you pick a point at random, there's a better than 50% chance that it will be in an inconvenient-to-read part of the map.

THE COLORIZED VERSION

The acrostic: HOW THE YELLOW PAGES BEGAN

The quote: The Wyoming Telephone... Company hired a printer for its first business directory. He didn't have enough white paper for the job...so he used the stock he had on hand—yellow. Other companies around the country adopted it too, not realizing it was an accident.

The clue answers:

A. HOPED
B. OPTION
C. WHITE TEETH
D. TED CASSIDY
E. HOWARD JOHNSON
F. EUGENE IONESCO
G. YOURE SO VAIN
H. EDOUARD MANET
I. LORENZO
J. LINDY
K. OFF THE COURT
L. WITHERSPOON
M. PITCH BLACK
N. ATHLETICS
O. GET SHORTY
P. ENCHANTMENT
Q. SHIRR
R. BRAINWASHED
S. EDDIE MURPHY
T. GOPHER
U. ADAPTATION
V. NEFERTITI

STILL CHANNEL SURFING

1. *Growing Pains*
2. *Cheers*
3. *All in the Family*
4. *Three's Company*
5. *Ironside*
6. *The Wonder Years*
7. *Night Court*
8. *Touched by an Angel*
9. *The Golden Girls*
10. *Veronica's Closet*
11. *Marcus Welby, M.D.*
12. *That's Incredible*
13. *Father Knows Best*
14. *Empty Nest*
15. *Magnum, P. I.*
16. *The Dukes of Hazzard*
17. *The Ed Sullivan Show*
18. *Joanie Loves Chachi*

LEARN JAPANESE IN ONE EASY LESSON!

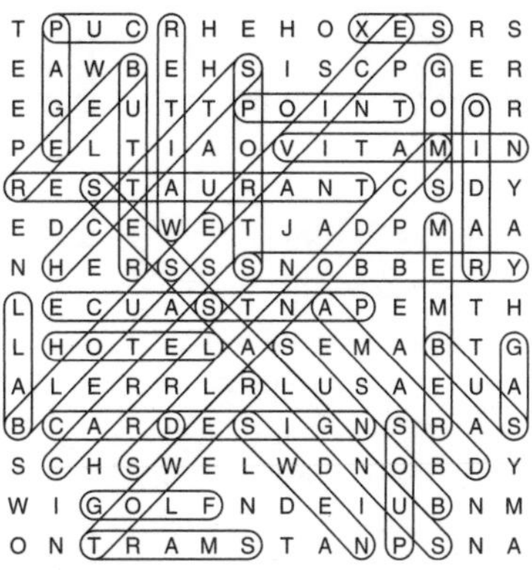

The list, with translations:

BASU (BUS)
BATA (BUTTER)
BIIRU (BEER)
BITAMI (VITAMIN)
BONASU (BONUS)
BORU (BALL)
BURAUSU (BLOUSE)
CARESU (CARESS)
DEZAIN (DESIGN)
DORAMA (DRAMA)
GASU (GAS)
GORUFU (GOLF)
HOTERU (HOTEL)
KADO (CARD)
KAPPU (CUP)
MAKUDONARUDO (MCDONALD'S)
MEMBA (MEMBER)
NYUSU (NEWS)
PANTSU (PANTS)
PEJI (PAGE)
POINTO (POINT)
RAJIO (RADIO)
RESUTORAN (RESTAURANT)
SABISU (SERVICE)
SEKKUSU (SEX)
SOSU (SAUCE)
SUMATO (SMART)
SUMOGGU (SMOG)
SUNGURASU (SUNGLASSES)
SUNOBBARI (SNOBBERY)
SUPOTSU (SPORTS)
SUPU (SOUP)
SUTECCHI (STITCH)
TAWA (TOWER)
WETA (WAITER)

The leftover letters spell: *The Horse Whisperer* played Japanese theaters as *Held by Wind in Montana.*

The word list in English:

BALL
BLOUSE
BEER
BONUS
BUS
BUTTER
CARD
CARESS
CUP
DESIGN
DRAMA
GAS
GOLF
HOTEL
MCDONALD'S
MEMBER
NEWS
PAGE
POINT
PANTS
RADIO
RESTAURANT
SAUCE
SERVICE
SEX
SMART
SMOG
SNOBBERY
SOUP
SPORTS
STITCH
SUNGLASSES
TOWER
VITAMIN
WAITER

MOST ADMIRED MEN

FYI: These thumbnails will help identify some of the names that—like General MacArthur's "old soldiers"— have faded from the limelight.

H	A	R	T					B							M									
O		E		W	A	L	L	A	C	E			G	R	A	H	A	M			B	U	S	H
P		A		A				R					O		N								T	
E		G		I		F	A	U	B	U	S		R		D		H	U	M	P	H	R	E	Y
		A		T				C			T		B		E		A						V	
K	E	N	N	E	D	Y		H		D	A	L	A	I	L	A	M	A		G	O	R	E	
							M		M		S		C		A		M			L			N	
	I	A	C	O	C	C	A		A		S		H				A	G	N	E	W		S	
					L		R	O	C	K	E	F	E	L	L	E	R			N			O	
	R	O	B	B	I	N	S		A		N		V				S			N			N	
					N		H		R					S	A	L	K		I		G			T
L		F		U	T	H	A	N	T								J	F	K		A			U
B		O			O		L		H	O	O	V	E	R			O		E		T	A	F	T
J	O	R	D	A	N		L		U								L				E			U
		D						T	R	U	M	A	N				D	I	R	K	S	E	N	

Bernard Baruch (1870–1965). America's "elder statesman"—the "go-to" guy for many presidents. Financier who amassed a fortune in the stock market. Never held public office, but served as an adviser to U.S. presidents Wilson, Harding, Coolidge, Hoover, Roosevelt, and Truman.

Everett Dirksen (1896–1969). Republican Senator from Illinois. With wavy white hair and a mellifluous voice, he was perfectly cast as the Senate minority leader during the Kennedy and Johnson administrations. He even had a hit spoken-word record called *Gallant Men*.

Orval Faubus (1910–1994). Governor of Arkansas (1954–1967), symbol of white defiance to integration—or, depending on your point of view, to "federal interference." Became famous when he defied a 1957 federal court order to desegregate schools and called out the Arkansas National Guard to "prevent violence" by blocking the entrance to Little Rock Central High School, preventing nine African American students from entering. In response, President Eisenhower mobilized 1,200 U.S. Army paratroopers to escort the students into the school. After leaving office in 1967, Faubus worked as a bank clerk.

Dag Hammarskjöld (1905–1961). Swedish economist and statesman who became the second secretary general of the United Nations (1953–1961). In one of the most dangerous periods in world history—with A-bomb scares, emerging third-world nations, Cold War tensions—he effectively used the United Nations to mitigate crises. Killed in a plane crash over the Congo in 1961 (during a civil war there) and was awarded the Nobel Peace Prize posthumously that same year.

Hubert Humphrey (1911–1978). Senator from Minnesota, 38th vice president of the United States (1965–1969), and Democratic presidential candidate in 1968 (lost to Nixon). Called "The Happy Warrior," his signature phrase was: "I'm pleased as punch to be here."

George Marshall (1880–1959). Army chief of staff during World War II and later U.S. secretary of state (1947–1949). His 1947 European Recovery Program became known as the "Marshall Plan" and is credited with saving post-World War II Europe. He received the Nobel Peace Prize in 1953.

Harold Stassen (1907–2001). Our favorite guy on the Most Admired lists. The wonder boy of the Republican Party in the 1940s, he became Minnesota's youngest governor and served three terms. He was Dewey's chief rival for the Republican nomination in 1948, but narrowly lost it. (Ironically, if he'd actually been nominated, he might well have been elected president, since Truman was considered extremely vulnerable.) Stassen never got over the loss. He became obsessed with the presidency and ran nine increasingly bizarre campaigns for it over the next 36 years.

Adlai Stevenson (1900–1965). U.S. political leader and diplomat who helped found the United Nations. Mainly remembered as the eloquent, witty Democratic presidential candidate who was crushed in 1952 and 1956 by Dwight Eisenhower. In 1961, he was JFK's ambassador to the United Nations.

Robert Taft (1889–1953) "Mr. Republican." Son of William Howard Taft, 27th U.S. president. U.S. senator from Ohio for 14 years (1939–1953). America's most prominent conservative for many years. Narrowly missed the Republican presidential nomination in 1952, losing to "internationalist" Dwight Eisenhower—interpreted as the defeat of isolationism within the party.

U Thant (1909–1974). In the 1960s, the United Nations was widely seen as a vital link to peace. Thant, a Burmese educator and civil servant, was the third U.N. secretary general (1962–1971). Often made news because he criticized both West and East for actions he considered threatening to world peace. Americans were fascinated that someone could have a first name like "U."

Terry Waite (1939–). British church official who was in the news when he successfully negotiated the release of British hostages in Iran and Libya. Then, while trying to arrange the release of U.S. hostages in Beirut in 1987, he was kidnapped by Shiite Muslims and held until 1991.

REDUNDANT AND REPETITIOUS

The leftover letters spell: The convicted felon was a unique individual who liked to circulate around.

The word list:
ADDED BONUS
ADVANCE WARNING
CLOSED FIST
DUPLICATE COPY
END RESULT
EXACT REPLICA
FOREIGN IMPORTS
FREE GIFT
JOIN TOGETHER
LAG BEHIND
PAST EXPERIENCE
PRIOR HISTORY
REVERT BACK
SUM TOTAL
TOTAL ABSTINENCE
TRUE FACT

F	O	R	E	I	G	N	I	M	P	O	R	T	S	T
Y	P	O	C	E	T	A	C	I	L	P	U	D	P	H
G	N	I	N	R	A	W	E	C	N	A	V	D	A	P
A	J	E	E	C	T	O	T	N	V	I	C	D	S	R
C	T	O	N	E	D	L	F	C	E	L	D	O	T	I
I	L	N	I	W	R	A	U	S	A	E	A	U	E	O
L	A	O	T	N	N	E	I	S	D	F	Q	U	X	R
P	G	E	S	I	T	N	V	B	E	F	E	D	P	H
E	B	I	B	E	V	O	O	E	R	R	I	U	E	I
R	E	D	A	U	D	N	G	E	R	A	D	L	R	S
T	H	W	L	H	U	F	E	E	O	T	L	N	I	T
C	I	I	A	S	K	G	I	E	T	D	B	T	E	O
A	N	O	T	C	I	I	R	S	C	H	U	A	N	R
X	D	L	O	F	A	T	E	A	T	R	E	O	C	Y
E	L	A	T	O	T	M	U	S	U	N	D	R	E	K

SETTING THE STAGE

F	A	M	E		M	A	M	B	A		R	A	S	T	A	S		A	O	L
E	D	I	E		A	D	O	R	N		E	T	H	E	R	E	A	L	L	Y
R	O	C	K	H	U	D	S	O	N		D	E	A	N	M	A	R	T	I	N
N	P	R		Y	V	E	S	M	O	N	T	A	N	D			B	O	N	N
	T	O	P	P	E	R			T	O	A	S	T		L	S	U			
T	I	D	I	E	S		F	R	A	P	P	E		C	A	U	S	T	I	C
A	V	O	N			G	O	A	T	E	E			I	N	N		E	A	R
P	E	T	E	R	L	O	R	R	E			J	A	C	K	B	E	N	N	Y
				B	E	T	T	E		C	H	O	R	E		O	L	D		
S	E	R	B	I	A				J	O	A	N	C	R	A	W	F	O	R	D
A	L	O	E		V	A	N	M	O	R	R	I	S	O	N		I	N	T	O
M	I	C	H	A	E	L	C	A	I	N	E				T	E	N	S	E	S
		K	A	T		B	A	R	N	S		R	A	I	S	E				
R	O	Y	R	O	G	E	R	S			J	E	R	R	Y	L	E	W	I	S
O	U	I		L	E	I			G	R	E	E	N	S			M	A	C	E
T	R	I	P	L	E	T		W	E	I	R	D	O		G	I	M	L	E	T
			O	S	S		M	O	A	N	S			M	E	T	A	L	S	
A	R	A	L			G	E	O	R	G	E	B	U	R	N	S		E	H	F
T	O	N	Y	C	U	R	T	I	S		Y	U	L	B	R	Y	N	N	E	R
O	U	T	P	A	T	I	E	N	T		E	R	N	I	E		I	D	E	E
P	E	Z		L	E	T	S	G	O		D	R	A	G	S		L	A	T	E

UNCLE POTATO HEAD?

a. Eggplant

MORE FREE ADVICE

1. A man is a fool if he drinks before he reaches fifty, and a fool if he doesn't drink afterward. (Frank Lloyd Wright)
2. Never go out to meet trouble. If you will just sit still, nine cases out of ten someone will intercept it for you. (Calvin Coolidge)
3. The only way to keep your health is to eat what you don't want, drink what you don't like, and do what you'd rather not. (Mark Twain)

LOONEY LAWS: THE QUIZ

1 – a (dentures)
2 – b (crocodiles)
3 – a (out of a bucket)
4 – a (in a bakery)
5 – a (your boots on)
6 – b (at men wearing striped suits)
7 – c (whistle underwater)
8 – a (shaving the chests of)
9 – b (working on a chain gang)
10 – c (play dominoes)

U.K. VS. U.S.A.

The leftover letters spell out: "An Englishman, even if he is alone, forms an orderly queue of one." —British humorist George Mikes

The word list:

ACCUMULATOR (BATTERY)
AUBERGINE (EGGPLANT— "aubergine" borrowed from the French)
BLACK TREACLE (MOLASSES)
BOBBY (POLICE OFFICER)
BONNET (HOOD—of a car)
BRACES (SUSPENDERS)
CANDY FLOSS (COTTON CANDY)
CARAVAN (TRAILER)
CASH DESK (CHECKOUT COUNTER)
CATAPULT (SLINGSHOT)
CHEMIST (DRUGGIST)
CHIPS (FRENCH FRIES)
CHUCKER OUT (BOUNCER)
CUBBYHOLE (GLOVE COMPARTMENT)
DRAUGHTS (CHECKERS)
FAG (CIGARETTE)
FASCIA PANEL (DASHBOARD)
FRINGE (BANGS—the hairstyle)
HOARDING (BILLBOARD)
HOOTER (SIREN)
LAY-BY (REST AREA)
LIFT (ELEVATOR)
LORRY (TRUCK)
MACKINTOSH (RAINCOAT)
NAPPY (DIAPER)
NOUGHT (ZERO)
PANTECHNICON (MOVING VAN)
PATIENCE (SOLITAIRE)
PETROL (GASOLINE)
POLKA DOTS (CHOCOLATE CHIPS)
PUSH CHAIR (STROLLER)
SOLICITOR (LAWYER)
SPANNER (WRENCH)
SPONGE BAG (SHAVING KIT)
TORCH (FLASHLIGHT)
TOWER BLOCK (HIGH-RISE APARTMENT)
TRACK (TREAD)
TUBE (SUBWAY)
VERGE (SHOULDER—of a road)
WAISTCOAT (VEST)
WING (FENDER)

A N T O H S G N I L S E N Y A W B U S
N R N G C H E C K E R S L E I S A H M
C H E C K O U T C O U N T E R A N N E
V E M P N I T F H F L A S H L I G H T
E I T R A S A T E R I A T I L O S G D
C L R E C I F F O E C I L O P O R A N
H E A L D F D O R N H I M S A N E S O
O S P L R O R D A C C S G S E R Y O R
C E M O U L R V N H D A H A T Y W L B
O S O R G Q G E U F E A N O R U A I B
L S C T G N R E Z R V R S D U E L N A
A A E S I W E O L I F E O H Y L T E T
T L V V S R E D N E P S U S B N D T T
E O O E T E B G R S V T T O I O T E E
C M L I S L K H H U M A A S O R A I R
H I G H R I S E A P A R T M E N T R Y
I O S T T A G F E N D E R O E V O R D
P G O E M R E G G P L A N T R U C K I
S K E D S T A O C N I A R E C N U O B

WILD KINGDOM

1. When you see dolphins nuzzling, you probably think they're expressing care for one another. And you're right. Dolphins use touch as a way to bond and to remove social tensions.
2. Elephants get vocal only when they're excited. Generally, the more excited they are the longer and louder they'll trumpet. At zoos, they'll give a short, sharp toot when they're impatient to be fed.
3. Animals play rough, so sometimes it's hard to tell whether two animals engaged in aggressive physical contact are angry or having a good time. But with crocodiles, it's no mystery: they're not getting along.
4. When salmon swim upstream, they're returning to the very place where they were hatched. And they apparently find the home stream by their sense of smell.

GIDDY-*UP*!

The quote: A horse expends more energy lying down than it does standing up.

The clue answers:

A. DEPOTS
B. TWEENERS
C. PAGANINI
D. NAUGHTY
E. DOMINOS
F. LENDS
G. HYDROX
H. GREEN

SURVEY SAYS...

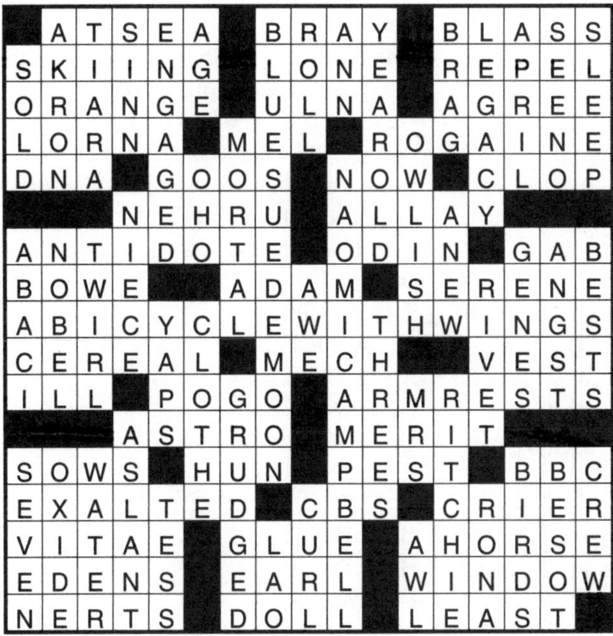

EVEN MORE GOOFY HEADLINES

1. MAYOR SAYS D.C. IS SAFE EXCEPT FOR MURDERS
2. JUMPING BEAN PRICES AFFECT POOR
3. BOYS CAUSE AS MANY PREGNANCIES AS GIRLS
4. TEENAGE PROSTITUTION PROBLEM IS MOUNTING
5. STORM DELAYED BY BAD WEATHER

YOU MUST REMEMBER THIS

1 – f (EBGDAE)
2 – e (Genesis, Exodus, Leviticus, Numbers, Deuteronomy)
3 – l (Io, Europa, Ganymede, Callisto)
4 – a (I, V, X, L, C, D, M)
5 – k (Kilo, Hecta, Deca, Unit, Deci, Centi, Milli)
6 – b (Kingdom, Phylum, Class, Order, Family, Genus, Species)
7 – n (3.1415926; the numbers are represented by the length of the words)
8 – j (Mercury, Venus, Earth, Mars, Jupiter, Saturn, Uranus, Neptune, Pluto)
9 – g (Norman, Plantagenet, Lancaster, York, Tudor, Stuart, Hanover, Windsor)
10 – c (occipital, parietal, frontal, temporal, ephnoid, sphenoid)
11 – h (parentheses, exponents, multiplication, division, addition, subtraction)
12 – i (Paleocene, Eocene, Oligocene, Miocene, Pliocene, Pleistocene)
13 – d (red, orange, yellow, green, blue, indigo, violet)
14 – m (talc, gypsum, calcite, fluorite, apatite, orthoclase, quartz, topaz, corundum, diamond)

GETTING THE LAST WORD

1 – q (Queen Elizabeth I)
2 – k (Lady Nancy Astor, when she woke briefly to find all her family around her)
3 – g (Florenz Ziegfeld)
4 – p (Pancho Villa)
5 – o (Pablo Picasso; this was the basis for a Paul McCartney song from the album *Band on the Run*—"Picasso's Last Words (Drink to Me)"
6 – m (Oscar Wilde)
7 – a (Anna Pavlova)
8 – j (Karl Marx)
9 – n (P. T. Barnum)
10 – h (François Rabelais)
11 – l (Leonardo da Vinci)
12 – f (Eugene O'Neill)
13 – c (Dominique Bouhours)
14 – e (Ernesto "Che" Guevara)
15 – d (Dylan Thomas)
16 – r (Thomas Jefferson; it was, in fact, the Fourth of July)
17 – b (Benito Mussolini)
18 – i (John Adams; Thomas Jefferson had actually died earlier the same day, but Adams didn't know it)

TWISTED TITLES 2

1 – d (A Fridge Too Far)
2 – i (Born Fred)
3 – h (Car and Drivel)
4 – f (50 Ways to Lease Your Lover)
5 – m (Nair)
6 – c (I Chung)
7 – b (I Get a Kink Out of You)
8 – a (Mrs. Doubttire)
9 – o (Preparation "I")
10 – j (Shorts Illustrated)
11 – g (The Cold Rush)
12 – e (Top Nun)
13 – n (Waa and Peace)
14 – l (What Kind of Food Am I?)
15 – k (When I Say Ho I Feel Guilty)

GOING, ABROAD

The leftover letters spell: Lavatories can be found in France by asking "Ou sont les toilettes?" But you might not like it when you get there since, as Billy Wilder said, "France is a country where the money falls apart but you can't tear the toilet paper."

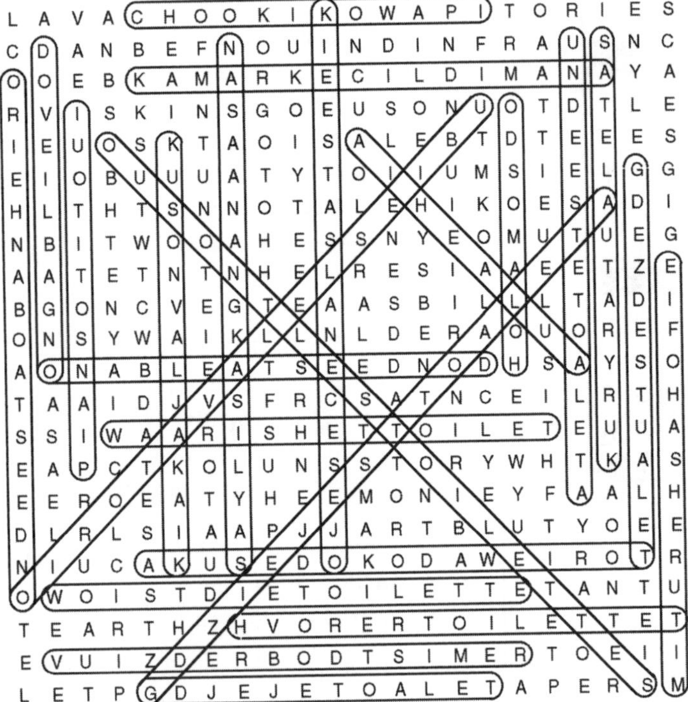

ANOTHER COUNTRY HEARD FROM

A	C	C	E	S	S	■	M	O	L	L	S	■	M	A	D	E	■	M	A	C
S	H	O	D	D	Y	■	A	R	I	E	L	■	O	P	A	L	■	U	F	O
K	I	S	S	I	N	G	Y	O	U	G	O	O	D	B	Y	E	■	S	R	I
S	A	M	■	■	C	O	O	■	■	■	V	I	E	■	■	M	U	L	A	N
■	■	I	D	B	E	D	R	U	N	K	A	L	L	T	H	E	T	I	M	E
I	D	C	A	R	D	S	■	S	P	I	K	Y	■	R	E	N	A	M	E	D
M	A	R	L	A	■	■	N	E	R	D	S	■	T	E	E	T	H	■	■	■
I	T	A	I	N	T	B	A	D	■	■	■	O	R	A	L	S	■	A	L	I
N	A	Y	■	■	R	U	B	■	H	E	P	C	A	T	S	■	I	N	O	N
■	■	■	C	H	E	R	■	G	E	L	A	T	I	■	■	A	L	T	A	R
I	V	E	B	E	E	N	A	L	I	A	R	A	L	L	M	Y	L	I	F	E
G	I	V	E	N	■	■	L	I	N	T	E	L	■	E	O	N	S	■	■	■
O	V	E	R	■	B	L	I	T	Z	E	S	■	A	I	R	■	■	R	C	A
R	A	N	■	M	A	I	N	Z	■	■	■	I	C	A	N	T	B	E	A	R
■	■	■	D	O	Y	L	E	■	R	U	B	L	E	■	■	C	R	E	P	E
H	A	V	E	N	O	T	■	M	A	R	E	S	■	L	I	B	I	D	O	S
I	T	S	C	A	U	S	E	I	M	L	E	A	V	I	N	Y	O	U	■	■
P	R	I	O	R	■	■	V	C	R	■	■	■	I	N	G	■	■	C	A	D
P	I	G	■	C	O	M	E	H	O	M	E	O	R	G	O	C	R	A	Z	Y
I	A	N	■	H	A	I	R	■	D	A	R	L	A	■	T	E	U	T	O	N
E	L	S	■	S	T	A	T	■	S	T	E	E	L	■	S	L	E	E	V	E

WHAT MAKES A GOOD VILLAIN?

The acrostic: ANONYMOUS STAR WARS STARS

The quote: David Prowse is a...former heavyweight wrestling champion. George Lucas saw him in *A Clockwork Orange* and offered him his choice of two parts, Chewbacca or [Darth] Vader. Prowse chose Vader because he didn't want to go around in a "gorilla suit" for six months.

The clue list:

A. APPROVING
B. NEVER NEVER LAND
C. ODDITIES
D. NAOMI WATTS
E. YOU DON'T OWN ME
F. MIKHAIL GORBACHEV
G. OUT OF AFRICA
H. UPSWING
I. SAGES
J. SCARECROW
K. THE THIRD WORLD
L. ACCORD
M. RUN OFF WITH
N. WHERE OR WHEN
O. AGGREGATES
P. ROCKFISH
Q. SOCIAL
R. SCAMPI
S. THE BACHELOR
T. AXIOMS
U. RADIOHEAD
V. SHOWCASED

POLI-TALKS

1. If B.S. was a dollar a pound, we would have paid off the deficit at about noon. (Rep. Jim Ross Lightfoot, R-Iowa)
2. Look, I'm trying to run for president! I can't sit here and debate free trade versus fair trade! (Pat Robertson)
3. The first law of politics: Never say anything in a national campaign that anyone might remember. (Eugene McCarthy)

EQUATION ANALYSIS HUNT

Answers to the equations:

1 = GIANT LEAP for MANKIND
1 = LIFE to LIVE
2 = QUARTERS in a HALF DOLLAR
3 = BEARS in "GOLDILOCKS"
3 = BLIND MICE
4 = QUARTS in a GALLON
4 = STARS for a GENERAL
4 = SEASONS in a YEAR
5 = FINGERS on a HAND
7 = WONDERS of the ANCIENT WORLD
8 = GREAT TOMATOES in a LITTLE BITTY CAN
9 = CIRCLES of HELL in the "DIVINE COMEDY"
9 = GREEK MUSES
9 = PLANETS in the SOLAR SYSTEM
9 = SYMPHONIES by BEETHOVEN
10 = HARDNESS of a DIAMOND on the MOHS' SCALE
11 = PLAYERS on a FOOTBALL TEAM
12 = NOTES in an OCTAVE
12 = SIGNS of the ZODIAC
13 = STRIPES on the AMERICAN FLAG
20 = NUMBERS on a DARTBOARD
40 = DAYS of RAIN in the GREAT FLOOD
40 = THIEVES (with ALI BABA)
54 = CARDS in a DECK (with the JOKERS)
88 = PIANO KEYS
90 = DEGREES in a RIGHT ANGLE
101 = DALMATIANS
1001 = ARABIAN NIGHTS

The leftover letters spell: Albert Einstein said, "Since the mathematicians have invaded the theory of relativity, I do not understand it myself anymore."

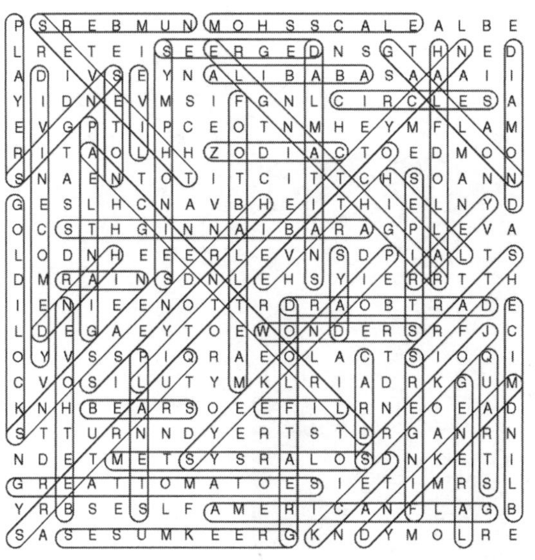

HIDDEN TALENTS

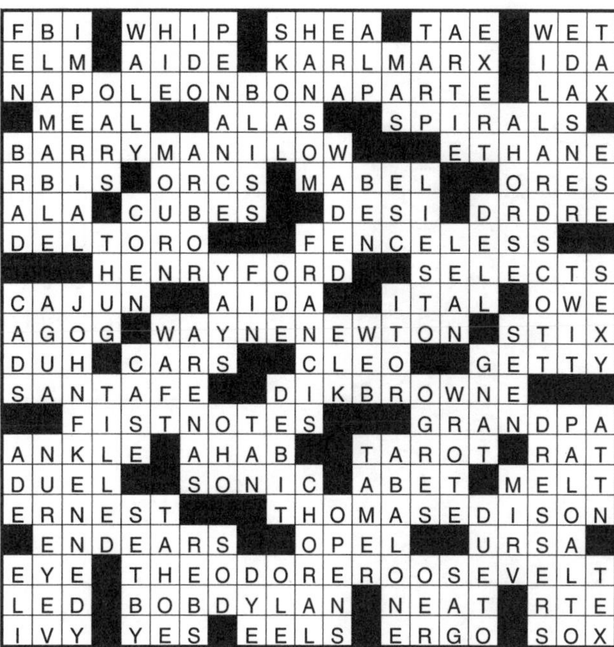

77 Across: In case you didn't recognize Dik Browne's name, he's the cartoonist who draws *Hagar the Horrible.*
117 Across: The sculptor, Kristofer Leirdal, created the statue for the 12th century cathedral when it was being restored in 1969. He based the figure on Dylan because "I saw him as a representative of American opposition to the Vietnam War…I thought it was appropriate to have a great poet on top of the tower."

INDUSTRIAL ESPIONAGE

DING-DING-DING!: Yo-yo promoter Donald Duncan also invented the Eskimo Pie and originated the Good Humor ice-cream truck.

A YEN FOR SUCCESS: A fortune-teller told Kichiro Toyoda it was good luck to change his product's name to Toyota and only use car names beginning with the letter "C."

WE LOVE HER, TOO!: CBS chose not to cover the Senate Foreign Relations Committee's hearings on Vietnam and instead aired reruns of *I Love Lucy* and *The Real McCoys.*

IT'S JUST A YELLOW WEATHER INVERSION: Dirty secret department: The *Los Angeles Times* bars the word "smog" from its real-estate section.

TO ORDER

Contact:

Bathroom Readers' Press
P.O. Box 1117,
Ashland, OR 97520
Phone: 541-488-4642
Fax: 541-482-6159
brorders@mind.net
www.bathroomreader.com

Shipping & Handling Rates:

- 1 book: $3.50
- 2 – 3 books: $4.50
- 4 – 5 books: $5.50
- 5 – 9 books: $1.00/ book

Priority shipping also available.
We accept checks & credit card orders.
Order online, or by fax, mail, email, or phone.

Wholesale Distributor

Publishers Group West (U.S.): 800-788-3123
Raincoast Books (Canada): 800-663-5714

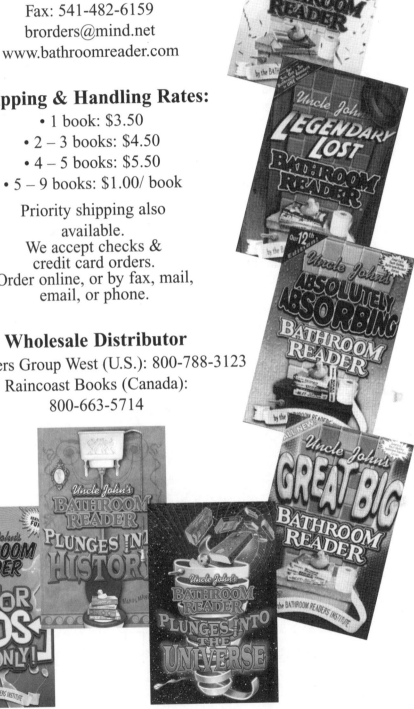